THE BOATMAN'S BIBLE

BY DAMAN C. FENWICK

TAB BOOKS Inc.
BLUE RIDGE SUMMIT, PA. 17214

FIRST EDITION

FIRST PRINTING—SEPTEMBER 1980

Copyright © 1980 by TAB BOOKS Inc.

Printed in the United States of America

Library of Congress Cataloging in Publication Data

Fenwick, Damon C.
    The boatman's bible.

    Includes index.
    1. Boats and boating. 2. Seamanship. 3. Navigation. I. Title.
VM321.F45   623.88   80-19912
ISBN 0-8306-9925-2
ISBN 0-8306-1231-9 (pbk.)

Other TAB books by the author:

No: 1061 *The Master Handbook of Boat and Marine Repair*
No. 1322 *Mobile Home Living: The Money-Saving Guide*

Contents

Introduction

The first law of life is survival. This is doubly true on water because the sea is hostile to Man. This makes survival so much more difficult, even under the best of conditions.

In gambling only a fool tries to beat the house at roulette because the mathematical odds are rigged in favor of the house. It is just a matter of time until the house wins all the fool's money.

In boating only a fool tries to beat the sea for the same reason. The odds always favor the sea. Try to buck those odds and the sea always wins—the Coast Guard and insurance companies record another statistic.

Nobody disputes these facts for the same reason that nobody disputes the mathematical fact that two plus two equals four. Yet millions of people every day all over the world try to beat the house at roulette, at blackjack, at a roll of the dice, or a game of numbers. The house always wins. Millions of boatmen every day all over the world try to beat the sea at impossible odds. The sea always wins.

Since the first law of life is survival, how do you keep the sea from always winning?

By changing the odds.

The sea is impersonal. It just doesn't give a darn and takes whatever you give. Every time you make a mistake, like cruising into new unfamiliar waters without a chart or like trying to run a coastal inlet at low tide, you change the odds. You just give the sea a bigger house edge and hasten the hour of reckoning when you become another loser like those 40,000 Americans who will have to be rescued by the Coast Guard this year at a cost of 1.5 billion to taxpayers because they will get into trouble on the water for "everything from bonehead mistakes to engine failure."

Of these 40,000 Americans who will be rescued this year, 1,500 will, unfortunately, be "rescued" too late. Their names will appear in the death notices of their hometown newspapers. Property damage will be over $15 million.

The purpose of this book is to show you how to cut down the house odds. This is the only way to survive on water— and the first law of life is survival.

Daman C. Fenwick

Chapter 1
Radio Communications

Once upon a time men went to sea with nothing but the stars to guide them (Fig 1-1). Even today Bedouin Arabs navigate that vast ocean of sand in Africa called the Sahara without any modern navigational aids. They never get lost. They never have problems with their camels colliding with other camels or objects.

BOATING, HOW IT WAS

The Chinese were the first to use the magnetic properties of the lodestone to navigate when celestial bodies were hidden behind clouds. As recently as World War II, shrimp, sardine and tuna fishermen spent weeks at sea with nothing but a simple magnetic compass, a chronometer in a wood box and a sextant (Fig. 1-2). A chronometer was necessary because at the time, it was the most accurate of timekeepers, and knowing the correct time is vitally important when shooting the sun at noon. An error of just seconds can throw you miles off your position.

With only these most basic of navigational aids, commercial fishermen never got lost. They never collided with other boats and they never went aground.

So who *needs* a book on electronics, piloting, seamanship and "Rules of the Road?" Maybe you don't. But currently there are members of the U.S. Congress who think that the U.S. Navy and the Coast Guard need *something*, maybe even this book. Does this shock you? Read on!

BOATING, HOW IT IS

Commercial fishermen today no longer go to sea with just a compass, a chronometer and a sextant. Nowadays fishing

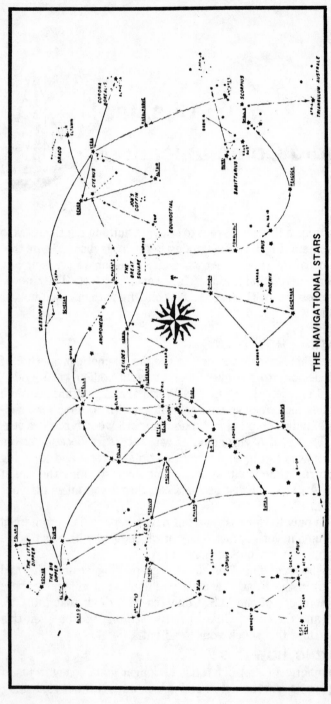

THE NAVIGATIONAL STARS

Fig. 1-1. This was the chief navigational tool that Christopher Columbus used to find the New World. Even today the Bedouin Arabs still use these same stairs to navigate that vast ocean of sand called the Sahara (courtesy of Celestaire, Inc.).

vessels are so loaded down with electronics and generating capacity that their boats had to be re-designed and built larger to provide more space for this gear. The average cost of just the electronics on these modern fishboats is around $100,000. Before World War II you could have bought five fishboats for this price, fully equipped and ready for sea. Something else had to also be re-designed larger—the mortgages. This made the Bank of America happy and also raised the price of canned tuna and other sea foods.

Fig. 1-2. The present day magnetic compass has been around less then a 100 years. The sextant has been around a little longer, just over 200 years, but still 240 years after Columbus discovered America. And even if the sextant had been available to Columbus, he had no reliable timepiece, without which the sextant is not too accurate.

Then came another momentous date in nautical history: the day CB radio went to sea. Some Coast Guard stations now monitor Channel 9. Since mobile CB units can be bought on sale at discount houses for $29.95, plus two bubble gum pictures of Roy Acuff, there will be CB whip antennas on rowboats, canoes and hollowed-out tree logs.

The question is—has all this brought greater safety on the water?

THE CB RADIO

The CB transceiver range is so short (about 3 miles) that it is of little practical use in the marine service. When some Coast Guard stations began to monitor CB Channel 9, it was expected that many manufacturers would rush to come out with special marine models designed to resist salt water corrosion. There is currently not one American manufacturer with such a model.

One manufacturer, *HANDIC-USA, INC.*, has a Swedish-made base station, Model Handic 3605, which is a combined dual function 40 channel transceiver that will operate on either 110 Volt AC or 12 Volt DC aboard ship or in an automobile (Fig 1-3). Another model, the Handic 240, is an AM/FM/MPX/CB. You can monitor CB and at the same time listen to your favorite AM or FM station. Combining CB chatter with an AM hard rock station will not help you make new friends in some yacht clubs. It might even get you killed. Handle this combination with extreme caution.

THE VHF-FM RADIOTELEPHONE

The old outlawed medium frequency (MF) equipment operated in the 2000/4000 kilocycle range, now called 2 kHz to 4 kHz. It was called "medium" frequency because it was above the commercial broadcast radio band, 500 to 1.6 kHz, and below the higher frequencies.

Low frequency radio waves are long in length and follow the

Fig. 1-3. No American manufacturer has come out (yet) with a special marine service model of his CB equipment. Handic-USA, Inc., imports this Swedish-made base station which they claim is designed for marine service. It also carries FM and AM radio broadcasts (courtesy of Handic-USA, Inc.).

curvature of the earth, which is why you get such distance, this is why radio station WLW in Cincinnati can be heard all over the United States. The wave "length" of WLW is measured in thousands of feet, or meters to be more precise. The wave "length" of VHF and UHF can be measured in inches.

Radio waves of short length do not follow the curvature of the earth, which is why VHF and CB have such a short range. This is why TV stations have their antennas either on high towers or high office buildings to get maximum coverage on which to base their advertising rate. The more TV sets that can pick up that signal, the more the advertiser pays. That is why the top of the Empire State Building is the most expensive TV tower in the world, next to the Sears Tower in Chicago.

Anything between 30 to 300 MHz is considered VHF, or Very High Frequency. The frequency in which you as a pleasure boat owner will work is 156 and 163 MHz.

An Explanation of kHz and MHz

I think it is time to explain the meaning of kHz, which you will be seeing a great deal of now that you own, or plan to own, a radiotelephone. Those three letters probably annoyed you because you hated to show your ignorance by asking their meaning. Whenever you get that feeling of embarrassment for being ignorant on something, always remember Mark Twain's words: "Everybody's ignorant, only on different subjects."

Once upon a time radio frequencies were called "kilocycles" or "megacycles" just like capacitors were called "condensers." The word "kilo" is Greek and means thousand. Mega is also Greek and means million. Kilocycles, therefore, means a thousand cycles and megacycles means a million cycles.

When you get up into the ultra high frequencies, where wavelengths are measured in inches, you start writing a lot of zeros. Radar frequencies go up to 30,000 MHz, or six more zeros after 30,000. Using the word "kilo" eliminates three zeros, "mega" eliminates six zeros, like 6 MHz for 6,000,000 cycles.

The word "cycle" is no longer used. In its place we use the letters "Hz", which is an abbreviation for Hertz. And why use the name "Hertz?" This name is used to honor German physicist Heinrich Rudolph Hertz who developed the first electromagnetic wave theory when he used the spark from an induction coil to produce and detect electromagnetic waves. These waves were later called "Hertzian waves." It was this discovery by Hertz, plus his later work in measuring velocity and wave length, which led to the discovery of radio.

Hertz, therefore, is the man who made it all possible—the multi-billion dollar electronics industry and all those Japanese radios. Instead of erecting a statue to honor this man who made so many people rich, the industry honors his memory in a different and novel way. Instead of saying "kilocycles" you now say "kilohertz." This is abbreviated one step further to "kHz." A million times every day all over the world a man's name is honored when people speak or write about communications frequencies.

Why Sailboats Have Better VHF Communications

Coast Guard Commander James Webb says that although sailboat ownership has increased tremendously in the past few years, there has been no increase in distress calls from this segment of the boating public—in fact, sailors are the least likely to get into trouble, and sailors have the best operating radio equipment.

There are good reasons for the above statement. Commander Webb, for diplomatic reasons, did not say it. But the fact is any damn fool can operate a powerboat because no special training is required by law. All you need is the ignition key and a push away from the dock.

However, it takes intelligence, training and a considerable amount of seamanship know-how to sail a boat. Bluntly put, sailors are just smarter and better seamen. That's why you will rarely ever hear a sailor go on the air with a Mayday. In fact, I personally have never heard a cruising sailboat make a distress call for help. But I have heard *hundreds* of powerboats make distress calls. I have gone to the assistance of a dozen power-boats in a Mayday situation. Not one one of the powerboat owners I aided had enough brains to batten down a sailboat hatch without falling overboard.

Although sailors make the least use of their radiophones for assistance or Mayday calls, their equipment usually functions the most efficiently and their radiated signal travels the far-thest. Since they are better seamen, they keep their gear in better shape. They also buy wisely and have their equipment installed properly.

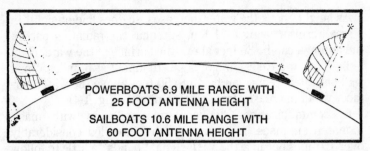

POWERBOATS 6.9 MILE RANGE WITH
25 FOOT ANTENNA HEIGHT

SAILBOATS 10.6 MILE RANGE WITH
60 FOOT ANTENNA HEIGHT

Fig. 1-4. Curvature of the earth is what limits the range of short wave transmission. To increase range, you raise antenna height. This is why TV transmitter antennas are always installed on high steel towers.

Getting More Range With VHF

Sailboats have a distinct edge in radio communications (Fig. 1-4). That main mast on a marconi rigged sloop makes an excellent antenna tower, which greatly increases the effective range of VHF.

High frequency radio transmission is strictly line-of-sight, which on water means as far as you can see before an object drops out of sight below the horizon. Sitting in a small outboard, only three feet above the water surface (Fig. 1-5), line-of-sight is only about 5 miles if you are looking for another equally small outboard. Of course, larger vessels can be seen at distances of 10 to 15 miles.

Fig. 1-5. Down close to the water surface, line-of-sight is very short, which is why the outboard radio is going to have a very short range, only about 5 miles to another outboard similarly equipped. This is considerably less than advertised ranges of 20 miles, but manufacturers don't base their claims on communications between two small outboards (courtesy of Hy-Gain Electronics).

As height above the water increases, so does line-of-sight. In a small cruiser using a 21 foot antenna, the radiating part of the antenna can be 30 feet above the surface of the water (Fig. 1-6). This increases line-of-sight to about 7.6 miles. In a sailboat the antenna can be 40 to 50 feet above the water surface, which increases transmitting range. (Fig. 1-4).

In communications between two sailboats with mast-mounted antennas, the range can be extended considerably over 10 miles because the VHF signal "bends" a little to follow the curvature of the earth before shooting off into space. Between two powerboats the range will be about 6 miles. Between two outboards, the range will be about 4 miles.

The above distances are practical day-to-day working ranges that you can depend on in any weather. They are not advertised ranges, which are ideal and totally impractical because they are based on the assumption that you will always be using your equipment under the best of conditions and that the equipment will always be properly tuned and maintained. This is a rarity with pleasure boats which, on the average, have radios that are neglected and badly maintained.

The above transmitting ranges do not apply when you communicate with a larger commercial vessel or a shore station. The shore station, including the Coast Guard, will have its

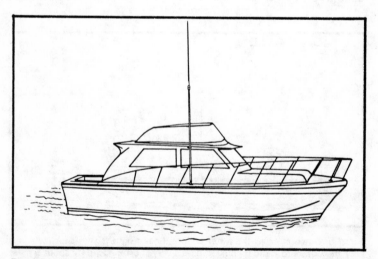

Fig. 1-6. Large cruisers can handle antennas up to 35-feet in height, which can increase range to almost 10 miles when communicating with another similarly equipped boat (courtesy of Hy-Gain Electronics).

antenna atop high towers or on some high building (Fig. 1-7). This effectively increases your transmitting range when you communicate with them.

The man in the outboard might have only a transmitting range of 3 miles when communicating with another outboard, but the marine operator at a shore station will pick him up at distances of 10 or even 20 miles. And the man in the outboard will be able to hear the shore station at long distances because of their high antennas and high-powered transmitters.

All these factors must be considered with VHF and you must not let yourself become discouraged when you read the true facts about transmitting ranges. Your true effective range depends on *who* you want to communicate with. If you plan to use your radiophone for socializing with other boats at the marina or club, you will not need more than a 10-mile range. When communicating with other boats during a group club cruise, range will not be important since all the boats will be close together, like camels in a caravan.

If you are one of those radiotelephone freaks who every Sunday afternoon pollutes the air with constant "signal checks," mainly to see how far the signal will reach, then you will not be happy with VHF-FM. Your only fulfillment would be with SSB, which will be discussed later.

If you want a radiotelephone for practical reasons, like safety and navigation, but feel that 10 miles is not a sufficient safety factor for the investment involved, remember again that you will have a range far greater than 10 miles if you ever get into trouble and need help. Remember, you are not alone in a Mayday situation. The people who will become involved in aiding you will be the very people that were mentioned earlier—the ones with the antennas on high towers and the highly sensitive directional receivers and the powerful transmitters, commonly referred to as the Coast Guard.

If you want greater range with your VHF "just because it's there," then there are two ways to affect this: first, get a better antenna and ground system, which will be elaborated on later; and second, buy a sailboat with a marconi rig. This will double or possibly triple your range—your *effective* range.

The Effective Range With VHF

You will see that word "effective" mentioned many times in radiotelephone talk. The "effective" range is what you can depend on seven days a week, in all kinds of weather, with an average installation, an average antenna/ground system and average losses between the transmitter and antenna. Advertised ranges of "20 and more miles" are entirely possible but rarely achieved because there are so many things that can stand in the way of you ever getting that kind of range when you want it just to talk with a friend back at the marina while on a cruise to Catalina.

Fig. 1-7. Coast Guard antenna systems are designed to hear all communications signals radiated within the station's area of responsibility. They have extremely sensitive receivers which, along with the high antennas, will pick up your signal anywhere in the station's territory.

The VHF wave is affected by thermal inversions, which can cause it to "bend" and follow the curvature of the earth. This, temporarily, can create conditions that may allow your signal to push far beyond its normal "effective" range. This factor may cause you to be surprised when, for example, you get a response, loud and clear, from the marine operator at KMB 393, Avalon on Catalina—*60 miles away!* Radio waves and smog are similar. Smog is caused by thermal inversions that push the air down, which prevents the pollution from dissipating. Inversions also push radio waves down, forcing them to follow the curvature of the earth before they dissipate into space.

You can not *depend* on thermal inversions to be available when you need them. It is a serious mistake, therefore, to consider your VHF capable of a 60-mile range. The advertiser is not misleading or making false claims when he uses the figure "20-mile range" because their claim is based on the assumption that radiotelephone equipment is to be properly, and *legally,* used for the ship's business and safety. This means *ship-to-shore* communications, and shore stations all have *high antennas.* When your vessel is in a hazardous situation, it is a *shore station* you will call, not a buddy over on Catalina. Your friend will not hear your distress call, but the marine operator on Avalon will hear you. Also, the Coast Guard will hear you, the Newport Beach marine operator will hear you, and all the ocean vessels in the area *will* hear you. In this respect, the advertiser is right, you do have the advertised range, and even more, sometimes much more. But for communications between small pleasure craft, you will have to be satisfied with a range of about 6 miles.

"GROUNDING" RADIOTELEPHONES

Nothing puzzles or confuses new owners of radiotelephones more than the mumbo jumbo they hear around the marina about "ground." And the reason they become confused is that they hear so much pro and con as to whether or not you really *need* a ground. Also confusing to the new owner is the fact there are a number of ways to install a good ground.

There is no problem on boating that has taken up more of my time than radiotelephones and grounding systems. I have exhaustively researched the subject of grounds to a point of no return. I don't think I have missed a single word on the subject that was written in the last 40 years.

I have studied the scientific test reports on all types of grounding methods (including the patented commercial types where a small block of porous sponge-like bronze is supposed to equal 12 square feet of copper. Well, if you believe that, then you also believe that Heaven will protect the poor working girl and honesty is the best policy).

Is a ground really necessary?

Yes!

Like it takes two to tango, it also takes two wires to operate anything by electricity. It takes two wires to radiate energy into the atmosphere because all MF antennas operate on the Marconi concept of *two wires*.

You are probably now more confused than ever because radio waves are not transmitted through wires. But they *are*, up to a point. The antenna is one wire and the ground is the second wire. They serve as the launching pads for the high frequency oscillations which are generated in your radio transmitter, modulated with your voice pattern and then allowed to *escape* from the two wires into the atmosphere. I use the word "escape" instead of "radiate" because I think escape more accurately explains what happens when you feed all that high frequency energy into two wires, with one of the wires, the antenna, going nowhere. When the energy is fed into the two wires, or "pushed" into them, they reach the end of the antenna, which is a dead end street. So the energy is literally "kicked" off into space.

As previously mentioned, in the Marconi concept, it takes two wires—and both of these wires must be in the same physical area. It makes no sense to buy the best antenna and then use a small guage wire for a ground connection to your engines. On your automobile you would never use No. 2 gauge wire for positive connection to your battery, and 14 gauge wire for a ground connection to the engine. As you well know, both battery cables are the same gauge wire. It is the same with your radiotelephone. It takes two wires, and for peak efficiency, they must be the same.

Is A Ground Plate Necessary

Will an automobile function without the battery ground connected to the engine? No! And neither will your radiotelephone. You must have battery power. However, once the battery ground connection is made, the transmitter does have some ground because the chassis is connected to the battery ground, which, in turn, is connected to the engines. So a radiotelephone will function without any additional grounding for the antenna.

The next question is how well will it function?

Transmitter efficiency is evaluated and measured by the amount of antenna current that is loaded, with minimum loss, to the top of the antenna. The more antenna current you get up there, the stronger the signal. And this is where you can *see* on a meter the importance of a good ground. In tuning the transmitter, the technician resonates and loads all the current he can get, and how much he gets into the antenna is determined by the quality of your ground. It's your ground that helps to push more current into the antenna. The more current you have, the stronger your signal will be when it leaves the antenna.

This is about as simple as I can make it, so I hope you understand. To reiterate briefly, your radio will work without a grounding system, but not as well as it could with one.

CB and VHF Grounds

The body of an automobile serves as the ground for CB transceivers.

With CB on a boat, if the hull is steel or aluminum, it would function as ground the same as an automobile body. An auto-type antenna could also be used (Fig. 1-8). However, in the marine environment, it is always best to use equipment designed specifically for the sea. Marine antennas are usually fiberglass with corrosion-resistant fittings sealed against moisture (Fig. 1-9). Special lay-down mounts are also available for marine antennas so they can be dropped when going under low bridges or into covered boat wells.

For wood or fiberglass hulls you will need additional ground, and how much depends on where you boat. By this I mean do you boat in fresh water, salt water, cold water, or warm tropical water? Why? It makes a big difference.

Salt water has high conductivity. Fresh water has poor conductivity. Water temperature also plays a role in conductivity. For example, cold fresh water has very low conductivity.

On the Great Lakes in April, water temperature is in the forties. The most current I could load into a friend's antenna was

Fig. 1-8. Automotive type CB antennas don't last long at sea, do nothing to enhance the appearance of a boat costing $30,000, and you don't save money when you must replace them after one season.

less than 2 amps. Four months later in Miami I re-tuned his transmitter and got over 4 amps of current into the antenna. That may not seem like much to you, but you would understand it better if you ever stood close to a transmitter feeding that kind of current into an antenna. If you were standing within three feet of the radio when it was transmitting, your flesh would tingle and the hair on your arms would actually move when the carrier was modulated by talking. That was one powerful signal. Yet the same radio caused none of this when used on Lake Erie earlier that Spring.

The warm salt water in Florida, and other tropical areas, has maximum conductivity. This makes for maximum efficiency.

Fig. 1-9. A regular marine CB antenna is well worth the extra cost because you only buy it once and it will last as long as your boat.

It also greatly simplifies the grounding of radiotelephones because just the underwater gear of any small cruiser, including the rudders, propellers, struts or shafts, will provide all the ground that is needed. Tests have shown that just one square foot of copper will provide adequate grounding for a radiotelephone in warm tropical salt water. You can get this much surface area with just one outboard drive.

In cold fresh water it will take 12 to 24 times as much metal surface area to provide an adequate ground. This still would not be as good as one lousy square foot in Florida.

Different Grounding Methods

Around the boatyard you can get all kinds of advice on how to install a ground for your radio. I have tried them all, and I have learned something: it is not necessary to put copper flashing material on the bottom of your hull. There is an easier and better way. Put it on the *inside* of your hull. In case you suspect this may be a typographical error, I will repeat: the ground plate does not need to be *in* the water. Metal-to-metal contact is not necessary when dealing with radio frequency. In fact, alternating current does not necessarily require direct metal-to-metal contact. In a transformer and condenser, there is no direct metal contact.

The copper ground material which you use in the bilges of your boat will become one plate in a giant condenser. The water outside the hull becomes another plate in the condenser. The wood or fiberglass separating these two plates becomes the dielectric.

You can transform your hull into a huge condenser which transmits RF energy just as easily as if the copper were in the water.

What To Use For Grounding Material

Some of the material I have seen used for ground plates includes aluminum flashing material, copper flashing, brass water pipe, copper water pipe and tubing, photo-engraver's 16-gauge copper plates (very expensive), sheets of Reynolds do-it-yourself aluminum, copper screening material and brass shim stock.

Do not ever use aluminum for a ground plate on the *outside* of your hull. Since the aluminum will be directly, or indirectly, in contact with other metals, (like the fastenings which secure it to the boat bottom, and the bronze through-hull fitting bolt), the aluminum will rapidly erode free of its fastenings due to electrochemical corrosion and it will rip loose from the hull and scare you to death when your boat starts steering erratically. You can use aluminum on the inside if you have a reasonably dry hull, but it will still corrode and become messy after a few years.

Copper Screen Grounds

There are many professional marine electronics installers who use copper screen material for radio grounds, especially in fiberglass hulls. Some manufacturers of fiberglass boats will lay copper screen down just before the last layer of cloth is gel-ed to provide a built-in ground for radiotelephones. This is fine because the ground is out of sight and does not become a dirt trap and collector of all kinds of crap that can get into the bilge.

For do-it-yourself installation, I do not like copper screen because you must do a great deal of cutting and soldering, and I do not like to solder in the confined area of a boat engine compartment. Even though copper screen is easy to solder, you still get a lot of smoke and noxious fumes. One more disadvantage of copper screen is that you must use a lot of the material to get sufficient surface area.

Brass Shim Stock For Grounds

My personal favorite material for radio grounds is brass shim stock, which can be purchased in 50 foot rolls, 6 inch widths. This adds up to 25 sq. ft. of surface area. The metal is thinner than the paper on which this is printed, which is one of its good features. You want *surface area* not metal thickness.

This brass material is easy to work with and can be layed down in any direction. It will shape easily right over the frames. You do not have to cut it. To make a 90 degree turn, you just fold it over like paper and secure it with either copper tacks on a wood hull or bronze staples. I used Arrow bronze staples, which are available on special order. Copper tacks are fine, if you can keep from banging your fingers.

On a fiberglass hull you can use 2-inch aluminum duct tape to hold down the brass stock. If you want 50 sq. ft. of ground, order two rolls of the stock, but solder the ends together *before* you go to work (Fig. 1-10).

Holding the brass stock in your hands like a roll of toilet tissue, you just lay it down between the frames, under the engines, going back and forth from side to side, or up and down, folding it tightly over the frames. To reverse direction, you just fold it over twice to make a full 180 degree turn.

Radio Connection To Ground

Before laying down the brass stock, you must plan and provide for a good connection to the radio—don't use wire. Make a 2-inch strap out of the shim stock and sweat solder it to the ground material.

The run to the ground should be as short as possible, so start laying down the brass as close as you can get to the area where the radio will be installed. This means you will start somewhere up under the decking. You make the final run from this point with the smaller 2-inch strap, which is easy to handle and can be held down with cloth tape. It should be available in colors that will match your woodwork. The radio is connected to the strap itself. If it is too wide to get through an opening, just fold it in half before you drill the hole.

The radio ground must be tied in to your boat's electrical bonding system (Fig. 1-11). Between the two of them, you will have a good freshwater radiotelephone ground system.

DO-IT-YOURSELF VHF INSTALLATION

The *Ray Jefferson VHF Model 1400* is a 12 channel 25 watt "package" unit with 7 full "pre-tuned" channels, plus two weather (W1 & W2) and a 6 db gain antenna with hardware.

The antenna and hardware "package" includes a specific length of coaxial antenna cable with coax connectors at each end. The transceiver is factory "bench-tuned" to the supplied antenna and coax cable, then dis-assembled and packaged for shipment.

The coax cable supplied *cannot* be shortened if it is too long, or replaced with a longer cable if it is too short. If the cable is changed, you must have the transmitter re-tuned. You must also re-tune if you change antennas—which you probably will. Why? Because all the experts around the club and marina will tell you that you must have a better antenna "to reach out farther". But if you try to pin them down on how *much* farther, you will get some very funny answers. So don't ask because you'll die laughing.

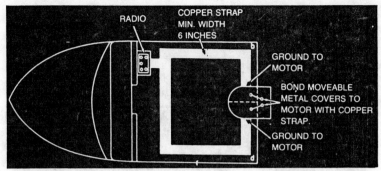

Fig. 1-10. Brass shim stock, thinner then the paper on which this is printed, is very easy to work with and doesn't have to be screwed or nailed down. Just ordinary aluminum duct tape can be used to hold it in place.

Installing a "packaged" VHF is so easy I could train a French poodle to do it in three easy lessons. You will need two screws to mount the set itself and two screws for the antenna hardware. Next, you will have to drill a hole for the coax cable, big enough for the connector end. Then, screw-fasten the coax cable connectors to the radio and antenna.

All that remains is to connect the power leads directly to one of your batteries. That's it! You now have a licensed radio station aboard ship.

But you may not be satisfied. The supplied coax cable will be either too long or too short. The thing will work, but when friends in the same marina or mooring basin tell you, "I read you, but not very well," you will be very unhappy and you will wonder why you spent all that money on a radio when your daughter needs braces on her teeth.

Factory "bench-tuning" produces radiotelephones that work, but not real well. You cannot set up and tune a transmitter on a factory bench, then transfer the equipment to a boat and get the same results you got on the bench. It's impossible! The grounds will be different and the surrounding area and interference will be different. At the marina there will be other antennas, sailboat rigging and electric and telephone wires that will all affect the transmitter tuning.

When and Where To Tune The Transmitter

I never tune my radio while tied up in the slip. The best time and place to tune a radiotelephone is out on the water, anchored with one engine running so the alternator is putting 14 volts into the battery that powers the radio. You will now be tuned and loaded for maximum antenna current, but most importantly, you will *stay* tuned for peak output—but only when you are out on the water with one engine running.

When you return to your dock, there will be a slight detuning of your radio, how much depends on how many saiboats and other influences there are in the vicinity. Your battery will

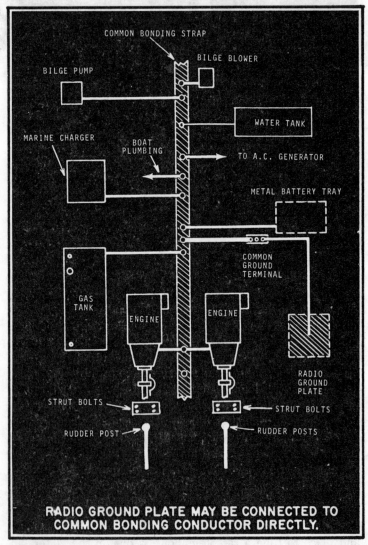

COMMON BONDING STRAP

BILGE BLOWER

BILGE PUMP

WATER TANK

MARINE CHARGER

BOAT PLUMBING

TO A.C. GENERATOR

METAL BATTERY TRAY

COMMON GROUND TERMINAL

GAS TANK

ENGINE

ENGINE

RADIO GROUND PLATE

STRUT BOLTS

STRUT BOLTS

RUDDER POST

RUDDER POSTS

RADIO GROUND PLATE MAY BE CONNECTED TO COMMON BONDING CONDUCTOR DIRECTLY.

Fig. 1-11. The boat's electrical bonding system, if done right, is itself a fairly good radiotelephone ground and in warm salt water is all you really need. However, in cold fresh water, you need more.

also be putting out only 12 volts, instead of the 14 volts you get with an engine running. All these things affect tuning and you must decide which is most important to you—peak signal strength when you are out on the water who knows where, or tied up in your slip safe and secure. You can't have both.

When you tell the radio technician with the second class commercial radiotelephone license that you want your radio tuned away from the dock, he won't like it because it takes more time and interferes with his working schedule. He may offer him an extra ten bucks, it will cure his seasickness.

"Packaged" radiotelephones are a good buy only if you are content to take what you get, install it and forget it. This what many week-end boatmen do after the novelty of the thing wears off. But if you are fussy about your boat, like all real boatmen are, you will not be happy with what you have bought because the supplied coax cable will be either too long or too short. You also won't be satisfied with the 6 db antenna and you'll have to change the coax cable length when you buy another antenna, plus you'll probably have the set re-tuned. These are things to consider because the "package" can become very expensive, especially when you junk some of it later.

The "packaged" radios are not for you if you have a sailboat and plan to install the antenna atop the main mast (Fig 1-12). You will require a special heavier gauge coax cable cut and tailored to your specific needs. The small 3 db antenna is always used on mast installation. In fact, the 3 db is called the sailboat antenna.

A "packaged" 25 watt radiotelephone will currently cost about $499.95.

A "packaged" 55 channel 25 watter will currently cost about $669.95.

A "packaged" 71 channel 25 watter will currently cost about $699.95.

You can buy a non-packaged VHF radio for considerably less than the above prices (Figs. 1-13, 1-14 and 1-15). You can still make your own installation because you buy your own antenna and hardware and you buy your own antenna feed line. Any electronics store carries coax antenna wire in all sizes. For power boats, where maximum length will not exceed 20 feet, RG-58 is used. For sailboats, where the feedlines may extend to a 100 feet, the heavier RG-8 is used. You will need a connector for each end. These are installed after you

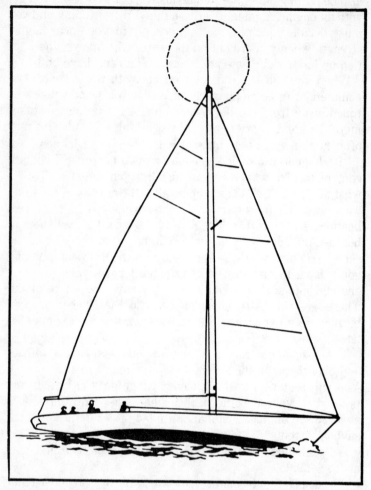

Fig. 1-12. Atop the main mast is where most VHF antennas are installed, even though it does cause an annoying problem with the co-ax cable slapping inside the aluminum mast. You must consider whether a few extra miles in range is worth the annoyance because nobody has yet figured out a way to stop that slapping (courtesy of Hy-Gain Electronics).

determine the exact length of you coax cable. When it's all put together, you have the set tuned.

Some manufacturers do have "packaged" VHF with coax cables in different lengths. Others just supply you with an 8-foot 6 db antenna and 20 feet of made-up coax cable. Even with the antenna mounted atop the mast on a small cruiser, this cable will be far too long and you will have a lot of excess wire looped and laying around in a non shipshape fashion.

VHF Antennas

Most packaged VHF equipment usually comes with an 8-foot 6 db antenna and 20 feet of coax cable. There are special sailboat models that come with a 3 db antenna which is about 54 inches in length and has 60 feet of coax cable.

If you stay away from the "packaged" radios and buy just a transceiver alone, you must then make another choice: which antenna to buy. If you think shopping for a new compact "gas-saving" car is nerve-wracking, wait until you go looking for an antenna. They come in all sizes, shapes, lengths and prices. And one thing in particular will puzzle you, the letters "db." The letters are used in conjunction with phrases like "full 6 db gain." This will impress you because you will imagine that "6 db gain" is twice as good as "3 db gain." However, this is not true. In fact, it may not even be as good because "db gain" is not a measure of range—it is a measure of relative loudness.

The Meaning Of "DB Gain"

Since all transmitted radio energy for communication purposes must be converted to sound, there has to be a way to measure this sound in terms of relative loudness, as heard by the human ear and not by some super sensitive instrumentation. The decibel (abbreviated to db) is the unit used to measure this loudness.

The human ear cannot accurately detect sound values. For example, if you increase transmitter power from 100 watts to 400 watts, the signal will only sound twice as loud to the human ear. Changing the sound level by one decibel is just barely detectable by the ear.

Fig. 1-13. This Raytheon Model 50-A is an example of a non-packaged radio-telephone. It has 55 transmit and 85 or 96 receive channels (courtesy of Raythoen Marine Co.).

27

Fig. 1-14. This Raytheon Model 55 is another example of a non-packaged radiotelephone. (courtesy of Raytheon Marine Co.).

Now you can see why numbers can be deceptive. The 6 db gain antenna will give a *measured* signal loudness twice that of a 3 db antenna, but it won't really sound much louder to the human ear. In fact, most listeners will hardly notice any difference at all. And should this happen to you, after replacing your 6 db with a "maximum duty antenna" of 10.5 db gain, you will wonder why you spent all the money. The "high gain"

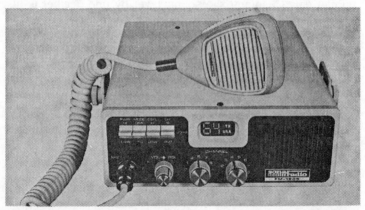

Fig. 1-15. This Sonar Model 1805 is also an example of a non-packaged radiotelephone. It too has 55 transmit and 85 or 96 receive channels (courtesy of Sonar Radio Corp.).

antennas are very expensive. For example, a 21-foot 9 db antenna will cost you around $230, compared to $80 for a 6 db.

How To Increase VHF Range

Instead of investing more money in antennas, there is a better and easier way to get more range with VHF—get the antenna up *higher*. Of course, the 24 foot 10.5 db antenna gets you up higher, but you can accomplish the same thing with a 3 db antenna by just putting an extension mast under it and raising it up as high as you wish (Fig. 1-16)

Extension masts of 8 and 10 feet are available from all antenna manufacturers, who are listed in Appendix A. The extension mast, which will perfectly match your antenna, has the proper threads on both ends to fit between your antenna and base. It is also hollow so that the coax cable can be run down inside to make a neat installation.

With a higher antenna, you will need additional mast support, as shown in Fig. 1-16. There is no limit to the number of extensions you can use if you can just figure out a way to support the mast so that it won't whip around excessively. The extra length increases leverage to such a degree that the deck mount can be loosened and pulled out of the decking.

Because of heel and masthead motion, sailboats are limited to the small 54-inch 3 db antenna. The prudent sailor with a masthead antenna always keeps a spare, either mounted aft (Fig. 1-17) or stowed, in case of de-masting at sea, or in case it fails to clear completely when passing under a bridge.

Why Too Much "Gain" Can Be Bad

Radio waves radiate from an antenna like light from an electric bulb—in all directions. As a result, most of the oscillating energy generated in your transmitter is wasted going in the wrong direction. "Gain" in a VHF antenna eliminates some of this waste by squeezing down the radiated energy to push it *out* rather then down or up.

The effect is much like the gain you get when a light source, a flashlight for example, is squeezed down to a narrow beam which you can project to a considerable distance.

This is both good and bad.

A little gain is good. Too much gain is worse then none because in a rolling powerboat or heeling sailboat, the squeezed down RF beam, just like the searchlight beam, can go off

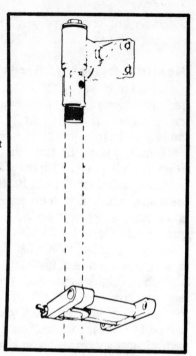

Fig. 1-16. You can insert as many mast extensions under your antenna as you wish, but the longer mast will have to be supported along the way as shown (courtesy of Hy-Gain Electronics).

target. This will cause fading and erratic reception of your signal. You will get reports like, "Your signal fades, then comes back strong. Are you running in the trough?"

High gain antennas are suited mostly for large craft, like freighters, which do not heel or roll violently in beam seas (Fig. 1-18). Think about this before you spend $300 for something that won't serve your purposes as well as the 3 db "sailboat antenna" for about $50. Spend the extra money on an extension mast, or masts. Forget about more "gain." The 3 db pushed up higher with two 10-foot extension masts will do a better job for you.

LONG RANGE COMMUNICATIONS AND SSB

On December 31, 1977, one year after the old AM medium frequency radiotelephones were outlawed by the FCC, the same thing happened to AM-Double Sideband (AM-DSB), which also became illegal in the U.S. Marine Service.

The year 1977 was a transitional period under International Law. It was a testing time for both double and single sideband marine radio communications all over the world. Single side-

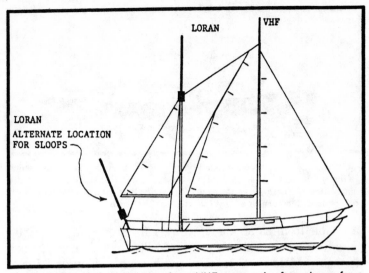

Fig. 1-17. The alternate location for a VHF antenna is aft as shown for a Loran or SSB antenna. From a practical standpoint, this is the best location because the masthead antenna is always being scraped going under bridges (courtesy of SRD Labs).

band won out and is now the official medium and long-range communications system.

If you bought one of the first DSB rigs, like I did, you undoubtedly were delighted with the performance and range of this equipment, and you undoubtedly were disappointed and bitter when this too was outlawed by the FCC.

If there is any small comfort, when you go to SSB you can still use your old MF antenna and ground system in the 2-3 MHz Lower Coastal frequencies, and your new SSB will perform just as well, maybe even better.

The big attraction, and advantages, of SSB is that you are not limited to just that 500 mile range you get in the 2-3 MHz band. You have all those High Seas Bands in 4, 6, 8, 12, 16 and 22 MHz which will give you reliable communications to just about anywhere in the world.

As you can see in the illustration (Fig. 1-19), that first band, which actually lies between 1.6 to 3 MHz, is the one often referred to as the Coastal Band. It is much used by workboat operators and commercial fishermen who operate offshore. With 50 to 75 watts of transmit power, they have dependable working ranges of up to 500 miles.

These low-end SSB rigs, like Raytheon's Model 1210, are

Fig. 1-18. Don't waste your money on expensive "high gain" antennas which are really not suited for small boats that heel, roll and toss about in even midly rough waters. These antennas require a steady base from which to project their concentrated wave patterns (courtesy of SRD Labs).

available from name manufacturers for around $700 to $800. The Raytheon set illustrated (Fig. 1-20) has 8 duplex channels in the 2-4 MHz band and puts out 65 watts. The term "duplex channels" means transmission and receive are on separate frequencies.

The next step up the frequency ladder would be something like Seatron's Model SSB-100 (Fig. 1-21), which has 10 channels and a frequency range from 2 to 9 MHz and an output of 125 watts.

For every step up the frequency ladder and channel range, you pay and you pay. Synthesized all-channel operation, with all antennas and couplers, will cost you around $600. The snob appeal alone is worth ten percent of the cost, and how much is a status symbol worth? Just owning such a piece of electronics sets you apart from the drones and menials who have to work

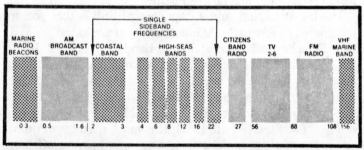

Fig. 1-19. The new "coastal band," 2-3 MHz, is actually in the same old area formerly used by the outlawed AM marine radio-telephones. That means, working in this band, you can still use that old Webster antenna you have gathering dust up in your garage rafters (courtesy of Fishing Gazette).

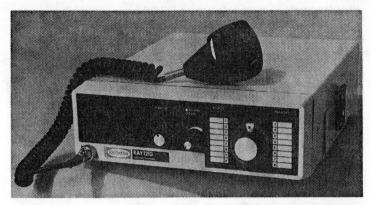

Fig. 1-20. This Raytheon Model 1210 is really all the radio communications that most pleasure boaters will ever need (courtesy of Raytheon Marine Co.).

overtime at the box factory to meet those mortgage payments on the boat.

You will understand someday why SSB is held in such awe and esteem by all Big Water boatmen when you start shopping for one yourself. Like womens *haute coture* footwear, SSB radiotelephones are smaller (much smaller), but they cost much, much more. Like women's shoes and bathing suits, the less material they use, the more they cost. The manufacturers explain that SSB radios are extremely complicated, the modulation circuitry is more complex and the frequency control requirements are ten times more rigidly maintained with things like the thermostatically controlled oven that keeps both the crystals and oscillators at a constant temperature. This results in excellent frequency stability far exceeding the FCC's specifications of ± 50 Hz.

Power Limits On SSB

You can have up to 150 watts with SSB. This is much more than you will ever need because the improved modulation in these new circuits gives far more "talk power." If you're loaded, nothing will dissuade you from buying 150 watts, if for no other reason than "it's there." Buy a 65 watter instead and save enough money to pay your son's first year tuition at college. And don't consider for a moment that you will be sacrificing power because you will still have a consistent range of 3,000 miles to other ships or to shore stations, both day and night. In the "High Seas" frequencies your range will extend out to 10,000 miles (Fig. 1-22). There will rarely be a day when you can't reach out at least 6,000 miles.

Why Doesn't Everybody Have SSB?

Not everyone *needs* SSB. Also, not everyone has the money. The boatmen on inland waters can get by very well with VHF, which is the reason the FCC will not issue an SSB license until the boat owner first owns a VHF station aboard his craft.

The offshore boatmen on coastal waters must survive in a far bigger and more hostile environment. A dead engine, a broken rudder or a de-masted sloop plus a strong offshore wind will send your Newport Beach sailor drifting on her way across the Pacific to who knows where. The captain could starve to death trying to reach somebody on VHF. With SSB he could get get help and still make it home in time to go to work the following morning.

What Is SSB?

Single sideband radiotelephones use the same 2-3 kHz band that was outlawed by the FCC for the old AM rigs. So why were they outlawed? They were inefficient and caused much interference. However, their inefficiency caused no troubles in radio communications 25 years ago because few pleasure boats *had* radiotelephones. In fact, they had nothing electronic aboard for the simple reason that nothing was available at that time for pleasure craft.

Fig. 1-21. This Seatron Model SSB-100 has 10 channels and a frequency range from 2 to 9 MHz and an output of 125 watts (courtesy of Seatron Marine Electronics).

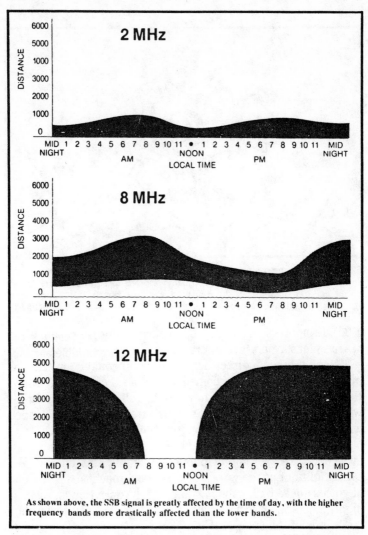

As shown above, the SSB signal is greatly affected by the time of day, with the higher frequency bands more drastically affected than the lower bands.

Fig. 1-22. With all-channel SSB up to 22 MHz, ranges of 10,000 miles are not unusual. In the much used 8-12 MHz bands, you can easily reach out 3-5,000 miles if you time your transmissions properly (courtesy of Raytheon Marine and Fishing Gazette).

The buying power of boatmen had yet to be tapped and exploited 25 years ago. In the marine bands, the only traffic you could hear was commercial, mostly tugs talking to freighters. The Coast Guard got most of its distress calls from freighters telling them they had seen a small boat off the channel near buoy 44 waving a white T-shirt on the end of a boathook (Fig.

Fig. 1-23. Not too long ago only large pleasure craft had radiotelephones. Small boat owners, disabled at sea, usually resorted to waving a white T-shirt on the end of a boathook or shooting off flares. New boaters don't know what you're talking about when you mention flares. (courtesy of U.S. Coast Guard).

1-23). Freighters just don't stop in narrow shipping channels to rescue pleasure craft in distress.

The only other indirect help a boatman could count on was his family. If he failed to come home at a specified time from a fishing trip to the reefs, they would call the Coast Guard—who, during the good fishing months, would always be flooded with telephone calls from anxious wives and relatives.

Then all this changed. Suddenly in a few short years, everybody had a radiotelephone—including this author. We came right out of the woodwork like cockroaches. The babble of voices got so bad, nobody could use the darn things. Even at night, fantastic skip ranges and harmonics caused interference thousands of miles away (Fig. 1-24).

The FCC was finally forced to do something. Out of their actions came the SSB.

The two major advantages of SSB is long range communications with minimum power, which leaves space for more new channels in already crowded bands without creating interference.

A radio wave has three parts. First there is the "carrier" wave, which is aptly described because it literally "carries" the message on its back. When nothing is being transmitted on the radio, the carrier can be heard. It sounds like the soft "sh-h-h" of a distant waterfall.

The carrier can be compared to a long river of moving water. The movement of water is useful and can be exploited for many practical purposes. In the lumber industry it is used to carry logs down river to the mills.

The radio "carrier" is used in the same way, to "carry" messages through space. To do this, another modulated and smaller frequency wave is imposed on the carrier to change its amplitude. When this is done, it is called "amplitude modulation," or AM.

A second and third part of the radio carrier wave are the sides, or "sidebands." This is the part of the carrier which actually carries the information. The carrier itself is just a lot of bull. It is a space and energy waster. The sides of the carrier take up little space and use less energy. Sixty watts of power in the sidebands goes a lot farther then when the same wattage

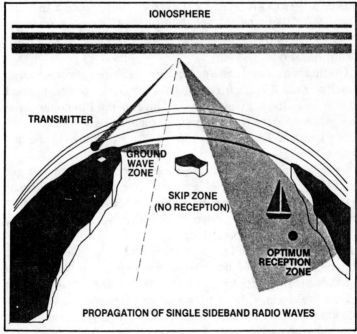

Fig. 1-24. Skip zone reception is the reason for those fantastically long communications with SSB. The ground wave has limited range, about 500 miles more or less. But the sky wave, reflected off the ionosphere, sometimes called the Kennelly-Heaviside Layer, is what makes it all possible (courtesy of Raytheon Marine and Fishing Gazette).

is pushing out the entire carrier, and it goes even farther when it is pushing out just one sideband.

So, using just a single sideband, with the lower sideband and carrier suppressed, you get more mileage with less gas. It's as simple as that.

Installing SSB

I am sorry to say that installing an SSB radiotelephone is not a job for the average do-it-yourselfer. There is far more to an SSB installation than just mounting the set on a bulkhead, screwing on the coax connectors and connecting the battery power leads.

Single Sideband places heavy demands on the ground and antenna system and getting the job done right is not easy. If you plan to use your old MF antenna and ground, be prepared to make improvements in both. Don't cut corners! Do the job right or have it done. If you want more information on this, write to NARCO KONEL, 271 Harbor Way, South San Francisco, CA 94080 and ask for their booklet *Down-To-Earth Explanation of Marine Single Sideband.*

Antennas For SSB

Getting a good antenna/ground for an SSB installation is so much work that when friends ask for my advice or assistance, I always beg off by saying: "I would love to, but I'm going to the hospital tomorrow to have my gall bladder removed."

My gall bladder has been removed twenty times in the last four years.

I don't mind writing on the subject because when you get mad later, you won't be able to get your hands on my throat (you will want to strangle *somebody* after spending all that money and then having to work so hard, or spend *more* money, to get the thing to work right).

If SSB was confined to the low coastal band, like 2-3 MHz, the installation would be so much easier and you would be so much happier with the results. But having lived with boatmen all my life, I know you will not be satisfied with just the low coastal bands. It's a status thing. It's being socially inferior. It's being unloved.

I can think of no other reason why boatmen, myself included, feel that they *must* have synthesized SSB with all the channels from 2 to 22 MHz.

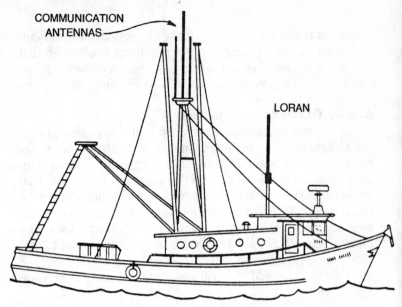

COMMUNICATION
ANTENNAS

LORAN

Fig. 1-25. To work the full range of all-channel SSB you need three antennas, with a separate coupler turning on each. Anything less will bring you nothing but disappointment and frustration, and with SSB, frustration is what you mostly get (courtesy of SRD Labs).

And that is what makes the installation so difficult—that wide range of frequencies. It is impossible for one antenna to handle that range. You will need three (Fig. 1-25). SSB antennas are big, running from 23-foot to 35-foot. But the antenna is only one third of the installation. The other two thirds are the antenna coupler and the ground, sometimes referred to as counterpoise.

You can see what the "coupler" looks like in the illustration (Fig. 1-21). It is almost as big as the transmitter itself. You will see radios advertised as having a "self-contained" coupler. They may save you some money, but I doubt if you will be satisfied with their performance.

The best location for the coupler is at the base of the antenna itself, thus eliminating any additional feedline to the antenna. The coupler has fine tuning circuits which resonate (tune) the antenna for each channel. Precise tuning can be done only on the antenna itself. If you mount the coupler inside, with perhaps 10-feet of additional feedline to the antenna, you will never achieve peak resonance.

Remember, making a good SSB installation is more art than

science or technology. So don't make the job any more difficult with a lot of unnecessary wire. If it bothers you having that delicate equipment out in the weather, make a cover for it just like you did for your searchlight and haler microphone.

Beware Of Backstay Antennas

The low coastal bands will require an antenna similar to your old MF rig that was outlawed. In fact, you can still use it. On sailboats the backstay is sometimes used as an antenna (Fig. 1-26). But you should be warned that there is a danger involved when you do this. When transmitting, the antenna is *hot* to the touch and will cause a stinging burn. If a guest or crew member, unaware of this, accidently touches the backstay at a critical moment, he might fall overboard. Another point to consider: backstays are stainless steel, which is a very poor RF conductor. You could lose half your antenna current overcoming the resistance.

Marina Maintenance

If you plan on having your SSB dealer do the installing, select one who has a proven reputation for making good SSB installations (not just some salesman's assurances that they

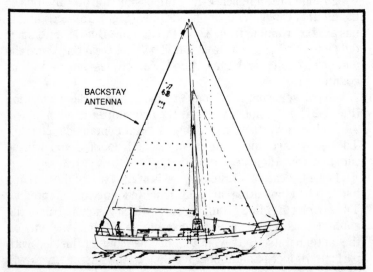

BACKSTAY
ANTENNA

Fig. 1-26. Regardless of what you may have been told, the backstay is not a good SSB antenna, for two reasons—stainless steel is a very poor RF conductor and through stainless steel, you will lose over half of your antenna current.

can do the job). Marinas have a notorious reputation for being big on promises, small on performance. Once they get your name on the bottom line, you wait and wait! And what you get eventually is far from what you were promised.

At this writing, a dear friend of mine, who a few weeks ago purchased a Pearson 365 cruising ketch, is waiting and waiting for the installation of all those electronic devices he bought at the same time. He hopes to be sailing *Jeddah* for her home port in Plantation Key, Florida within two weeks.

It has saddened me to watch my friends, Wanda and Bud, as they make plans, lay in stores, buy charts for all the waters along the way because I know exactly what is going to happen to them. They will still be here two months from now, their traveling schedule in shambles, as they wait for all their electronics and accessories to be installed and checked out.

To date, nothing that they bought and paid for, totaling over $26,000, has been delivered or installed, and it was all purchased from the biggest commercial boating operation on Western Lake Erie, a conglomerate-owned marina grossing millions.

Among the many electronic items my friend ordered was Loran-C and all-channel synthesized SSB. I happen to know that this marina, and all other marinas in this area, does not employ anybody with experience in Loran-C or SSB. In fact, very little SSB or Loran is sold on Lake Erie for the simple reason that you don't need it. Lake Erie, at its greatest width, is 60 miles, which means that at no time can you be more than 30 miles from shore. An SSB station license is not automatically issued like CB, or even VHF, without questions. You can't even apply for an SSB license until you first have a VHF station aboard. And, in your application, you must state that you will be taking your boat to Florida for extensive fishing offshore.

The modern boatyards and marinas all have big labor turnovers. Nobody stays around long enough to learn anything about boats. The kid who climbs up on your boat in the Yard with boxes and some tools to, as he says casually, "install a depthfinder" will probably be working somewhere else next week.

You happen to know that this kid just got the job at the Yard and that his previous boat experience was gained at a big supermarket where he bagged groceries. The only other practical experience he has is expertly throwing a Frisbee to a dog.

This kid is now the Yard "electronics technician" who is going to install your depthfinder. And when you watch him preparing to drill a hole for the transducer in your $60,000 boat, right at the point where the hull angle is 45 degrees, you come close to having a cardiac seizure when you realize he is preparing to drill the hole *straight!*

I am not dramatizing or exaggerating and the above is not an unusual or isolated case. Boatyards and marinas are not unionized. Since they must hire so much inexperienced labor, they do not pay good wages, which is the reason they no longer have "experts" for specific jobs. In today's marina, everybody on the payroll is an "expert."

Buying An "Equipped" Boat

What is the solution to the previous problem?

Don't buy a new boat off the showroom floor. These boats are usually delivered without even a compass. Everything that you want, like auto-pilot, AC generator, electronics, etc., must be added on to the boat *after* it is built. This is not always easy to do because so many areas of a finished boat are hard to reach or work in. The same jobs can be easily accomplished while the boat is under construction, and the job can be done right with the workmanship being first class.

If you are ever in the market for a new boat, order it delivered from the factory with all the accessories you want. Don't every buy a stripped boat with dealer installed accessories. If you ever examine a Chris Craft with factory installed equipment and electronics, you will understand and appreciate what I mean. I have never cared too much for Chris Craft boats, but I have always greatly admired the quality of workmanship in Chris Craft-installed accessories and electronics. Their electrical and electronic work is absolute perfection.

Since you already own a boat, how do you go about getting an SSB radio properly installed?

Don't buy an SSB radio, then go looking for somebody to install it. Forget about brand names, discounts and "good buys." Shop instead for a dealer with an established reputation for making good installations. Then buy whatever brand of SSB he sells.

Grounding For SSB

You have probably heard, or read, about new antennas which are "self-grounded," or "counterpoised." This is still a controversial matter and best left alone, unless you like being a guinea pig.

The matter of grounding was covered earlier in this chapter. Read it again. How much grounding you will need for SSB depends on where you boat (fresh water or salt water)

A typical SSB installation will cost around $1,000. Most of this is for installing the ground system. This is where you can save some money by having the ground system ready when the technician comes to install the transmitter and antenna.

Where To Install SSB

Warning! Don't tell the technician you want the SSB transmitter installed way up there in the flying bridge. He may tell you to go jump off the dock. He may even walk off the job. This is the reason why I am always having my gall bladder removed when friends ask for my help with SSB. They always want the antenna, or antennas, installed in the wrong place. The same with the transmitter. When you say it can't be done, they want to argue. I don't like to argue with friends. And don't start an argument with the technician when he tells you where he is going to install the antennas and the couplers.

Think about this for a moment. Do you really *need* High Seas communications way up there in the flying bridge?

There is an understandable and practical need for VHF communications on the flying bridge for short range talking to lock tenders, for docking in crowded ares and for contact with other boats in a club cruise. And VHF is easy to install just about anywhere, even on top of tuna towers (Fig. 1-27), because grounding is not so important when you work with those tiny waves of 156 MHz. Another important point, VHF has low power requirements, which does not call for heavy #4 gauge wire to the batteries. SSB radio is available in power ranges from 50 watts to 2000 watts. Since the cost is astronomical beyond the $10,000 for some 150 watt sets, very few pleasure boatmen even think beyond 150 watts.

The SSB radio is almost always used *after* a day's run, when you are snug at anchor, tied up in a guest slip at some yacht club in Bimini. The kids are running around with the dog on a leash, looking for an acceptable place for him to go

Fig. 1-27. VHF radiotelephones can easily be installed on flybridges, even tuna towers, because grounding is not so vitally important when you work with those tiny little waves up in the 156 MHz band. But SSB belongs in the deckhouse, close as possible to a good ground connection.

while your wife thaws out the frozen fried chicken in the micro-wave oven and warms the Van Camps baked beans, which is standard boat fare in the United States.

It was a long, hard run and you are unwinding with a Scotch on ice, reviewing the mistakes and miscalculations you made. And this is when you make use of the SSB radio—in the air-conditioned comfort of your deckhouse. You decide to call your sales manager back in Oak Harbor, Ohio to find out if your employees are robbing you blind in your absence. This is what SSB is mainly used for by pleasure boat owners, to keep in touch with their business operations while they fish for marlin. When the day's fishing is done, they call their lawyers and board directors back home. They never make these calls from the flying bridge.

You now have presented all the reasons, other than technical ones, why your SSB radio should be installed in the deckhouse, close as possible to the ground connection and antenna coupler. You are also closer to a 12 volt power supply, which is considerable for a 150-watt transmitter. Most radios have imput voltage requirements of 13.6 VDC ±15%. That 15% means a voltage variation of 2.04 volts, which really screws things up when it comes to tuning.

Maintaining Efficiency With SSB

For the best reliable efficiency and power output with SSB, the transmitter should be tuned at a specific voltage and used at that same voltage all the time. This is impossible if the radio is getting its power from one of the engine batteries. With the engine running, the alternator is putting about 14 volts into the battery—and *that* is what the radio is getting. Later at dockside, with other accessories running off the battery, voltage will drop, sometimes to less than 12 volts under heavy load. All this voltage fluctuation is bad for output and tuning.

To get a steady, reliable 12 volts for the radio, you must have a separate battery for it. If you keep this battery charged when not in use, it will deliver a clean steady 12 volts under load. If the transmitter is tuned at this unvarying voltage, out on the water away from interfering objects, it will stay tuned and deliver an unvarying output.

This is one of the most misunderstood problems in radiotelephone operation and the main reason for so much dissatisfaction, so much re-tuning and so much annoyance with radio technicians who get testy when you complain about their prices and their last tuning job.

There is also a little bonus to maintaining an extra and separate battery for the radio. Since this battery is not hooked up to an engine and is not tied in to the boat's electrical, bonding and ground systems, you pick up less garbage and interference. That's what is meant by "clean 12 volts."

MAINTENANCE ON RADIOTELEPHONES

If you already own a radiotelephone, you are not interested in what the new models do or cost. You are interested in keeping your radio in operational condition. You want to know how to service and maintain it.

You don't!

Why?

It isn't necessary. All marine communications equipment manufactured within the past two years requires no yearly maintenance because there are no components in them to wear out. Everything is solid state. There are no moving parts to corrode, make poor contact or get loose. If the equipment didn't break down the first year of operation, it never will—provided you keep it dry and away from salt spray.

Transistors don't wear out. The few switches and relays are not used enough in a typical boating season of 50 to 100 hours of actual running time to suffer from wear. In normal boating use, the equipment should last as long as the boat.

There is, however, a possible source of erratic performance with your VHF. Did you buy some "bargain priced" crystals last summer? The communications market today is flooded with poor quality crystals due to the fantastic boom in CB.

As always happens, everybody wants some of the action, which leads to price-cutting, then quality-cutting. Most of the new sellers were marginal suppliers who got their components from marginal manufacturers who worked out of sampans or junks in Hong Kong, Korea and Singapore. Quality crystals made in America by name manufacturers are very expensive. This created a market, in the boom era of CB, for the "economy priced" electronics equipment, which includes crystals.

Poor quality crystals have a tendency to drift off frequency, which results in a weak signal. You are, in effect, being tuned out. You may never know this is happening, until someone on the receiving end of your transmission tells you that "you're drifting away." This drifting off frequency is more noticeable on transmit than on receive. When a boatowner learns about this, he usually blames "that guy who tuned my radio."

I feel no great compulsion to defend those "licensed technicians" who tune radiotelephones and mess up teak decks with the oil they pick up on their shoes from oiled gravel roads in marinas, but this time I must say something in their defense. If you bought some "economy priced" crystals last summer when you took that long cruise, you are kicking the wrong dog.

If your crystals are original components that came with the equipment, and you still get reports of a "weak signal," then it is time to check out the system. The radio itself is only one part of a "system" which includes the transmitter, two coax connectors, the coaxial cable itself, the antenna and the ground.

There are checks you can make yourself which do not require a second class commercial radiotelephone license. Anything on the outside you can work on all you wish. You can even go into the equipment and fool around with the receiver, if you know which part is the receiver. This is difficult to do unless you can read a schematic because in the new transceiver radiotelephones, the transmitter, receiver and power pack are enclosed in one cabinet; but they share many components. Since you don't transmit and receive at the same time, many components do double duty.

I could devote space in this chapter showing and explaining how a transmitter is tuned, but this isn't really necessary because everything you need to know about tuning your own transmitter is right there in your owner's manual. I'll probably get a warning letter from the FCC for revealing "classified information." So I'll tell you something else: if you get the urge to tune your own radio, you will not be the first or the last boatman to do this.

Your VHF transceiver, if it survived the first season, will require no maintenance, other than wiping off the rings left by beer cans and cocktail glasses. But that area from the coax connection at the back of the radio to the coax connection at the base of the antenna does require an occasional check. If you have a power loss, it could be there.

You will need an SWR watt meter to check out the antenna system. The letters "SWR" mean standing wave ratio. The meters are used to rate antenna efficiency. You might be able to borrow one, but don't borrow, or use, a CB meter. It will not work with VHF. If you decide to buy one, Heathkit has an excellent meter for $39.95.

You make a check with the SWR meter at the back of the set, *between* the coax connector and radio. Then you do this again at the antenna. If the energy transmitted by the antenna equalled the amount received through the coax cable from the transmitter, that would be a standing wave ratio of 1:1, which is perfect. This is also impossible. For practical reasons, on which another book can be written, you will never radiate all the high frequency oscillations which are amplified in the final PA stage (power amplifier). Those high frequency radio waves are escaping before they even leave your radio.

To illustrate this, think of ordering a sizzling steak at a restaurant. In the trip from the kitchen to your table over 10 percent of the heat in the steak will have dissipated into space.

Before you even finish eating the steak, all the heat will have dissipated. Heat loss from the kitchen to your table can be reduced with a metal cover over the sizzling steak. This metal cover would serve the same function as the special cover put on transmission lines and called "coaxial" cables. This special covering holds down dissipation loss. With the old MF radios, coax cable was not used. As a result, the transmission wire from the radio to the antenna was in reality an antenna itself, wasting most of the power output before it ever got to the whip.

When you check your coax connections, the best you can hope for is an SWR of 1.5:1 at the base of the antenna. This means that only 50 percent of your signal strength was dissipated along the way through the cable. That is very good—in fact, it's almost perfect. Most losses will be 2.5:1 and even 3:1.

If you get a low reading at the radio and a very high one at the antenna, you very likely have a defective antenna. A long coax cable that is filled with water can absorb power without increasing the SWR reading. In fact, it can even give you a low reading, which can fool you. That is why a high reading usually indicates losses in the antenna itself. This rarely ever happens because quality marine antennas are rugged and trouble-free; until you forget to lower them going into a covered slip or under a low bridge.

Give everything a good eyeball check. Tighten the connectors, after thorough cleaning. Look for water leaks and corrosion. When re-assembling, apply silicone lubricant to connectors. This helps to keep out moisture and makes it easier to disassemble.

If you are still putting out a weak signal, then the final place to look is the radio itself. I have already mentioned "bargain priced" crystals. Next check supply voltage with a volt meter. Check the voltage before transmitting, and during transmitting.

With a fully charged battery, before pressing the microphone button, the supply voltage to the radio should be about 12.75 volts. When transmitting, voltage should not drop below 12.5 volts. The slightest drop in voltage can make a big difference in power output of the transmitter. Power amplifier plate voltages are very high. The 12 volts from the battery might be stepped up fifty times to produce the working voltage. If the battery voltage is down only a ½ volt, when you multiply this fifty times, it becomes a drop of 25 volts.

If you have a good battery and have maintained it at full charge, then you are probably asking yourself—why isn't that voltage getting to the radio? There has to be a reason. This is a very common problem when radiotelephones are installed up on a flying bridge. This is a long distance from the power source. Owner-installed equipment will almost always have wire too small for the job, like #12 or #10 gauge, which, of course, is much easier to work with when you have to feed the wire through holes and around tight corners. This is another reason why I, personally, would never install a radio up on the flying bridge of a boat after it was already built. The wiring with #6 gauge wire should be done while the boat is under construction. If you ever tried to push #6 wire through a small hole and work it around corners and bends, you understand what I am trying to explain.

If VHF is difficult to wire to battery power, SSB is almost impossible because the power requirements are so much greater. To get battery power up to the flying bridge for SSB would take at least #2 gauge wire.

A better alternative to the heavy wire would be to install a separate battery up in the flying bridge for the radio alone. You could even have a separate charger for this battery, also up in the flying bridge. This would be much easier than fighting with that heavy wire.

RADIO USE

The chief advantage of CB over traditional marine radio is that here are no limits on what you can talk about on CB. Well, there are two restrictions: no music and no profanity. But, as mentioned earlier, even these two rules are ignored (Fig. 1-28).

The radiotelephone, in the marine service, is restricted to "ship's business."

If you have ever listened to a marine channel on any summer weekend, you know that "ship's business" means many things. Calling the Coast Guard for a signal check is "ship's business." Calling anyone to check out your equipment is "ship's business." Calling other boats to check on the weather, on water conditions, on fishing, on gas availability, on dockage or anchorage is also "ship's business." The list is endless.

Women can discuss their shipboard recipes for fried chicken and baked beans. The galley is an important part of every vessel and so is endless gossip. As long as the women occasionally mention something about the boat, like how they made new drapes for the head or how they got rid of the smell in that same area, it's all "ship's business," and the FCC is powerless to prevent it. Ship's business on a pleasure boat is an entirely different thing than ship's business on a tug or coal freighter.

The marine radiotelephone is not supposed to be a long-range vehicle for improving social relationships between pleasure boatowners, but somehow it has turned out to be just that, and the FCC is almost helpless.

Radio Licenses

In marine communications, two licenses are needed. Any vessel with radio communications aboard must have a station license. This license can be issued to a U.S. citizen or an alien, but not to a foreign government, or its representative. Corporations come under special rules, as outlined in section 82.23 of the FCC Rules.

Application for a station license must be made on Form 502 and mailed to the FCC, P.O. Box 1040, Gettysburg, PA 17325.

Fig. 1-28. The Citizen's Band radiotelephone belongs to all Americans, including children, and it's use is not limited to "ship's business," like the conventional marine service bands.

The FCC maintains field offices in major cities and if you live close to one of these offices, you can take the application there personally, or you can pick up a form 502 at the field office and fill it out while you are there.

It usually takes about 30 days to get the station license if it is mailed to Gettysburg. I drove to Detroit to fill out Form 502 and was immediately issued an "Interim License," which allows immediate use of the station. The fee for a five-year station license was $4 and the fee for an interim permit was $6. I say "was" because on January 1st, 1977, all fees for station licenses and interim permits were suspended by the FCC until further notice. That is still where it stands at this writing.

Operator's Permit

You now have a station license, but you still can't personally use this station until you also get an operator's permit. This is a personal license that is required for the operation of a marine band radio station. And it is a *personal* license, meaning it does not include your wife or children. If your wife wants to use the station when you are not around, she must get her own license. The same with your children. Your family can still talk over the station without a personal license, but you must be present to actually operate the station.

There are two classes of operator's licenses available to you, the *Restricted Radiotelephone Operator Permit* and the *Third Class Radiotelephone Operator Permit.* There is little difference between the two as to what you can or cannot do. What little difference there is will be only in the physical size of the paper issued to you. The restricted permit is just a small card which you carry in your wallet. The third class permit is an impressive document that resembles a common stock certificate from General Motors. It can be framed and displayed next to your bowling trophies and Good Conduct Medal Anyway, it will impress your guests.

Anybody can apply for the restricted operator permit. You don't have to appear in person at any FCC office or take any tests. You just make a "declaration" on the application that you are at least 14 years of age. You must also "declare" that you understand and can transmit messages in the English language, or even some foreign launguage which somebody else could translate into English. You must declare that you will keep a log in English, or a translatable foreign language; that you understand our maritime treaty provisions and other applicable laws; that you will at all times keep yourself knowledgeable and informed on all rules and regulations.

You say "I do" to the above, sign the application and mail it off to Gettysburg, PA. There was a $4 fee for this also, but at this writing, the fee is still suspended until further notice.

I urgently advise that you check on this fee matter before mailing the application, *any* application, because by the time this book appears in print, Congress might have decided to balance the national budget by raising the fees on everything.

There is no age limit on the Third Class Operator Permit. There is, however, an examination. Don't panic! The examination questions are on non-technical matters like operating rules and procedures. Test questions are multiple choice, like "If someone falls overboard, which of these three things would you do: throw and anchor, throw a life ring, or throw a Bible?"

If you want that Third Class license, but still fear the examination, there is a free *Study Guide* available to you on request. Just write to any FCC field office.

Rules For Radio Operation

As a new boat owner with his first station license and operator's permit, you must allow yourself, for a moment, to be awed and impressed by the rules and regulations promulgated by a federal regulatory agency called the *Federal Communications Commission* (FCC). These rules, the agency says grandly, are for the purpose of "bringing order out of chaos."

If this makes your nose itch, it means you are already slightly familiar with FCC "Rules and Regulations" through ownership of CB in your automobile. And you are most likely wondering if marine radio will be better than CB. In fact, you are probably silently praying that it will be better.

Your prayer will be answered, to a small degree.

Marine radio will be better. But not much.

The reason it isn't as bad as CB is because marine radio has yet to catch up to the sheer volume of numbers with CB. But it will and when it does, it will be just as bad.

The main reason why I like SSB so much is because on the High Seas bands you meet a better class of people. I'm serious. CB radio is "The Pits" of electronic communications. You hear Americans at their worst.

SSB communications is the union club—the man who has everything—the executive suite. On the High Seas bands you can eavesdrop on crooks with class. You can listen to some wheeler-dealer, trolling for Blue Marlin in the Caribbean on his $500,000 sportfisherman, talking to his lawyer and partner in New York. From half of the conversations you hear, you will learn that a proxy take-over is being planned. This is a euphemistic way of saying some corporation is going to be stolen.

You can spend many interesting hours on your boat just listening to SSB. You can learn how to steal with class. What do you learn listening to CB or VHF? You learn how to carry on a 2-hour conversation using just 10 words of the English language, "you know," "okay," "no way," "tell it like it is."

The FCC blew it in their Rules and Regulations when they stipulated that radio use be confined to safety and ship's business. Those two words "ship's business" opened up a loophole big enough for an aircraft carrier to pass through. It opened the flood gates for millions of calls like, "Hey, Joe, where do you buy booze in this town on Sunday?"

Replenishment of a ship's liquor stores is *vitally important ship's business!* Before the great naval battle at Trafalgar, three ships of the line would not leave Falmouth until their allotment of six casks of rum were hoisted aboard. How chould they "splice the main brace" and toast the King's health without rum?

The traffic on the marine radio any summer weekend will annoy you because it seems unnecessary. But if you just stop to evaluate what is being said, you will find that it is necessary and it DOES touch upon safety and ship's business. Two women discussing tuna fish salad is ship's galley business and it is just as important to the crew's health and tranquility as the daily rum ration.

Think of this next Sunday when you curse the chatter on your VHF. Some day you will run out of booze and you will go on the air to borrow or buy a fifth to tide you over the crisis

Use of the marine radiotelephone in safety situations will be thoroughly examined in a later chapter on Seamanship. Good seamanship entails many skills, one of which is proper use of the radio, especially in distress and Mayday situations.

Chapter 2
Depth Sounders/ Scanning Sonar

Bora-Bora! Pago Pago! Tahiti!

Be there man with soul so dead who never to himself has said: "I'm gettin' out of this rat race someday. I'm gonna sail my own boat to Pago Pago, lay under a palm tree and eat coconuts."

I can't remember how many times I myself have said those same words, or how many times I will say them again. But another man, Thoreau, said: "Most men live out their lives in quiet desperation."

But some men don't. Some men actually quit "the rat race" and set sail for those magic islands in the South Pacific. You read about these men in the newspapers, quitting their jobs, selling everything they own, buying a ketch to fulfill a dream. And you often wonder what happened to them, what happened to their dreams.

Well, most often those dreams are shattered on some reef, and this fact you will rarely read about in your local newspaper. Even today yachtsmen must navigate in the waters of the South Pacific around those famed dream islands using very poor charts. Last summer four American yachts broke up on the reefs near Huahine Island northwest of Tahiti. It was the end of their dreams. It was back to the "rat race" for them.

Fig. 2-1. This 51-foot ketch is one of the few American yachts that did not break up on the reefs 15 miles west of Tahiti, a well known graveyard for deep keeled sailboats (courtesy of Wesmar Marine Systems).

SAVING DREAMS

There was one American dreamer who did not break up on those reefs. He is Harry Rothchild, skipper of the *Ono,* a 51-foot Morgan Out Islander ketch (Fig. 2-1). Harry credits Wesmar scanning sonar with saving his yacht from disaster on Moorea Island, 15 miles west of Tahiti.

"In this area," Harry says, "even when charts show breaks in the reef, it's still very hard to identify the opening by sight. We used full-color postcards taken from about 12,000 feet instead of the charts because you could tell the depths and see the reefs much better.

"At Moorea, the opening through the reef into the harbor is 75 feet wide. My boat is 15 feet wide. That's not a lot of room. Heading to sea, on the starboard side the reef breaks and has a sand dome which extends completely across the mouth of the harbor. You must clear the reef, then bear strong to port. But you can't bear too strong because there's a pinnacle there, which you must clear before bearing to port.

"My boat has a 60-foot stick. I had one man standing on the top spreader, two others standing on the second spreader, two men on the bow, my helmsman at the wheel and I was on the sonar. The three men on the spreaders were literally steering the ship. But the sun came down on the horizon, blinding them and obscuring their vision.

"As we started to make the exit, I wasn't even looking at the sonar, I was so scared. There was a yell from the top spreader,

'Turn to port! To port!' We did, and the sonar went bananas. I told my helmsman, 'There's something wrong with this sonar.'

"But there wasn't. About 10 seconds later, the men on the spreaders were screaming, 'Starboard! Starboard!' They had misjudged. Even 60 feet above the water they could not identify that pinnacle, but the sonar did" (Fig. 2-2).

Adds Rothchild: "I am thinking about buying a larger sonar. In any waters where you have reefs or uncharted shoals with rocks, sonar is a must."

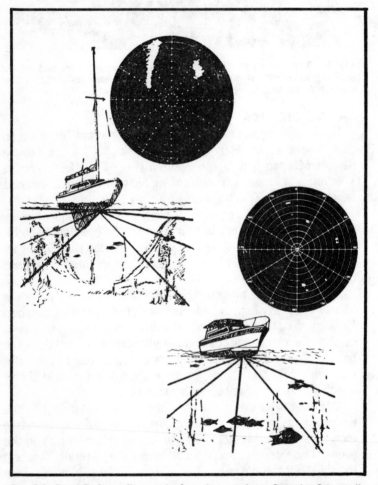

Fig. 2-2. Depthfinders tell you what's under your boat. Scanning Sonar tells you what's up ahead and on the sides, which is what saved the ketch "Ono" as it moved through the reef (courtesy of Wesmar Marine Systems).

Frank Rowland is a power boatman who likes to cruise the Georgian Bay in his 44-foot Trojan cruiser *Oblio*. This is some of the finest cruising waters in the world, but, like in the South Pacific, not too well charted—with apologies to Canada because Canadian charts are, on the whole, excellent. But Canadian charts don't show you rocks in shoal areas like American charts do.

According to Rowland, who is a Canadian himself and lives in Toronto, "The waters I like to cruise in are mostly uncharted with rocks sometimes only 6 inches below the surface. It makes your blood boil to be going along and suddenly see rocks ahead. That's where the sonar does an excellent job. It tells me what's up ahead of my boat (Fig. 2-2). Twice I have made serious errors in navigation, thought I was in one place, but was actually someplace else. The sonar got me through and into safe water again."

I am, believe me, the least likely person in the world to promote depth finders, sonar, etc., because I was the last of the stubborn hold-outs who resisted buying "electronic toys," as I always called them. I own one now, but I still have little confidence in sounding devices because I don't need a $300 gadget to tell me how deep the water is after I hit a log and bend a shaft. All of the many misfortunes I have suffered through in boating have been the kind that no sounding device could have prevented, such as running over floating objects just below the water surface where neither you or any sounding device can see them. This is the reason why I am still biased in my writings on depth finders. This is the reason why I presented the opinions of Harry Rothchild and Frank Rowland, who have had good experiences with sonar. My experiences have all been unfavorable. So for the rest of this chapter, I will present only the opinions of others.

DEPTH SOUNDERS

Depth sounders haven't been around too long. They were one of the fringe benefits that came to the maritime services from the German U-boat undersea war on allied shipping. The familiar sonar blip was used by both the hunters and the hunted.

The "blip" is actually an echo in water. In the air, sound waves travel roughly 1100 feet a second. You can accurately gauge distance by timing the echo. After shouting, if your echo

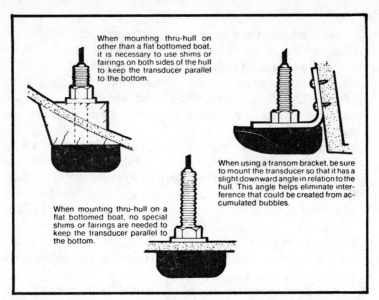

When mounting thru-hull on other than a flat bottomed boat, it is necessary to use shims or fairings on both sides of the hull to keep the transducer parallel to the bottom.

When using a transom bracket, be sure to mount the transducer so that it has a slight downward angle in relation to the hull. This angle helps eliminate interference that could be created from accumulated bubbles.

When mounting thru-hull on a flat bottomed boat, no special shims or fairings are needed to keep the transducer parallel to the bottom.

Fig. 2-3. Transducers are mounted on hull bottoms in three different positions, as shown. It is desirable to have the transducer up forward rather than aft where the bottom is almost flat, even though it is easier to install in this area. Forward boat sections are V-shaped, which means fairings or shims must be used (courtesy of Ray Jefferson).

returns in 3 seconds, then you know that your voice bounced off some object 3300 feet away.

In salt water, sound travels 4945 feet a second, in fresh water 4800 feet. Most manufacturers use 4800 feet in calibrating their instruments, which means you will get a slightly shallower reading in salt water. But this, slight as it is, can be considered a margin of safety when navigating in shoal waters.

The transducer attached to the bottom of the boat hull (Fig. 2-3) is the "antenna" which transmits low frequency oscillations of 200 kHz, which is the same vibration coming from the cone of a loudspeaker. The transducer itself is usually a piezoelectric ceramic element which vibrates when an electric current is passed through it. Like radio crystals, the ceramic element can be cut and shaped to vibrate, or oscillate, at any frequency desired.

Most transducers act like directional antennas with the vibrations radiating in a cone-shaped beam straight down to the lake or ocean bottom at a speed of 4800 feet a second (Fig. 2-4). The silent vibrations bounce or reflect off the bottom back to the transducer at the same speed. Total elapsed time for the round trip is calibrated on a dial to show you the depth in feet or fathoms.

The first depth finders available to pleasure craft were the flashing light type. They were hard to read in bright light and they were confusing when you had three lights flashing at various points on the dial. But, with experience you did learn how to read them.

It was about 25 years ago that these first flashing light depth sounders, or finders, were made available to pleasure boatmen by Raytheon. In fact, the Submarine Signal Co., now a part of Raytheon, developed and tested the first electronic sounder over 50 years ago. The first commercial fathometer installation was made in 1924. It created a sensation when it recorded a line of soundings showing the ocean floor from 5 to 1150 fathoms with the ship moving at full throttle.

Then the American advertising industry went to work and created a market and a need for depth finders. If you, like me,

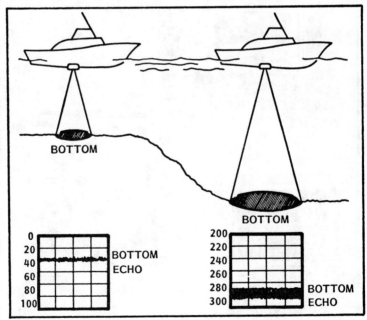

Fig. 2-4. The transducer signal radiates in a cone-shaped beam straight down to the bottom. The angle of this beam varies with different types of sounders and models. For simple depth measurements, a narrow beam is best. However, for fishfinding you want a broad beam to cover a greater area (courtesy of Raytheon Marine Co.).

didn't have one on your boat, you were considered odd. But this never bothered me because I have always been considered "odd." But most Americans have a fear of being considered different. They want to conform, to do what everybody else is doing, and everybody else in boating was buying depth finders. They were even clamping them on the transoms of rowboats and rubber rafts.

Today there are more than 100 companies manufacturing depth measuring devices in a variety that will blow your mind when you go shopping for one, and you eventually will (Fig. 2-5). The flashing neon finder is now the cheapest to buy and you can pick up a portable "fishfinder" at discount and close-out prices for $69.95.

Meter Reat-Out
Metered sounding devices, with a numbered dial face like an

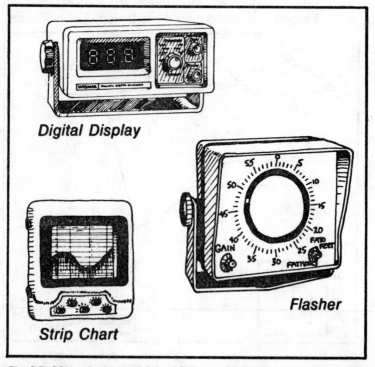

Fig. 2-5. Of the three types of depthfinders available today, the original flashing light sounders, dollar for dollar, are the best buy. They are the least expensive to buy and provide all the information the pleasure craft owner needs in a more digestable manner (courtesy of Wesmar Marine Systems).

ammeter, were next on the scene. They are an improvement on the neon light because they can be easily read in a bright light. Since open flying bridges are the thing today, who wants to look at a neon light in bright sunlight? The new meter sounders also had two scales, one for shoal water and one for deep. The shallow scale would read 0 to 10. The deep scale would read 0 to 100 or 0 to 200, depending on how much you wanted to spend.

The blips, or pulses, transmitted by meter sounders are of a much higher frequency—ultrasonic, which puts them above the audibility range of the human ear. These oscillations, 12 pulses per second, are produced by a silicon-controlled rectifier or thyraton. Two additional circuits control these pulses. The scale of the sounder is a highly damped milliameter.

It takes 1/12 of a second for the needle on the meter to deflect full scale to 200 feet. When the transducer picks up an echo signal during that 1/12 second period, a second circuit stops the needle's advance across the dial and it will stop somewhere at a lower figure. This figure will be the water depth. This is repeated 12 times a second, which is why the read-out is steady and continuous. If the echo is broken by a school of fish, the needle will fluctuate up and down the scale.

The meter sounders are popular with owners of small cruisers, 20 to 35-feet, and they are reasonably priced from $125 to $175. You could call them the working man's depth sounder because you will never see one of these sounders on a corporation-owned boat, and all Fat Cat boats are corporation-owned.

Digital Read-Out

The way the world of instrumentation is going digital surprises even people in the industry because digital wristwatches are not new. A mechanical display digital wristwatch first appeared over 30 years ago "and took off like a lead balloon," a jeweler told me.

Electronics is what made the difference, just like electronics and miniaturization launched the computer Age. What really started the digital revolution in instrumentation was the electronic high speed counter, a super-fast stopwatch that could measure and count in millionths of a second.

There is one of these electronic stopwatches in the digital depth sounder. When the high frequency pulse leaves the

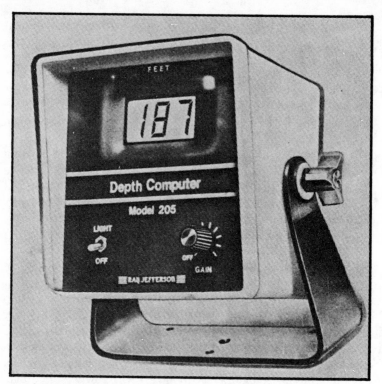

Fig. 2-6. Digital sounders, like metered types, give you no information other then water depths. If this is all you want, then digitals may be worth the extra cost to you (courtesy of Ray Jefferson).

transducer, the stopwatch is triggered to start counting the thousanths of a second that elapse until the returning echo hits the transducer and stops the counting. On the dial face, twinkling numbers show the depth.

The display duration is usually about 2 seconds. This gives the skipper 30 new displays every minute. However, this can be adjusted on most digital sounders by simply turning a dial to increase or decrease the number of soundings and the time at which they are displayed.

What you will pay for a digital sounder (Fig. 2-6) depends on its depth reading capacity. For depths up to 200 feet they will cost from $300 to $400. Greater depth capacity will cost you about $500. Digitals for commercial craft will run over $1,000.

Digital sounders do only one thing for you, they give you a continuous read-out of the water depth under your hull, and *nothing else*. They give no indication of bottom formation (like soft mud, irregular and rocky, hard bottom or clay bottom), which is useful information for anchoring purposes. If you want fishing information, digitals are not for you. Waste no time with them because you're going to have enough confusion to wade through considering all the other "fish-finders" that are available.

Cathode Ray Tubes

For the fisherman, commercial or sport, the cathode ray tube depth sounders are the ultimate tool for men who go down to the sea in ships to hunt for fish (Fig. 2-7). In fact, they should be declared illegal because foreign factory ships roam the world hunting school fish with their electronic eyes and already certain types harvested by New England cod and mackerel fishermen are showing a sharp population decline. Other species in other areas are also declining in volumes harvested. The supply of food fish in the seas, like Middle East oil, is not an inexhaustible resource.

The cathode ray tube (CRT) is just a smaller version of the picture tube in your TV set (Fig. 2-8). Miniaturization is the big factor behind the fantastic growth of marine electronics. Older equipment was just too big, too heavy and too bulky for boats 20 to 35 feet in size. Electronic micro-miniaturization and the use of microprocessors (the same type used in tiny pocket calculators), has reduced the physical size of CRT sounders down to 7½ x 7½ inches for one popular make which is capable of recording depths down to 200 feet in a straight line display. This equipment, which will easily fit into a tackle box, is practical for the smallest of fishing boats.

Some CRT sounders have "zoom" capability, which means you can change the scale so you can get a closer look at the schools of fish. You can even determine their size with this instrument. The new Ross SL 500 has the power to maintain extreme resolution (the holding of fine detail) at great depths, according to Hy Pollack of Ross Laboratories. Individual fish in tightly packed schools can be picked out, even if they are small bait fish.

Do you really need all that? If you do, then you are almost certainly a Lake Michigan coho salmon fisherman because all coho fishermen are slightly mad. You can sell this peculiar breed of fishermen almost anything if it will help him catch a big salmon. Lake Erie pickerel fishermen are almost as bad,

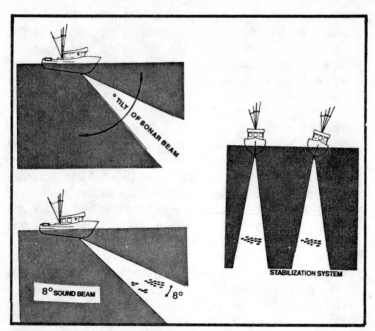

Fig. 2-7. With cathode ray sounders it is possible to not only find schools of fish, but even pick out individual fish, identify them and determine their length and weight. (courtesy of Wesmar Marine Systems).

Fig. 2-8. Cathode Ray Tube (CRT) sounders are completely revolutionizing "sport" fishing (courtesy of Wesmar Marine Systems).

but not quite to the point of madness like coho fishermen. You won't see as many CRT sounders on Lake Erie as you will on Lake Michigan. I think every manufacturer of CRT sounders has a major distribution center somewhere on the eastern shore of Lake Michigan.

Against such odds, my sympathies are with the fish. What chance does a poor salmon have pitted against a technology that helps the enemy find him in the deepest waters of Lake Michigan, and then measures him for trophy size and weight? It's like hunting polar bear in the heated comfort of a helicopter. But who said fishing was a sport?

So now you're all excited and want to buy a CRT fish finder. So what should you buy?

The CRT Fish Finders

If you fish Lake Michigan for coho, you don't need any help from me on what CRT fish finder to buy. Just ask any bait dealer on the eastern shore of Lake Michigan or ask any fisherman—even one in the smallest rented boat. You can see these strange characters every weekend drive up to the boat livery in an old 1966 Volkswagen. He will have a large tackle box manacled to his wrist, in the manner of diplomatic couriers. He will lift a 20-year-old beat up Mercury outboard motor off the back seat, carry it to a rented boat with one hand, hanging on to the tackle box with the other arm as if it contained 10 pounds of uncut heroin. Then he will go back to his car, return carrying a heavy 12 volt truck battery and put it in the boat. Only now will he remove the shackles from his wrist and open the tackle box. And what do you suppose is in that tackle box? Uncut heroin? Wrong! Out of that box he will take a $1,500 CRT fish finder and clamp-on transducer.

This man will have the soulful look of a saint as he hooks up that fish finder to the battery. He may not dress too well. He may not live too well, but he is sublimely happy. He is going off to catch a coho with the help of his fish finder.

All coho fishermen are slightly mad.

If you are not a coho fisherman or a pickerel fisherman, but you still would like to buy a CRT fish finder, and don't know where to turn to for unbiased opinion, I will try to help. However, I can't help too much because my opinion is also biased. I don't like fish finders for the same reason I don't like "sportsmen" who hunt and shoot polar bears out of helicopters.

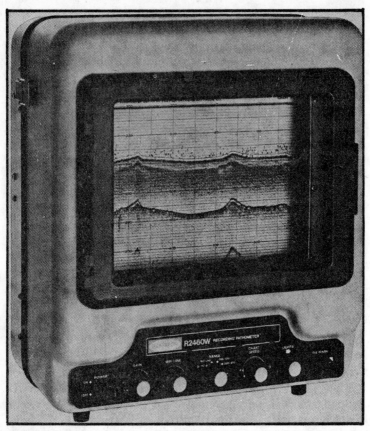

Fig. 2-9. This is strictly a recording fathometer, very expensive, very bulky and suitable mainly for commercial vessels that like to keep written records of every inch of bottom they work over. This type is not too popular with owners of pleasure boats (courtesy of Raytheon Marine Co.).

Recorders

There is still one more type of fish finder—the recorders (Fig. 2-9). This type shows water depth as dots or lines on a moving paper chart, which provides a cross section picture of everything from the surface to the bottom. The advantage of this is you have a written record of the bottom contour and the fish you passed over. You also have a record of the schools you located and caught. Recorders, for that reason, are much preferred by corporate fishing operations, and by foreign fish factories that want records of everything so that if they have a bad season, they can explain why back home. If a Soviet factory ship has a bad season, it can be blamed on the Japanese. If the Japanese have a bad season, it can be blamed on the Soviets.

Why a pleasure boat owner would need such a record I will not try to explain. I just don't know. Yes, I have seen many recorders on the boats of coho fishermen, but this still does not explain anything because these are not normal, rational people. The only thing that saves them from being committed to some mental institution is that coho fishermen, once removed from Lake Michigan, immediately revert to full normalcy and become good decent citizens, good husbands and good fathers.

Where To Buy A Recorder

The best place to shop for a fishfinder, CRT, or recorder, is in the commercial marinas and bait stores on the eastern shore of Lake Michigan. During the coho season, you will find every

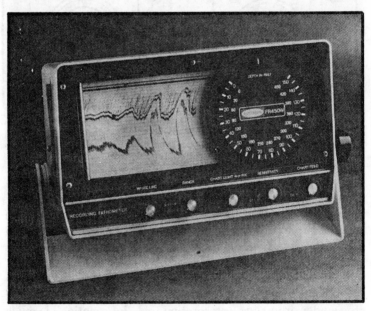

Fig. 2-10. This is a combination recording fathometer and flashing light depth sounder. You don't have to waste paper recording when all you want is depth information. This is the type you will see on many coho fishing boats (courtesy of Raytheon Marine Co.).

model and make on display in even the smallest boat livery and bait establishment (Fig. 2-10). They even accept Master Charge and Visa. But don't look for discounts during the coho season. In the off-season, you can find discounts of

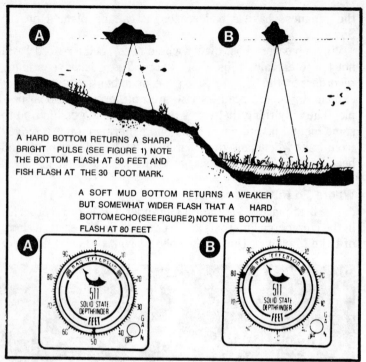

Fig. 2-11. (A) A hard bottom returns a sharp, bright pulse. Note the bottom flash at 50 feet and the fish flash at the 30 foot mark. (B) A soft mud bottom returns a weaker, but somewhat wider flash than a hard bottom echo. Note the bottom flash at 80 feet (courtesy of Ray Jefferson).

maybe 10-15 percent if you wait until after the Christmas shopping season.

If you cannot visit the eastern shore of Lake Michigan, then consult Appendix A where you will find full information and prices. If you want even more data, write to the manufacturers and they will send brochures.

If electronic bafflegab bores you, wait until you see the displays on fish finders—the lines, the squiggles, the blobs and the spider droppings. Interpreting this "information" is much like reading tea leaves, which is why I say that this is not every man's cup of tea. Some men like it. Some men never stop being confused like a personal friend who has this CRT fish finder mounted on a bulkhead in his cockpit. Up in the flybridge he also has a meter depth finder. His sounder in the cockpit is monitored while drift fishing for pickerel.

Does it work? All I get is shrugs when I ask. My friend is

fascinated by the fish finder, even though he doesn't really understand everything on the display, but he catches pickerel anyway. So he's happy and he loves his fish finder because it's a wonderful conversation piece when he has guests aboard.

Best Buy In Depth Finders

The depth finder is the most popular and most widely owned boating accessory. It is the first thing that a new boat owner buys, almost the day he takes delivery. For that reason my advice is frequently sought by new boat owners, and always they ask: "Would you recommend a good depth finder?"

And always I answer: "They're all good."

This always befuddles them, until I add: "But some are more good than others."

Their eyes always brighten at this. "How?" they ask.

"By giving you the same information more expensive finders do, for less money."

And that is how I measure a *good* depth finder. *Consumer Reports* does the same thing, only they call it "Best Buy."

So what is a "best buy?"

The old flashing neon light depth finder, introduced to pleasure boating over 25 years ago, is still the best buy. Why? Because it will give you more useful information for less dollars invested than anything else on the market today. It will tell you the depth and it will tell you whether the bottom is soft mud, hard clay, or rock. It will also show you individual fish and schools of fish (Figs. 2-11 and 2-12).

What more do you need?

You can spend up to $5,000 for a recording fish finder and not get any more useful information necessary for pleasure boating.

Two of the Best Buys in flasher neon light finders are the Ray Jefferson Model "511", 0 to 100 (Fig. 2-13), and the Raytheon Model F 360-D, 0 to 60 feet and 0 to 60 fathoms. Both of these models sell for around $129.95. Considering the deflated value of money and how little a hundred dollars buys, you get a lot of value for your money. I recommend these finders to everybody.

A second "Best Buy" would be Ray Jefferson's "Echo-Larm" Model 5125. If you do much cruising and over-night anchoring in strange waters, the "Echo-Larm" will help you get some sleep because an alarm will awaken you if the wind shifts and your boat swings around into shallow water. When running a compass course, the alarm can be set to warn you the water is getting shallower (you may be off course). This model costs $199.95 and is worth every cent.

SCANNING SONAR

I have left scanning sonar for the last because this is a piece of marine equipment of much complexity and many uses. In

Fig. 2-12. This sounder has a new and unusual feature. It shows flashing light signals in three different colors — red, yellow and orange. The red flash indicates bottom depth, the yellow flash indicates fish, and the orange flash indicates depth of grass, weeds, debris, etc. (courtesy of President Electronics, Inc.).

fact, a book could be written on just this subject alone because, until just recently, it was used only on very large commercial vessels and U.S. Navy ships. As a result, little has been written on the subject "for the lay press," as the expression goes. In the trade, "lay press" means books like this written by "lay writers" like me.

The equipment for scanning sonar was so huge and complex

Fig. 2-13. This depthfinder and Raytheon's F 360-D, which is similar in performance and price, are the two Best Buys because they give you all the information you need at affordable prices. (courtesy of Ray Jefferson).

it resembled a bank of computers for General Motors Chevrolet Division. But that was before WESMAR MARINE SYSTEMS developed a mini-mini version of their scanning sonar which could be easily "owner-installed" on pleasure boats as small as 30-feet (Fig. 2-14).

What Is Scanning Sonar?

Somebody asked this question at a marine dealer's convention in Chicago and an engineer in one of the display booths answered: "Scanning sonar is just an ordinary depth sounder with a transducer like an owl's neck (an owl, because of its very flexible neck, can turn to see in any direction, almost 360 degrees)."

That was a good description. Scanning sonar, using a combination of mechanical and sonic energy, can also turn its head to look 360 degrees all around your boat up to distances of 1200 feet at a horizontal angle of either 4 degrees above the horizon or below the horizon. This angle of view can be adjusted downward to scan the bottom like any other depth sounder (Fig. 2-15).

How Far Can It See?

How far scanning sonar can see completely around a boat depends on the size and design of the particular model. WESMAR's top of the line Model 220 has transmitting power of 2000 watts and a range of 3000 feet, which is over half a

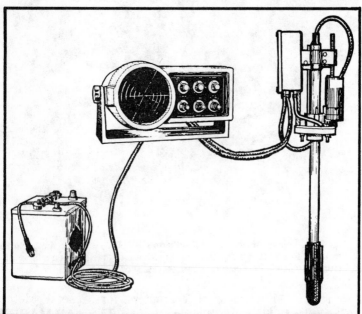

Fig. 2-14. This is the complete working package of Wesmar's scanning sonar. The transducer is the key to the system (courtesy of Wesmar Marine Systems).

mile. This impressive piece of equipment has an equally impressive price tag of $9,000. They do have an "economy model," the SS90, at $1,900. This model has transmitting power of 200 watts and a range of 800 feet. There are other models in between this price range.

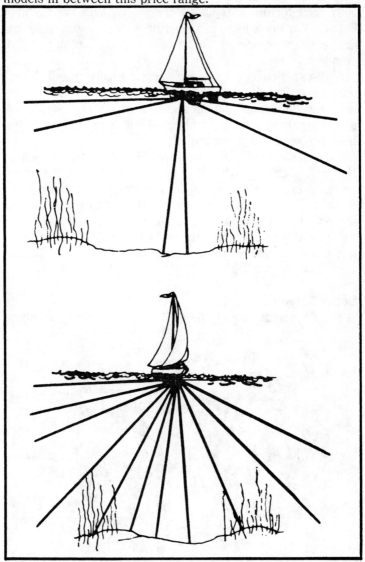

Fig. 2-15. Like a swivel-necked owl, scanning sonar can "see" in all directions, or it can concentrate on a specific spot or area, like a reef to starboard (courtesy of Wesmar Marine Systems).

Is Scanning Sonar Easy To Use?

The answer to: is scanning sonar easy to use, has to be yes and no. For some people just reading the various dials on an automobile instrument panel is difficult, which is why some auto manufacturers replaced the instruments with "idiot lights." You don't just push a button with scanning sonar and get easily understood information, like blinking digital numbers.

With experience, a sonar operator can learn to tell the approximate size, the distance from the boat, the relative bearing, the depth and the range of an object the boat is approaching. But, as you can see in the illustration (Fig. 2-16), this does require a few calculations.

It was scanning sonar which saved from disaster the yacht of Harry Rothchild leaving Moorea Island through the coral reefs. An ordinary depth sounder would have been useless in a situation like this because it was the water on each side of the narrow channel that presented danger, not the water under his yacht. With scanning sonar the reef on each side of the channel was clearly visible on the CRT display screen, as the illustration shows (Fig. 2-17).

Sonar Screen Displays

The display picture on the CRT screen is not a continuous

Fig. 2-16. There is more to the operation of scanning sonar then just switching the equipment on. There are knobs to turn and adjustments to make. But if you can adjust the picture and color on TV, you can handle the adjustments on sonar. (courtesy of Wesmar Marine Systems).

74

full screen picture, but, like a radar screen display, comes and goes as the trace line sweeps around a 360 degree circle. For example, in the illustration (Fig. 2-18), when the trace line reaches the 6 o'clock position, targets which appear at 12 o'clock will have temporarily faded from the screen until the next sweep. However, the full 360 degree scan period is short enough that you don't lose a mental image of the whole picture.

In tricky passages, like the Rothchild yacht going through the reefs, you can select smaller scanning segments, like 180

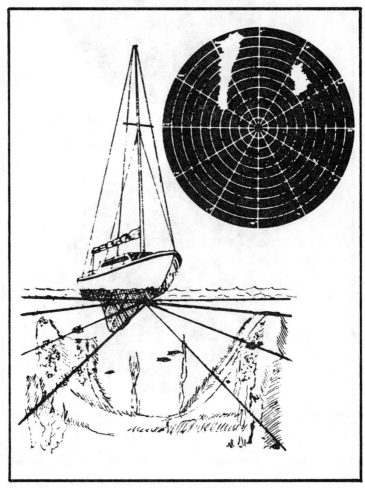

Fig. 2-17. The sonar here is scanning both sides, with the reef clearly visible on the CRT screen (courtesy of Wesmar Marine Systems).

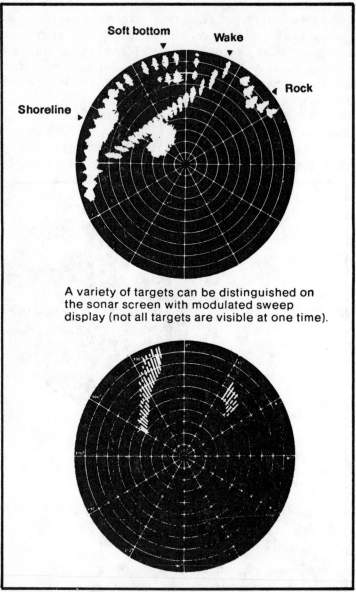

A variety of targets can be distinguished on the sonar screen with modulated sweep display (not all targets are visible at one time).

Fig. 2-18. The targets are not visible all the time, and they start to fade slightly by the time the trace line makes a full 360° sweep. If the target is dead ahead, as shown here, the trace sweep can be reduced to a smaller 180° segment, which will keep the target from fading (courtesy of Wesmar Marine Systems).

degrees which is only half of a full circle. This shortens the time you lose the picture. You can narrow down to 45 or 30 degree spot wedge. You can scan 90 degrees, 45 degrees on either side of the bow, or just one side of the boat in a 180 degree sweep from bow to stern. When running a tricky passage, or entering a strange harbor without local charts, if you know that danger lurks to port, there is no need to scan starboard. If potential danger lies dead ahead, there is no need to know what is behind you.

The Importance Of Sonar Wave Frequency

Scanning sonar as used by the U.S. Navy would be unsuitable for pleasure boats because of the big difference in sonic wave frequency used. The greater the frequency, the smaller the waves. The better the resolution, the smaller the objects that can be detected (small fish is an example).

The U.S. Navy is not interested in detecting small fish. The U.S. Navy is interested in detecting larger "fish," like submarines. For that reason Navy sonar uses low frequency sonic waves which can cover much longer distances, like thousands of miles, but with considerably less clarity and accuracy. When seeking out large submerged objects, fine resolution is not important.

Fine resolution and good detection of small objects is very important in commercial fishing. As you can see in the illustration (Fig. 2-19), low frequency sonic waves, which are quite large, would pass right over small fish. For this reason, scanning sonar for the commercial fishing industry, and for pleasure craft, uses high frequency sonic waves. This greatly limits range, but greatly increases clarity to where you can almost count the scales on some fish.

What Will Scanning Sonar Do For Me

Scanning sonar eliminates the need for a conventional depth sounder because it will do this work also by just projecting the beam straight down. But this is only the beginning. Scanning sonar is better for fish finding. Why? Fish will often be spooked when a boat passes over them. Also, as all scuba divers know, sonic pulses from a depth sounder can be "felt" when a boat passes over. Now, if scuba divers can "hear" the sonic pulses passing over, then why not fish?

Scanning sonar locates fish *ahead* of your boat. With the information on the CRT screen, you can calculate relative bearing, range, depth and approximate size of the fish while still hundreds of feet away. And if the school is moving, you can track them until they stop moving.

Scanning sonar can be very useful to scuba diving enthusiasts (Fig. 2-20) because it enables them to make extensive surveys of diving sites for old wrecks, cliffs, coral reefs and submerged rock outcroppings. Commercial fishermen always scan the bottom carefully for old wrecks because their very expensive nets can foul up on them.

What Size Boat Do I Need For Scanning Sonar?

Look at the illustration in Fig. 2-14. What you see represents the entire package of Wesmar's Model SS90. The central console will be on your bridge. The battery you already have. The transducer (in scanning sonar it is called "soundome") is quite an elaborate device and probably the most expensive compo-

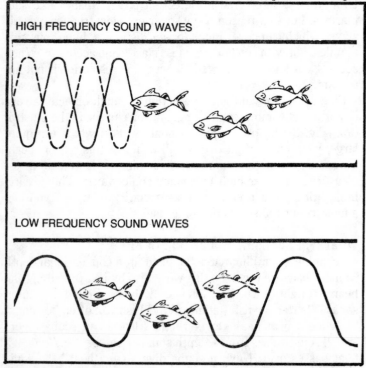

HIGH FREQUENCY SOUND WAVES

LOW FREQUENCY SOUND WAVES

Fig. 2-19. Navy sonar is designed to reach out at long distances and pick up large submerged targets like submarines. The low frequency waves used in Navy sonar are of little value to private craft and commercial fishermen who are interested in picking up small targets like fish. High frequencies used in fish detection have a short range (courtesy of Wesmar Marine Systems).

nent in the system.

Wesmar states that their Model SS90 is designed expressly for "small pleasure boats." But, it is not designed for planing boats whose front hull sections constantly slam down hard on the water surface. Also Wesmar does not recommend the installation of scanning sonar on a rubber raft.

Owner Installed Scanning Sonar

The question is frequently asked: "Can I install it myself?" The answer is: yes, it can be owner-installed, and so can a nuclear war-head be "owner-installed" on the bow pulpit of a sailboat or cruiser. After all, everything you need to know for a do-it-yourself bomb can be researched in libraries. But I wouldn't advise you to make plans for a do-it-yourself sonar installation on the next lousy wet weekend.

Fig. 2-20. Good diving sites for scuba divers can be found by scanning the bottom at an angle of about 8°. This covers a large area and more easily detects objects like old wrecks on the bottom (courtesy of Wesmar Marine Systems).

79

Wesmar provides excellent instructions for a do-it-yourself installation, and it can be done. But it won't be easy. There's more to it than just drilling a hole through the hull. There is a lot of precise workmanship required after you drill that hole, and it's not going to be a small hole. It's almost 4 inches in diameter. Is you hull wood, steel, aluminum, fiberglass? Well, the soundome housing is a bulky object and projection. It will have to be faired over. That means working with wood, steel, aluminum or fiberglass. Did you ever try to weld aluminum? Did you ever try to put toothpaste back into a tube? It's about the same.

Can you understand instructions and drawings? Just for size, try reading some of these instructions which come with Wesmar's Scanning Sonar Model SS90:

"The SS90 sonar has a 3.1" (7.88cm) diameter sound-ome assembly which houses the sonar transducer. To insure satisfactory sonar performance, care should be taken when installing the sounding assembly."

"When not being used, the soundome is designed to be retracted back inside the hull into a 3.00 to 3.11" (7.90cm) inside diameter pipe known as a "sea-chest." The sea-chest is supplied by the customer and can be 3" scheudle 40 steel pipe or fiberglass."

"The outside diameter of the soundrome is ribbed. A small amount of the plastic ribbing can be removed from from the ribs to accomodate a sea chest with only 3" (7.62cm) inside diameter."

"The sea-chest is normally placed between midship and a point ⅓ back from where the bow enters the water."

"Mounting the sea-chest too far forward increases the probability of air turbulence which will interfere with sonar performance."

Mounting the sea-chest too near the engines and propellers increases mechanical noise which can interfere with sonar performance."

"Do not mount the sea-chest behind obstructions on the hull which can cause turbulence around the soundome."

"One a sailboat the sea-chest is normally mounted just in front of the keel."

"The sea-chest should be securely mounted using standard shipyard techniques."

"On a fiberglass boat the sea-chest is often mounted in the center fo the keel."

"The maximum distance between the bottom of the sea-chest and the bottom of the keel is 2" (5.08cm)."

"To facilitate repair of the soundome without hauling the vessel out of the water, a 3" (7.62cm) inside diameter gate valve can be installed. A minimum 12" (30.48cm) extender pipe above the gate valve must be used. The soundome is pulled into the extender pipe, the valve closed, and then the soundome can be removed for servicing."

"When the sonar is turned on, the soundome is automatically lowered and should be a minimum of 4.5" (11.43cm) below the keel."

"The SS90 sonar system consists of console, hoist assembly, bronze packing gland, soundome with 10 feet of cable, 35 feet of interconnect cable, junction box, 3 feet of stainless steel tubing, viewing hood, trunnion mounting, miscellaneous hardware and owner's manual."

Who Makes Scanning Sonar?

Wesmar is not the only manufacturer today of scanning sonar. I have devoted a lot of space to this particular manufacturer's Model SS90 because it is the only equipment of this type designed and *priced* for small pleasure craft. Price is important to the private citizen boat owner who does not have the tax advantages of corporation-owned boats.

The tax laws of this country have always been written by men of wealth for men of wealth, and most wealth is derived from those entities called corporations. It is impossible for a private individual to earn great wealth, and keep it. But if he controls a corporation, he can. And then he can own the biggest yacht in the marina, the 65-foot Hatteras or the 75-foot Burger with all the electronics, and he doesn't have to ask when he orders a depth sounder, "how much does it cost?"

But if you do not control major stock in a corporation, you buy and pay for your own boat and you buy your own electronics. You even install it yourself. And you never stop asking: "How much does it cost?"

Narco Konel, a division of Narco Scientific, San Francisco, CA., also manufacturers scanning sonar, but not for $1,900. Their sonar, a very fine piece of equipment, is for that guy in the 65-foot Hatteras who never asks: "How much does it cost?"

Konel's Model FH-105 is a 1000-watter with an effective picture size (with supplied magnifier) of 12 inches, as compared to a 5-inch picture size with Wesmar's Model SS90. The Konel sonar "is designed for all commercial vessels engaged in the taking of fish." And, as you must certainly know, such "commercial vessels" are owned by corporations.

I hope that I have not offended Konel because they have helped me with this book, for which I thank them. If I were very rich, I would order a 75-foot Burger in aluminum with a lot of Konel electronics factory installed, especially scanning sonar. But, I am not rich and I will never own a Konel or a Wesmar scanning sonar. I will just dream because scanning sonar is the stuff of which dreams are made. I also wish to thank Wesmar for bringing their sonar, at $1,900, just a little closer, to where I can at least touch it.

Which To Buy

I feel sorry for the first-time boat owner who wants to by his first depth sounder. The market is so flooded with this particular boating accessory (the variety, the complexity, the price of some so great) that a man could blow his mind trying to make a decision. I know what you are going through because I've been there, so I'm going to narrow your choice down to about two or three.

Ninety percent of the people who own boats rarely cruise more than 100 miles from their home port. This is a statistical fact. The Chesapeake Bay boatman stays in the Bay. The Lake Ontario boatman, on the Canadian side, stays in Canadian waters. The Western Lake Erie boatman never sees the deeper water on eastern Lake Erie. The Cincinnati boatman stays in the Ohio River. The St. Louis boatman stays in the Mississippi. That's how it is wherever boatmen boat or sailors sail. The Harry Rothchild's, who chuck it all and set sail for the Society Islands in the South Pacific, are a very small elite group who most of us would like to join, but our wives won't let us. I had the same trouble as a little boy. I wanted to ship out on a tramp steamer as a cabin boy, but my mother wouldn't let me.

Since it is a statistical fact that you will not use your boat in shallow fresh water one week, and deep salt water the next week, the type of depth sounder you need has already been narrowed down considerably.

There are four basic types of boatmen. There are fishing boatmen, cruising boatmen (power and sail), water-sport boatmen (ski and racing) and summer-cottage boatmen. If you own a boat, you fall in one of the above basic categories.

Let's first look at the last two categories. The water-sport boatman is so busy racing around the lake at 60-miles-an-hour, or towing 4 skiers, that he hasn't the time to watch a depth sounder, and he doesn't really care anyway because his fast planning hull will float on a heavy dew. This man is not thinking about investing $600 in a recording fish finder because he has no use for it.

Next we have the "summer cottage boatman," of which there are now almost 2 million in America. This is a recent phenomenon which started with the houseboat craze in the early seventies when the first models that appeared were reasonably priced. You could buy a 50-foot houseboat for around $20,000 to $25,000, with living accomodations for 10. A conventional cruiser in this size would start at $60,000. Today it starts at over $100,000.

The buyers of these houseboats were people who normally would have bought a summer cottage up on Devil's Lake, or at the seashore. But land with water frontage has become scarce and expensive. A small lot, with riparian rights on undeveloped land, can cost $100,000. Later, when the land is developed with sewers, streets and sidewalks, the assessments will push that lot up to $200,000, and there is still no summer cottage on the lot.

The buyers who used to be looking at these lots are now looking at boats, which are a quicker and cheaper way to get a summer home on the water. Next to corporate buyers, almost all of the big boats, 40 feet and up, are being sold today to people in this category. These people are not in the least bit concerned about gas prices or availability because they just aren't going anywhere. They rent themselves some water space at a yacht club, which has all the amenities like a swimming pool, bar, dining room and plenty of activities, and they remain tied up to the dock all summer.

If you are the owner of such a boat, why do you need a depth sounder? I have no further advice for you.

Two categories remain—fishing boatmen and cruising boatmen (power and sail).

These two types of boatmen can legitimately rationalize the

purchase of a depth sounder. I'm not saying they need this equipment, I just say they can present a terrific selling campaign to their wives as to why it is more important to buy a depth sounder than it is to have their daughter's front teeth straightened.

I don't know what we American boatmen would do without Madison Avenue's help in conning our wives. Without their help I wouldn't have anything on my boat except an old lousy compass in a wood box that my wife picked up in a Flea Market for $2. Big deal!

So, you are a cruising sailor and the skipper of a deep-keeled yawl drawing almost 6-feet, and you think that investing money in a depth sounder will help to keep that keep off the mud banks. And you're right, it will.

And you, Mr. Powerboat Owner, think the same thing. This past May, with the boating season hardly started, the Coast Guard has already pulled four powerboats off sandbars and mud banks, but not one sailboat. Why? Is it because the sailboats all have depth sounders? Yes, they all did, but that is not what keeps their keels off the mud banks. Then what did? It was seamanship. Sailors trust their charts, not their depth sounders.

It is always dangerous to take a vessel into unfamiliar waters, for which you have no chart, trusting electronic gear to keep you out of trouble. Most manufacturers will warn you of this. Wesmar Marine Systems sounds this warning repeatedly in their literature and manuals: "Important note! Scanning sonar should not be used for navigation except by a trained and skilled operator, and then only in conjunction with other navigational aids."

It is the last part of that warning you must never forget: "... *in conjunction with other navigational aids.*"

What does "other" mean?

I will go into that later in this chapter. First, you want to buy a depth sounder. First you must understand that how much you pay for one has no relationship to what you will get in value. A sounder costing $5,000 will serve your particular needs no better than on costing $129.95. Why? You are not interested in fish. You just want to know how deep the water is under your boat.

It's the same with cruising sailors, with one exception. Sailors do a lot of gunkholing, which means anchoring in little

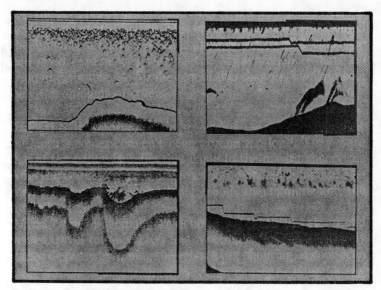

Fig. 2-21. This is what you get for your money with a typical recording sounder. Some boaters just never learn to make sense out of what they see on the paper. Yet, other boaters swear they understand every smudge and flyspeck (courtesy of Fishing Gazette).

off-the-beaten-path coves. Sailors want bottom information, like is it mud, sand, rock or solid stone. This is very important information, which you do not get with meter and digital sounders.

For sailors, therefore, the choice narrows down to any of two or three flashing light (LED) sounders, reasonably priced from $129.95 to $199.95. For powerboats, either the flashing light, meter or digitals will serve adequately, and the less you pay for them, the better. I say this not disparagingly, but pragmatically. Your boating dollar will stretch just so far, so don't stretch it too hard to buy a depth sounder. There are other things in boating far more important.

Our last category is the fishing boatmen. This is where we open the can of worms. All those 100 manufacturers of depth sounding electronics have aimed all their big guns at you, and the commercial fishing industry. As they say, that's where the action is.

Everybody in the industry, depth sounders and fishing tackle, gear their selling strategies on the proven fact that all sport fishermen are crazy, and coho fishermen are the craziest. So they contrived all sorts of goodies for you, one of which is the recording depth sounder.

I could write a book on just this one subject, but I won't because some of my dearest friends are coho fishermen, and they have been set upon enough. These poor men need understanding, kindness and love, not more exploitation.

Before you lay out 500 bills for a recording sounder, check your responses to a few recordings. Are you good at reading tea leaves? If you are, reading the four sounder graphs in the illustration (Fig. 2-21) will be easy for you. Write down what you think you *see* in each of the four graphs. Then turn to the next page and read what the graphs *really* say (Fig. 2-22). How did you score?

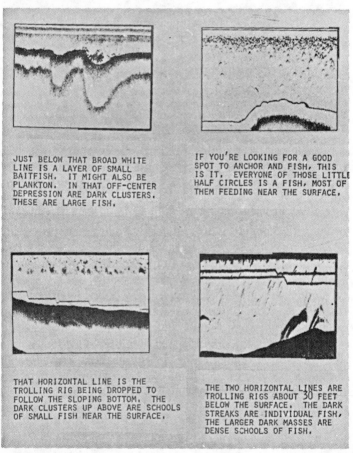

JUST BELOW THAT BROAD WHITE LINE IS A LAYER OF SMALL BAITFISH. IN THAT OFF-CENTER DEPRESSION ARE DARK CLUSTERS. THESE ARE LARGE FISH.

IF YOU'RE LOOKING FOR A GOOD SPOT TO ANCHOR AND FISH, THIS IS IT. EVERYONE OF THOSE LITTLE HALF CIRCLES IS A FISH, MOST OF THEM FEEDING NEAR THE SURFACE.

THAT HORIZONTAL LINE IS THE TROLLING RIG BEING DROPPED TO FOLLOW THE SLOPING BOTTOM. THE DARK CLUSTERS UP ABOVE ARE SCHOOLS OF SMALL FISH NEAR THE SURFACE.

THE TWO HORIZONTAL LINES ARE TROLLING RIGS ABOUT 30 FEET BELOW THE SURFACE. THE DARK STREAKS ARE INDIVIDUAL FISH, THE LARGER DARK MASSES ARE DENSE SCHOOLS OF FISH.

Fig. 2-22. Here are what the Sounder graphs shown in Fig. 2-21 mean. Did you read them correctly? (courtesy of Fishing Gazette)

If you got two right, you passed. If you got one right, welcome to the club because that's what I got, one right. If you got none right, congratulations! Nobody's perfect.

I wish I could give you some testimonials from owners of recording sounders which might prove something. I can't, even though I tried. All the opinions I get cancel each other out. One fishing friend tells me the recording sounder is the greatest invention since sliced bread. But another friend just shrugs and says: "Who needs it? I caught just as many fish without it."

My own personal experiences with recording sounders, on the boats of fishing friends, are also inconclusive. I would dearly love to own one because nobody enjoys boating toys more than I do. But I would never buy one. I would also dearly love to own a Navy de-commissioned headed-for-scrap World War II vintage submarine. But I would never buy one.

INFORMATION ON TRANSDUCERS

Nothing has been said so far on transducers (Fig. 2-23). Much of the problems and limitations of depth finders is in the transducer itself. It will not work at high speeds. There is too much water turbulence. Barnacles around the transducer will also cause water turbulence and reduce its effectiveness.

To get around water turbulence problems, some boat owners will have special fairings made and installed ahead of the transducer. This reduces turbulence and makes possible depth readings at higher speeds.

Another device, most often used on fiberglass hulls, is to install the transducer *inside* the hull and enclosed in a special oil or water-filled container or cofferdam. It works, but less that 100 percent. If you can be satisfied with about 75 percent efficiency you might try this.

Paired Transducers On Sailboats

Under sail, a sailboat heels. With only one transducer, 50 percent of the time it will not *see* the bottom because of the angle of view. The solution to this is to have two transducers, one on each side of the hull installed at an angle so that when heeled the lee transducer will point straight down.

Limitations Of Depth Sounders

Much is written in the consumer-oriented boating magazines

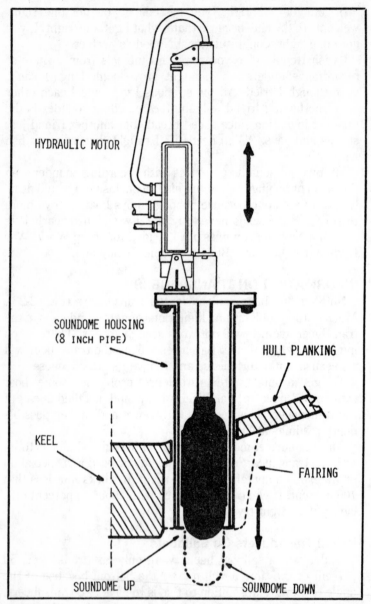

HYDRAULIC MOTOR

SOUNDOME HOUSING
(8 INCH PIPE)

HULL PLANKING

KEEL

FAIRING

SOUNDOME UP

SOUNDOME DOWN

Fig. 2-23. The transducer for scanning sonar is called a "soundome." Because of its large size, it is raised up when not in use, as you can see in the drawing. But it is subject to the same problems and limitations of ordinary depth-finders and their transducers in that they will not work at high speeds, and they will not warn you of a log floating just under the surface dead ahead (courtesy of Wesmar Marine Systems).

about all the wonderful things you can do with a depth sounder, like navigating for instance. Don't you believe it. Why? Many manufacturers, like Wesmar, strongly warn against doing this, and for good reason. Running aground happens very quickly. One moment you're in deep water. Then, pow, you hit a rock and the vibration shakes your boat so hard the beer cans fall off the dinette table.

Ninety percent of the claims filed with marine insurers are for damage to underwater gear, like shafts, rudders, propeller and struts. But this is not always because the vessel went aground. It can happen very easily in deep water when you run over a water-soaked log floating just below the surface. It happened to me three times one bad season. It can happen to you, with or without a depth sounder.

PILOTING WITH A DEPTH SOUNDER

Yes, you can use a depth sounder in piloting, up to a point. Then why not in navigation? Because piloting and navigation are not quite the same thing. Entire books are written on just piloting alone. Piloting with a depth sounder will be thoroughly examined later in the book.

Chapter 3
Position Finding
Systems

Sometimes I envy Big River boatmen, especially those on the Mississippi. All those endless miles of wonderful cruising waters, with never a fear of getting lost. You always know exactly where you are.

The offshore boatman, once beyond sight of land, can never really relax. He is always haunted by nagging doubts, insecurity and fear. No matter how big their boats and no matter how much they have gone to sea, some men never lose their fear of Big Water. And I am one of those men.

The first time you see the Gulf Stream off the coast of Florida, you are awed. It is a sight you will never forget, for many reasons. If you are in a powerboat and cut your engines for just five minutes, you're lost! You must go back to the chart, re-plot your course to allow for your drift for those five minutes your engines were idle. If you are under sail, you are never sure excactly where you are, unless you are an exceptional navigator. And who is? If you are a worrier like I am, you keep wondering if your made enough allowance for the Gulf Stream current, or did you make too much? Questions like: Was your starboard tack too short against the current or should you make a shorter tack to port by way of compensation, are always on your mind.

Why all this confusion?

It is a necessary part of "pleasure boating."

Your position at any given moment is determined by many factors. Sometimes you get the feeling that you have made a mistake in calculations and doubts begin gnawing at your guts because it is, to some men, a frightening thing to be uncertain of a boat's position at sea. Some boatmen, like me, are absolutely paranoid about this. We are what some in the youth culture refer to as "chicken-in-a-boat."

The boating industry is well aware of this paranoia, so they have provided us "chicken-in-a-boat" sailors with the electronic wizardry of four *Position Finding Systems* to keep us constantly informed as to where we are. But all these infernal machines have big price tags.

Peace of mind does not come cheap my fellow "chicken-in-a-boat" sailors and yachtsmen.

One of these "infernal machines" that has been cleverly devised to separate you from money is called the *Radio Direction Finder, RDF* for short. There are two basic types of RDF, hand-held and stationary. Hand-held is the cheapest—starting at $125.00.

RADIO DIRECTION FINDERS

I will not say that it is necessary equipment, but if you cruise off shore in any coastal waters of the United States, an RDF is a very comforting thing to have aboard. I use the term "off shore" to mean beyond sight of land on any ocean.

I refuse to say, as some do, that it is mandatory you have this equipment for off shore cruising because fresh in the news is the story of that lone American sailor, Gerry Spiess, who sailed across the Atlantic in a boat smaller than a bathtub in some motels. There was no room in that tiny 10-foot boat for anything but food, water and Gerry Spiess.

In 1965 when my friend and fellow newspaperman, Robert Manry said he was going to sail his 13½-foot *Tinkerbell* across the Atlantic, I was certain he would never work again on the copydesk of the Cleveland *Plain Dealer*. Like many of his colleagues, I was certain that Bob Manry had finally cracked up and had lost all of his marbles when he ignored my advice to have an RDF and small radio transmitter aboard.

So Robert Manry made a fool out of me. He also taught me something: never make positive, dogmatic statements when writing about the sea and boats. Always hedge a little bit. You now understand why I now say you don't really *need* a *Position Finding System* on your boat, but, as somebody once said: "Oh God, the sea is so big and my boat is so small."

It will give you much aid and comfort to have at least an RDF on your boat.

There is nothing to fear. There is nothing complicated or mysterious about an RDF. It's just an ordinary table model radio, with a few added functions. In fact, some portable radios were sold a few years ago that doubled as radio direction finders. And they're still available! You can currently buy the Ray Jefferson Model "RDF" Radio and Direction Finder for $179.95 (Fig. 3-1).

To function as an RDF, a radio must have a rotatable anten-

Fig. 3-1. This type of RDF, which doubles as a portable radio, was quite popular a few years ago. This is the only one still around (courtesy of Ray Jefferson).

na, a calibrated antenna bezel and a highly sensitive signal strength meter.

The Meaning Of Null

Operation is surprisingly easy and it is even easier with the higher priced models that eliminate fine tuning for *null* detection. Don't let the word null scare you. It just means that after you have picked up some AM broadcast or Coast Guard Beacon Band station on the radio part of the equipment. But you can manually turn the rotation antenna until the signal strength meter reads a weak or minimum signal, and that is null.

When you find null, you note the reading on the calibrated bezel. You must have a chart and a course protractor to make use of the reading. You place the protractor hole right over that beacon station you have nulled on the radio. You set the protractor arm to the compass heading you took off the calibrated bezel and draw a pencil line from the beacon station out into the sea. Somewhere along that pencil line is where you are.

You could, if necessary, just home in on that beacon station. However, if you want to plot a course in a different direction, you need still another pencil line on that chart.

So you tune in a second beacon station in the same manner. *What* beacon station, you ask? Don't worry about it. The U.S. Coast Guard maintains hundreds of radiobeacons along all our coastlines. Just tune in the next beacon down the coast a ways and draw another pencil line. Where the two lines intersect on your chart is your *exact* position.

If you are disabled and need a tow into port, the first thing the Coast Guard radio crewman will ask you is: "What's your position?"

And he doesn't want an answer like: "I'm about half way between Newport Beach and Catalina."

That is a typical answer the Coast Guard will get on a Sunday afternoon from the "boat jockeys" and "cowboys." An answer like that stamps you as a novice owner of a new boat "still under a 90-day warranty."

The Coast Guard would be pleased to hear something like: "I'm adrift with a disabled engine 9 miles, 240 degrees from Newport Beach."

That's a lot better. But it could be even better if you said: "I

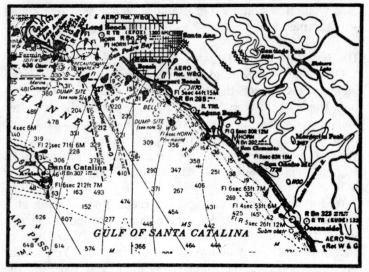

Fig. 3-2. Harbor charts in heavily populated areas, like the west coast between Los Angeles and San Diego, are loaded with good reference points for dead reckoning and radio fixes. The Gulf of Santa Catalina chart shows three radio station antenna towers. Oceanside KUDE is at the lower right.

am adrift with a disabled engine 12 miles, 300 degrees from Oceanside KUDE radio tower.''

Why is the above better?

The radio tower is a precise, minute spot on the Gulf of Santa Catalina chart. So is the radio tower at Laguna Beach and KFOX at Long Beach. Cities and even small towns are not good reference points for course plotting because they cover so much area.

With the KUDE radio tower as a reference point on the chart (Fig. 3-2), anybody who hears your radio call for assistance can lay down a protractor, measure off 12 miles at 300 degrees and pinpoint your position in all that water. Since you are adrift, they will make tone of wind direction and speed. Soon you will have a tow.

If for no other reason then the previous example, RDF is worth the money to a one-engine powerboater who has no knack for mechanics and who thinks the Coast Guard, like some state highway police, carries spare gasoline for boatmen who run out of fuel.

WHAT RADIO BROADCAST STATIONS TO USE

Just because I mentioned three AM broadcast stations does

not mean that you can tune in just any old radio hard rock station for direction finding. You must *only* use radio stations whose transmitter towers are shown on your chart. Many radio stations will not be on the chart. You might be asking: Why can't I use them anyway? What should I use for a reference point? The answer concerns the fact that the station location may be in a city, but *where* is the antenna tower? It is vitally important for direction finding purposes that you know the exact location of the broadcast station's tower.

What Bands Are Necessary?

Although some RDF radios have 5 or 6 bands, only two are usable for direction finding, so don't let yourself be "over-sold" on something with more bands. The Beacon Band (150-400 kHz) and the AM Broadcast band (535-1605 kHz) is all that you really need.

There is some practictical need for one other band, VHF/FM, which enables you to monitor marine transmissions. The CB band is also on some radios. If you are a masochist who likes to suffer, you can listen to CB all day. However, there is a danger in this. Many direction finding radios operate on self-contained batteries. You can exhaust those batteries monitoring CB or VHF all day. Then when you really *need* the direction finding capabilities of the equipment, all you will get is expensive nothing.

The logical way to avoid winding up with a dead direction finder is to carry a spare supply of at least eight 1.5v "C" batteries. But who remembers to carry spare batteries? A better answer to the dead battery problem is to buy an RDF which operates off the boat's 12v D.C. system.

AUTOMATIC VERSUS MANUAL

There are some people who will always have difficulty with the fine tuning required to establish null. They will sometimes wind up with what they think is null on the opposite pole of the compass, which is a 180 degree bearing error.

These are the same people who could never learn to tune the color on TV, or to read the instruments on an automobile dashboard. This is why they put idiot lights on cars and automatic color on TV. Now they have automatic null on direction finders (Fig. 3-3).

In the automatic mode, the antenna rotating ferrite loop is turned by a small motor, which eliminates hand turning and

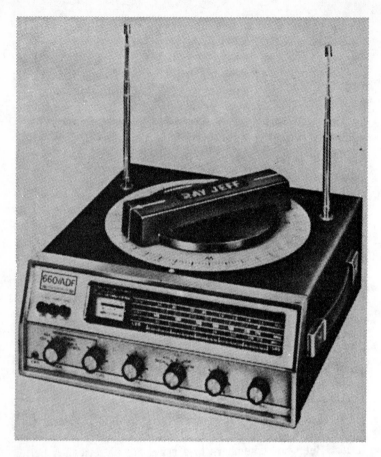

Fig. 3-3. The Ray Jefferson Model "660" is both an automatic and manual RDF with "sense" antenna, all in one unit. All you do is tune in the AM station or beacon signal. The rest is automatic. This is nice to have, if you can afford the $500 price—double what a non-automatic without sense will cost you (courtesy of Ray Jefferson).

null detection. A built-in "sense" antenna eliminates the chance of a 180 degree bearing error due to the signal being heard twice. These direction finders can also be operated manually, just like automatic 35mm cameras can also be used manually. Professionals, like myself, scorn the automatic mode on their cameras and claim they use them only on manual. When nobody is watching, I switch mine to automatic.

Hand-Held Direction Finders

Not too long ago the convention RDF equipment was a

monstrous thing with a barrel-size loop antenna, a metal cabinet and a chassis that looked like it weighed a ton (Fig. 3-4). I watched two big men lifting one off an old Wheeler yacht one time when suddenly one of them slipped. The equipment dropped to the dock and broke two 1-inch oak boards. That probably accounts for the fact that very few pleasure craft used to have direction finders. They were something of an oddity.

The new direction finders are amazingly small and vastly im-

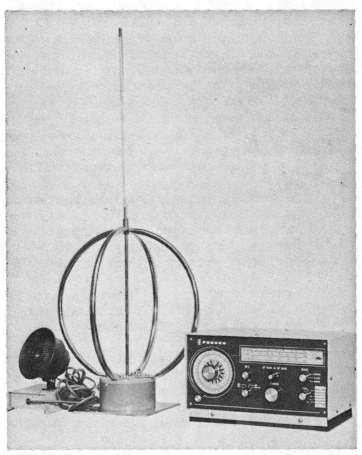

Fig. 3-4. This is a moden version of oldtime RDF that is used on big yachts and commercial fishboats that go to sea. The fixed-loop antenna with vertical sense antenna at center, and loud speaker, are separate units. Fishboats use this type of RDF for homing in on their radio-buoyed fishtraps in fog and at night (courtesy of Furuno Electric Co., LTD).

proved. Ray Jefferson's automatic Model 660 only weighs 9 pounds and costs $499.95. Their non-automatic Model 640, a pound less in weight, costs $289.95

The hand-held direction finders are the marvels of direction finding systems, considering their size and price, and also what they can give you in return for your dollars invested. Sure, you get a lot more information with other systems, like Loran and Omega, but you don't get more per dollar invested. And you don't buy Loran or Omega equipment for $125, which is where prices start for hand-held RDF.

Most of the hand-helds are practical instruments which do only one thing, but they do it extremely well. However, when you are not position finding you can't tune in a hard rock or country western station for entertainment and you can't monitor VHF or CB. If these extra functions, which are available on all stationary models, are important to you, then forget about hand-helds. But if you like ease of operation, fool-proof accuracy and portability, you will prefer the hand-helds. I wouldn't trade mine even-up for the most expensive RDF on the market.

The lack of multi-band capability may seem like a disadvantage, but actually the elimination of VHF, AM and CB bands provides for a sharper null on hand-helds. Broadcast frequencies produce more distorted bearings than radio beacons, which is why they are not used by professionals for bearing taking. The AM broadcast stations are preferred by the amateur because commercial radio is something with which he is familiar. Radio beacons, with their Morse Code identification, tend to turn the amateur off. He feels more comfortable with country western music.

As previously mentioned, you will not find all AM radio station towers listed on charts, and even when they are listed, their location on the chart is not always too accurate. The tower could be a few hundred feet off in either direction. Radio Beacons you can depend on for pin-point accuracy in position finding.

The *Seamark* direction finder (Fig. 3-5) operates from 180 to 400 kHz with no extra crystals to buy. It will receive all beacon ranges published in the Light Lists and because of its low power drain on 4 penlight batteries, it will give approximately 100 hours of continuous use.

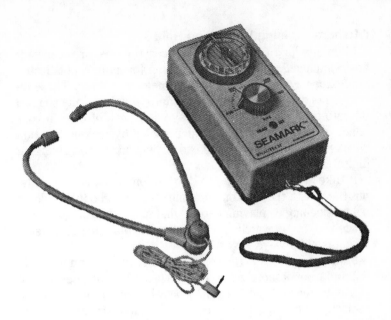

Fig. 3-5. Hand held RDF equipment is small, inexpensive and easy to operate. Since they have their own internal power supply, they can be used right at the helm when homing in on a beacon (courtesy of Nautech Maritime Corp.).

Homing In On A Beacon

The hand-helds are used a lot for homing in on a beacon in areas where heavy fogs prevail, rather than steering by a compass. All you do is point the unit to where you want to go. This is a lot easier to do than running down below to check your bearing on a fixed RDF unit. And where traffic is heavy, or in fog, you don't dare leave the wheel.

Compass steering is all right when a course is set from a known position. When not steering from a known position, you could be headed 240 degrees and still be hundreds of feet to the left or right of where you thought you were going. When homing in on a beacon, you will often be surprised to learn that had you instead used a compass bearing, you would have missed the beacon by a 100 yards.

Homing Away From A Beacon

When leaving a harbor, you can also use a radio beacon to steer a course in the opposite direction. You just point the unit behind you, null in on the beacon, and head in the opposite direction.

Offshore Cruising With Hand-Held

Making a long run up or down a coastline requires constant position checking, which is the reason for more sophisticated (and expensive) gear like Loran, Omega and Omni. These instruments do the checking for you automatically while you run on auto-pilot and try to stay away with a can of beer in your hand. You can stay awake much easier by making position checks with a hand-held instead of watching those blinking digital numbers.

It takes time, of course, to do position checking manually, but then, with the boat on auto-pilot and everybody else down below sleeping or playing cards, what else have you got to do? Since you are on watch, it is *your* responsibility to stay awake, which is not always easy.

Making long coastal runs on auto-pilot can be a stupefyingly dull and a monotonous grind. That's a fact. All you can see around you is water and the horizon, which is why an object on the horizon is always a thrill. In fact, the most thrilling sight in long-range cruising is to see your landfall suddenly, as if by magic, appear dim on the horizon. These are the moments of excitement you live for in boating.

At sea, objects on the horizon move like glaciers, 1-inch an hour. Time seems eternal, you wonder if you're ever going to get anywhere. This is the reason watches are kept short. This is the reason why I, personally, like to have something to do while on watch. Taking position bearings can be a big relief from tedium. The more money you spend for position finding systems, the less you have to do. Maybe you like it that way, I don't.

THE VECTA RDF SYSTEM

All of the hand-held direction finders today are the tunable type, where you either dial a specific frequency or push buttons, like you do on the digitally tuned APTEL DDF300. This instrument has a button keyboard resembling a telephone. With the tunable types, a whole range of radio beacon frequencies are available to you. This is both good and bad. Tuning can sometimes be difficult and confusing in rough seas and you have to listen very intently for the identifying sequence, especially if there is some interference from an adjacent frequency.

With the VECTA system of hand-held direction finding,

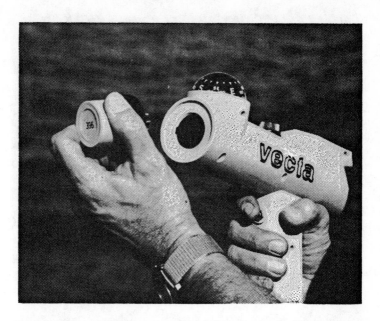

Fig. 3-6. With the VECTA system, all you do is plug in the 396 module, an then sweep the horizon (courtesy of VECTA Sales Corp.).

there are no tuning difficulties because this is a *fixed-tuned* RDF which operates with plug-in modules for different frequencies. For example, if you are in the Gulf Stream and want to check your position, this is the instrument to have. The Bimini radiobeacon broadcasts on 396 kHz, the Miami on 322 kHz. All you do is plug in the 396 module (Fig. 3-6), and then sweep the eastern horizon with the VECTA and you will immediately hear the identifying signal of the Bimini beacon. Sweep the horizon again slowly and you will get both an audible and visual null when the VECTA is pointed directly at the beacon (Fig. 3-7). Read the built-in compass and you have the magnetic compass bearing from where you are in the Gulf Stream to Bimini, and only Bimini because the 396 kHz module will not receive any other transmission in that area.

The VECTA, which costs about $250, comes with two modules. Others are available at about $15 each. If you do all your boating in a certain area, you could get by with about 4 or 6 modules (Fig. 3-8). But if you cruise much in other waters, you will need many more. This is the major drawback to fixed-tuned. This is the same drawback you have with non-synthesized 12-channel radiotelephones. If you cruise exten-

Fig. 3-7. You sweep the horizon with the VECTA hand-held until you hear the signal and get a null (courtesy of VECTA Sales Corp.).

Fig. 3-8. If you remain in home waters, 4 to 6 modules will serve your needs. If you cruise to other waters, you will need many more (courtesy of VECTA Sales Corp.).

sively, you must be continually buying new crystals, and new modules.

Hand-helds have one other drawback. Because of their small size and portability, they are often dropped overboard. If you buy one, be sure to have it attached to a lanyard, and keep it away from the kids.

RANGE AND ACCURACY OF RDF BEARINGS

Position finding by radio is effective up to 100 miles from shore. The U.S. Coast Guard maintains hundreds of radio beacons along all our coastlines. Radio beacons are also maintained by other countries all over the world.

Accuracy of radio bearings is not perfect, but it is very good. This means you can expect bearing accuracy within 2 degrees five miles from a beacon. At a distance of 70 miles you can expect 5 degree accuracy. Translated into something you can understand, this means that if you took three position sights 90 miles out to sea, your position would be narrowed down to a triangle about 2 miles wide. This is not perfect, but considering the vastness of the sea, it is almost a pinpoint.

HOW TO OBTAIN LISTS OF RADIOBEACONS

The quickest and easiest way to obtain a list of radiobeacons for your area of boating is the marina store where you probably dock your boat. Various government agencies and the Government Printing Office designate marine supply houses, boat sellers, marinas and boat liveries as official sales agents for their publications. However, these local agents will usually only stock charts and other navigational aids for their specific area. In other words, if you dock your boat on the western shore of Lake Huron, you won't be able to buy anything but Lake Huron charts for American waters. The same for light lists and radiobeacons. For more information on government publications and where to obtain charts and cruising information for ALL waters, see Appendix C.

SOME FINAL NOTES AND WARNINGS

The most accurate RDF bearings are taken during daylight hours and the most inaccurate ones are taken at night.

Be especially careful of bearings taken both at sunrise and sunset. Atmospheric changes cause refraction (bending) of radio waves. This causes false null readings.

Never take bearings on *inland* AM radio stations. The low frequency waves of commercial radio stations also refract, or bend, passing over land. They are also affected by buildings and mountains, all of which will cause null errors.

Radio direction finders have super-sensitive receivers which are doubly affected by engine ignition systems and other electrical accessories, even bilge pumps and windshield wipers. This interference can be so bad that it can seriously affect your ability to hear a station, identify it and obtain a null.

These are all things to think about before you rush out to buy a radio direction finder (See Appendix A for information on where you can purchase a radio direction finder).

LONG RANGE NAVIGATION SYSTEMS

Radio direction finding is fine for short distances up to a 100 miles, but what do you do beyond that distance?

Celestial navigation with the sextant (Fig. 3-9) is still the most widely used method of determining position at sea— excluding, of course, the navies of nations and their merchant marines.

There are two other more sophisticated methods of long range navigation, Loran and Omega. But they are so expensive that up until just recently, only navies and merchant marine vessels could afford them. Today, in the consumer market pleasure boat field, only the well-heeled yachtsman can afford them.

But it was the same way with the first calculators and quartz digital wristwatches. Pocket calculators that cost $300 just five years ago are now being given away free by banks and savins & loans if you open up a savings account. It is reasonable to expect that Loran and Omega prices will also drop.

LORAN

The word "Loran" comes from the cannibalization of three other words, *LO*ng *RA*nge *N*avigation. It is an advanced electronic navigation system that enables ships to accurately determine their position at sea by using shore-based radio transmitters and special on-board Loran receivers.

LORAN-C

By the time you read this, Loran-C coverage, as you can see

Fig. 3-9. The old sextant is still around, even as backup equipment on vessels carrying all the latest in navigational electronics. It is also the basic and only navigational tool in many parts of the world because, like the compass and chronograph with which it is used, the sextant is dependable, affordable and is never out of service because of breakdowns (courtesy of Celestaire, Inc.).

in Fig. 3-10, will completely cover coastal waters around the United States and Canada, with the sole exception of the North Slope of Alaska. Great Lakes coverage became operational in the spring of 1980, completing the Coast Guard expansion plans for U.S. coastal waters and the Great Lakes.

All Loran-A stations were to have been closed by December 31, 1979. However, studies conducted by Oregon State University indicated that the original closing dates of Loran-A service would have created hardships for commercial fishermen because the schedule coincided with peak operating seasons. So the closing of Loran-A stations on the Atlantic Seaboard, Gulf of Mexico and Caribbean stations were extended six months to June 31, 1980.

Bad Loran Signals

The Coast Guard is compiling a list of potential sources of radio interference which may interfere with the Loran-C signal. If you are having difficulty tuning in the Loran signals in your area, the reason is very likely interference.

The Coast Guard list, which will include transmitters operating in the 70 to 130 kHz band, should be completed and ready for you by the time this is printed. The list will be divided into regions, including: Alaska, West Coast, Gulf of Mexico, Southeast Coast (to North Carolina) and Northeast Coast.

If you suspect an outside source of interference, this list will be helpful. When writing to the Coast Guard, ask for their *LORAN-C Interference List.* Also specify your region. You will find an address to write to in Fig. 3-11.

Pleasure Boats And Loran-C

Who uses Loran? A study made by Oregon State University found that in 1978 more than 50,000 U.S. civilian mariners

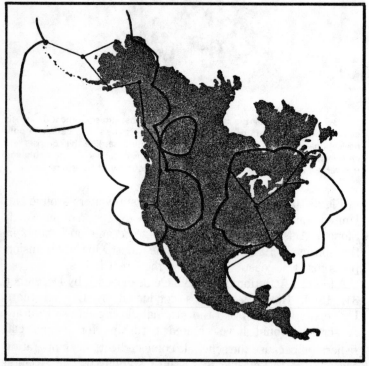

Fig. 3-10. Loran-C serves a much larger area than Loran-A with higher accuracy and no gaps in marine coverage (courtesy of Oregon State University Marine Advisory Program).

WE HAVE THE RIGHT
ANSWERS FOR YOUR
QUESTIONS ABOUT LORAN-C

Confused? Got a question about Loran-C you can't get an answer for? Write it down on a piece of paper and send it to us. We'll find the answer and present it in this column. The only questions we can't answer are the ones we don't receive. Send your questions to: THE LORAN-C BULLETIN, U.S. COAST GUARD (G-WAN/73), WASHINGTON, DC 20590.

Fig. 3-11. Loran is the Coast Guard's own little baby and they will go to surprising lengths to help you. The U.S. Coast Guard has always been the most friendly and coooperative agency in the vast Federal bureaucracy. So don't be afraid to write or phone if you have troubles with Loran, or with piloting and aids to navigation, over which they have jurisdiction (courtesy of the U.S. Coast Guard).

used either Loran-A, Loran-C, or a combination of the two. The number has been increasing quite rapidly since the study. And listen to this: pleasure boatmen are the largest group of marine Loran users, numbering more than 32,000. However, this study will soon be obsolete because Loran sales have really taken off in the last few years.

Of the entire U.S. commercial fishing fleet, only about 25 to 40% use Loran. This represents about 15,000 vessels. It is believed, however, that many fishermen held off on Loran until the Coast Guard completed the change-over to Loran-C. The total will soon be considerably higher. No one stands to gain more from Loran then commercial fishermen.

Other vessels equipped with Loran include about 1,800 (60%) commercial sportfishing charter boats; about 500 (96%) merchant marine ships; about 600 (56%) offshore petroleum service vessels; 300 (34%) tow and tugboats; and about 600 other varied types of vessels.

Loran-C Installation

Installing Loran-C is going to be a big financial bonanza for many commercial marinas, most of which are nothing but franchised dealers for many lines of equipment. Most of these marinas farm out the installation work to some private entrepreneur who operates his business out of a Volkswagen bus with an attached magnetic sign reading: Marine Electronic Specialists. This kid probably learned all about "electronics" working for his father-in-law repairing television sets. He most likely went through a crash study program with questions-and-answers books, took the FCC exam for a 2nd Class Commercial Radiotelephone License and then set himself up in business working the waterfront.

I am not suggesting that these technicians do not know the business of electronics. They do. The just don't know boats, or the sea.

My advice is this: Do not buy a Loran/installation package deal from anybody unless they have a proven record and reputation for making good installations using their own employed personnel.

When the installation is farmed out, that is when the problems start. I have seen friends work themselves into nervous breakdowns in situations like this. Who is responsible to whom? The installer is not working for you and he doesn't really work for the dealer, he works for himself. If his work is unsatisfactory, you reach him through a third party, the dealer. You can blow an entire boating season fighting to get the matter resolved. Who needs it?

If you buy from any dealer who has no proven record, or has no experienced personnel to make installations, get it down in writing on the purchase order that if the installation is not made in a manner to assure proper operation, you will get a full refund on demand.

Why all these precautions?

The greater accuracy and range which have been promised are achieved only with proper installation on Loran-C equipment—so says the Coast Guard. At 100 kHz, there are more interference sources to be dealt with and the antennas are a lot less efficient. This means their placement is very critical, especially on boats that are already bristling with antennas. Before you spend all that money ($2000-$3000) ask yourself: "Where do I put the antenna?" If you own a sailboat,

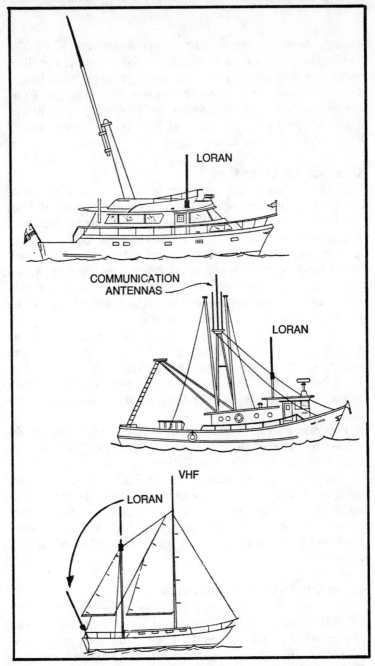

Fig. 3-12. The Loran antenna is a problem to install, especially on sailboats with all those stays and aluminum masts. Height is not important, isolation from metal is. Of the two sailboat installations in the drawing, the aft location, away from the mast, is the best (courtesy of SRO Labs).

your problem is compounded by all those stays and wires. The general rule with Loran antennas is to keep them in the clear, well away from all other antennas and wires (Fig. 3-12). Height is not as important as being in the clear. You may have to re-arrange some of your other antennas. Whatever you do, just be sure that the Loran antenna is at least 10 feet away from all metal objects, stays, wires (Fig. 3-13).

Grounds For Loran-C

At the low operating frequency of 100 kHz which Loran-C uses, ground is very important—in fact, it can be critical. Both the Loran receiver and the antenna coupler must be connected to a good ground, and *here* is where there can be big trouble. The ground lead could become a part of the antenna and pick up all kinds of garbage and interference from the boat. When checking for interference sources, this is the first place I look. There can even be serious damage to the Loran receiver if the ground is shared with a radio transmitter.

Some manufacturers use the capacitance of the antenna as part of a tuned circuit. Changing the length of the antenna can result in poor sensitivity or incorrect cycle selection. Lengthening the antenna, as is sometimes done to increase sensitivity in couplers which have a broad band input, can cause trouble.

The manufacturers installation data on this point should always be followed to obtain best performance. Too often the technician making the installation has his own ideas on grounds and antennas because he has had good success with what he is doing, so he keeps doing the same thing on all in-stallations whether the boat is wood, steel, aluminum, ferro-cement or fiberglass. You just can't do that with Loran because ground is different on boats made of wood, metal, fiberglass.

Loran Interference Suppression

Electronic interference is a much more serious problem at 100 kHz than at higher frequencies because the oscillations generated in motors, generators and spark plug ignitions is also of low frequency, almost harmonic with Loran frequency. This is where you can blow your mind, tracking down and sup-pressing all the noises you will get. This is where a technician who knows his business is worth anything he charges because there are so many sources for electronic interference, and so many ways to control it.

The surrounding environment itself can sometimes be a source of interference. We will ignore that. Just concentrate on the boat's electrical system, both AC and DC. Anything that functions or moves when you turn on the electricity can be a source of interference. When I say "move," I am referring to the physical movement that you get when an electrical motor is put into operation. When you turn on a toaster, or an incandescent light bulb, nothing moves. There is no spark arcing. When you switch on a windshield wiper, a motor is turning and sparks are arcing. It is that arcing voltage that causes the cracking noises in radios.

The things that must be suppressed are alternators, generators, ignitions on gasoline engines and electric motors of all types. These include bulge blowers, bilge pumps, fans, air-conditioners, flourescent lights, radars, television sets, and many other devices too numerous to mention.

Suppressing this noise is going to require a lot of ingenuity, perserverance and detective work. It will also require the installation of many by-pass condensers, filters, traps, shields, resistance wire and capacitors.

How much will the job of noise suppression cost?

Plenty!

Why?

Because it takes time to do the job, and "time" in many marinas and boatyards is evaluated at $20 to $25-an-hour.

How much "time" will it take?

It took me a week to suppress interference noise on my own boat, and I know where everything is. And I don't have even a fraction of the accessories and electronics you will find on the modern 50-foot cruiser today.

Some Practical Tips On Loran

Beyond the base Loran-C receiver, there is a wide range of accessories and "features" available to the buyer.

Don't buy more than you need just because you can "afford the best." And don't buy less than you need.

There is a good reason for this, according to the Coast Guard who state in their *Loran-C Bulletin:* "Some Loran-C receivers have more features then are essential to the full realization of the published performance capabilities of the equipment (Fig.

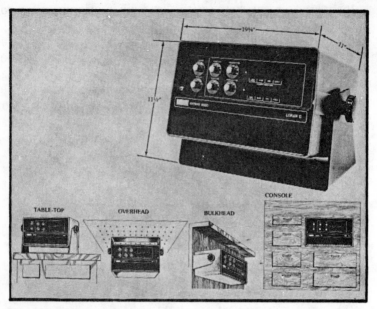

Fig. 3-13. Here some typical installations on pleasure craft are shown. There is one important thing to remember — ventilation! It doesn't matter where the equipment is installed just so heat build-up can be dissipated. Usually this is not easily done in a console. (courtesy of Raytheon Marine Co.).

3-14). Though this additional automation may be convenient to the owner-user, it can *downgrade the accuracy* of Loran-C position measurements."

The previous italics are mine.

"The propagation of Loran-C signals over land introduces some errors into the time differences measured in the coverage area. Loran-C charts include compensation for these errors when they are significant.

"Some of the more sophisticated Loran-C receivers have special features like microprocessors which compute latitude and longitude directly from the time differences measured within the receiver. These computations, in many receivers of this type, do not account for propagation errors and may contain other minor computational errors."

The above errors can be corrected—if you *know* about them. But why buy the errors in the first place because without all the extra "features" you wouldn't have any error to be corrected.

Before you buy, try to get a live demonstration of Loran-C on a boat *similar* to yours. For example, if your boat is fiberglass,

DEPARTMENT OF TRANSPORTATION
U.S. COAST GUARD

LORAN-C BULLETIN

--Compiled from Volume I, Issue Numbers 1, 2, 3; Volume II, Issue Number 1

The Loran-C Bulletin is a regular publication containing Loran-C related items of interest to users and potential users. This publication shall not be considered as authority for any official action and is non-record material. Questions or comments and items for possible publication in the Loran-C Bulletin may be submitted to Commandant (G-WAN/73), U.S. Coast Guard, Washington, D.C. 20590

Fig. 3-14. The Loran-C Bulletin is free. Send for it. You can learn things that will save you money (courtesy of the U.S. Coast Guard).

you should learn how the equipment works on fiberglass hulls, not steel or aluminum. Be wary of dealer showroom demonstrations on so-called "live" antennas. They tell you nothing about the biggest problem with Loran-C, the background radio noise, or "grass" as it is called in trade jargon. This noise can be so bad on a fiberglass hull that with manual acquisition, you will never be able to match envelopes visually because to do this you must be able to see the signals above the grass. When the signal is twice as loud as the grass, it is called a *signal-to-noise-ratio* (SNR) of 2:1. If the grass is three times higher then the signal you have an SNR of 1:3. Fortunately, the signal in most coverage areas will be stronger then the background noise, but you *will* run into occasions when it will not be stronger.

You will never get full Loran-C coverage unless the receiver can acquire and track signals for you when the SNR is 1:3 or even 1:1. Receivers that *acquire* signals automatically also *track* them automatically.

You have an important decision to make—manual or automatic. This is why a live demonstration on a boat similar to yours is so important. If the dealer has made many installations, he can arrange this very easily with one of his satisfied customers. Boatowners are always pleased to show off and demonstrate their toys. This was probably one of the main reasons why they bought them in the first place.

I have a friend who owns a 60-foot houseboat on the Ohio River. He has $30,000 worth of electronics on that boat which he doesn't need, like scanning sonar, radar, recording fathometer, Loran-C, SSB and Omega. He hardly ever moves his boat from his fancy dock downriver from Cincinnati. But when you come aboard, you get a 2-hour lecture and demonstration of all his electronics. And he becomes visibly annoyed if you show lack of interest.

I have never met or heard of a boatman who refused to let anyone see his new auto-pilot, his new depthfinder, or his new Loran-C. All you have to do is ask, but be careful not to get your arm broken when he quickly pulls you aboard.

If you're going to buy a Loran, you better start looking around marinas for Loran antennas and asking for a look and a demonstration.

When you get your demonstration, *ask questions!* Ask about noise levels and about ease of operation, especially if the receiver is manual acquisition. There are many operator actions required with manual, like:

- Turn on set
- Select chain
- Set notch filters
- Acquire master
- Select secondary
- Match envelopes
- Match cycles
- Set gain control

114

If the set is automatic, ask more questions. How automatic *is* automatic? Some automatics you just turn the set on. Others still require you to perform a few manual functions like: select chain, set notch filters, select secondary chain.

All the information you get from dealers on Loran performance and specifications is supplied by the manufacturer. There is no standard testing procedure, no common base for making numerical comparisons. What I am trying to say is: *Let the buyer beware!*

If you are in the process of collecting literature and sales brochures from manufacturers, then you must learn something about the language, or electronic jargon.

Receiver Band Width

The frequency used by Loran-C is 100 kHz, but this is the average or peak signal. The actual working frequency spreads from 90 to 110 kHz. Therefore, the receiver must have sufficient band width to work within that range spread. If the receiver band spread capability is too broad (as it is with some equipment), the receiver will pick up unwanted signals and garbage. If the band spread capability is too narrow (as it is with some equipment), there will be signal distortion and errors in time-difference read-outs.

Notch Filters

To obtain optimum performance, every Loran-C receiver has from 2 to 4 electronic controls which reduce the effect of interfering signals, most of which come from some human source. This means they are either radio stations or special stations like Decca. The Coast Guard has a list of all known interfering signals, grouped by region. They are available on request by writing to an address given later in this chapter and asking for: *Loran-C Interference List.* The "electronic control" device which removes this interference is called a "notch filter" and it must be set properly in the receiver.

Sensitivity

The greater the sensitivity of a receiver, the greater the range, or distance from a transmitter, it can be used from. Put another way: sensitivity determines how long you can use the equipment before background noise drowns out the signal. SNR again (signal-to-noise-ratio), plus sensitivity is a determining factor in Loran-C usefulness.

Dynamic Range

Sensitivity determines how far from a transmitter you can function.

Dynamic range determines how close to a transmitter you can function.

Differential Gain

A Loran receiver works with two signals, a Master and a Secondary. They are not always the same strength. The maximum difference in strength between the two signals the receiver can handle is called the *differential gain*. When you work close to a transmitting station, as pleasure boats often do, high differential gain is a desirable feature.

Power Consumption

Power demands of Loran-C receivers vary widely with some using only 10 watts, while others demand 100 watts. This is an important consideration with small boats, which are often already loaded with electronics and accessories. Most equipment designed for pleasure craft is DC with AC as an option.

Display

The Loran-C display is something you should *see*, not something you read about in books or sales brochures. This is why the on-boat live demonstration is so important.

A lighted display is what gives you information, like time-difference readings. Some sets have one display and some have two. If the receiver is tracking two secondaries, and has only one display, it will show the readings alternately. If the receiver has two displays, you can see both readings at the same time.

To get full Loran-C accuracy, you need a display that shows time increments in at least *tenths* of a microsecond. They don't all do that.

Other questions to ask yourself are: is the display easy to read? Will it be readable in bright sunlight? Can you dim it at night? How frequently is the display time-difference updated?

Number Of Secondaries Tracked

The cheaper Loran receivers track only one secondary. This is fine for one reading. But if you want two readings for a position fix, you must start all over again, by going through the acquisition and matching for a second Loran time-difference read-out.

If the receiver is capable of tracking two secondaries at the same time, you get all the information with one shot. Like automatic transmission on automobiles, this is a nice convenience to have, but it costs money.

All of the above features are important, which is why I listed and explained them. There are many more, which I will also mention, but I will not go into them in detail.

Additional features include: cycle-step switch, memory button, alarm indicators, blink alarm, lost signal alarm, cycle alarm, remote read-out display and track plotters.

INFORMATION SOURCES FOR LORAN-C

Loran-C User Handbook, U.S. Coast Guard Publication CG-462, available from U.S. Government Printing Office, Washington, D.C. 1974.

How To Get The Most Out Of Loran-C, Oregon State University Extension Service, School of Oceanography, Corvallis, Oregon 97331.

Financial Considerations In Switching From Loran-A To Loran-C. If you want more information on the principals of Loran, two good sources are: *American Practical Navigator* by Bowditch, U.S. Government Printing Office, 1962 edition and later; also *Dutton's Navigation And Piloting,* 1969 or later edition, U.S. Naval Institute, Annapolis.

HOW TO GET ANSWERS TO TRICKY LORAN PROBLEMS

One of the things I like about Loran is that you are never alone (like you are with a damn sanitary holding tank in a small town marina). If you have problems with Loran, you always have a sympathetic ear waiting to listen and help you. For example: a TD reading on your display jumps 10 "mikes" over what it should be. This happens whenever a station in another chain is testing. You wonder, is *that* the reason? You would like to know. Who do you ask?

Call or write the U.S. Coast Guard Loran-C Regional manager. He is qualified to answer specific questions and solve problems of an operational nature. If the problem is technical, he will steer you to someone who can solve your problem.

For tricky Loran problems on the U.S. West Coast, Canadian West Coast, Gulf of Alaska, North Pacific, Northwest

Pacific and Central Pacific Loran-C chains, contact:
CDR Cyrus E. Potts
c/o Commander (ptml)
Pacific Area, U.S. Coast Guard
San Francisco, CA 94126
Phone: (415) 556-8627

For the same tricky technical/operational Loran problems on the East Coast, Southeast Coast, Gulf of Mexico, Northeast Coast and Great Lakes Loran-C chains, contact:
CDR Francis W. Mooney
c/o Commander (atml)
Atlantic Area, U.S. Coast Guard
Bldg. 125, Room 204
Governors Island, N.Y. 10004
Phone: (212) 264-1272

Note: The phone numbers listed above are also FTS numbers after deleting the area code.

HOW TO GET LORAN-C STATUS REPORTS

The U.S. Coast Guard provides instant and continual updated status reports on all Loran-C stations, and they are all available by telephone.

Current information on the operational stations within the 9930 chain (east coast) will be provided to Loran-C users by recorded messages. Just call (607) 869-5395. A second recorded message regarding the 9930/7980 chain expansion can be obtained by calling (904) 569-5241.

If more information is needed then that provided by the recorded messages, contact the *Coordinator of Chain Operations* at LORAN-Station, Carolina Beach, North Carolina: (919) 791-0501.

I have hardly scratched the surface on Loran, and yet, for the average American boatman, I have told him far more than he really wanted to know. For this reason I have covered only the things a knowledgeable buyer should know before he goes into the marketplace to spend his money. Loran is not a small investment.

For the few boatmen who will want more information, I have supplied sources. I have also listed names and addresses of all manufacturers of Loran equipment .

Chapter 4
Radar

The word "radar" comes also from the cannibalization of other words, like the phrase *RA*dio *D*etection *A*nd *R*anging. It was coined by the U.S. Navy in 1940 and was quickly adopted by our allies in World War II as the official name for a new radio detection and position finding device that was to change modern warfare.

WHAT IS RADAR?

Radar made possible a means of gathering information on distant objects by aiming and projecting very high frequency radio waves against them, and measuring and timing the echoes which are reflected back.

The ultra high frequency of radar produces radio wavelengths measured in inches, some only 1 centimeter, which is less than a half-inch (0.39). Compare this with the wavelengths used in Omega, around three miles per wave. These tiny waves travel with the speed of light. They also behave like light waves in that they can be focused down to a tight beam, and then bounced and reflected off distant objects like speeding automobiles in a speed trap.

HOW RADAR WORKS

There are two basic types of radar—primary and secondary. The primary type is the only one of interest to boatmen, so I will skip the other one which is of interest only to the military.

Primary radar uses the true echo which is a reflection of radio waves from an un-cooperating object, like enemy targets, natural hazards, icebergs, mountains and hurricanes (and even speeding automobiles in a traffic control zone).

All radar systems, regardless of their type, use high frequency transmitters to send out a beam, usually in short pulses. Anything in the path of that beam pulse will be reflected back to a receiver (Fig. 4-1).

Radio waves travel at 186,000 miles per second, which calculates down to 1,000 feet per microsecond (millionth of a second). A variation of just 1 microsecond in measuring the round trip calculates to an error of 500 feet in range. Variations in time lag can be measured down to 1/30th of a microsecond, which calculates to a range error of 5½ yards. It is this time-lag error which makes it possible for police radar to calculate your speed in a car. It is based on the time it took your car to go through the radar beam.

Radar Antennas

Because of the narrow transmitted beam, radar antennas are highly directional. This beam is in direct proportion to the wavelength. The shorter wavelengths (5/8 to about 4 inches) have narrower beams. The longer wavelengths from 10 centimeters to 1 meter (4 inches to over 3 feet) have broad beams which can cover large areas, like a hurricane for instance.

Since the radar beams cover such a small area, they must be moved for a better view. This is called scanning, rotating the antenna in a complete circle, slowly and continuously. (Fig. 4-2).

Radar Receivers

The radar reflected signal, or echo, is so weak when it returns to the receiver that it cannot be satisfactorily amplified directly. So it is done indirectly, by changing it to an intermediate 50 MHz frequency where it can be easily amplified by a superheterodyne circuit. Because of the ultra high frequencies used, radar oscillators and mixers require special precision and manufacturing techniques which is why the equipment is so expensive.

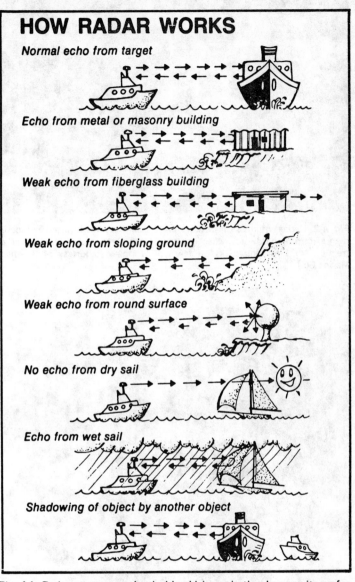

HOW RADAR WORKS

Normal echo from target

Echo from metal or masonry building

Weak echo from fiberglass building

Weak echo from sloping ground

Weak echo from round surface

No echo from dry sail

Echo from wet sail

Shadowing of object by another object

Fig. 4-1. Radar serves as an invaluable aid in navigation because its performance is unaffected by darkness, fog or bad weather of any type. (courtesy of Bonzer, Inc.).

Radar Indicators

This is the part of radar with which most boatmen are familiar (Fig. 4-3) because they have seen it so often in the

Fig. 4-2. Radar antennas on pleasure craft look more like inverted washbasins then electronic hardware, which is a good thing perhaps because it has no attraction for birds and picks up few gull droppings (courtesy of Raytheon Marine Co.).

Fig. 4-3. Radar sends out a signal and "hears" the echo when it returns from electrically conductive surfaces. The echo off the object, or target, is displayed on the indicator scope, which is a cathode ray oscilloscope (courtesy of Furno Electric Co. LTD.).

movies and on TV Late Shows.

The screen that you view in radar is called a cathode ray oscilloscope, also commonly refered to as "scope." There are two types of indicator displays. In one, the *Deflection Modulated Display,* a spot of light on the scope shifts in position to show size and bearing of objects.

In the second type, *Intensity Modulated Display,* the spot of light on the screen stays put but grows brighter or dimmer according to the information being received.

The first type, also called A-scope, is the simplest to use. In the absence of any signal, all you see is a straight horizontal line across the scope. When some object is detected, there will be a vertical deflection, or *blip* from that horizontal line. The height and size of the blip determines the target's size and its range.

After a target has been detected, on the northeast segment of the screen for example, the operator can change the antenna scanning sweep so that the entire scope can be used over a smaller range for greater accuracy.

Plan Position Indicator

This type of radar, also called PPI, combines the best features of deflection modulation and intensity modulation. It is the most useful and most popular among both pleasure craft owners and commercial boats. If radar is in your plans for the future, this is what you will buy.

In PPI radar, the horizontal line is not stationary, but rotates around the scope as the antenna turns and scans the horizon. One complete sweep will take from two to three seconds. But the image is not lost as the sweep passes because the inner surface of the scope is coated with a phosphorescent material which remains luminous for several seconds.

When there is no target, no object on the horizon to detect, the scope or screen remains dark. But when an echo bounces off some object, a white outline is literally painted like a map on the screen. You can see the coastlines, cities, ships, lighthouses and river mouths in bold relief, that is, once you have learned to recognize them (Fig. 4-4).

Radar will give you information, but it will not spell it out for you.

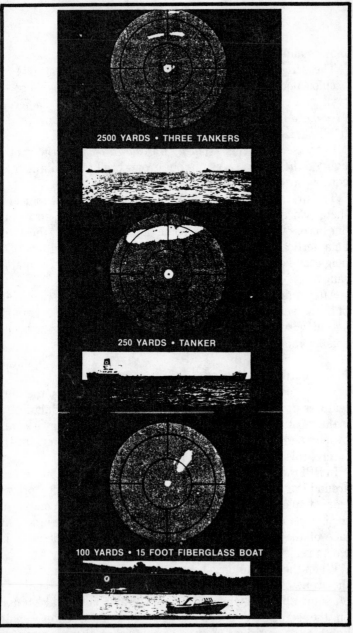

2500 YARDS • THREE TANKERS

250 YARDS • TANKER

100 YARDS • 15 FOOT FIBERGLASS BOAT

Fig. 4-4. Here are three radar targets as they appear on the scope at ranges of 2500, 250 and 100 yards. That white spot in the very center of the scope is your boat. You see the targets in the position they are in relation to your boat (courtesy of Bonzer, Inc.).

WHY BOATMEN BUY RADAR

Many of the new owners of radar thought that this all-seeing magical eye was going to banish all their boating fears, that they would never again be afraid of being on the water at night.

I am one of those boatmen who have radar, and I am still afraid of being on the water at night.

Then why did I buy radar?

content and happy. We are not content. Deep inside we all suffer from the feeling of insecurity and we all worry constantly about the safety of our families and the seaworthiness of our boats. When some boatman flounders at sea or loses his boat, it touches every one of us.

When we read, or hear, that there was some electronic gadget that could have prevented some mishap on the water, we are deeply impressed. So we all rush out to buy that electronic thing, no matter what it costs.

Ten years ago I don't remember seeing a single radar antenna on a small pleasure boat. Recently, in the marina where I live every season, I counted 19 radar antennas, and it is only the last of April, with most boats still to be launched.

All it takes is a freak boating accident involving some prominent citizen in the community. Then add a TV news interview and you could start panic buying of some piece of electronic equipment which will supposedly prevent such boating mishaps.

Some years ago, Western Lake Erie was in one of its 7-year low water cycles. It was a bad time for marine insurers, but it was a good time for marinas who did propeller repair work, and who had franchised dealerships for depth sounders.

It was a time when just about everybody who had something that floated bought a depth sounder, and not just because of the shallow water.

It was the news stories and TV interviews about another prominent citizen whose 55-foot yacht ripped open its bottom on a huge boulder which normally would have been under six feet of water. But that day it was covered by only about 15 inches of water.

The yacht sank down to just an inch below its decking. News photos showed the owner standing on the wet deck, glowering as he waited for a salvage boat.

When interviewed on TV he said: "Never again will I go out

in this damn lake without a depthfinder."

His quote sold thousands of depth sounders on the shallow end of Lake Erie.

Radar sales also got a big boost in the same manner after the publication of a 5-column news photograph showing a brand new $150,000 yacht sitting up on a rock-covered beach 20 miles east of La Salle, Michigan.

The yacht had been returning from a shake-down cruise to Put-In-Bay late at night in heavy fog. But the wealthy owner of the boat, undeterred by zero-visibility and the presence of many fishtraps, had been running at full throttle and was steering manually by compass.

How did he get the yacht up on those rocks?

When interviewed on TV he said a guest had put his beer can down right next to the compass, causing an error of about five degrees. This had pulled him way off course and had caused the boat to run up on the beach at a speed of about 27-miles-an-hour.

He also said: "If my radar equipment had not been delayed in shipment, it would have been installed in time for this cruise and this mishap would never have occurred because I would have seen the approaching shoreline on the radar scope and been alerted that something was wrong with the compass. Believe me, after this experience, I'll never be without radar. It would have saved me last year when I was running in heavy fog and hit a lighted buoy in the ship channel."

The owner of the yacht was right in the first instance. Radar would have warned him and saved his boat from the rocks.

WHAT RADAR WILL NOT DO

The owner of the yacht was wrong in the second instance. Radar would not have warned him in time to avoid hitting the lighted buoy. Why? Because radar is useless in close quarters, such as picking up buoys in a narrow ship channel or inlet passage.

Most privately-maintained passages through dangerous waters into a bay or river will be marked by wood posts stuck in the mud. You will get no echo from them at any distance.

About 95 percent of all boating mishaps to pleasure craft occur within a range that is too close to be seen on any radar. The other 5 percent are also beyond the reach of radar, like things *under* the water's surface.

In Fig. 4-4, those three tankers at 2500 yards, or the single freighter at 250 yards, present no hazard to a pleasure boat. Neither does the fiberglass boat at 100 yards. But if that fiberglass boat, in heavy fog, approaches to within 50 feet, it *will* become a potential hazard. But at that close range, it will no longer be visible on the radar scope.

Although the freighter at 250 yards presents no immediate danger to a pleasure craft, it would be a serious threat to another *freighter*. Why? Because of the difference in reaction time. A pleasure boat can react quickly and stop within its own length. Large freighters react slowly and must calculate every move minutes or even an hour ahead of time. Super oil tankers can't be stopped in less then a mile. That is why radar is so important to ships with long reaction times.

When foreign vessels enter the Great Lakes, professional pilots take over. When there is heavy fog, you can hear them on the radio with their voices snapping. Their voices really snap when they see a large moving object dead ahead in the 1500 yard range on the radar screen.

These professional pilots go by the book, but the "domestics" and "locals," as the pilots call them, sometimes play it by ear. This infuriates the professional pilots because they are always thinking one mile ahead. They become very nervous when they see a moving vessel suddenly stop right in their path at 1500 yards.

You can feel the biting sarcasm in a professional pilot's voice when he goes on the air with something like: "Eastern Star, 1500 yards on your scope, approaching down river and due at Middle Grounds in 20 minutes. To the vessel sitting in the river, would appreciate a summary of your plans for the evening. Over."

"Thunder Cay to Eastern Star. We're being turned around by two tugs. Stop worrying. When you get here in 20 minutes, you'll have plenty of room."

"Appreciate that Thunder Cay. And thanks for the Security."

"What security?"

"The security call you didn't make. Eastern Star. Over and out."

The above exchange actually took place because I heard it. Those professional pilots get very upset when they don't know what's going on one mile ahead of them.

WHAT RADAR WILL DO

Radar is an important piloting tool for large vessels who must see a mile ahead so that they have time to react. At that amount of distance, they have options. But at the 100 yard range, if a smaller vessel suddenly turns 90° and cuts across their bow, all they can do is give a single horn blast to warn them that they are maintaining course and speed because they could never stop in that short of a distance.

That is exactly what happened when the Argentine Freighter *Santa Cruz II*, saw on their radar that the Coast Guard cutter *Cuyahoga* suddenly changed course and had cut across the path of a privileged vessel. The freighter could not stop in that distance. The smaller Coast Guard boat could and did. The *Cuyahoga* reversed engines and stopped, right in the path of the freighter.

Wasn't the freighter visible on the *Cuyahoga's* radar? It was. Then what happened?

The *Cuyahoga* was on a routine training cruise with 16 officer candidates aboard, one of whom was assigned to the radar. He was a former Indonesian navy officer who couldn't speak English and had no former experience with radar or the Chesapeake Bay area. The freighter was visible on the radar, but so were many other things, like land masses, buoys and fishing boats. All those funny globs of white can be very confusing and they are subject to some funny interpretations (Fig. 4-5).

That is what you, too, will get from your radar unless you make the effort to learn what all those white globs *mean*.

LEARNING TO INTERPRET THE DISPLAY

There is only one way to learn how to interpret radar display—practice! There is no other way. If your home waters is Puget Sound or Chesapeake Bay, then *that* is where you should practice and practice until you can come home in heavy fog and be able to recognize familiar landmarks as they appear on the scope.

Here is what one manufacturer of small boat radar, *Nautic-Eye*, advises in their Owner's Manual:

"Practice in good visibility conditions using your *Nautic-Eye* and compare what you see on the scope display with actual targets.

"One useful practice is to locate your boat near a target such

128

Fig. 4-5. Radar is useless until you learn to interpret the meaning of all those white blobs on the scope. Look at the scope above. If you didn't see the boats in the background, would you have guessed that you were looking at a crowded boat anchorage? (courtesy of Furuno Electric Co., LTD.).

as a buoy, a stationary boat anchored and fishing, or a small land mass or island. Identify the target on your scope at the shortest possible range setting. Then slowly move your boat away from the target and continue to view the display and the target at other range settings until it is no longer visible on the display.

"This practice will help you compare the actual target with what you see on the display at various ranges. It will also give you an indication of the type and size of targets that can be viewed at different range settings."

Piloting With Radar

Off shore piloting is where radar is most useful, especially when used in conjunction with other aids, like a depth-sounder, a compass and a chart. Radar adds a new dimension to dead reckoning because it can see through fog for those necessary bearing sights on land objects.

Entering a harbor in heavy fog is where radar pays for itself.

The harbor range lights, which normally line up your entry into the harbor, are useless because you simply can't see them. But you *can* "see" the harbor opening between the two land masses, and you do know the compass bearing of the rangelights, even if you can't see them. Your chart shows you the water depth when entering the harbor on the range bearing.

However, one piece of information is missing—where is the channel?

You can see on the radar display the harbor opening at the 250 yard range, and you are approaching at the right compass bearing of 278°, but you could still be left or right of the channel and headed for dangerous shoal waters.

This is where the chart and depth sounder go to work and earn their keep. Water depths always grow shallower away from a channel (Fig. 4-6). If they didn't, there would be no need for a channel and range lights to keep you in that channel.

With the depth sounder, you work your way gradually into the deeper water of the channel. Once in the channel, the compass bearing of 278° and the radar display will bring you into harbor safely.

Radar In Close Quarters

Once you get into the confined quarters of the harbor or marina, radar becomes less useful as you approach within 50 yards of other objects. The radar angle of view shrinks down and is often too narrow at ranges closer than 100 feet.

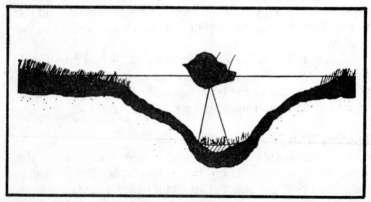

Fig. 4-6. With the depth sounder you find the deep water of a dredged channel entering an inlet or harbor. After that, the range lights compass bearing and radar will keep you in the channel (courtesy of Ray Jefferson).

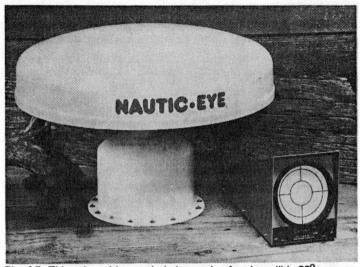

Fig. 4-7. This radar, with a vertical view angle of an incredible 28°, can see targets at a minimum range of 30 feet. This is what you need on small pleasure craft, more so then seeing targets at 1500 yards (courtesy of Bonzer, Inc.).

Radar Angle Of View

The manufacturer claims for minimum angle of view are a little like auto maker claims for gas mileage on their new models.

Minimum angle of view is very important because it determines how close you can get to a target before losing it on the display.

The usual horizontal angle of view is about 2-3°. This angle is not too important because the antenna is continuously sweeping at about 24 rpm. The vertical angle of view is usually about 20°. Rotating the antenna does not increase the up and down view, and the higher the antenna is mounted, like on a sailboat, the more limited the view on close range. On large merchant vessels, and Navy ships, the very high mounted antennas miss anything closer than 200-300 yards.

The Bonzer Company manufactures a radar expressly for *small* pleasure craft. Their *Nautic-Eye*, which sells for $1,695, weighs only 5¼ pounds and has a 5-inch scope in a 6½ x 5½ cabinet. I mention this equipment because the manufacturer claims their *Nautic-Eye* (Fig. 4-7) has a vertical angle of view of 28° with a minimum range of 10 yards.

This is really amazing because it opens up a whole new area of usefulness for small pleasure craft who spend a great deal of time maneuvering in close proximity to other boats and other objects. This means that you can come home to your harbor in heavy pea-soup fog, maneuver your way in and around all the other boats at their moorings and, finally, even pick up your own mooring.

OWNER — SKIPPER
ANDREW M. GAULT
PORT ARANAS, TEXAS

PROMESA II

90th & Cody
Overland Park,
Kansas 66214
(913) 888-8760

RADAR
By
BONZER

Fig. 4-8. The mizzen mast on a yawl or ketch is the ideal location for the radar antenna because the spreaders are not up so high. Getting the antenna up too high reduces close range viewing, which is the chief advantage of this particular unit (courtesy of Bonzer, Inc.).

To appreciate how wonderful this is, you have to experience the fears and uncertainties of entering a quiet mooring basin in heavy fog. You're happy to have made it home safe, but you're still not all the way home, tied up to your own mooring.

On the radar display you can see hundreds of white marks, which are boats at their moorings. But these are all beyond the 100 yard range mark. As you get closer, you begin to lose them on the display.

What do you do now?

This happended to me once. If you do not own a Bonzer *Nautic-Eye*, you should perhaps do the same thing I did. I dropped the hook, made some coffee, and watched TV until the fog lifted.

INSTALLING THE ANTENNA/ROTATOR

With a small radar unit like *Nautic-Eye*, the owner can do the installation work himself. The display indicator is so tiny it can be installed just about anywhere. But the antenna/rotator will take some work and improvising. In fact, radar antennas always require ingenuity and improvising when being installed because the superstructure of small pleasure craft currently being built of fiberglass makes it hard to install a radar antenna.

Small cruisers built of wood just a few years ago had rakish-looking masts slanted back off the top of the trunk cabin. It made an ideal place for a platform to hold the radar antenna. However, this mast, like the watch pocket in men's pants, was scrapped on marine designer drawing boards, and nobody seems to have noticed but me. I wonder why.

Installing Radar Antennas On Sailboats

On a small cruiser, or sailboat, some sort of mast and platform must be devised, as in Fig. 4-8. A flybridge with a hardtop makes a good platform for the antenna. There must be no boat structure to shadow the radar beam. It should be mounted so that it "sees" over the top of any large obstruction (Fig. 4-9).

If you're wondering about the aluminum mast of sailboats, strangely enough, they have not been found to seriously affect performance, even with masts of 4-inch diameter, one inch from the rotating antenna.

On sailboats, the antenna/rotator is always mounted about

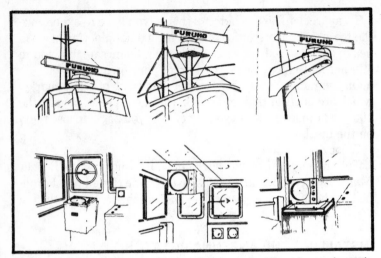

Fig. 4-9. On some cruising boats, a platform or pedestal may have to be made to hold the antenna. Shown also are various methods of installing the display unit (courtesy of Furuno Electric Co., LTD.).

half way up the mast and on the forward side facing the bow. Any clutter caused by the mast will be on a display area of the scope which is where the boat has *been* and not where it is *going.*

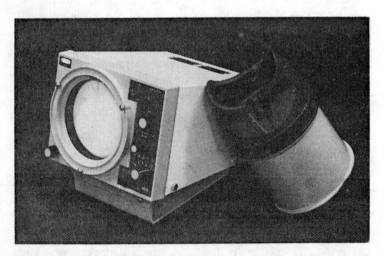

Fig. 4-10. Raytheon's Model 2600, like Bonzer's Nautic Eye, has a minimum of knobs to turn. The viewing hood is helpful in daylight viewing, like running in fog (courtesy of Raytheon Marine Co.).

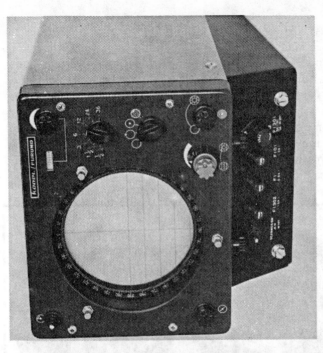

Fig. 4-11. The more you pay, the more knobs you have to turn. This is both good and bad. Some people like to control things while some people like everything done automatically for them. For the automatic buffs, Bonzer's Nautic-Eye, with just two knobs, is best (courtesy of Furuno Electric Co., LTD.).

OPERATION

Some radar units are easy to operate (Fig. 4-10), they have just two knobs. Some are not so easy. Some have 4 to 8 knobs to turn, adjust and evaluate (Fig. 4-11). Radar picks up a lot of clutter from precipitation and waves. There is a knob for tuning out the clutter, or grass as it is also called. There is also a fine tuning knob for optimum response; a gain control for brightness level; a centering adjustment; a bearing cursor adjustment; and a heading marker alignment control to synchronize the scanner and display unit. And finally, there is also a range selector knob.

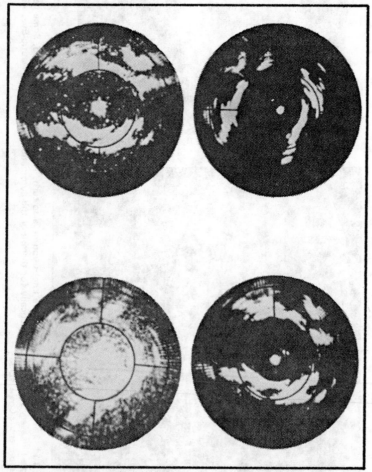

Fig. 4-12. The sensitivity "gain" control on radar determines what you get on the scope (courtesy of Bonzer, Inc.).

Bonzer's *Nautic-Eye* has just two knobs. The one knob turns the set on/off and also adjusts gain or sensitivity. The other knob selects ranges of 100, 250, 1,000 and 2,500 yards. The unit has no clutter control knob since this is all eliminated automatically.

The sensitivity, or "gain," control is common with all radar equipment and Fig. 4-12 shows you how it is used to get optimum display.

POWER REQUIREMENTS

This is where you stop and ponder, when considering the purchase of radar. What is the *real* reason you want this gadget?

Small cruisers, under 30 feet, have limited self-sustained electrical capacity, and all of those in the 12 volt DC variety produce their electricity by one or two alternators while the engines are *running*.

With a peak power output of 40 watts, *Nautic-Eye* uses only 30 watts. This you can live with. This makes Bonzer's radar ideal for cruisers as small as 25-feet with one engine.

The range of 2500 yards is not much by commercial marine standards, but it is more then sufficient to meet the needs of small boats in the 25-to-30-foot class who will not be using radar to scan the shipping lanes of the Great Lakes or the Atlantic Ocean.

To get more range, like 32 miles with the Seatron Model "32M", requires a transmitter with 5 kw (5000 watts) of peak power output.

The Konel "KRA-124" has a range of 24 miles with a 7 kw (7000 watt) transmitter (See Appendix A for information on where to purchase radar equipment).

Chapter 5
Miscellaneous

The word "autopilot" is a misnomer. There is no such thing as an automatic pilot, and there never will be.

"AUTOMATIC PILOTS"
Mechanical contrivances that will steer your boat to a pre-determined compass course have been around for over 40 years, but they don't really pilot your boat because only you know where the boat is going. The skipper pilots the boat. The mechanical steering device merely follows your orders and holds the compass course you have plotted and set. When there are changes to be made in a heading, as there always are, you will make the change, not the brainless mechanical slave.

Since the word "autopilot" is so established by usage, I will continue to use the word, but only as a name and not as a description, for all mechanical steering devices.

The Hunting Type
When the first automatic steering system was developed in the 1930s, it was called a *hunting* pilot. If you ever saw one in action, you would understand why. It was a very busy little machine that never stopped moving the wheel back and forth as though it was hunting for the right course but couldn't quite

find it.

All this back and forth movement of the wheel averaged out and you eventually arrived where you wanted to go, but you traveled a zigzag course to get there. Under sail you expect this, but under power it is a waste of time and fuel. It also puts unnecessary wear and tear on the equipment and drains a lot of power from the boat's batteries.

With all its faults, the hunting type autopilots (Fig. 5-1) are simple and very reliable. They are also the least expensive to buy because they have the fewest parts and components.

The Non-Hunting Type

A new breed of autopilots was developed about 10 years later in the '40s, the non-hunting dead-band type. With this type there is no constant port/starboard movement of the wheel, which remains stationary until the boat strays off course.

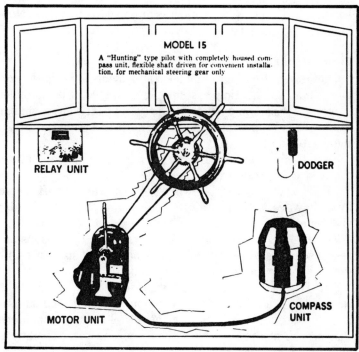

MODEL 15

A "Hunting" type pilot with completely housed compass unit, flexible shaft driven for convenient installation, for mechanical steering gear only

RELAY UNIT

DODGER

MOTOR UNIT

COMPASS UNIT

Fig. 5-1. The "hunting" type autopilots are still the most widely used because they've been around a long time, they're simple, easy to install and maintain and the least expensive to buy (courtesy of Wood Freeman).

The amount of stray or variation in compass heading is called the *dead-band*. It is an adjustable window, or area, that the heading can vary before the autopilot corrects it by moving the wheel.

The non-hunting type works well, but only at a certain speed for which it is geared. When a boat is moving slowly, as in heavy seas, a human helmsman will move the wheel hard and quick to keep on course. But the autopilot keeps on correcting the same way as if the boat were moving along at a moderate speed with strong water pressure on the rudders and instant response.

At high boat speed it over-corrects and overshoots the course heading. At low speeds in heavy seas it corrects too slowly. Only at the one speed for which the pilot has been geared will it steer a straight course, with the wheel being moved only when the boat passes out of the dead-band area.

In other words, at slow or faster speeds you still travel a zigzag course. The chief advantage of non-hunting is less wear and tear on the equipment and less drain on the batteries. Non-hunting also costs more to buy.

Proportional Rate Non-Hunting

The newest thing in autopilot status symbols is the *proportional rate* non-hunting system. In this type, the autopilot moves the wheel only when the boat strays off course, similar to the second type, but it does this in three better ways than the dead-band type.

First: there is no window, the pilot corrects instantly at the slightest course deviation.

Second: at slow speeds, or when the boat is pushed off course by a big wave, the pilot adjusts by swinging the wheel harder and faster.

Third: at high speeds in calm waters, when there is instant response to the wheel, the pilot again adjusts by making a slow gradual correction to prevent over-shooting.

This is what is meant by proportional rate. It operates the same way as a human helmsman would. This device adjusts the response and movement of the wheel to meet conditions that prevail at the moment, such as speed, water conditions and the amount of error.

Proportional rate non-hunting is like a human hand on the wheel—in fact, even better because its eyes never stray from

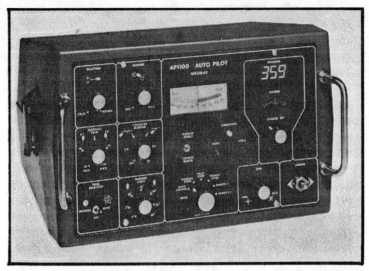

Fig. 5-2. The Wesmar AP1100 is an impressive automatic steering system and a gadgeteers delight with all those dials to play with. If you can afford the options, especialliy the digital compass, it will impress your guests (courtesy of Wesmar Marine Electronics).

the compass due to boredom and weariness as so often happens with a human helmsman. This is why tricks at the wheel are purposely kept short by wise skippers. Helm duty can be a drag on long runs. This is why an automatic pilot is one of the most useful conveniences aboard slow-moving powerboats. The autopilot never gets bored, never dozes off and never complains about having to take the helm while everybody else is below playing cards and drinking beer.

The proportional rate autopilot also consumes battery amperage at a rate in proportion to its corrective action. With a boat moving at high speed in calm seas, the pilot drive motor might consume only 1 ampere of current at 1/10th RPM. But at slow speeds in rough water, the drive motor works harder and consumes 5 amperes of current at 10 RPM.

All modern powerboats being built today, with factory installed automatic pilots, are coming through with the proportional rate non-hunting systems. This does not suggest that the two other types have become obsolete. On the contrary, they are more in evidence then ever because there is a special need in certain types of installation for the hunting and non-hunting. Also, they are less costly and more easily installed by boat owners themselves.

Affluent boat buyers today (the only ones who can afford the Big Name fiberglass luxury cruisers in the 40-foot and up class) do not quibble about cost of accessory equipment. They demand the best that is available, so builders install one of the proportional rate autopilots like the Benmar "Course Setter 21" or the Wesmar AP1100. If I was loaded I would dearly love to own that Wesmar with all those knobs and switches to play with (Fig. 5-2).

HOW AN AUTOPILOT WORKS

There are three basic components common to all automatic pilots—a compass, an electronic control unit and an electric motor to move the rudders.

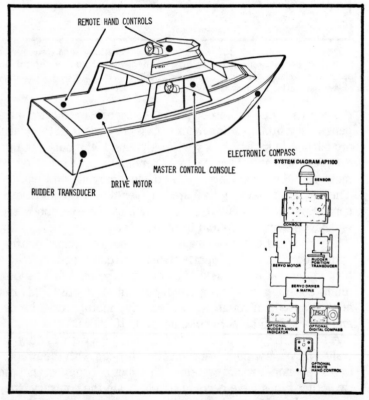

Fig. 5-3. The Wesmar autopilot system, as the above diagram shows, is more complicated and has more components. However, three of the above, 6, 7 and 8, are really unnecessary since they are optional extras (courtesy of Wesmar Marine Electroncs).

The compass "senses" the course heading and relays the information to the control unit which converts this to an electronic signal. The rudder position is also "sensed" and converted to an electronic signal. If the rudder and compass signals do not match, an error signal is generated. After being amplified, the error signal, through relays and transistors, actuates an electric motor linked to the boat rudder system. When the rudder is back on course, the error signal is nulled, and remains so until the compass sends another port or starboard error signal.

The above is an over-simplification, but it is basically what all autopilots do to keep a vessel on course. Each manufacturer develops his own refinements and improvements to this basic principle (Fig. 5-3).

THE AUTOPILOT COMPASS

The compass is where big improvements have been made, especially in the small pleasure boat field. The compass is the brain of the whole automatic steering system and for over 40 years mechanical compasses have been the only thing that was available for small boat pilots.

A mechanical compass is nothing more than a round card balanced on a jeweled pivot and completely enveloped (damped) by some fluid. The fluid is there to give the card stability while it remains pointed north, regardless of the boat's point of direction.

Down through the years all kinds of improvements have been attempted, and made, to compensate for the inherent weakness of all magnetic compasses—its tendency to "swirl" in rough seas. This over-activity is sometimes derisively referred to as "a busy little compass."

A good compass is a steady compass. The card moves *only* when the boat changes course. It follows the boat's movements slowly and smoothly and it never bounces or swings back and forth, but stops instantly.

This type of compass is available, but it is not sold in auto supply stores with dashboard mounts.

With mechanical compasses all sorts of methods have been devised to "pick off" course information which could be converted to an electronic signal and then be "read" by the control unit. A popular method used by three manufacturers uses lights and photo cells. Another method is an inductive pick-off.

Wood Freeman autopilots use two unique pick-off devices on both their hunting and non-hunting systems, which they call direct contact "catwhisker" sensors.

The hunting type models, 11 and 15, have one "catwhisker" which produces either a *left* or *right* signal without neutral or "null." This system uses a reverse steering motor of 1/8 h.p. which runs, or *hunts*, continuously.

Double "catwhisker" sensors are used on their non-hunting models 420 and 423, which produce a signal for *left* or for *right* or for both *off* (null signal). The null width is adjustable at top of the compass. Solid state transistors are used to amplify the catwhisker signals. There is a mechanical feed-back from the steering system. On hydraulic steering systems, the feedback is through push-pull cable.

An entirely different pick-off is used on Wood Freeman non-hunting proportional rate autopilots. The sensor in their 500 Series pilots is a Hall-Effect crystal. This crystal detects the magnetic field of the compass magnets and generates a DC voltage whose polarity depends on the direction of turn from the selected heading. Amplitude of this voltage is dependant, or proportional to the heading error. The more error, the more voltage.

Feed-back from the rudder is determined by another Hall-Effect crystal and magnet in a sealed encoder unit that is installed close to the rudder. The magnet is turned by a mechanical coupling to the rudder post.

The Hall-Effect sensor models, all 500 Series Wood Freeman Automatic Pilots, are designed to automatically compensate for variations in the steerability of nine out of ten boats when all control knobs are set to "average." For that remaining one boat that has special steering problems, compensating adjustments can be made, assuming that the boat responds to the rudder.

THE GYROCOMPASS

Large vessels have no problems with mechanical compasses because they don't use them. Gyrocompasses are used by navel vessels and merchant fleets all over the world because they are free of all the inherent weaknesses of the magnetic compass. The gyrocompass points to *true* north; the magnetic compass points to *magnetic* north. This alone simplifies navigational computations because it eliminates all those endless deviation and variation corrections that must be made when plotting a course.

The gyrocompass is not entirely without error, but its error is more easily corrected. The gyrocompass can be integrated into complex navigation systems where computers do all the work and solve all the tough problems. An example is the use of a gyrocompass to operate accessory equipment, an example being the gyropilot. There is no gyrocompass in a marine automatic pilot. The ship's gyrocompass electronically supplies signals to the gyropilot, in another part of the ship, which steers the vessel.

Only very large vessels use gyrocompasses and gyro-integrated automatic pilots. They are monstrous pieces of equipment unsuited for use on anything but the largest vessels. The gyrocompass alone will cost more then many yachts.

THE "SATURABLE CORE SENSOR" COMPASS

A new type of compass has been developed by Wesmar Marine Systems. They call it a "saturable core sensor," or electronic compass. It has no floating disc or moving parts enclosed in fluid. It is entirely transistorized and functions by sensing the "earth's horizontal flux field." Since the sensor is electronic, responses to heading changes are instant and there is no need for a "pick-off" system.

Magnetic compasses are usually installed in the pilot house. However, on steel boats they must be installed as high as possible to avoid the steel hull effect. The saturable core sensor, according to Wesmar's installation instructions, must also be installed at least 3 feet from any magnetic interference. On steel hulls they suggest installing the sensor on a mast if necessary.

Relays

The weak link in all older type autopilots was the relays, which are electro-mechanical switches. Any mechanical device made of metal which opens and closes to pass electricity is subject to burn-out caused by arcing at the point where electrical contact is made.

Because of the constant course adjustments, relays are busy little devices which frequently go bad at the most inopportune time. The relays in non-hunting (off and on), autopilots can be subject to 20 times the normal wear and tear in other applications and service. This makes autopilot relays subject to Murphy's Law (if anything can go wrong it will).

In Wood Freeman autopilots, heavy duty mercury relays are now used. Fluid mercury is the electrical "contact" point in the switch. This eliminates arcing and contact deterioration. Other manufacturers have replaced relays with transistors, which make the ideal "switch" because there is no metal-to-metal contact and no wear and tear. Theoretically, transistors should last forever because there is nothing moving and therefore nothing to wear out.

Just getting rid of those old troublesome mechanical relays has been a major improvement in automatic pilots because it eliminated the cause of most break-downs.

Rudder Position Feedback

No two boats steer alike, especially in following seas. Autopilots will not function satisfactorily without rudder information tuned to the particular steering characteristics of the boat. This is why a rudder-position transducer is a necessary component in any good autopilot. It is usually installed near the rudder stock and quadrant.

Terminal Box

Older type autopilots were trouble-prone. I know many yachtsmen who have autopilots but never use them. If you ask them why, some will ignore the question and change the subject. They get upset just talking about them, and who needs high blood pressure.

Any complex system for automatic steering of a boat that is hand-wired and functions with mechanical relays is going to be trouble-prone. This is especially true with older hunting autopilots where mechanical relays can get eaten up and expire of old age in one short summer of cruising. In a 10-hour run in heavy weather, those switches will open and close thousands of times. No mechanical switch can take that kind of service without starting to malfunction.

Older systems were hand-wired with everything terminating in a wiring center, which was usually the pilot house control console. Hand-wired systems are always more difficult to service and maintain then the newer systems today with plug-in cables, connectors and circuit modules. These are all centered in either a terminal box, an interconnecting matrix or a junction box that is usually located in the engine room.

WHAT TO LOOK FOR WHEN BUYING

Steering torque differs, even on similar size boats. Be sure the system you buy can handle the torque of your steering equipment.

Steering torque changes with the weather. Be sure the system has controls to adjust for sea conditions.

Some systems are difficult to understand because they have an endless number of knobs and switches which require you to make many complicated adjustments.

Some questions to ask yourself are:

- Do you set the course in the pilot house, or in some remote location where the control compass is installed?
- How much maintenance does the system require, and is everything accessible?
- Will you have to replace relays and photo-cells? Will you have to carry spare parts? Are they easily available?
- How many "accessories" must you buy, like remote hand controls, to be fully equipped?

THE AUTOMATIC PILOT ON SAILBOATS

Weekend sailors are not interested in self-steering devices, some even bristle at the mere suggestion that some mechanical gadget can handle the tiller better then they can. They sail for the pure joy of sailing, for the satisfaction that comes from personally controlling their boats as they steer and maneuver for that last ounce of energy from the wind.

Why Some Sailors Dislike Autopilots

When I asked one sailor his opinion on a home-made self-steering device he replied: "Steering is half the fun of sailing. I get no pleasure of just sitting in my cockpit watching a guest at the tiller steering my boat. I'd feel the same way about an automatic pilot."

Another sailor told me: "The weekend sailor dislikes autopilots mainly because he isn't going anywhere, which after all, is what weekend sailing is all about. You just go out on the lake or river and sail! At the end of the day you return, under power, to the location from whence you started. Like the squirrel on a treadmill, you were on the go all day, but went nowhere. Under such conditions, who needs an automatic pilot?"

Why Some Sailors Like Autopilots

An oldtime sailor told me: "Show me a sailor who goes someplace and I'll show you a sailor who has a tiller or wheel self-steering device on his boat, even if he made it himself."

And that is the reason why some sailors do and some do not like automatic pilots. What it all boils down to is, if it's fun, you do it yourself. If it's work, you get somebody else, or something else to do it.

Sailing for a few hours on weekends is fun. Sailing short-handed on a long cruise is work. Sailing on a long ocean cruise, when somebody has to be at the helm 24-hours a day, weeks on end, is absolute drudgery.

My friend, Robert Manry, who spent 78 days crossing the Atlantic alone in a 13½ foot boat, told me: "The boredom was mind-numbing."

Tiller Autopilots

Tiller rudder control is the most popular type of steering on small sail boats under 25 feet. Young novice sailors get their first lessons with a tiller in their hands. When they graduate to larger boats or when they enter Class boat racing, they will still steer with a tiller in their hands.

The *Tiller-Master*, an automatic pilot that was originally designed for tiller-arm self-steering on small sailboats, is a joy to use and own, mainly because of its utter simplicity and ease of installation (Fig. 5-4). It doesn't take two engineers from Cal Tech to get it working right on your boat. And once it is install-ed and working right, you don't spend hours reading the Owner's Manual trying to learn how to make all kinds of com-plicated adjustments.

There is only one dial (for setting the course) and one switch (for ON and OFF) on the non-hunting *Tiller-Master* which, in-cidently, is the only type recommended for sailboats. A hunt-ing pilot would work itself to death before the boating season was half over.

Installation of "Tiller-Master"

I don't know of any marine operational gear that is easier to install then *Tiller-Master*. You drill one ¼ inch hole in the top

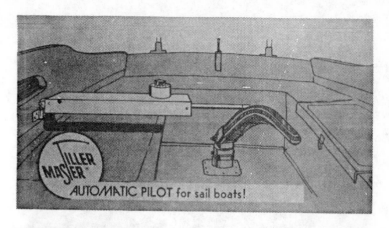

Fig. 5-4. This is the only auto-pilot on the market today that can be used on either tiller or wheel steering, and it can be owner installed in an hour with the simplest of tools. There is no crawling around in the bilges, and no high hourly labor charges (courtesy of Tiller-Master Automatic Pilot).

of the tiller itself for a stainless steel ball pin and two screw holes to mount an oarlock socket on the cockpit seat or coaming. Wire up to a 12 volt battery and you're ready for a sea test.

If you want to go manual, just lift the *Tiller-Master* off the tiller ball pin and out of the oarlock, and stow it away. Servicing this gear is easier then the installation. The entire electronic package is plug-in.

Fig. 5-5. Tiller-Master is also easily installed on pedestal wheel steerers with the use of a special wheel adapter kit. For the single-hander on a long cruise, a helping hand at the tiller or wheel is something you have to sail without to appreciate (courtesy of Tiller-Master Automatic Pilot).

Although originally designed for sailboats with tillers, this simple autopilot is also available for wheel steering (Fig. 5-5) by purchasing a special wheel adapter. These adapters are available for wheels made by Edson, Yacht Specialties and Don Allen Wheels with destroyer-type rims up to 40 inches in diameter.

The *Tiller-Master* autopilot sells for $425.00 direct from the manufacturer. A wheel adapter costs $67.50 and a course dodger is available at $27.50.

Address of the manufacturer is listed, along with others, in Appendix A.

There is another tiller-type autopilot, similar in operation to the above, and sold by Manhattan Marine. It is called *Firstmate Sailboat Autopilot.* It, too, is available for both tiller and wheel installation.

The tiller system sells for $559.00. The wheel system sells for either $649.00 or $695, depending on model.

Conventional Sailboat Autopilots

Sailboats in the small-to-medium size range don't have too much working space or accessibility below decks in the area where you have to work to install an autopilot. The best time to prepare for such an installation is when the boat is being built, not after.

This is why I always advise against buying sailboats, or powerboats, off dealer showroom floors. These are basic stripped boats. Anything extra you might want must be added on after you sign the papers. Dealers just love this because they make their real profit on the things you buy and have installed after you pay for the boat. And the salesman will fawn and drool all over you as he makes lavish promises on how quickly all the extra equipment you order will be installed. May the good Lord help you if you believe him.

A friend of mine, owner of a new Pearon 365 ketch, which he purchased in March off a dealer showroom floor, is still waiting in the last week of August for installation of an autopilot.

Even if you don't want an autopilot factory-installed, if you specify that you plan to install one at a later date (which many buyers do for financial reasons), the builder can make such an installation a lot easier for you, even to the point of having an autopilot drive unit already mounted in the right place, and it

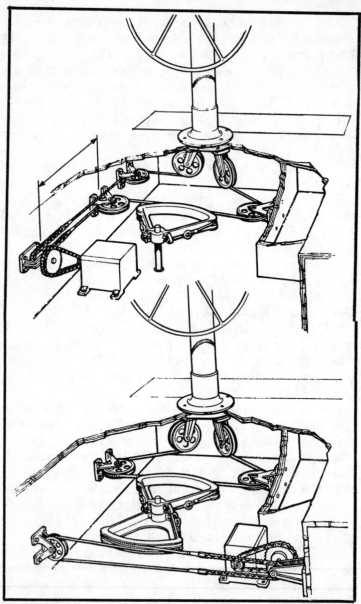

Fig. 5-6. It is very difficult, and labor cost is high, to install all these sheaves and drive units to a fiberglass hull after it is built. You just don't screw-fasten big sheaves and drive motors directly to fiberglass without backup reinforcement, usually blocks of wood fiberglass encapsulated. However, during the layup process, this is easily done and builders will even provide all these reinforced areas if they know you plan to install an autopilot later (courtesy of Teleflex Yacht Specialties).

may not even cost you anything.

Installing a drive unit later can be difficult, especially on a fiberglass hull because where the drive unit must be mounted there is nothing but 10 layers of fiberglass cloth layed up in resin. This area will first have to be strongly reinforced with at least a one-inch block of wood, bolt-secured from the outside and then covered by fiberglass.

In the drawings supplied by Teleflex Yacht Specialties (Fig. 5-6), you can see different autopilot drive units in place. The box with the chained pulley is the actual business end of the pilot system. Once it is properly installed, the rest is all down hill.

PEDESTAL WHEEL DISC STEERERS

Pedestal wheel steering systems (Fig. 5-7), are a big thing right now and you can't hardly buy a sailboat over 26 feet off a dealer showroom without a pedestal, destroyer wheel and "beverage" caddy. The pedestals come in three basic types—disc, quadrant and push-pull cables. The disc is the most popular because it is the easiest to install and it does not require a battery of sheaves around which the cable must travel (Fig. 5-8). It is also the least expensive.

Anything which must be fastened to thin-skinned fiberglass is potential trouble, unless there is strong reinforcement, like encapsulated wood, to hold fastenings for the sheaves and drive units.

The one disadvantage of disc steerers is that there is no flexibility for alignment of the cable into the disc groove. The drive shaft of the rudder must be perpendicular, straight up and down, for this system to work smoothly. Some rudder posts have a certain amount of rake, which requires a different type of pedestal further away from the disc.

Another disadvantage is that stops must be secured to the hull at some point for the disc to hit against when the rudder reaches the end of its full swing, port or starboard. There is a built-in extension or protrusion on the quadrant or disc which hits the stops.

For do-it-yourself installation of pedestal-wheel steering on a sailboat, radial types are the most popular and they work very smoothly with a minimum of friction since there are no sheaves. Also they give you a "feel" of the helm.

Installation kits are available for around $375.00, not in-

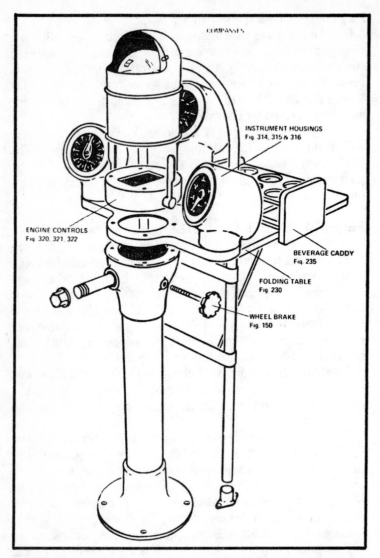

COMPASSES

INSTRUMENT HOUSINGS
Fig. 314, 315 & 316

ENGINE CONTROLS
Fig. 320, 321, 322

BEVERAGE CADDY
Fig. 235

FOLDING TABLE
Fig. 230

WHEEL BRAKE
Fig. 150

Fig. 5-7. The "pedestal" is more then just something on which to hang a big steering wheel like they have on destroyers. It is the control console, the pilot house, the booze holder and dispenser all in one package (courtesy of Teleflex Yacht Specialties).

cluding the wheel itself. Destroyer-type wheels cost from $75.00 to $125.00.

THE QUADRANT STEERER

As previously mentioned, it can be pretty crowded below

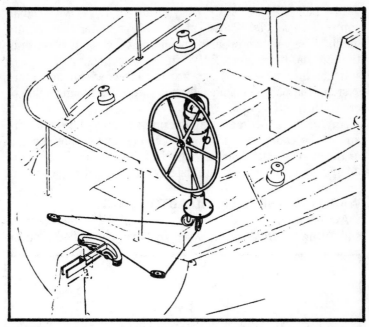

Fig. 5-8. The disc drive, also called radial, is preferred on fiberglass hulls because of the sticky problem of securing all those extra sheaves on other systems. You just can't screw fasten anything directly to fiberglass without some backup reinforcement, like blocks of encapsulated wood (courtesy of Teleflex Yacht Specialities).

decks in the aft of a sailboat and sometimes you just can't make a straight run from the pedestal to the disc because there may be things in the way—like exhaust lines, tanks and cockpit drains. To get around these objects it becomes necessary to use sheaves, as in the quadrant steerer illustration (Fig. 5-9). This is the type system you will see most on larger boats with raked rudder posts.

Kit prices for quadrant steerers run a little higher, from $400.00 to $450.00, not including the wheel.

PUSH-PULL CABLE SYSTEMS

There are two types of cable systems: one uses a single push-pull cable while the other uses two separate cables around a disc. This type is caled a *pull-pull* system because both cables exert a pulling force on the disc.

The *push-pull* system is used mainly on light displacement small boats with outboard rudders, as in the illustration (Fig. 5-10).

The pull-pull cables are used on larger boats with radial-controlled rudders. These cables, always under tension, are much stronger than ordinary push-pull types, and because of the tension, there is no "play" in the wheel action.

If conditions below decks are too crowded for any other system, the pull-pull can easily be routed around an engine or other obstruction.

Any of the above pedestal steering systems will work with any of the conventional below-decks automatic pilot controls or the above-decks tiller and wheel steerers. Manufacturers of all such automatic pilots are listed at the end of this chapter.

WARNING! THE LAW AND AUTOPILOTS

Autopilots do not relieve a boat owner of his legal responsibility under *Rules of the Road* to have a qualified man on

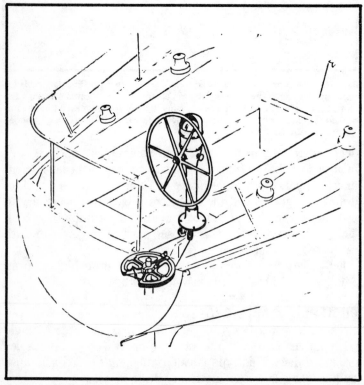

Fig. 5-9. The quadrant is used on both inboard and outboard rudders, and is more common on larger boats with raked rudder posts, angled instead of perpendicular (courtesy of Teleflex Yacht Specialties).

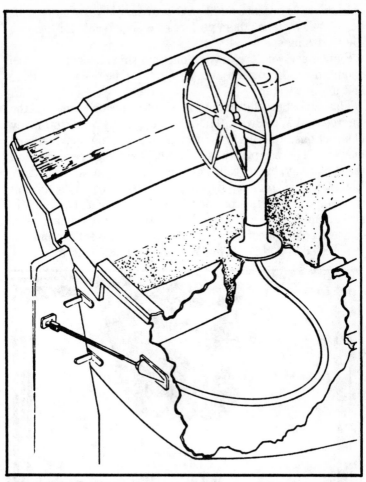

Fig. 5-10. Push-pull cable systems are resorted to in crowded below decks conditions where conventional sheave-cable systems cannot be used because of obstructing equipment and machinery (courtesy of Teleflex Yacht Specialities).

watch whenever his vessel is underway. The primary function of an autopilot under the law is to *assist* the man on watch in maintaining a designated course set by captain.

An autopilot should never be used in busy commercial ship channels. Some ship channels can run a compass course for 15 to 25 miles straight out to sea, and this would seem like a logical time to put her on "auto," sit back and relax, but *don't!* These channels are marked on both sides by hundreds of navigational markers like cans, nuns, spars and lighted buoys. And there are always fishermen in small boats anchored near ship channels because numbered buoys are always in the same place, which makes them perfect reference points for locating "hot" fishing spots.

Remember, you are never alone in a ship channel. A vessel should never be put on automatic pilot unless you are alone and in open water.

This almost precludes the use of autopilots on rivers and the Intercoastal Waterway. There is too much traffic, too many obstructions, too many shoals and too many navigational markers. There is plenty of what looks like big open water on the Waterway, but it really isn't, even when you can't see land. You may be surrounded by water on all sides as far as you can see, but you are still confined to a marked channel, which is nothing more than a dredged lane in shoal waters. I have seen cruisers and sailboats stuck in the mud who went around the wrong side of a channel marker by only a few feet.

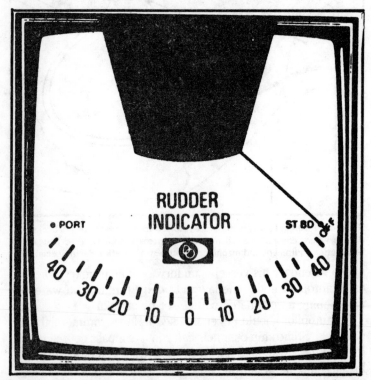

Fig. 5-11. You can spend $500 for an electronic rudder position indicator. This one costs less then $30 by mail, and does the same thing (courtesy of Manhattan Marine).

RUDDER POSITION INDICATOR

The tiller of a sailboat makes a perfect rudder position indicator, the wheel does not.

So, if you change to pedestal wheel steering, you very likely will be thinking about installing one of the many devices available to show you the angle of your rudder. This is necessary information when backing out of a gas dock or slip in close quarters, and what gas dock isn't in close quarters?

This is also necessary information for twin-screw boat maneuvering, especially by engines alone. And when you back up with a single-screw boat, you better know where that rudder is, even if it does seem almost useless at times.

Rudder position indicators are standard equipment on all large vessels and tugboats, but rarely seen on pleasure craft, perhaps because boatowners don't know that something is available or perhaps because marina stores do not stock this item. If you want it, you must ask for it, and they will order it.

There is a less expensive indicator available from Manhattan Marine for $29.75 (Fig. 5-11), with extra station costing $8.95. The small sending unit of this indicator is easily installed at the rudder post. Wires are run to a calibrated meter at the helm which shows the rudder position in degrees, port and starboard.

A Home-Made Rudder Angle Indicator

To the owner of a boat with a $3,000 autopilot, a simple home-made rudder position indicator costing a few cents will spark no interest. But there are still quite a few powerboat owners around who want very much to save bucks so they can buy gas. To them I offer this rudder angle indicator which is so simple and so inexpensive that I am almost embarrassed to offer it.

The illustration (Fig. 5-12) tells you everything you need to know. Starting with the basic idea, you can modify or improve it when you adapt this for your own use.

For example, instead of screweyes, you might use small pulleys or tiller rope guides. Instead of cord, you might use rigging wire and instead of a moving bead as a marker, you might use a small turnbuckle swaged into the wire rope. The turnbuckle could put tension on the wire and serve as the moving marker over a calibrated scale to show the degree of swing to port or starboard.

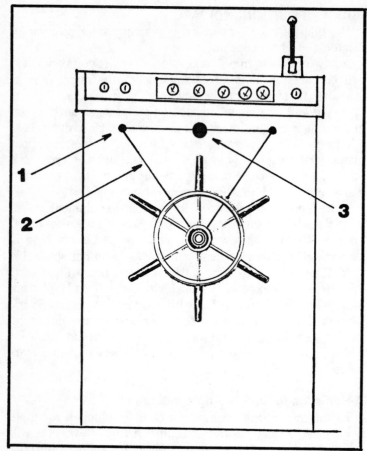

Fig. 5-12. This home made rudder position indicator can be rigged up with odds and ends out of your dock box. (1) this is a simple eye screw or tiller rope guide. (2) this can be heavy cord or tiller wire. (3) this marker or indicating device can be a small turnbuckle with a reference mark.

No matter how much you improve on this basic idea, it won't work any better because it already works perfectly. What more can it do but show you where your rudder is at all times?

FUEL VAPOR INDICATORS

The world's best gasoline fumes detector doesn't cost a dime. It's your *nose!* However, few boatowners think to make use of this natural fume sensing device but prefer to rely on man-made mechanical detectors (Fig. 5-13) which, though they work very well, are far from infallible. If you decide to buy one, please remember that the fume detector does *not* eliminate the continued need for electric bilge blowers.

I was an eye-witness to a tragedy at the gas docks of a well known marina in Detroit which proves the above statement. A big cruiser, with many people on board, had finished taking on gas. I was waiting for the boat to back out so I could move in. Suddenly there was a tremendous explosion that sent bodies flying ten feet straight up in the air and then into the water. Debris fell on boats a 100 feet away.

There are big signs at this marina's gas docks warning of gas fumes dangers. They also warn that boat engines must NOT be started until bilge blowers have ventilated engine compartments for at least three minutes.

The owner of the cruiser that blew up had neglected to use his blowers because he had just himself installed a fuel vapor detector and since it had given no warning, he had assumed that everything was all right down below.

Installing a fuel vapor detector is easy, both electrically and mechanically, but installing it *right* is not so easy. For example, the vapor detector sensing head, in the boat that blew up, had been installed in the lowest part of the bilge where gas fumes, being heavier than air, will normally settle. I say "normally," that is if the fumes can get there.

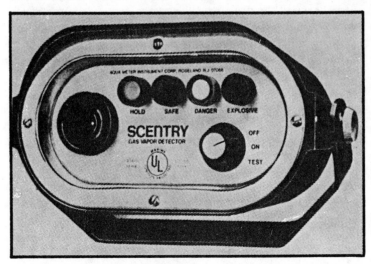

Fig. 5-13. Gas vapor detectors, like this popular model by Aqua Meter, are completely reliable when properly installed, but many are not. The sensor must be where the gas vapors are, and there is more then one place where vapors can accumulate (courtesy of Aqua Meter).

On this particular boat, the lowest part of the bilge was not directly under the engines, but up ahead under the cabin. The two bilge areas were separated by a bulkhead with only large limber holes on each side of the inside keel for water to drain through to reach the bilge pump. These two limber holes, after considerable sawing and drilling, had become plugged with bilge debris, sawdust and dirt. Gas fumes in the engine compartment could not reach the detector sensing head, which is why it gave no warning.

Where Sensors Should Be Installed

This is why a gas fume detector is not a positive guarantee that you will be warned in time, or even at all unless you have more then one remote sensor, with three being the minimum. Why three?

One sensor should be installed low in the gas tank area to detect a leak in the filler hose connections, copper lines and main filters.

Those 2-inch filler hoses from deck plates to gas tanks are almost always out of reach and out of sight where you can't even make a visual inspection to see if there is a leak around the hose clamps. And frequently this is because all manufacturers ground the gas deck filler plates, which in turn grounds the gas pump filler nozzle when you take on gas (Fig. 5-14). This is an important safety feature, but the way some manufacturers ground the deck plate only creates another safety hazard.

On one of my Big Name boats, the manufacturer ran a strip of thin gauge metal down the length of the gas filler hose, folding it *under* the clamped hose ends so it made contact with the gas tank at one end and the deck plate at the other end. This produced electrical continuity and grounding, but it also produced a very slow, seeping gas leak at both clamps, even after they were further tightened.

Fortunately, I only got the mysterious gas fumes when taking on gas, which was when my gas detector (my nose), warned me, and I would run the bilge blower for five minutes. After that I would have no more trouble with gas fumes until the next time I took on fuel.

I know that there are many other manufactured stock boats with gas deck plates grounded in the same way, and with the same potential for a seeping leak. If you have a mysterious gas

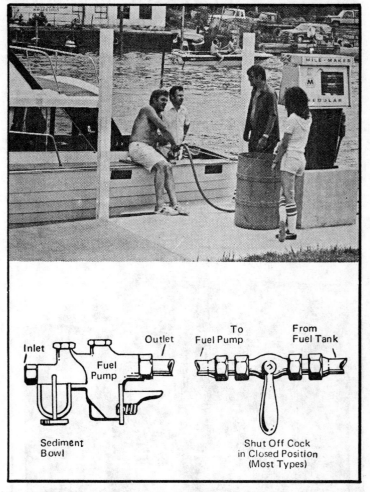

Fig. 5-14. (Top) Grounding of the deck filler plates is an important safety factor on boats because static electricity is generated when gas moves through the gas pump hose and metal nozzle. In the past, a chain was attached to the nozzle and dropped into the water to ground it. Boat builders now routinely ground deck plates, but some do it badly and only create a gas leak. (Bottom) The glass sediment bowl attached to the fuel pump is a potential gas leak if improperly seated in its gasket. The shut-off cock and flared fittings leading into and out of it are also seeping leak possibilities.

fumes problem on your boat, and can't find the leak, try checking those filler hoses.

A second sensor should be installed under the engines close to the fuel pumps and engine gas filters. If there is ever a gas leak on the engines, it will be in this area. Carburetors on

163

modern down-draft marine engines create no gas fume hazard because if the carburetor is ever flooded, the gas just runs down into the engine intake manifold where it can do no harm.

The most likely place a gas leak might occur is the fuel pump and small filter. This second gas filter and sediment bowl in the boat's fuel system is a small glass-bowled device (Fig. 5-14) between the fuel pump and carburetor. When the engine is running, the gas is under pressure from the fuel pump to the glass bowl and it will leak past the gasket if the bowel isn't clamped on properly. In fact, it can even squirt out of there in a stream and spill down into the bilge. A sensor in this area will instantly warn you of this gas spill.

A third sensor should be in the lowest part of the bilge, where all gas fumes eventually settle. If you are away from the boat for a week or so, this is where the major concentration of fumes will be when you finally come aboard to be greeted by

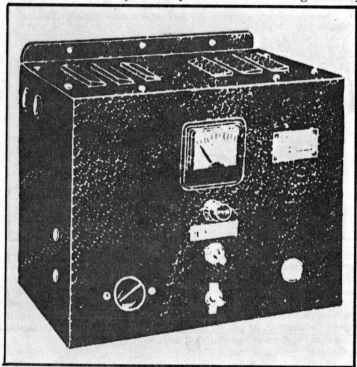

Fig. 5-15. There is a misconception regarding marine converters. Many boaters believe that they are just fancy over-priced battery chargers. Converters do charge batteries, but they do it unattended and with 100 percent safety, which auto-type battery chargers do not. (courtesy of Manhattan Marine).

an audible warning from the detector.

If you plan to install a gas fume detector, do it right or don't do it at all because to rely on something that won't do the job is more danger than you afford. Without a detector you at least won't be lulled into a false sense of security like the man whose boat blew up in that marina gas dock. Without a detector, after gassing up you will (I hope!) raise your hatches and use your nose.

THE MARINE CONVERTER

With dockside electricity almost universally available, modern power and sailing boats come factory-wired for 115-volt AC. But there is still a great need for 12-volt DC electricity to power all the accessories and electronic gear which inevitably is installed by the owner. Use of this equipment dockside eventually runs down the batteries.

The proper way to prevent this happening is with a marine converter. But many new (and old) boatmen today are confused by the word "converter," some even suspect the word is just a euphemism for battery charger.

In other words, many boatmen think "converters" are just high-priced battery chargers, and you can't really blame them for thinking this because that's the way it is in boating. The poor boatman is exploited, gouged and over-priced by everybody. An electronic voltage regulator can be bought at any K-Mart store for $9.95. I recently bought three, one for my car and two for my boat. This same voltage regulator is selling at a fancy marina store in Detroit for $67.50.

Converters And Battery Chargers

I understand the reason why many boatmen resent having to pay $365 to $555 for what they think is just a fancy battery charger with a new name when the Sears catalogue lists big heavy-duty garage-type chargers for just a little over a hundred dollars, and smaller heavy-duty types for considerably less.

However, "converters" and battery chargers are not quite the same thing.

Converters are called by that name because that is what they truly do—they convert 115-volt AC to 12-volt DC.

Battery chargers also do this, but not to a constant unvarying 12 volts. Also, battery charger voltage is *not* 12 volts and it is not constant but varies with internal battery resistance.

Ordinary consumer type auto battery chargers are not safe in the marine environment unless you monitor them closely. *Never* leave them unattended. The confined space of engine compartments presents entirely different conditions then those under an automobile hood where there is free movement of air.

Lead-acid batteries, during charging cycles, emit gases and hydrochloric vapors as a result of electrolysis, which, in turn, creates hydrogen gas which is highly explosive. It is not safe to hook up a boat battery to an auto-type charger before you leave the club or marina Sunday evening in the mistaken belief that when the charger "tapers off" to a safe trickle charge, no harm will be done when you return to the boat a week later. Not one of the major manufacturers of lead-acid auto batteries consider "trickle charge " as being safe or necessary. And a battery under a so-called "safe" trickle charge is *still* producing explosive hydrogen gas.

This is still another reason why boats are equipped with bilge blowers and why some boat manufacturers even hook up an exhaust blower with flexible 4-inch duct pipe to the covered battery compartment. This is to get hydrogen gas out of the bilge in a hurry!

Auto type chargers can still be used on your boat, but use them carefully. Keep a close watch on the charge rate meter. When the charging rate tapers down to about 2 amps, *turn it off!* This means internal resistance in the battery is high, which is why the input amperage has dropped so low. This is why charging voltage will be so high, sometimes 14 to 16 volts.

What this means is that the battery has reached the limits of its capacity and further "trickle" charging will accomplish nothing but generate more electrolysis and hydrogen gas, which you do not need on a boat.

The converter, as expensive as it is, is a better way to safely maintain *all* your batteries and provide you, at the same time, with all the 12-volt electricity you need dockside to operate shipboard refrigerators, bilge pumps, lights, electronic gear, accessories and starter motors. The marine converter/charger is the only type of charger you can safely leave unattended for weeks or for months to operate your bilge pumps and ventilating fans, and still keep *ALL* your batteries at peak capacity.

Fig. 5-16. The over-charging of lead-acid batteries in the confined engine compartments of small boats can be more dangerous then leaking gasoline. So-called "trickle charging" is over-charging, which generates highly explosive hydrogen gas. Marine converters, like this one by Ray Jefferson, never over-charges, by automatically turning themselves off (courtesy of Ray Jefferson).

How Converters Charge Batteries

The constant 12 volts from a converter will not charge a battery. So how is the job done?

The Stickell Converter is actually two completely separate circuits—one to charge your batteries at the proper voltage and another to adapt shore 115-volt AC to the proper voltage directly to your boat's 12-volt DC lights and accessories. Only the *Stickell Converter* has this dual feature (Fig. 5-15) .

The non-commercial consumer type battery charger has the limited capacity to charge only one battery at a time. Converters will charge a bank of three 12-volt batteries and monitor the state of charge of each individual battery "120 times a second" according to the claims made by one manufacturer (Fig. 5-16).

Converters have front panel controls to adjust output voltage to match your battery system. Also, they automatically compensate for normal line voltage variations, giving constant output. They have current limiters which automatically hold output current to the charger's rated capacity, thus eliminating blown fuses.

Converters constantly monitor the condition of all your batteries and when they are as fully charged as they will ever be, the converter does not continue with a trickle charge, but automatically shuts itself completely off!

AC Current And Boats

Marine converters are designed for the sea. This means they have isolation transformers, which consumer-type battery chargers do not. Why is this important?

The sea and AC current just don't get along too well. When you plug in your boat's "umbilical cord" to 115-volt AC shore power, you open the door (as Hamlet said) to a sea of troubles which you must forever take arms against. The "isolation transformer" is just one of the battles you win in a sea of troubles because it protects you both from high voltage shock and electrolysis.

This one feature alone makes converters worth their excessively high prices to me because I am scared to death of high voltage AC on a boat.

INVERTERS

If you were confused by converters, you will be even more confused by inverters because at first glance they seem like a crazy contradiction. First you spend a bundle to convert 115 volt AC to 12 volt DC. Now you must spend another bundle to invert 12 volt DC *back* to 115 volt AC.

"Why?" you ask.

When you unplug your umbilical cord from that dockside 115 volt receptacle, you go back in time to the wonderful Dark Ages of boating when we used ice for refrigeration.

Even the smallest of fiberglass day cruisers and sailboats have electric refrigeration today, which operates through an umbilical cord on 115 volt AC. But you can't store AC in a storage battery. How do you run the refrigerator when the umbilical cord is pulled?

There are three things you can do to keep running the refrigerator, but two of them cost a lot of money.

If you have adequate space below, you can install a gas-driven Onan or Kohler AC generator; if you don't have adequate space below, you can install a 115-volt AC generator which runs off a special dual belt pulley on the front of your engine; or you can buy an inverter.

The first two choices will cost you from $2,000 to $4,000.

The third choice, an inverter, will cost you about $570 and up, depending on the optional equipment you buy with it.

The last inverter I had only cost about $120. I got it for $85, and it didn't require any optional equipment to turn it off when there was no load demand or to automatically turn it on when the umbilical cord was pulled, whether intentionally or accidentally. Now these are costly options.

My inverter was used to operate an icebox refrigeration conversion unit which required 115 volts AC. I could easily have bought a 12-volt conversion unit instead of the 115 volt unit. But whichever I chose, something else costly had to be bought to run the thing at dockside or at sea.

With the 12 volt DC unit I would have required a converter for dockside operation. The converters, at the time, cost three times as much as the $85 I paid for an inverter. So I went the cheaper route because I was a poor boy at the time who was only getting a penny-a-word for what he wrote.

The inverter worked out very well, so long as the engines were running. I checked it out once at dockside to see how long I would have refrigeration running off a 100 ampere hour battery before it pooped out. I had refrigeration for almost two days.

But that was in the spring when bilge air temperature was low, which made the compressor fan heat dissipation more efficient. This resulted in longer off cycles.

In the summer, bilge temperature gets pretty high, especially after the engines have been running. This means poorer heat dissipation and longer run cycles. In these conditions, I doubt if I could have gotten more than six to eight hours of refrigeration off that one 100 ampere hour battery.

A marine inverter will operate any refrigerator, or small air conditioner (not both together) indefinitely while the engine is running, or about 6 to 8 hours if you stop the engine to fish for a while.

Summing up, the marine inverter is a very useful and worthwhile piece of equipment and a far better alternative if the only need you have for 115 volt AC is to operate a refrigerator or small air conditioner.

A gas engine-driven Onan/Kohler is a considerable investment, both to buy and install. Ask yourself, is it really worth it when you can get the same convenience with a marine inverter, or even two inverters stacked—one to run the refrigerator and one for the air conditioner (Fig. 5-17)?

One last warning: I am writing about *marine* inverters, not those silly little things you buy at auto stores to operate your electric shaver. The marine inverter is a heavy duty beast that is specially designed to handle the heavy starting surge requirements of compressors. The inverter must be able to handle momentary surge loads of up to 1500 watts and continuous duty loads of 800 watts. Anything less then this will not work with any refrigeration or air conditioning compressor.

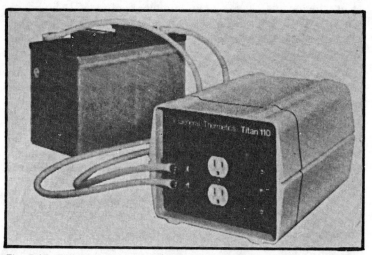

Fig. 5-17. This inverter, costing $570, will give you refrigeration after you yank the umbilical cord at the dock. I used one similar to this for 10 years. It still works. They never wear out, they never break down and they don't use gas (courtesy of Manhattan Marine).

Chapter 6
Seamanship

Seamanship is hard to define because like an elephant it is so big, and like a circus tent, it covers so much. Ask a sailboat owner, a tugboat skipper or a Coast Guard crewman to describe seamanship and you will get answers like those given by the three blind men who "saw" an elephant by touch for the first time, and were asked to describe what an elephant looked like.

One blind man felt the elephant's trunk. "An elephant is long and round like a stove pipe."

The second blind man felt the body. "An elephant is big and broad like a barn door."

The third blind man felt the tail. "An elephant is long and thin like a rope."

WHAT IS SEAMANSHIP
What seamanship is depends on which part, or which area you touch. The subject is so broad it can never be covered in one chapter, or even one book. Seamanship is *everything* that Man does in the marine environment of oceans, seas, lakes and rivers on vessels propelled by mechanical power or sail. It is sail handling and power handling. It is taking care of a boat, and knowing that boat. It is understanding things like the use

of lines, knots, splices, anchoring, docking, maneuvering, running a breaking inlet, running in the trough, before a following sea and into a head sea. It is handling emergencies, adverse weather condintions, man overboard, and much, much more.

The Ordinary Seaman

Anybody can buy a boat, use a boat and sail a boat. There are no examinations to take, no tests to pass and no license to carry in your billfold. All you need is a good credit rating and cash for the down payment and you are an instant Leading Seaman, which in the old British and American merchant marines was two grades above Ordinary Seaman and Able Seaman.

Even the lowest grade, Ordinary Seaman, had to be qualified to perform routine duties at sea, and routine duty at sea required many seamanship qualities. For a would-be sailor to pass himself off as a qualified Ordinary Seaman when signing on, and then later failing to cut it, was cause for demotion, degradation and abuse, not only by the officers, but by the crew as well. This would-be sailor was banished to the filthiest part of the fo'c'sle, where he was placed in charge of all the buckets that were used for the collection of body wastes. And when he wasn't emptying and cleaning these, he was being bullied and abused by the ship's cook. And that is what they did in the days of sail to would-be sailors who couldn't cut it.

You can walk through any marina today, and even if you are a non-boatman, you can easily pick out the boats whose owners are would-be sailors passing themselves off as Ordinary and even Able Seamen just by the general appearance of the boat and its dock lines. How a boat is tied up in its slip tells much about the owner's seamanship abilities and whether he qualifies only for that special job in the fo'c'sle with the slop buckets.

In an average marina of 400 boats, only about 50 will be owned by boatmen who could qualify as Ordinary Seamen, possibly ten would qualify as Able Seamen, and maybe two would qualify as Leading Seamen (rated equal to a Boatswain's Mate—bosun for short).

The remaining 335 boats in that marina will be owned by people who just like to "play around" with boats. These are the people who like to fish, or who like club social life and flying a burgee on the bow mast. These people usually enjoy the status symbol of belonging to some plush yacht club. A small portion of this group will be those refugees from urban pollution who originally wanted a summer cottage on some lake, but settled for a big boat permanently tied up at some social boating spa on the water. About 20 of these boats, huge things in fiberglass, will be owned by corporations, ostensibly for corporate entertaiment and improved employee relationships. The only seamanship you will ever see here is when the hired crew takes over.

By this time you may gather that good seamanship is a rare thing in a nation that last year spent more money on boats and boating activity then the combined national budgets of six new Developing Countries in Africa. If you suspect this, and want facts, the U.S. Coast Guard has them because they are the federal agency directly involved when millions of Americans decide to become sailors and yachtsmen, but neglect to learn which side of the boat is port and which side is starboard. The Coast Guard had to rescue 32,000 boatmen last year who got in trouble on the water through "bonehead maneuvers," to use their words.

And private citizen boatmen are not the only ones who make "bonehead maneuvers" and lack seamanship abilities because when the National Transportation Board investigated the tragic Chesapeake Bay collision between the Coast Guard Cutter *Cuyahoga* and the Argentine coal freighter *Santa Cruz II,* they learned that the young Coast Guard crewman who was on watch just before the mishap didn't know which side of the boat was port and which was starboard.

Boat Language

Boat talk has always been the butt for much humor, as this old newspaper cartoon graphically illustrates (Fig. 6-1). To a non-boatman it's hard to take boat talk seriously, like "batten down the hatches" or "put a long splice on the main sheet."

Would it be more understandable to just say "close the doors" and "tie those two ropes together?"

No! It would be more confusing and more humorous. For example, tie *what* rope? And what is *tie* supposed to mean?

Boat language is not funny, at least not to people who live and work on the sea in ships. It is a highly utilitarian system of communication that evolved over countless centuries from common usage by ship crews of all nations.

173

"Mizzen the poop! Fo'castle the yardarm! Mains'l the brace! That does it, we're going sideways at a nice clip!"

Fig. 6-1. To be understood, a certain amount of sea language is necessary. A certain amount is not, mainly because of obsolescence and the passing of the great square-rigged sailing ships of yesterday. Use only boat terminology that is relevant to today's boating, or you will look and sound laughably ridiculous (courtesy of The Blade, Toledo).

Sailors evolved their own way of speaking, which in turn found its way into the terminology used by officers in giving commands, like "make fast there with the aft spring," or "lay to on the main sheet."

Once you learn the language, there is no mistaking what the above commands mean. There are miles upon miles of rope on a sailing vessel, serving hundreds of different purposes, but there is only one *main sheet.* There is no possible way a qualified deck hand can make a mistake, in an emergency, by grabbing the wrong "rope." That is why every piece of rope on a boat *must* be called by its right name.

It is not necessary to carry boat talk to such an extreme that your wife and children will become alienated to boating, and they will if you shout orders like a Captain Bligh whenever they come aboard. Boating is supposed to be fun, not Mutiny on the Bounty revisited. Use only the boat langage that is absolutely necessary, like calling things by their right names (Fig. 6-2), and all physical things do have proper names.

MARLINESPIKE SEAMANSHIP

Old sailing vessels were operated and controlled by literally

174

miles of rope. Marlinespike seamanship deals entirely with rope (Fig. 6-3) and all the ways of working it by hand and through systems of blocks and winches.

Nothing more quickly stamps you as a lubber, or rank amateur, then how you handle rope and what you call it. The term "rope" is used only in nine very minor applications, a few of which are tiller ropes, bell ropes, bucket ropes, etc. The general term for rope is *line*. And try not to forget that, and try not to compensate for your ignorance by being too nautical because it makes us old salts wince with pain when you saunter jauntily into the club bar wearing your new white yachting cap and ask for a flagon of rum to "splice the main brace."

All lines on a boat serve a specific purpose, which is even further narrowed down in identification. For example: docking lines refers to all the lines used in securing a vessel to a pier or dock. But these are further broken down in classification as port and starboard bow lines, forward and aft spring lines, port and starboard stern lines and forward and aft stand-off lines.

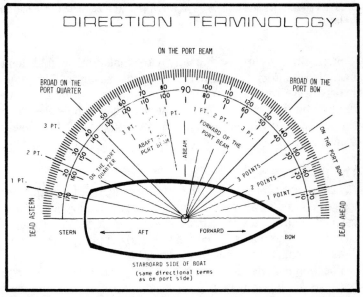

Fig. 6-2. Much sea language today centers around points of direction. For example, you go "aft," you do not go "to the back." You go "forward," you don't go "up front." You look "off the starboard beam," you do not look "over there to the right." This is not a nautical affectation, but a practical necessity.

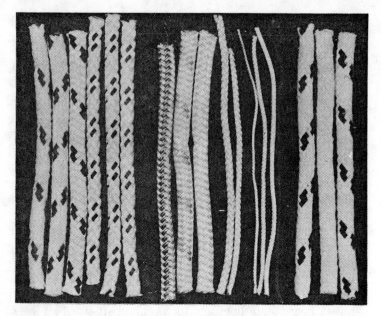

Fig. 6-3. The world of synthetics has revolutionized marine cordage. Each type has advantages and disadvantages which you must consider depending on its usage.

Stand-off lines are used mainly with small craft to hold them away from a dock when the tide is rapidly rising to above normal because of severe winds. This can raise water levels so high that a boat can wind up on the dock when the water later drops. Stand-off lines prevent this by holding the boat away from the dock.

The Bosun's Locker

The Boatswain's Mate, the First Sergeant of deckhands, was in charge of all vessel equipment, tackle, cordage, ship's carpentry and damage control. He had the keys to the ship's storeroom where all such equipment and supplies were stored. This was called the "bosun's locker."

The biggest inventory in the bosun's locker was cordage because the life expectancy of vegetable fiber rope, the only kind available at the time, was short in a salt water environment. But today we have over a half dozen synthetic substitutes for manila and other vegetable fiber ropes, and new types are coming out every year.

TYPES OF ROPE

The vegetable fibers are manila, which comes to us from the Philippines where it is made from the abaca plant; sisal is made from a Mexican and Central American plant; linens is made from flax; cotton is made from cotton; and hemp is made from a widely cultivated Asiatic herb of the mulberry family.

Among the synthetics, the two polyesters are nylon and Du Pont Dacron. The polyolefins are polyethylene and polypropylene.

The two polyesters have taken over completely in the world of sailing because of their proven superiority. No sailor today would use anything but Dacron for his sheets and halyards. Nylon is used for dock lines and anchor rode. Why these specific applications?

The two synthetics are alike in one respect, they are stronger then any of the vegetable fibers, but they do not kink or swell when wet and they are more resistant to rot. However, there the similarity ends. Nylon is elastic and stretches. Dacron does not stretch, which is why it is preferred for halyards and sheets.

The elasticity of nylon makes it ideally suited for applications where stretch is desirable, like in anchor lines, dock lines, tow lines or *painters* on dinghies. For anchoring, elasticity is actually a good thing because it reduces the shock when a boat strains at the line in rough seas. Also when tied up at a dock, a boat will strain and snap at its lines after the wash of a passing boat causes it to roll violently. In fact, before nylon it was common practice to use rubber snubbers belayed in manila dock lines to ease the shock. Nylon does this without the snubbers.

Nylon loses some of its strength when wet, Dacron does not. This is another reason why Dacron is almost universally preferred by both racing and cruising sailors.

Sailors, like auto racers, are the darlings (and guinea pigs) of industry design and engineering. Anything new in the marine field, or automobile, was first tried out on a racing sailboat or race car.

The New Synthetics

There is a new type of synthetic fiber rope, referred to as 2-in-1 double braid, and it is designed expressly for sailors. This rope reminds me of coaxial radio cable in the way it is made, an inner braided core of polypropylene and an outer braided core of nylon or Dacron.

This new rope is not-rotational, which makes it free running. No matter how you throw it around or handle it, when you pull it through a block it runs smooth and does not kink, which is much loved by sailors. Also, the double braid provides a greater bearing surface, which makes it grab better on winches. It also retains its flexibility wet or dry over long periods of use.

The Economics Of Rope

When the votes are all in, the final verdict of choice is an important matter of economics to more boatmen then meets the eye. There is an old Indian saying: "Do not judge a man until you have walked in his mocassins for two moons." A modern version of that: "Do not judge a man who owns a boat until you have made his mortgage payments for two months." Sometimes you want nylon, but you buy manila.

The most expensive rope is the pre-stretched English Terylene which is used for halyards on racing boats. A 100 feet of this in ½ inch diameter will cost you a hundred bucks at least.

The favorite sheet of sailors is the 2-in-1 Yacht Braid. In ½ inch, 100 feet will cost you about $70. However, when you go up a little in diameter on these exotic ropes, the price doesn't just double for one inch, it quadruples to about $230. When you go from ½ inch to ¾ inch, the price doubles to $140.

The last time I bought manila, the ½ inch size was selling for $10 for 100 feet at a discount house. The ¾ inch size which I bought cost me $25. for a 100 feet, and I thought even that was a lot of money.

How Rope Is Sold

Cordage is sold in two different ways. If you buy a standard coil or reel (Fig. 6-4), it is sold by the pound. But if you buy a cut length, as almost all boatmen do, it is sold by the foot, but at a higher price. Why? Cutting the rope entails a certain amount of waste due to unraveled and frayed ends. Then there is time and labor involved in taking rope from a coil, measuring out lengths and cutting it.

The size of marine fiber rope is measured by its circumference, but yachtsmen have always bought and referred to rope by diameter, so that is the way it is sold on the retail level to customers.

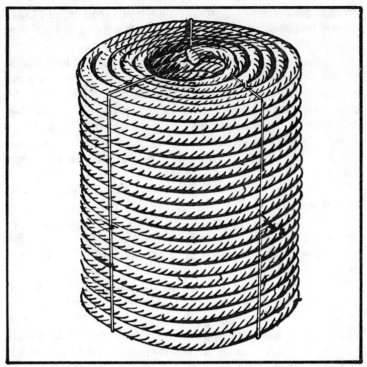

Fig. 6-4. This is the best most economical way to buy rope. In coils like this, it is sold by the pound, which often is half the price you will pay by the foot. This is how most boaters buy their rope.

Hazard Warning On Synthetic Rope

There is a little understood, rarely mentioned, potential hazard in the use of synthetic rope called *cold flow*. When a heavy load is put on a synthetic line over a long period of time, as in anchoring during a storm or in towing, the fibers will stretch and elongate to a different diameter size. When a ¾ inch line is stretched out, it will become a ½ inch.

In mild weather the line will usually recover and return to its original size. But there are times when it will not. And *that* is where the hazard lies.

Air and water temperature affect *cold flow*. Some synthetics are affected more then others, like in anchoring or towing in cold weather, and they will *not* recover.

After any sustained load in cold weather, synthetic lines should be checked for diameter. When a ¾ inch line is stretched out permanently to ½ inch diameter, breaking strength also is reduced proportionately. Instead of the 14,000 pounds breaking strength you think you have, you may only have the 6,000 pounds of a ½ inch line.

Does this mean that all that expensive line must be discarded? No! It is still perfectly usable, so long as you understand about the reduced break strength and do not subject the line to a sustained load exceeding its new capacity. And you can always cut it into shorter lengths for extra dock lines when cruising or gassing up. There are so many uses for extra line that it will never go to waste. Just be warned that there *is* a hazard.

Wire Rope

Wire rope is almost universally used today for standing rigging on sailboats, even very small ones, because once the rigging is tuned in the Spring, you're finished with that chore for the rest of the season.

Wire rope is also used a lot for running rigging on larger boats. The wire is made from plain steel, which will corrode, and galvanized steel which will not. If you can afford it, wire rope is also available in stainless steel, but anyone who can afford a Gulfstar 47 at over a 100 Gs is not going to fuss about the high cost of stainless steel.

There is wire rope available with a hemp core. This makes the wire more flexible and also acts as a shock absorber when the rope is subjected to stress or heavy loads.

Preventing Kinks

Wire rope is not for everyone, especially the Sloppy Joes of boating who keep unused lines laying around like piles of wet macaroni (Fig. 6-5). You just can't do that with wire. Wire rope should always be stored on a reel, then reeled off when needed, *not* slipped off over the ends like rope. This is necessary to prevent twisting, which causes kinks. Once you kink a wire rope, it's ruined.

There is no way you can coil wire rope in your hand like fiber. Even fiber rope can be damaged by kinks and strain over sharp bends.

Handling Rope

The proper handling of rope was once a basic skill for acquiring recognition as a qualified Ordinary Seaman. If you couldn't handle rope, you were worse then useless on a sailing merchant vessel because even the most menial task, like the overboard emptying and cleaning of slop buckets, required the use of rope.

The many ways we handle, store and use rope today were learned by trial and error over countless centuries. Therefore, everything that is done with rope has a reason, and is not done for show or neatness.

FAKING TO HEAVE A LINE

The first time you ever try to heave a line, either to someone on a dock or to another boat alongside, you will learn how difficult it is to do this unless the line at your feet is properly faked down to play out easily. If it is not, when you heave the line, it will stop short of the target because of a tangled mess of line at your feet caused by a kink.

Before you can heave out a long length of line, you must first fake it down on the deck as illustrated (Fig. 6-6) in a continuous series of figure 8s.

Line should never be dumped in a heap, it must always be ready for instant use, and how can you use it in a hurry if you

Fig. 6-5. You could never do this with wire rope. When wire rope is left sloppily laying around, tangled up in this manner, it will almost certainly twist and then kink, after which you can throw it away.

HANDLING

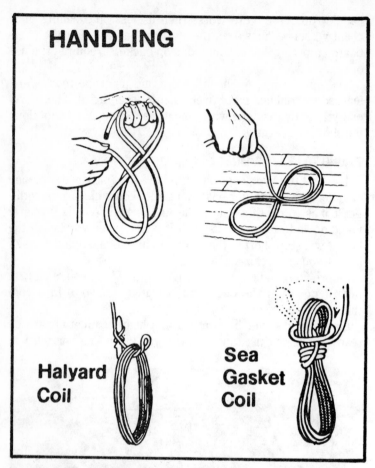

Halyard Coil

Sea Gasket Coil

Fig. 6-6. One of the first things you must learn, and quickly, is how to heave a line. Either you, your wife or your children will be doing this every time you approach a gas dock, where someone will be waiting to take your lines. You can look very foolish if you do this wrong. The secret to heaving a line is in how you prepare the line before you heave.

have to spend five minutes untangling a bird's nest? That is why line should be neatly coiled (Fig. 6-7). By coiled I don't mean wrapping it around a hand and elbow as many do. Each turn around the elbow puts a twist on the line which, in turn, causes kinks and tangling when you try to heave the line. The coil must be turned as you wind to avoid twisting.

KNOTS

When you buy your first boat, you quickly learn that a simple square knot is not the way to tie up at a gas dock. You will need to add about five or six new knots to your marlinespike skills. There are many more, but since you are not boning up on knots for another Boy Scout Merit badge, you can disregard them. Why?

It is an utter waste of time learning to tie knots that you will never use often enough to keep from forgetting how to tie them. For example, the bowline is considered the most used of knots, yet I never use it, and I have been around boats all my life. The bowline is basically a loop on the end of a line. But I always preferred *spliced* loops on my lines. As a result, I fre-

Fig. 6-7. Many tragedies occur on the water every year because rope is not ready for use when needed.

quently forget how to tie a bowline, which embarrasses me when someone asks me to show them how to tie it.

I can think of only one use I might make of a bowline— helping to heave a line in high winds or long distances. When you put a bowline loop on ⅞" manila it will be so bulky and heavy you can heave it across the Ohio River.

The tempo of life today in socialized boating leaves little time for learning how to tie more knots then you really need to know about. These few will get you by very nicely (Fig. 6-8):

The Figure Eight. This knot, like the simple overhand, is used on the end of a line to keep it from unraveling. It is better then the overhand because it will not jam. Also, two figure 8 knots in series on the end of a line will make it easier to heave.

The Clove Hitch. I consider this knot more useful then the bowline. You will never forget how to tie a clove hitch because you will use it every time you buy gas and tie up to one of there 4 x 4 standoff posts. It is quick to tie and untie.

Two Half Hitches. This is my favorite knot for tying up to gas dock posts or pilings. It's an easy knot to remember, it's easy to untie and it will not work loose or jam.

The Anchor Bend. This knot is sometimes called the Fisherman's Bend. After you make an extra turn around the ring of an anchor or spar, this knot resembles two half hitches. In some areas, like the Mississippi Delta country, they prefer this knot to a thimble or splice for attaching line to an anchor. Fishermen also use this knot in fastening line and leader to hooks and sinkers.

The Square Knot. This is the most common of all knots, the first you learned to tie as a child. It is used for everything from tying cord on packages to fastening two lines together. But do not try to tie two lines of different sizes together because it will slip. This knot has one bad drawback, it will sometimes jam so tight when wet it can never be untied without cutting.

The Sheepshank. You will be surprised at how often you will use this odd-named knot. I find it far more useful then the bowline. The sheepshank is like a zoom lens on a camera which gives you dozens of different focal lengths. Many times you will need a short length of rope, maybe 10 feet, but all you have is longer lengths like 20 and 30 feet. You hate to cut anything or weaken it with a knot. You don't have to. A sheepshank will instantly give you that shorter length without cut-

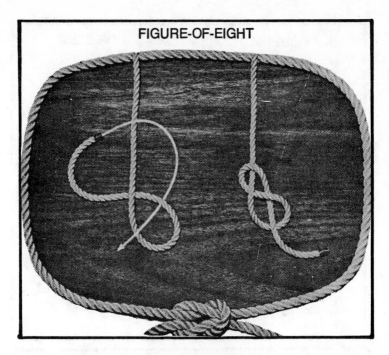

FIGURE-OF-EIGHT

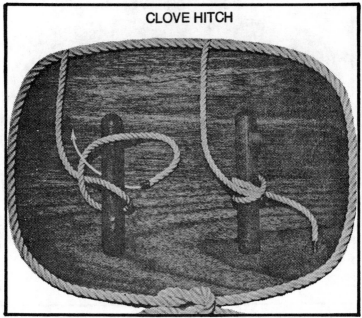

CLOVE HITCH

Fig. 6-8. Learning to properly tie knots is a very important part of boating.

185

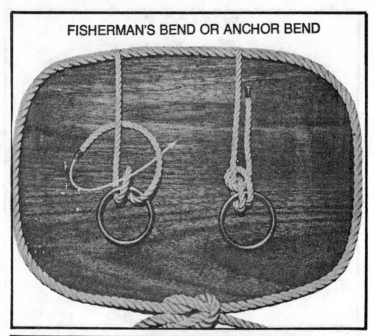

FISHERMAN'S BEND OR ANCHOR BEND

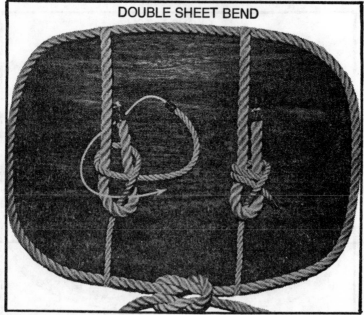

DOUBLE SHEET BEND

Fig. 6-8. Learning to properly tie knots is a very important part of boating. (continued from page 185).

BELAYING

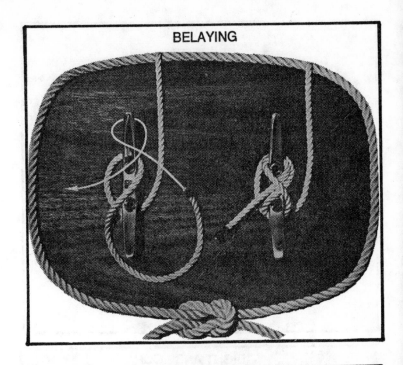

ROLLING HITCH

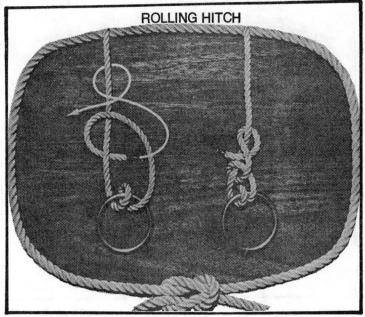

Fig. 6-8. (continued from page 186).

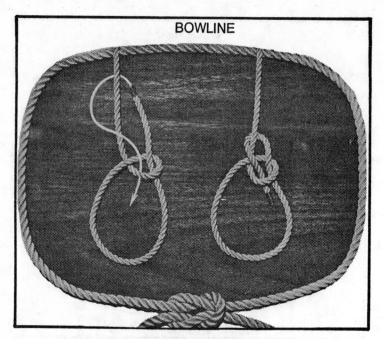

BOWLINE

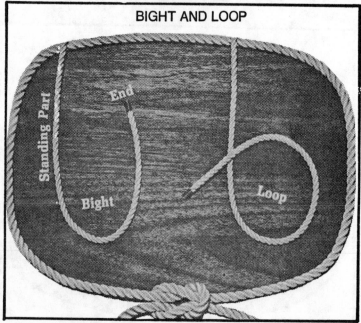

BIGHT AND LOOP

Fig. 6-8. Learning to perperly tie knots is a very important part of boating. (continued from page 187).

ting or weakening a line with tight knots. When finished with the shorter length, the sheepshank quickly releases and you are back to your original length, good as new.

The Sheet Bend. If you ever have to tow another boat, this knot will be useful. When the boat to be towed heaves you a line, the sheet bend is used to secure it to one of your spliced dock lines. On the other hand, if they heave you a line that is spliced, you just reverse your dock line and sheet bend to their splice. This knot holds well even when there is a great difference in the sizes of the two lines, like the ⅜ line of a small outboard to the ¾ line of a cruiser.

EYE SPLICING

One of the first things I learned to do with rope in my boyhood days down in Delta country south of New Orleans was to make a long splice with short lengths of rope. I didn't have the money to buy rope, so I scrounged odd scrap lengths that were thrown away and by long splicing was able to make up a usable anchor line for my fishing dory.

Up in waste-economy America, where I now live, splicing odd lengths of line just isn't done. I mention it now only for the nostalgia freaks among boatmen who also renovate old cars and go to turkey shoots with cap and ball rifles.

PACKAGED LINES

Like frozen TV Dinners, "packaged" lines can be purchased today ready for instant use, beautifully spliced and whipped with rubber gook. Of course, "packaged" lines cost more money—quite a bit more money!

"Packaged" lines sales promotion is aimed at the junior executive market, those busy young men who just don't have the time "to splice and all that jazz." Unmarried junior executives by Mystic Catboats and O'Day 22s as investments in their futures. The boat enables them to join yacht clubs, make social contacts and, hopefully, go sailing with the boss's daughter.

MAKING YOUR OWN LINES

If you have the time and like to save money, buy your rope right off the reel at foot prices, or better still, buy the whole reel at pound prices which can be 20% less then the foot price. You can make up your lines at a fraction of "packaged" prices.

The eye splice is really quite easy, if you get started right. A splicing fid (Fig. 6-9) is helpful I have been told, but I never had one. I made my own out of wood. Don't use a screwdriver

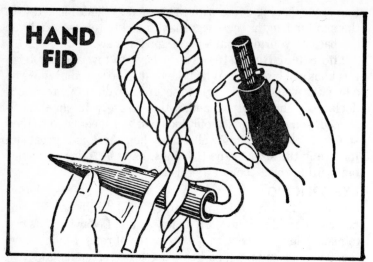

HAND FID

Fig. 6-9. New rope, especially manila in sizes over ½-inch, is stiff and hard to unlay. For this, the fid is helpful, but not really necessary. Don't use a screwdriver, like so many do, because the sharp metal edges can damage inner fibers. You can make a perfectly good fid with any round wood handle or one-inch wood dowel stock. Just taper the end as in the drawing (courtesy of Mannhattan Marine).

with sharp edges to unlay the strands because it can cut the small fibers and make the splice messy with little strands of fiber sticking out.

There is an easy and a hard way to splice (Fig. 6-10). The hard way, with nylon, will blow all your brains out through your ears. Make up your mind right now to do it the easy way for the sake of your family.

First you measure off the length of dock line you need, but do not cut it until you tape about a 3-inch area where the cut will be made. I like to use white Mystic Tape for this because it looks better on nylon than black electrician's tape.

With a very sharp knife, or single-edge razor blade, cut about on the one-inch mark. You will have two clean severed portions, one with a two-inch end neatly whipped, the other with only an inch whipped. Why not cut right in the middle? Because you will *remove* the tape on the end to be spliced, but you will do this very gently so as not to disturb the fibers. Be especially gentle with nylon because just breathing on the threads loosens and spreads them.

With manila, after you remove the original tape for cutting, gently separate the three strands and then *retape* each of them close to the end.

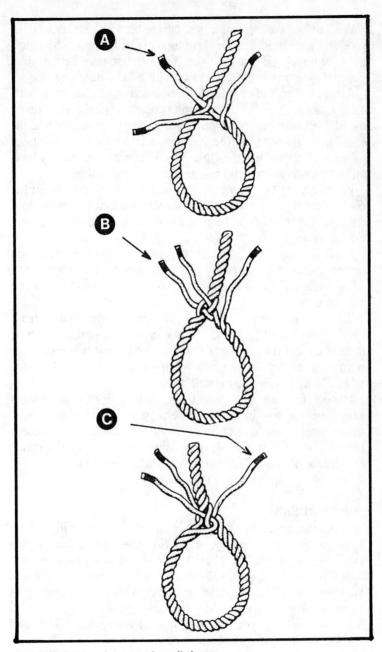

Fig. 6-10. Splicing three-strand manila is easy.

With nylon, you very gently separate the three strands while you hold your breath, then slip a loop of string about a half inch below the end and draw it tight. You can use tape for this, but you will only disturb the threads with all the handling.

After each strand of nylon is looped and tightly knotted, with a cigarette lighter burn the ends of each until the strands of nylon melt into one big blob. I use a small propane torch, instead of a cigarette lighter, because it takes considerable heat to melt the nylon into the right size blob which will firmly hold all the thread so you can make a tight, neat splice.

Be careful at this point not to touch the melted blob until it cools. I got a nasty burn on my thumb once that was very slow healing. You don't have to burn the ends of manila strands, the tape is enough.

Look at the drawing (Fig. 6-10). Note the three strands under which you will make the first very important tucks. I always start with middle strand "A". I then use "B" as the second tuck.

The first two tucks, "A" and "B", should give you no trouble. It's that third tuck, "C", that can screw you up. In fact, it always causes trouble for a first time rope splicer because the natural tendency is to reach *up* for a strand to tuck under when, in fact, you must reach *down*.

Once you make these first three tucks properly, the rest is easy because you just keep repeating what you did at least three, preferably five, times. Then you cut off the excess strand ends, leaving a half inch. With manila, soak the splice in water and then roll it around and it will dry into a neat splice. With nylon, nothing more is necessary.

The Short Splice

If you can make an eye splice in a dock line, you will have no trouble splicing a thimble, or making the short splice to join two lines together. The short splice is just an eye splice done twice in two directions. It is a better way to permanently join two lines together then any of the various knots because all knots, to some degree, reduce the strength of rope (Table 6-1). The short splice gives 85% efficiency; the eye splice 95%; and the square knot only 45%.

The one drawback to a short splice in sailing is that big lump which will not go through a sheave or block. To splice lines together so they will go through a block, you must make a long

Table 6-1. The Percentage of Strength By Rope In Knots and Splices.

Knots	% of efficiency
Normal rope	100
Anchor bend	76
Timber hitch	70-65
Round turn	70-65
Two half-hitches	70-65
Bowline	60
Clove hitch	60
Sheet bend	55
Square knot	45
Splices	*% of efficiency*
Eye splice	95-90
Long splice	87
Short splice	85

splice, which is more complicated. Nobody makes a long splice any more. Why? For the same reason American women no longer save bits of cloth material until they have enough to make a Crazy Quilt blanket, and why little boys, with patches on their pants, no longer scrounge short pieces of rope to splice together for an anchor rode.

We are not a string-saving nation any more and no self-respecting sailor would risk the embarrassment if it were gossiped around the club that he used spliced Dacron sheets on his Columbia 10.7 meter.

Splicing Wire Rope

Yes, you can splice wire rope, but you're crazy if you try. This work, which requires special vises and tools, should be left to professional riggers at sail lofts where they make up wire halyards and standing rigging to specifications. Nobody splices wire rope any more. The modern way is swaging and patented swageless wire rope terminals. You can buy swaging tools and make up your wire rope rigging. Everything you need for this is available from Manhattan Marine in New York.

CARE OF FIBER ROPE

The useful life of rope can be doubled or tripled with proper care. There are many things you can do to make your lines last, at least until you pay off your loan at the bank to finance the last season of boating and club socializing, especially the bar bills.

● Keep your lines clean, this means free of mud, sand and grit which can cut the fibres. Hose them down gently so as not to force sand into the fibers.

● How you stow rope has much to do with life expectancy. Natural fiber ropes, like manila, cotton, sisal, linen and hemp will rot if stored wet or damp in areas of poor ventilation. The synthetics can be stored wet, but they shouldn't be because this only creates musty odors below decks and in lockers. Also, wet nylon will pick up rust marks from chains, thimbles and shackles. Direct sunlight is hard on synthetic lines and so is intense heat, so keep them away from exhaust pipes and batteries.

● Beware of kinks, the biggest destroyer of boat lines. New rope is unruly and prone to kinking. Putting a heavy strain on a line that is kinked can damage it to such a degree that it will no longer be safe to use for anything but hanging bumpers over the side. Under load, a kink overstresses the fibers where they are sharply bent. The rope will rapidly disintegrate at that stress point and, at the most inopportune time, even break apart. Rope kinks when handled the wrong way (like coiling it the way a housewife coils up a laundry line—wrapping it around her open hand and elbow). Every turn around the elbow puts another twist on the line. Later when you try to pull line off that coil, it kinks.

Manila is troublesome to handle when wet because it both shrinks in length and swells in diameter, which causes all kinds of stress where it is knotted. Knots can be just as damaging to manila as kinks because when it swells, the knot gets tighter, and the stress increases. Table 6-1 shows which knots cause the most damage.

● Chafe is another enemy of rope, and that includes all rope whether synthetic, fiber or wire. Boats are always in motion, to a varying degree depending on weather and wind. When a boat is anchored, moored or tied up at a dock, motion makes things rub together. That means friction, wear and tear. Lines take a terrible beating from chafe when the wind blows and they strain hard against mooring bitts and cleats. But lines take their worst chafe where they lay free in a bow chock (Figs. 6-11 and 6-12) to rub back and forth constantly. If they are not protected at this chafe point, they can part in one night of heavy winds.

Fig. 6-11. This line is a double chafe hazard since it is wearing away at both the rope fibers and the fiberglass deck structure on this boat.

● On sailing boats, a synthetic line can be ruined in one day of heavy sailing by careless handling. Holding a line against the revolving drum of a winch or hoist can create enough heat to melt synthetic fibers. Sudden jerks as line is snubbed can also damage fibers. Stretching and straining against a cleat can melt fibers so they will stick and grab running through blocks. Rope has a hard life on sailing boats.

195

Table 6-2. Typical Strength and Weight Comparison
for Yachting Ropes.

SIZE	NYLON		DACRON*		MANILA	
Diameter	(Lbs.) Weight Per 100 Ft.	Lbs. Breaking Strength	(Lbs.) Weight Per 100 Ft.	Lbs. Breaking Strength	(Lbs.) Weight Per 100 Ft.	Lbs. Breaking Strength
¼"	1.6	1800	2.2	1800	2.0	540
⁵⁄₁₆"	2.6	2900	3.5	2900	2.9	900
³⁄₈"	3.7	4000	4.6	3800	4.1	1215
⁷⁄₁₆"	5.0	5400	6.3	5200	5.3	1575
½"	6.6	7100	7.9	6500	7.5	2385
⁹⁄₁₆"	8 3	8900	10.0	8300	10.4	3105
⁵⁄₈"	10.5	11000	12.8	10.400	13.3	3960
¾"	15.0	15000	18.0	14.400	16.7	4860

Weights and strengths shown above are based on figures supplied by the cordage industry using Du Pont nylon and "Dacron". This is typical data Actual weights and strengths may vary between manufacturers of rope and cordage. Some will exceed these values by 10% to 15%.

*Du Pont registered trademark for its polyester fiber

● There are all sorts of tables (Tables 6-2 and 6-3) published by manufacturers to show exactly what service you can expect from their different types of cordage. One table usually shows minimum breaking strengths. For example, half inch manila has a breaking strength of 2650 pounds. Remember, this figure is for *new* rope not weakened by kinks or knots. To determine the safety factor when selecting rope, multiply the expected load by 5. If the rope must handle a working load of 1,000 pounds, select a rope with 5,000 pound breaking strength. Rope must never be subjected to a load beyond 75% of capacity. In the above example, the proper manila rope would be ¾ inch; nylon and Dacron would be 7/16 inch and polypropylene would be 9/16 inch. Each of these ropes, in the sizes specified, has a breaking strength of approximately 5,000 pounds.

Table 6-3. Weights, Tensile Strengths, Working Elasticity and Working Loads for Various Cordage.

DIA	CIRC	POLYESTER WT LBS/100	POLYESTER AVG TENSILE STRENGTH LBS	POLYESTER MIN TENSILE STRENGTH LBS	POLYESTER WORKING LOAD LBS	POLYESTER SAFETY FACTOR	NYLON WT LBS/100	NYLON AVG TENSILE STRENGTH LBS	NYLON MIN TENSILE STRENGTH LBS	NYLON WORKING LOAD	NYLON SAFETY FACTOR	COVER/CORE WT LBS/100	COVER/CORE AVG TENSILE STRENGTH LBS	COVER/CORE MIN TENSILE STRENGTH LBS	COVER/CORE WORKING LOAD LBS	COVER/CORE SAFETY FACTOR	POLY/POLYPRO WT LBS/100	POLY/POLYPRO AVG TENSILE STRENGTH LBS	POLY/POLYPRO MIN TENSILE STRENGTH LBS	POLY/POLYPRO WORKING LOAD	POLY/POLYPRO SAFETY FACTOR
3/16	5/8	1	1300	1040	210	5															
1/4	3/4	2	2300	1840	370	5	1.6	2300	1840	370	5										
5/16	1	3	3400	2870	575	5	2.6	3400	2780	575	5										
3/8	1 1/8	4.4	4900	4140	830	5	3.7	4900	4140	830	5						4.8	5200	4400	880	5
7/16	1 1/4	6	6600	5630	1125	5	5.1	6600	5630	1125	5						6	6700	5700	1140	5
1/2	1 1/2	7.9	8500	7360	1470	5	6.6	8500	7360	1470	5						8	9000	7650	1530	5
9/16	1 3/4	10.7	11500	9800	1960	5	9	11700	10000	2000	5						10	11600	9850	1970	5
5/8	2	14	14600	12400	2480	5	12	15200	13100	2600	5	11.8	16000	13600	2700	5	13	14500	12300	2460	5
3/4	2 1/4	18	18400	15600	3120	5	15	19100	16600	3300	5	17	23000	19600	3900	5	20	21200	18000	3600	5
7/8	2 3/4	27	27000	22900	4580	5	22	28300	24700	4940	5	23	31500	26800	5400	5	24	25000	21200	4240	5
1	3	32	31400	26700	5340	5	26	33600	29400	5880	5	30	40700	34600	6900	5	28	33500	28500	5700	5
1 1/8	3 1/2	43	42800	36000	7200	5	36	45000	40000	8000	5	38	50700	43100	8600	5	37	38200	32500	6500	5
1 1/4	3 3/4	49	48000	40800	8160	5	41	52000	46000	9200	5	47	62800	53400	10700	5	42	43200	36700	7300	5
1 5/16	4	56	54400	46200	9240	5	47	59000	52300	10460	5	56	74400	63200	12600	5	54	54000	45900	9200	5
1 1/2	4 1/2	71	68000	57000	11400	5	60	74000	66200	13240	5	66	88400	75100	15000	5					
1 5/8	5	88	83800	71000	14200	5	74	91000	81800	16360	5	81	100000	85000	17000	5					
1 3/4	5 1/2	106	100000	85000	17000	5	89	110000	97600	19520	5	97	121000	102900	20580	5					
2	6	126	117800	100000	20000	5	106	131000	115000	23000	5	115	144000	122400	24500	5					

WEIGHTS are average with maximum 5% more than listed

TENSILE STRENGTHS are for new rope of standard construction, tested under Cordage Institute Standard Test Methods

WORKING ELASTICITY see information on reverse side

WORKING LOADS are calculated from listed safety factors applied to minimum tensile strengths. They provide guidelines for rope in good condition for use in non-critical applications and should be reduced where life, limb or valuable property are involved, or for exceptional service such as shock or sustained loading, severe abrasion, etc. For special applications working loads are not necessarily intended to apply where a thorough engineering analysis of all conditions of use has been made and these conditions will not be exceeded in service. In such cases, tensile strength, elongation, energy absorption, behavior under long term or cyclic loading and other pertinent properties of a rope may be evaluated to allow selection of the rope best suited to the requirements

Table 6-4. Rope and Fiber Durability Comparisons.

	Manila	Nylon	Dacron	Polyolefins
Mildew, rot resistance	Poor	Excellent	Excellent	Excellent
Acid resistance	poor	Fair	Fair	Excellent
Alkali Resistance	Poor	Excellent	Excellent	Excellent
Sunlight Resistance	Fair	Fair	Good	Fair
Solvent Resistance	Good	Good	Good	Fair
Melting point	380° (burns)	410°	410°	300°
Floatability	only when new	None	None	Indefinite
Abrasion Resistance	Fair	good	Excellent	Poor

● Keep chemicals away from your lines. Table 6-4 shows the resistance of various rope fibers to chemicals, organic solvents, sunlight and heat. When checking batteries with a hydrometer, remove all lines in the vicinity. One drop of sulphuric will instantly burn manila. Nylon and Dacron can also be burned, it just takes a little longer. It's like when you spill battery acid on your trousers. You notice nothing at the time. The next day there's a small hole in your pants leg. Be careful when using bilge cleaners, which are powerful solvents. It takes an alkali like sodium hydroxide to break up dirty engine oil and emulsify it so you can pump it out. Get all lines out of your engine compartment and far enough away so you won't splatter them if you hose down the engine compartment. Fumes and rust also affect rope, especially when wet. This is another reason why rope should not be stowed until thoroughly dry.

● The only thing worse then a block too small is a block too large. If the block is too small, the line will stick and chafe against the sides, or cheeks. Then there is increased internal friction caused by the sheave that is too small in diameter and which turns too fast. Both friction and chafe are at work to damage the fibers. On the other hand, if the block is too large, the line will slip off the sheave and jam between it and the cheek. Table 6-5 shows how to match blocks to rope. For rope ⅜ inch in diameter, the block should have a shell length of at least 3 inches, 6 inches for ¾ inch and 9 inches for 1 inch rope. Small sheaves in steering systems, where they get heavy duty service, can be a source of trouble because they never stop turning. A small sheave quickly wears down the pin on which it turns causing it to corrode and stick. A sheave frozen on its pin can ruin a steering cable in one long run in heavy weather, which is the worst possible time to have steering troubles.

● Don't try to improve on the way cordage manufacturers treat their product to preserve it and retain its strength. The rope you buy, whether natural or synthetic, already has all the oil and preservative it will ever need and any oil or solution treatments you add will do more harm then good.

● Manila rope absorbs water which, if it freezes, can so seriously damage the fibers that it would be dangerous to ever trust that line again, especially if it is an anchor rode. This happens more often then you might think. In fact, it happened to me one lay-up season when we had an early cold snap around the beginning of November. My boat had just been hauled and was resting in its cradle up on the beach uncovered. It was a beautiful warm day when it was dropped into the cradle. I had my lines laying on the decks to air out and dry. The next day it rained, turned cold and snowed until I had three inches of the stuff on my boat. My lines all froze, so I threw them away. But, if no strain is put on frozen rope and it is thawed before being used, it need not be discarded. On the other hand, synthetic rope absorbs very little moisture, which is why commercial fishermen, who go out in freezing weather, have all switched to nylon.

ROPE SAFETY CHECKS

The Coast Guard Auxiliary will give your boat an annual safety check, but they will not inspect your ropes. You can

Table 6-5. Proper Rope And Blocks Sizes

Size of Block (length of shell)	Diameter of rope
3″	3/8″
4″	1/2″
5″	9/16″-5/8″
6″	3/4″
7″	13/16″
8″	7/8″-1″
10″	1 1/8″
12″	1 1/4″
14″	1 3/8″-1 1/2″
16″	1 5/8″

NOTE—Some larger blocks could accomodate rope in a larger size, but this is not recommended since it causes more strain on outer fibers, increases internal friction which reduces rope life.

Fig. 6-12. These lines are weakening themselves by chafe to the danger point.

pass all the routine safety checks (proper bilge ventilation, approved fire extinguishers, approved life jackets, proper navigation lights) and *still* be a hazard to someone's health.

Who will inspect the wire rope on your rigging or the synthetic rope on your running rigging? A broken backstay in a blow could de-mast you, even knock one of your crew overboard. Have you ever been on a boat in high winds when it was de-masted? All that confusion and yelling and wind blowing, do you think you could come about in time to find the man overboard?

If you are a sailing skipper, you alone are responsible for determining the safety of all your ropes, including the wire rope in the standing rigging and the synthetic rope in the running rigging.

Wire rope of ordinary steel is subject to corrosion. Even galvanized rope will rust and corrode when the galvanizing wears off inside where the strands flex and rub. When you see rust stains seeping out, that is the reason.

Stainless steel wire rope is the answer to rust stains and corrosion, but even stainless steel is subject to wear. Check closely the outside diameter of the single wires that make up a strand. Compare them with a piece of new wire. When the diameter of these individual wires is worn down to half their original diameter, the rope is a definite hazard and should be replaced.

Another sign that wear is catching up on your wire rope is those tiny broken wires called "meat hooks" that sting when

200

they cut up your hands. This is another warning that it is time for new rigging.

Care Of Rope

I still use the word "rope" because that's what cordage is when you buy it, but after you cut it up into usable lengths, splice one end, whip the other end so it will not unravel, it becomes a "line" from that point on.

Although the synthetics have pretty well taken over in Class boat racing and yacht club fiberglass yachtsmanship, there are still many old wood boat traditionalists around who continue to use manila, and if you have ever sailed in the Chesapeake Bay, Long Island Sound or Martha's Vineyard, you will understand what I mean. I said synthetics have proven their superiority, true—but not to everybody. You would be amazed at how many wood boats there are around that still use alcohol stoves for cooking and kerosene for lights.

My last cruiser, which I bought for $20,000 just 13 years ago (factory new), had an alcohol stove and an ice box, plus, as standard equipment, 200 feet of manila anchor line and four dock lines, also of manila. The alcohol stove and ice box sound like something out of the Dark Ages of boating today, but yet it seems like just yesterday when these things were used by everyone.

Don't knock it or turn up your nose. The Philippine Islands are still exporting all the abaca fiber they can produce to be twisted or woven into manila rope and sold to the merchant fleets all over the world, and to nostalgia freaks like me. In the commercial field, and merchant marine, the synthetics are just too costly. Can you imagine the cost of a 3-inch hawser in nylon? A freighter will use as many as eight of these lines, 300 feet long, to tie up alongside a dock. An ocean liner will have hawsers as big around as a baseball bat. Just one of these hawsers in nylon would cost more then some small pleasure cruisers.

There is nothing wrong with manila, you just have to work more with it, which, in some respects, is a good thing because discipline and orderliness is necessary training for those who go to sea in ships. Too much of boating today is promoted and sold around the *care-free, maintenance-free, trouble-free* myth created by the hucksters.

It is actually dangerous to believe what the hucksters delude you with because there is no such thing as boating free from trouble and work. If there was, what would be the pleasure? What is the satisfaction in just hosing down a boat, coiling up the wet lines and walking away into the setting sun? This is the theme music that accompanies all advertising for fiberglass boats and synthetic rope.

Rope of natural fiber will deteriorate if stowed away wet, or even damp in a poorly ventilated anchor chain locker, where it will rot.

Manila shrinks when wet, so much that it can damage a boat by pulling out cleats and mooring bitts. This is still such a serious threat that many boat owners, myself included, have working arrangements with the Yard or marina to have some employee check on the lines after a rain. These lines must be loosened when wet and shortened when dry.

It is the same with manila sailboat rigging where the shrinking can cause serious structural damage. This is what I meant by manila requiring more work. The *work* is in the extra things that you must do, the extra maintenance, the extra vigilance, the checking of lines and the drying.

But this has always been a necessary part of boating just like coffee grounds were always a necessary part of coffee drinking, until somebody invented Instant Coffee. Now coffee grounds are a drag, and so is drying out manila.

Fiber ropes should be given a feel and eyeball test at the beginning of each season. With manila the "feel" test can tell you much. New manila has a feel of life, stiffness and strength. Old, worn out manila has all the vigor and stiffness of a cooked strand of spaghetti. Even without a visual inspection, you should know that the rope is no good. But yet I have seen rope in this condition being used as dock lines on 50-foot houseboats. Then when the lines broke and the houseboats swung over to bang against neighboring boats, the assessed damage was later attributed to "high winds."

Bad, worn-out rope (Fig. 6-13) used for dock lines is the cause for more damage to boats then any other thing except hurricanes. Even in hurricanes, bad rope is a contributing factor in many instances.

ADVICE FROM AN OLD SALT

If you don't want to be bothered with annual "rope inspec-

Fig. 6-13. This dock line, chafing in the bow chock and on the rub strip, has been weakened to the danger point. In a strong blow, when boats lash and jerk at their dock lines, this line will break and the ensuing damage can be considerable, especially when neighboring boats are involved.

tions" or you are afraid to trust your judgement, then follow the advice of the late Bill Harrison, founder of Harrison's Marina on western Lake Erie. A salt of the old school, Harrison told me: "Use dock lines for two years and then throw them away. Then take your anchor rode, cut it up into shorter lengths and splice it for new dock lines. Buy new rope for anchoring. Two years later, repeat the process."

I have personally found this to be good advice and have followed it for years.

Dock lines get heavy service in a season, both from chafe at one end, and the constant bending around cleats, spars and pilings at the other end. Weather, salt and the sun are also eating away at your lines.

Anchor rodes see very little service on pleasure and cruising boats so it makes sense to discard the much used dock lines and cut up the little used anchor rode to make new lines. It's like rotating the tires on your car.

SOME TRICKS OF THE PAST

Many new boatmen in their gleaming white fiberglass are not turned on by marlinespike seamanship of the Moby Dick era. But for the few who are, I will discuss a few old tricks.

WHIPPING ROPE ENDS

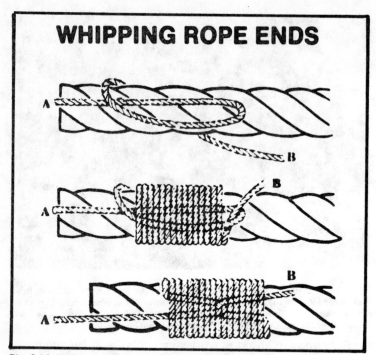

Fig. 6-14. Whipping rope ends is the traditional way of preventing rope from unraveling and fraying at the ends to become cow's tails. However, this is tedious work and takes up a lot time.

Going over these old tricks makes me wonder, is anybody interested in making a back splice on the end of a line to keep the strands from becoming cow's tails, and to make the end of the line double in diameter, thus easier to heave?

You can treat rope ends much faster and easier by dipping them into a red vinyl liquid called "Whip End Dip" (Figs. 6-14 and 6-15). This stuff quickly seals and binds the fibers into a solid flexible mass.

Is anybody interested in protecting their lines from chafe in the old Yankee Clipper way of serving, parcelling and worming? Worming means running small twine into the lay of the rope to keep out the moisture and to fill in and make level for parcelling, which is winding over-lapping strips of canvas on the rope. Serving, the last step, means covering all the above by wrapping seine twine to the lay of the rope. This involves a lot of work, but this is how rope was protected from chafe in the days of sail.

But why should you do all that work when you can buy rub-

204

ber chafing sleeves (Fig. 6-16) and patented "Chafe-Guard" that will do the same thing?

I don't think you will ever care about worming, parcelling and serving and so I will not bother to elaborate on it any further.

Most men that I know can't sew worth a darn, and furthermore they don't ever want to learn how. In sailing, you sometimes have to make emergency repairs and according to most experts who write on boating subjects, every sailor should be able to sew canvas. That's what they say. They also say you should have aboard a "ditty bag" (Fig. 6-17) containing all the essentials like an assortment of seven needles, beeswax, sail twine, awl, knife and a sailmaker's palm, which serves the same purpose as a seamstress' "thimble."

If you ever want to buy a sail repair kit, or "ditty bag," just to have on your boat as a conversation piece, you will find this favorite of the nostalgia freaks like myself, listed in the *Manhattan Marine* catalog for about $16, which is a bargain.

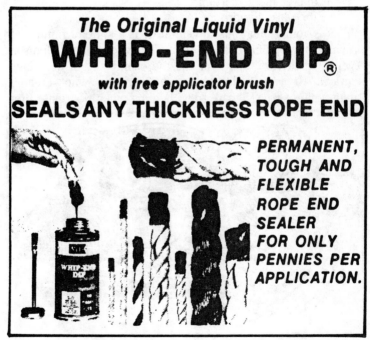

Fig. 6-15. "Whip-End Dip" makes whipping rope ends faster and easier (courtesy of Manhattan Marine).

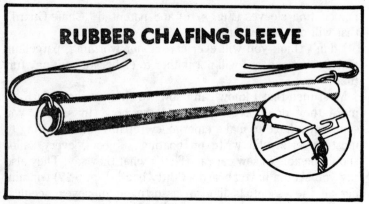

RUBBER CHAFING SLEEVE

Fig. 6-16. Rubber chafing sleeves protect your lines from wear and tear.

And while you're at it, be sure to also order from Manhattan a few rolls of *Seaboard Ripstop Tape,* which is nylon spinnaker cloth with an adhesive backing for temporary repairs of sails.

When the occasion arises that you must repair a sail, I am certain it is the tape you will use, and not the ditty bag.

What makes me so certain?

The Fiberglass Syndrome.

This is something I just invented. It is a state of mind that prevails in popular boating today spawned when Madison Avenue hucksters took over the merchandising of all things nautical. It was advertising copywriters who created "maintenance free," "care free" boating when fiberglass first

Fig. 6-17. These items are considered "essentials" on a sailboat because they can be used to make emergency repairs.

appeared on the boating scene about 30 years ago.

Traditionally, ownership of a wood boat always meant hard work. They never called it pleasure boating when I was a boy. The word "pleasure," a Freudian device, was added only 20 years ago to help sell the new fiberglass "fun boats" for beautiful young people, especially girls in bikinis. But you never see those girls in bikinis splicing rope, sewing Dacron sails or scrapping loose paint off boat bottoms. Fiberglass was supposed to take all the drudgery and work out of boating and replace it with fun and carefree days in the sun.

Old fashioned marlinspike seamanship belongs to the old image of work, scrape, sand, caulk, paint and varnish. The fiberglass boatmen today just won't buy "all that crap," as they say. As one young junior executive told me: "Why should I waste valuable boating time learning how to braid loops in rope when right down there in the marina store they sell it already braided and looped by machines that do a far better job?"

This is why I am certain the new boatman in the fiberglass sloop will make only temporary repairs on his sail with tape, then later drop it off at the Sail Loft for permanent repair by so-called professionals.

And the ditty bag he bought will join the other memorabilia of the days, he will tell guests, "when he sailed before the mast," like Joseph Conrad.

BLOCKS

Blocks were a major step up the ladder of human progress for Man (Fig. 6-18). Blocks are marvelous mechanical contrivances that give one man the strength of many. Without them, sailboating would be almost impossible in anything larger then a sailing dinghy.

One of the things that still baffles engineers and historians is how the Egyptians built the pyramids without blocks and pulleys. How did they handle and lift those huge stone blocks weighing hundreds of tons? It was over 1000 years after King Tutankhamen was entombed before the Greek geometrician, Archimedes, discovered the principle of the lever and reportedly said: "Give me a lever long enough and a place to stand and I can move the world."

It was not until the 1st century A.D. that pulleys and cords were used as gearing to lift heavy weights. The handling of sail

Fig. 6-18. Without blocks, sailing as we know it today, would be impossible because it would take too much manpower.

on merchant vessels began to change in the 2nd century A.D. as blocks and tackle were devised that could better control sails then sheer manpower.

Today, 1800 years later, there has been little change in blocks because, like the wheel, after it was invented, not many improvements were left to make? The big wood blocks that you can see today on old sailing ships have changed little from those used on merchant vessels sailing the Mediterranean while the Caesars still ruled over the Roman Empire (Fig. 6-19).

The traditional block is made of a wood shell, or frame, inside which a metal wheel called a sheave rolls on a pin or shaft. This pin today can be plain, self-lubricating or roller bearing and both the shell and sheave can be some tough plastic material. This is about the only modern improvements in block, which is really not an "improvement," but a substitution of construction materials. The block made of plastic today functions no differently then one made of wood 1800 years ago.

Block types are designed according to the number of sheaves they contain, like single, double or triple. The more sheaves, the more leverage and the greater the ratio of force to weight.

Size of block and sheaves is determined by the circumference of rope for which they are designed. The block must be three times the circumference, while the sheave must be twice as large. For example, 2-inch rope (⅝″ in diameter) would require a 6-inch block and a 4-inch sheave.

Table 6-5 will help you match rope with blocks.

TACKLE

The word "tackle" is a blanket term that covers everything that is used to increase lifting power, which means blocks, hooks and chains wrapped around beams and the rope.

Types of Tackle

You will learn to recognize the various types of tackle and the names they carry by the number of sheaves in the blocks. Some of these were handed down from centuries past, like Spanish-burtons, luff-tackles, gun-tackle and watch-tackle. There are many more.

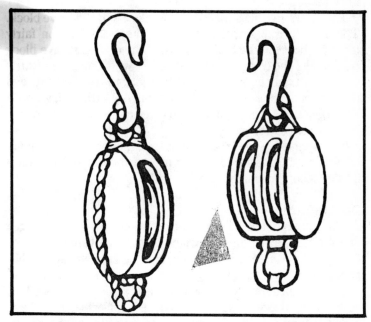

Fig. 6-19. Blocks come with one, two or three sheaves. There have been no real basic improvements in blocks in the last 2,000 years. They just make them with different materials, like plastic instead of wood and iron. They don't last any longer and they don't work any better.

The Single Whip

This is just one block that gives no increase in lifting power and is used mainly to change direction of pull.

In all common tackles, one block is fixed and one block, attached to the object to be lifted, is movable. The hauling part (the end of the rope you pull) can be on either block, but the power ratio will be greater when it is on the movable block attached to the load being lifted or moved as in a sail boom.

Gun Tackle

This is two single blocks which will give either a ratio of 1:2 or 1:3 power increase, depending on whether the hauling part of the rope (the end you pull on) is on the lower or upper block (Fig. 6-20). This type of block arrangement is used on small day sailers under 20 feet to control the boom. There will always be a third and a fourth block to change the direction of pull, and on larger boats, the hauling part will end up on some type of winch to further increase the pull power.

Luff Tackle

This is one double sheave block and one single sheave block. This is an arrangement popular for sheet handling on fairly large sailboats in the cruiser class. If the double sheave block is movable, the force gained will be 1:4, which means one little girl could trim the sail on a 28-foot gaff-rigged catboat, and that's a lot of canvas to muscle. But that one little girl, with 1:4 leverage on the sheet, would need three more little girls to help her muscle that boom.

If the single sheave block is movable, then the leverage gained will be 1:3, still enough for a man to trim the sail on a 30-foot sloop or marconi rig.

Double Tackle

This is two double-sheave blocks, which will give leverages of 1:4 or 1:5, depending on which block is movable.

With a five-force leverage gain, and the hauling part further snubbed to a winch, the biggest sail can be handled with ease.

Without these marvelous mechanical devices and winches, single-handed ocean sailing would be impossible. Men have sailed around the world alone on 70-footers because a single-handed sailor is not really "single-handed." The term is misleading because all those blocks and winches are extra "deckhands" helping him.

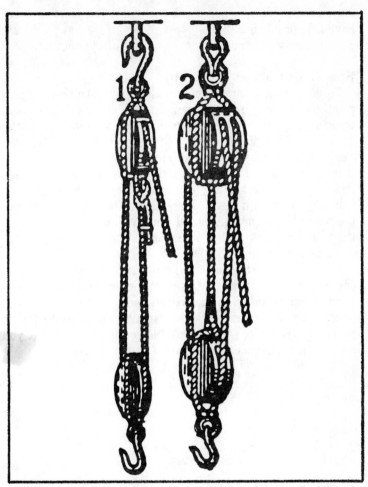

Fig. 6-20. These are two common tackle arrangements on small sailboats to handle jib and main sheets. (1) This is called a "gun tackle," two single blocks providing either double or triple force. (2) This is a "luff tackle," providing a 1:3 or 1:4 power increase, depending on whether the upper or lower block is movable.

Triple Blocks

Yes, there are triple blocks with three sheaves, but you will never see them on pleasure boats because with all the wonderful winches available with power gains of up to 50:1, there is no need for them. On a triple block, the hauling part must always be run on the middle sheave. If this is not done, the block will twist to one side which can cause the rope to jam. In extreme cases it can even break the block. But you will never have this problem because you will never see a triple block. You will only see double blocks and beautiful winches.

How To Use Blocks Efficiently

To get the most out of your blocks, they must be used efficiently, which may not always seem to be the most convenient way to you. However , you have many alternatives . If the angle of pull on the sheet does not suit you, the direction can easily be changed with another single block.

With a single and double block tackle for maximum leverage and efficiency the hauling part of the line should always run from the block with the most sheaves. If both blocks are double sheave, then the line should run from the *movable* block. If the tackle is single and double sheave, then the double block should be on the movable end.

There is no rule that says you can't do it any other way. You can do just the opposite of the above and the tackles will work, but not as efficiently. What matters most is convenience. It's your boat and your tackle so you should use whatever tackle arrangements make you comfortable because the leverage you lose in the tackle is easily made up on the winches.

Chapter 7
Powerboat Seamanship

The instant you step aboard any vessel, no matter how small, that is power or sail propelled, there is a degree of seamanship involved—not only in your own survival, but the survival of others who may have to come to your rescue.

"They're paid to do that," you say.

But they are not paid to *die*.

The U.S. Coast Guard has a long Honors List of crewmen who died in the line of duty, often rescuing boatmen just like Novarro.

"No man is an island, entire of itself," John Donne wrote over 300 years ago. Nowhere is this more true then when you go to sea in a boat. Every mistake you make touches the lives of others. What Donne was saying is that you can't even stupidly throw away your own life without involving other people. If you don't give a darn about your own life, give a thought to the lives of others who must give a darn about your life.

How Is Seamanship Involved?

Seamanship is paying attention.

"Attention to what?" you ask.

Weather warnings for one thing. When the Coast Guard runs up the small craft warning (Fig. 7-1), a single red pennant by day, red light above a white light at night, seamanship means staying home.

Fig. 7-1. When the Coast Guard runs up the small craft warning, seamanship means staying at home.

This is the reason why powerboaters are held in such low regard by sailors, especially in those clannish little communities called "yacht clubs." I have heard it said so many times at these clubs that all powerboaters are dedicated lubbers who don't have the brains to stay at their moorings when the wind blows.

To skipper a powerboat you don't have to prove anything to the authorities to be issued a registration number for your boat, which, in turn, automatically makes you the legal skipper of the registered vessel. But that doesn't prove anything to your peers at the club or marina. To them you are a lubber, and always will be a lubber until you prove a passable grade in seamanship.

How To Start Learning

You are involved in seamanship the instant your signature is on that Purchase Agreement and you take possession of something that is propelled through the water by an engine. You are excited. Your kids are excited. Your wife is chain-smoking, looks worried. You can't wait for them to drop you in the water so you can turn the key and take her out.

This is your first lesson in seamanship—*don't*.

Curb your impulses when the salesman gives you the keys, shows you how to flush the head and then waves gaily as he leaves saying, "Have fun."

You will not, I promise, have any "fun" if you take that new boat out into Big Water without any prior doctrination and instruction from somebody, even if it's only your parish priest offering blessings and God's help.

Warning! Remember *Murphy's Law!* If anything can go wrong, it will (it always will on that First Day with your wife and kids). Your first, and one of your most important lessons in seamanship is *don't take her out* the first day (Fig. 7-2), which is Jinx Day for all lubbers.

Have the marina run your boat over to your dock or mooring and show you how to tie her up. But don't expect too much from marina employees on seamanship because the kid who is handling the lines for an older man at the wheel of your boat probably just started working at the marina.

Spend the first day getting acquainted with your new boat, open up all hatches, pull out drawers and look into everything. It is very important that you know *everything* about your boat and where everything is. Boats are a lot like women, they have character, personalities and they respond to love and care. But not all of them respond in the same way. That is what you must learn—how the boat responds to your touch.

Practice starting the engine and watch the tachometer. This is something American auto drivers rarely see, a tachometer,

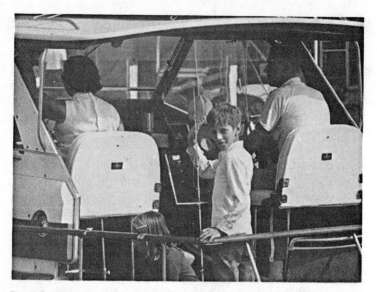

Fig. 7-2. When the keys are finally turned over to you by the former owner of the 10-year-old 29-foot cruiser that captured your heart, don't expect any help, other then instructions on how to light the alcohol stove and flush the head.

which shows your engine rpm's, or revolutions-per-minute. When the engine is warmed up, push open the throttle to 1500 rpm for a second, and then back it off quickly to the stop point. If properly adjusted, the engine will slow down to about 500 rpm without missing a beat. Many times, with a new boat engine, it will stall. That's very bad. But it is a good thing to know *before* you take her out for the first time. It can be very scary when an engine stalls approaching a gas dock or going into a slip.

You may think it nit-picking, all this fuss about a trivial, minor mechanical adjustment on the throttle controls.

There are no such things as "trivial or minor" adjustments on a boat because the safety of your boat and crew depends on these "minor adjustments." That's what good seamanship is. On a boat, the engine and reverse gear is the only way you have of stopping. It is your brakes! If the engine stalls at a critical time, you have no brakes.

There is another way of stopping a boat. You just ram your stem into a steel bulkhead. I saw a friend do this with his new $85,000 Matthews, only he didn't do it intentionally. Coming into a covered boathouse, he revved in reverse to slow down, then backed off on the throttle. The engine stalled, but he hadn't reversed long enough and his boat kept on moving and banged into a steel bulkhead.

He just stood there, white and shaking, staring at his beautiful new yacht with the badly damaged stem. Then he got in his car, bowed his head on the steering wheel and cried like a baby. And I almost cried with him because I love boats.

New engines are especially prone to this type of stalling, after being revved up to high rpm's and then quickly backed off on the throttle to the stop point, the engine is actually gasping for air, which is why it stalls.

It will be necessary to adjust the idle to a higher rpm, like 600 or even 700, to prevent stalling (and prevent it you must before you go out for the first time). If the marina mechanic makes this adjustment, make sure he does it right.

Bear in mind that you also have to dock that new boat for the first time. Learning to dock can be a little hairy and you will almost certainly make a few bad approaches. If so, reverse to stop, and back off to try again. And again! And again! For this reason you must be sure that your brakes will work. They will *not* if your engine stalls.

THE IMPORTANCE OF WEATHER

Good seamanship is knowing the weather. There will be a full chapter on weather for the boatman, which should indicate the importance of this subject.

Nobody, not even farmers, worry and fuss about the weather more them people who own boats. Our whole lives are compressed down into so many weekends, plus three or four weeks of vacation. There are so many lost weekends because of bad weather.

What Is Bad Weather

The words "bad weather" do not mean the same thing to all people. For example, a boatman's "bad weather" might be perfect weather for golf or a family picnic. When a boatman says "bad weather" he means the wind is blowing from the wrong direction on the lake or offshore causing three to five foot waves. On eastern coastal waters, strong offshore winds are bad for small outboards with one engine and no radio communications (Fig. 7-3). Engine trouble could be disastrous because the offshore wind will blow them into the Gulf Stream.

Pleasure boats are *small* boats. All small boats cease to be "pleasure" boats when weather forecasters say on the 6 o'clock evening news: "Winds on the lake and bay tomorrow will reach 15 knots with waves running about four feet. Small craft warnings have not been posted at this hour, but it is expected they will be early tomorrow."

The above weather report will be good news for racing sailors, but it will be bad news for owners of small powerboats. It will also be a test of seamanship, not in proving how good you are at handling those seas, but in having the good sense to not go out. Here is where you separate the lubbers from the seamen. Seamanship means avoiding confrontation with bad sea conditions whenever possible, but being able to handle them when absolutely necessary. The lubber doesn't have the good sense to do this. He goes out anyway. He goes out when he doesn't have to.

There is probably a question on your mind, like "Are four foot waves dangerous?"

Fig. 7-3. These are the vulnerable boats: one engine, no communications, heading out to sea, and an offshore wind blowing briskly. On eastern coastal waters it is always dangerous for such craft under these conditions. Should the one engine become disabled, the boat would be blown out to sea and into the Gulf Stream.

No. But they are damn uncomfortable!

Why make your family miserable? Are you a sadist? Boating is supposed to be fun, a family thing. Boating is sheer hell and misery when you fight 4-5 foot waves in a small boat. Running in the trough, you roll violently, your kids get seasick. Loose objects go flying in all directions, dishes, cups and food slide off tables.

A standard food fare aboard pleasure craft is chili, bake Van Camp beans, wieners, fried chicken and potato salad. These dishes don't look very nice when splattered all over a cabin shag rug.

Seamanship is thinking of your family's comfort. It is building a fire on the beach to roast the wieners and heat the beans for a picnic ashore instead of going out to fight waves. The kids will gripe and call you a chicken sailor for being afraid to go out, but your wife will understand and love you all the more.

WHAT IS A GOOD SEA BOAT?

If you read boating magazine advertisements, then you have certainly seen those claims made by many manufacturers that their product is a good *sea boat*. And in the advertisements you will always see the boat planing beautifully over water that is gently rippled like a fish pond with a bikinied girl becomingly sprawled over some cushions aft. But you never see the boat struggling in a steep chop being literally drowned in spray.

The words "good sea boat" is nothing but a catch phrase, a Freudian trick to sell boats. Don't let yourself be conned by these Madison Avenue Siren Songs written by "seafaring" men who never went to sea. There is absolutely no way to define what is a "good sea boat" without sounding like a pompous ass who thinks he knows it all. Although I have been around boats all my life and have built and designed them, I still can't tell you exactly what a good sea boat is.

Why is it so hard to define?

No matter how I define a good "sea boat," somebody will produce historical records and technical data to show that I am wrong. For example: would you consider a 10-foot sailboat to be a good sea boat? Would you consider it safe enough to sail 3500 miles across the Atlantic? You say no! You are wrong! That ridiculous little boat, smaller then some bathtubs, did safely sail across the Atlantic and survived severe storms that would have foundered many larger vessels.

Would you consider a steel passenger liner with a gross tonnage of 46,328 and designed to carry over 2200 passengers as being a good sea boat? This particular ship was considered by naval architects and engineers as the largest and safest vessel ever built and, according to its owners, *The White Star Line*, was virtually unsinkable because the new type hull construction was compartmentalized with water-tight bulkheads. The flooding of even four or five compartments would not sink the vessel.

But this perfect sea boat that was "unsinkable" failed to pass its first real sea test. The *Titanic* never made it to New York on her maiden voyage. It seems the designers overlooked the possibility that all the compartments might be holed and flooded. That is exactly what happened when the *Titanic* sideswiped an iceberg ripping a huge gash along the length of its hull.

If success and survival at sea is the standard of measurement for what is and what is not a good "sea boat," the American sailor Gerry Spiess's 10-foot *Yankee Girl* is a good sea boat. It is even better then the ill-fated *Titanic* because at least the 10-foot boat made it safely across the Atlantic through hell and high water.

Which brings us back to the original question: what is a good sea boat?

The answer: anything that floats.

History will bear this out. Men have survived long sea passages in the most incredible contraptions imaginable, from hollowed-out logs to rafts made of palm leaves and reeds. Even as I write this, the Boat People of Indo-China are going to sea in dilapidated unseaworthy hulks that are so over-loaded with humanity that the gunwales are awash. Yet they are surviving in that most hostile of environments—the sea.

What does all this prove? There are no bad sea boats. There are only bad sea skippers. And when you get down to the final line, *seamanship* is what makes a good skipper—and a good sea boat.

Types Of Good Sea Boats

Since anything that floats is basically a good seaboat, does this mean that the boat buyer can go blindfolded into the market place with no fear that he will make a bad choice? Ab-

Fig. 7-4. Labels are attached to boats by people who don't know what they are talking about. All round bottom "soft chine" hulls, they claim, are "rollers." This is a ridiculous label because all boats roll. They just do it differently. However, the so-called "rollers" have compensating features. This particular displacement hull, with its sharp forward entry, is a soft riding boat in head seas and never "pounds."

solutely not! Do you go blindfolded into the market place to buy an automobile? All automobiles are basically good, but some are better then others for you. The mini-compacts are great for people who are four feet tall. For me, over six feet tall, they are not very comfortable.

It's the same with boats. Some are better then others for you.

Some people insist that the minute they step aboard a soft-chined hull (round bottom), they get seasick because the boat rolls too much (Fig. 7-4). Do round bottom boats really roll more then other types? True or false?

If you said "true" you were wrong. All boats roll, but not in the same way. The roll of a round-bottomed hull is smooth, easy and steady like the swing of a pendulum on an old grandfather clock. The roll of a semi-V is quite different, it recovers more quickly at the end of a roll, and the movement is faster. It can be a very tiring roll, even give you a stiff neck after a long day of fishing over an anchored spot. The hard chine semi-V roll is just as uncomfortable to some people as the easy round bottom roll is to others.

Some people think that semi-V hulls (Fig. 7-5), which are designed to plane on the surface, are not as seaworthy as round bottom displacement hulls which push *through* the water rather than *on* the water. True or false?

If you said "true", you are wrong again.

The semi-V hull is designed to plane on the surface when *conditions permit.* But that isn't too often with a small boat under 30 feet. The ideal conditions for planing is when the water surface is rippled with small waves of about one foot.

When on plane, the V-hull encounters minimal water resistance and a speed over the surface is limited only by engine horsepower. The more horses you have, the faster you can go. The semi-V hull, pioneered by Chris Craft, revolutionized marine engine technology which produced smaller engines with more and more horsepower at higher and higher RPMs.

Pre-World War II yachts usually had only one engine which would weigh several tons. This monstrous piece of iron had pistons bigger then gallon oil cans, but yet only developed about 25 horsepower at 600 to 800 RPM. However, these huge

Fig. 7-5. This semi-V, hard chine hull, which has almost a flat foreward entry, will slap on small 1-foot waves and it will hammer your guts on 2-foot waves and all the pistons in your engines will change holes when you hit 3-foot waves. Yet, with all the discomfort, these are "seaworthy" hulls.

engines developed enough shaft torque to swing enormous 30-inch wheels that would push the displacement hulls through the water at a respectable 10 knots.

When water conditions do not permit, the planing hull must

Fig. 7-6. The semi-V hull with a sharp forward entry, as above, will not pound at non-planing speeds. In addition, when it has flared topsides, as above, water will be deflected away so it will not blow back on the bridge and windshield, making for a drier ride.

be driven at reduced engine RPMs, which means it becomes just another displacement hull pushing through rather then on the water. When operated correctly, the V-hull is no less seaworthy then any other type hull.

Seamanship means understanding this and not playing the fool by forcing a hull to plane in six-foot seas. When some clown does this, the V-hull is not "seaworthy", but neither is the *Queen Elizabeth* if she is pushed beyond her structural design limits by being driven at flank speed (maximum power) in a severe Atlantic storm.

Some people say that V-hulls make their buttocks sore because they pound in choppy water. True or false?

If you said "true" again, you were right this time. The V-hull does pound, and some pound more then others. Why? The "V" up forward can be narrow or broad. A sharp V entry (Fig. 7-6) will help ease the pounding, a broad V foreward section, as in many houseboats, will increase the pounding.

This was the main reason for the fall and decline in popularity of houseboats on the Great Lakes (Fig. 7-7), especially the shallow western end of Lake Erie which produces steep seas that run close together. This type of sea is murderous on small boats and will hammer the life out of a houseboat. The twisting

Fig. 7-7. For a short period in the early seventies, houseboats were hotter then Texas chili on the western end of Lake Erie. Today this is one of the few left, and it sat on the beach all summer with a "For Sale" sign waiting for a buyer. The broad V entry, flat bottom, shallow draft of houseboats is ideally suited for river boating.

224

and pounding causes structural movement, which, in turn, cracks the glass in all those big windows on houseboats. On smaller outboards only a masochist would sit up foreward and take the beating. The only way to stop the pounding is by reducing speed, getting off plane, and bringing the foreward sections down so the bow pushes *through* the water like a displacement hull. If the boat is slowed down too much, spray coming over the bow will drown you. There is an optimum throttle setting which every skipper must learn for himself to keep his bow up just high enough to hold down spray, yet not so high that it will pound.

In short, the V-hull becomes a displacement hull, which is how it is run most of the time on any of the Great Lakes. It is only on rivers and small inland lakes where planing hulls can plane at will. Offshore on the ocean, forget it.

There is a stock boat race which is run from Miami to Bermuda for fast planing hulls. But this is more an endurance test then a true "race" because the boats are pushed to their structural limits regardless of sea conditions. As a result, very few of the entrants each year even survive long enough to finish.

Boat builders enter this "race" mainly to prove the durability of their hulls. The funny part is so few have the structural "durability" to survive the race and the builders would be far better off if they stayed out of the race and just let the advertising copy writers explain "durability" to boat buyers.

HANDLING THE SINGLE-SCREW INBOARD

Some people say that the single-screw inboard in a light planing hull is the most difficult of all boats to handle when docking. True or false?

Absolutely true.

I have handled many single-screw hulls, both shallow and deep draft. The light shallow drafts, if there is wind and a strong current, are the most unmanageable of beasts ever created by man, and I "created" one of them, built in my garage.

Plywood was, and still is, a popular hull planking material and many stock boats were built of this material in the 1950s and sixties. Many had no keels or skegs. They also had small rudders. Boats planked with ¼ and ⅜ plywood were very light and floated high in the water like corks or balsa wood. A typical 27-foot cruiser would have 6-inches of hull below the waterline and seven feet above to act as a sail in the wind. With one engine and a small rudder, you can see why they were impossible to control on windy days. Even the lightest wind would blow them sideways almost as fast as they moved forward entering a slip.

You never docked one of these single-screw hulls on the first pass. You always, stopped, backed off, tried again until you made the correct allowances for wind drift and current. Even then you occasionally miscalculated by inches and banged against pilings or a neighbor's boat. Those were days when I spent much time repairing damaged sheer rails and gouged topsides. In fact, it is the reason why I am so good at repairing hull damage. I got a lot of practice.

Deep Draft Single Screw Powerboats

A keel, deep skeg and 24 inches of hull below the waterline (Fig. 7-8) makes a big difference in the handling of a single-screw inboard powerboat. It's all a matter of water pressure; the same pressure that makes sailing possible. Without water

Fig. 7- 8 . You will rearely see this type of single-screw hull anymore, but they were the easiest to handle and dock. The rudder and propeller are protected from groundings. Since the propeller shaft is almost horizontal, rather then severely angled as on most modern hulls, there is almost no uneven thrust in reverse. Since the rudder surface area is large, helm response is quicker, which means you get almost instant steerageway in reverse.

pressure on the rudder, keel and centerboard it would be impossible to sail because you would be at the mercy of air movement, going in the same direction as the wind. But water pressure on the keel and rudder from one direction equals air pressure on the sails from an opposite direction.

To understand what happens, take a bar of soap, squeeze it between two fingers, what happens? The soap squirts out in a different direction from the two opposing pressures of water and air. And that is what makes a sailboat sail and a single-screw deep draft powerboat so much easier to control and dock. You are no longer at the mercy of every wisp of air current.

The Single-Screw Propeller Problem

There is one little peculiarity of single-screw propellers that you must be warned about. I am being kind when I say "peculiarity." Handicap would be a better word because that's what you have with an inboard single propeller, a built-in handicap.

You are one strike up before you even turn the ignition key. When you try to back out of your slip under right rudder, your stern will go *left!* To call this disconcerting is an understatement. Panicsville is a better word.

If you looked under your boat before it was launched, you surely must have noticed that the propeller shaft came out of your hull bottom at a sharp angle. Obviously, that puts the propeller also at an angle and drastically changes the pitch of the blades as they turn. On the right side (starboard), the blades lose some of their bite on the water because of that angle. On the left side (port), they gain more bite. This gives the propeller more thrust to port and is the reason why the stern swings in that direction when first starting to move astern.

You don't notice this unequal thrust moving forward because the propeller is pushing water against the rudder, which holds the boat on a straight course. But when you start to move astern, you get no immediate response to the helm because the propeller is pushing water in the opposite direction *away* from the rudder. So, until you gain steerageway (moving fast enough to put water pressure on the rudder), you have no response to the helm and your stern swings to port with a right-hand wheel.

You get this type of propeller thrust only on single engine in-

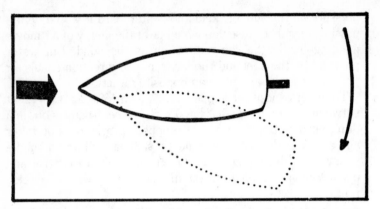

Fig. 7-9. Regardless of rudder position, when first starting to move in reverse, unequal thrust of a R.H. (right hand) propeller will swing your stern to port, as above. It will continue to do this only until there is sufficient water pressure on the rudder to give you rudder response (steerageway).

boards where the engine and shaft must be installed at an angle. With a right-hand wheel (Fig. 7-9), your stern will swing to port on reverse. Moving ahead, the stern will swing slightly to starboard, but this movement is never noticed because you are correcting it at the helm. With a left hand propeller, the actions are just the opposite (Fig. 7-10).

All propellers are stamped on the hub with the letters "RH" or "LH." If you are confused as to how propeller rotation is determined, stand at the transom of your boat. If the propeller turns right going ahead, you have a right hand wheel.

Right hand wheels on single engine installations are almost a standard thing with builders of stock boats. The only time you will find a left hand wheel is when an engine has been replaced. I did this once. My replacement engine came from a twin screw boat, after its first shakedown run. The port engine blew a connecting rod. It was immediately replaced with a new engine and it went back to the factory to be "remanufactured." I was able to buy this engine for less than half the original price. However, the port engine in a twin-screw installation is always left-hand-rotation. The starboard engine is right-hand-rotation.

Once you understand what is happening, it is easy to adjust so you can live with the "peculiarities" of engine screw inboards. It is only ignorance and surprise that creates monsters out of gnats. Losing control of a boat in a crowded marina filled with expensive yachts can be a traumatic experience to a new boat owner. I have known men who were so shaken by the experience that they were never able again to take the wheel without breaking out into a cold sweat.

Boats tied up in slips secured by lines all around are like tigers in a zoo. They look so gentle and so harmless that you can hardly resist reaching in to pet them. But once you cast off those lines, a boat suddenly seems to acquire a mind of its own. It can even become a tiger on the loose.

Seamanship is knowing, understanding and learning how to control the tiger once you throw off those lines at the dock.

The Art Of Single-Screw Boatmanship

Handling single-screw boats is simply a matter of adjusting and adapting; it even includes using to your own advantage all

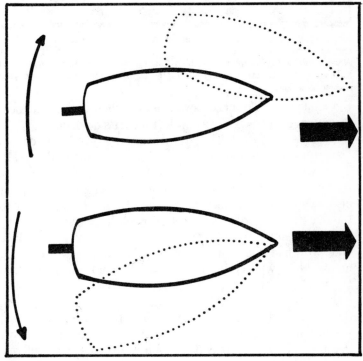

Fig. 7-10. Moving ahead from dead in the water, with a left-hand wheel the stern will swing to port as above. With a right-hand wheel it will do just the opposite, it will swing to starboard. But you don't notice this tendency moving ahead because you have instant rudder response and you are correcting at the helm. In reverse, you do not have instant rudder response and for a few moments your stern is not moving in the direction you wish.

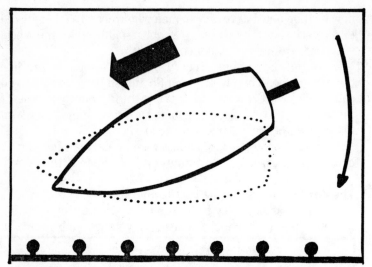

Fig. 7-11. A port side dock is the easiest for a single screw boat to get into, and sometimes the hardest to get out of if there is wind or tidal currents. When wind or tide current is pushing you against the dock, you must start to leave with your stern swung out in the same manner as above and your rudder hard right.

the faults of single-screw power. First, when you rent a dock, if you have a choice, always select a port-side dock.

A port-side dock will be the easiest for you to enter and leave. You always approach such a dock at an angle (Fig. 7-11). Then when you reverse engine to brake to a stop, you get a free bonus. Reversing the engine not only stops your boat, it also swings your stern, sticking way out there, right over to the dock just as pretty as if you planned it that way.

When backing out of a port dock, you adjust again. Have your wife hang on to a bow line holding it close to the dock momentarily while you push the stern away from the dock to about the same angle as when entering. At this point, everybody let go and start backing out. The push away from the dock at the stern gives you time to gain steerageway, which will stop the stern from swinging any further to port because once you are moving at a fair speed, your boat will respond to the helm as you move astern. However, how much control you have depends, as always, on wind direction.

If wind is off the starboard beam, blowing you against the dock, the push may not be enough and you will need more help in controlling that stern. The engine and rudder are still able to give you all the help you need. But wait until you are clear of your dock, then swing hard left rudder and hit it with a good blast of water pressure by revving the engine in forward gear. These blasts of water pressure must be hard and short. You don't want to reverse movement and start going foreward again. Just hit the rudder and back off quickly. You'll be amazed at what you can do with your stern. It can be made to almost jump out of the water.

Give her another shot in reverse, then another hard blast on the rudder. Repeat this as often as necessary. While you are doing this, you will be making almost no backward or forward progress in the water, but you will be slowly swinging your bow to port so you can leave in that direction.

However, if the wind is strong off the port beam, blowing you away from your dock, you will have no trouble in backing out, but you should *never* swing that bow to port so you can leave in that direction. Don't even try. Never forget this: in close quarters where there is little sea room to maneuver, don't ever try to fight the wind with your bow. You can't control the bow in strong winds, but you *can* control the stern. With the wind on your port side, you will have to back *into* the wind and *stay* into the wind until you have backed up to an area when you have more sea room to turn and get the bow into the wind.

Turning 180 Degrees

There is only one way you can turn a single-screw hull 180-degrees in a confined area. You stay in one spot and pivot a half circle. This is a neat trick easily done by twin screws, but it can also be done with one propeller.

To get that bow around 180 degrees you use the push-pull, forward-reverse technique (Fig. 7-12). Your rudder should be hard to starboard. *Leave* it there. Now alternately hit the rudder with a blast of water pressure, then a hard reverse thrust, then another blast, and another reverse thrust. Keep repeating this until you have made a 180-degree pivot—but remember my earlier warning about not changing gears while the engine is still revving up at high RPM. Always bring that throttle back all the way *before* changing gears.

With a little practice you will be able to do this smoothly and easily. But you must learn this technique of blasting the rudder to kick the stern, either to port or starboard, so that you will have control.

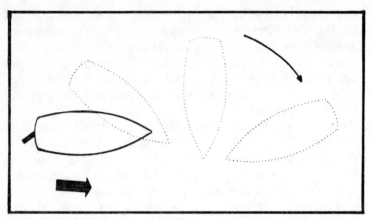

Fig. 7-12. Alternately revving the engine forward/reverse is how a single-screw boat is turned 180° in tight quarters, which is a mighty handy maneuver to know when you enter a strange marina or yacht club and run down a blind alley. However, there is a danger here if you are careless. You can damage the reverse gear if you don't back off on the throttle to idle speed before you change gears. Never change gears at high rpm.

Plan Ahead Before All Maneuvers

A single-screw boat is controlled by the stern. That's where power and direction are centered. An automobile is steered by its front wheels, and the rear wheels just follow. The opposite is true in a boat. The stern determines direction, the bow just goes where it is pointed. This is something new boatmen are slow to learn, often only after they have banged their sterns

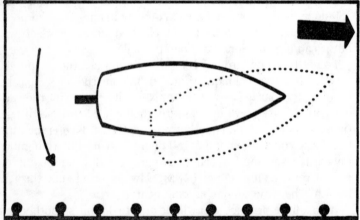

Fig. 7-13. When maneuvering in tight quarters, always think about your stern before you make a move. If you don't make allowances for stern swing on a turn, you're going to hit something or somebody.

against pilings, steel bulkheads and other boats while making a hard turn left or right.

When you swing the helm hard to port, the stern immediately swings right (Fig. 7-13) and unless you have planned ahead to make sure there is sufficient sea room to starboard, you are going to hit something!

A beautiful illustration of this was in the Cary Grant movie *Mother Goose*, where Grant was alongside an Australian minesweeper in his cabin cruiser. The Australian skipper gave the command: "Hard to port." This so surprised the exec that he had to repeat the command. As the minesweeper moved off, the stern swung over and ripped a big hole in the topside of Grant's cruiser, which was about ten feet away.

Advantages Of Single-Screw

Having just one propeller to worry about isn't all bad. For one thing, you save a lot of money each season on haul-outs to change shafts and propellers that were damaged when you hit some debris. That single propeller behind a skeg and keel is less vulnerable (Fig. 7-14) because it's out of the line of fire so to speak.

Fig. 7-14. The owner of this steel yacht went to considerable trouble and expense to protect his one propeller from the shallow waters and floating debris of western Lake Erie. But it didn't save his rudder which was knocked out of its lower support and bent.

Fig. 7-15. When a semi-V hull, with flat aft sections, runs over floating debris, the junk gets pushed back right into the propellers on twin-screw boats. On single-screw boats, the debris will go harmlessly past the wheel and rudders, which is why you will rarely see these boats hauled out in the slings during mid season for a wheel change.

When a hull runs over a piece of floating debris, the forward and aft V-sections shunt it off to one side where it harmlessly slides along under the hull about midway between the keel and chine. This is the area that I call the "line of fire" because that's where all the debris travels when you run over something. It never gets to the propeller on a single-screw. But twin-screw propellers are right in that "line of fire" where they suck in all the floating junk and you hear that sickening "clunk" and then the vibration, which means you just bent the shaft (Fig. 7-15).

When I owned single-screw boats, I never had to haul out in mid season for wheel changes. With twin-screw, I have hauled four times in one season. I average two a season.

The single-screw boat is far less expensive to buy, to maintain and to fuel for a season. One engine makes far less noise and you get very little fumes and steam blown into the cockpit when you run with the wind on your back. And you have so much room in the engine compartment to work. I have seen twin screw 32-footers where a little boy had to be hired to change the oil filters, at five bucks each. And if the boy weighed more then 60 pounds, he was too big to get down there.

I once changed the oil filters on Flagship engines, where it is in the most inaccessible of locations to the right of the flywheel on the lowest part of the engine. I had to go down there like a pearl diver, head first, and actually stand on my head while I unscrewed the filter. Then I couldn't get out. I yelled for about ten minutes until a neighbor heard me and pulled me out.

That was not good seamanship and I tell you this only that you might profit from my stupidity; never go down head first into a cramped, crowded engine compartment when you are *alone* on the boat. That's almost as bad as going swimming when you are alone.

If you have ever serviced twin engines, or watched marina mechanics cursing under their breaths as they work on them at $25 an hour, you will understand why twin engine service bills are so high . A simple 30 minute job will often take two hours because the mechanic is working in such a confined area, where so many things are hard to reach with the tools he brought. So he makes countless trips back to the shop for some special tool.

Coping With A Starboard Dock

Single screw boat handling was once a fine art because *everybody* had one engine. That meant half the boatowners in any marina or club got stuck with a starboard dock. It's surprising what you can do when you have to.

Many single screw skippers solved the starboard dock problem by *backing* into their slips at an angle, and then braking with a short burst of forward right rudder, which kicks the stern over closer to the dock.

Using Boat Levelers To Control Reverse

Docking on the starboard side with one engine gives some skippers more trouble then others (Fig. 7-16). Some skippers, in fact, actually prefer the starboard dock because they like to *back* into their slips. But I have found that many of these skippers, who do it the reverse way, have boat levelers installed on their boats (Fig. 7-17).

The primary function of boat levelers is to eliminate stern *squat*, bring the bow down for a more level ride, increased effi-

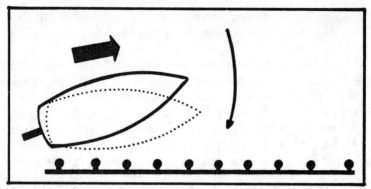

Fig. 7-16. A starboard approach in this manner will get you nothing but heartburn because when you reverse to stop, your stern will only swing further away from the dock. This approach is all right only if you can get a spring line off quickly to one of those posts, then hard reverse will pivot your boat so that the stern swings away and the bow swings toward the dock.

ciency and fuel economy. However, the levelers are also useful on single engine inboards when reversing, an important feature overlooked by many skippers. By dropping the starboard leveling plane (Fig. 7-17) about two or three inches into the water, a drag is created when moving in reverse which balances off the uneven thrust of the propeller. As a result, with that starboard plane down, there is no swing to port and the boat stays on a straight course at all times when reversing.

Fig. 7-17. Stern levelers like these are used on single screw inboards to counteract unequal thrust in reverse. With the starboard plane dropped 2-3 inches into the water, a drag is created and the boat can be made to reverse in a straight line.

Now comes stopping. We're still discussing backing into a slip.

With the rudder dead ahead and a forward burst of power, the stern would normally swing to starboard and *away* from the dock, which you don't want. To prevent this, you must quickly swing the wheel hard to starboard *before* giving a burst of power to stop boat movement in reverse. This will both stop the boat and swing the stern toward the dock.

I know it sounds complicated, but so was parking an automobile when you took your driver's license test. But you learned with practice. It also takes practice to smoothly manipulate the throttle, the reverse gear and the rudder in all boat handling, whether single or twin engine.

Backing into a port side dock is even easier with stern levelers. You don't have to make a fast rudder change before using forward power to stop. Just keep the rudder dead ahead, give her the forward thrust and the stern will swing to port and your dock.

Disadvantages of Single-Screw

I discussed the advantages of single - screw first because they are more important and easily offset the few disadvantages. The first and most often mentioned disadvantage of one engine power is that when, and if, it breaks down, you have nothing.

True, but I don't like that word "nothing." You are never in a situation where you have "nothing." You do have communications. You are never alone in today's world of boating where almost everybody has some form of radio communications aboard, whether CB or VHF. The only serious consequence of engine failure today is the acute embarrassment of seeking help from the Coast Guard.

The Coast Guard does not operate a free marine "tow-truck" service with no questions asked. They have a job to do, and they have statististics to keep. After towing you in, there is paperwork. Your boat is given a thorough safety check. If there are violations, you are cited, and you become another Coast Guard statistic and a small news item in the local newspaper.

All this can be painfully embarrassing, but it is the worst that can happen to you with engine failure.

I don't like the words "engine failure." This is not true.

Engines don't "fail." They sometimes won't start if the battery is depleted running the refrigerator through an inverter while anchored fishing. But this, more accurately, is seamanship failure rather then engine failure. Good seamanship encompasses every phase of boat operation, including the battery which starts the engine.

Engine failure is a scare tactic used to motivate buyers into boats with two engines. The modern pleasure boat, in itself, is a strictly non-essential recreational vessel of little more importance to the individual in our society then campers or bowling balls. They're all nice to have, but you can live very well without them.

I personally own a twin-engine pleasure boat and I have owned many with only one engine. I like the convenience of two engines but I have never deluded myself into believing that two engines were absolutely necessary for my safety and well being. They are an expensive non-essential luxury and I know it. And I am sure that many other boatmen know this also as gas becomes more costly.

MANEUVERING WITH TWIN-SCREW

The skipper has such complete control of his boat with two engines that there is no need for those power bursts to kick the stern to port or starboard. The boat can be steered, maneuvered and docked without ever touching the wheel.

The reason for this control is those two propellers which are rotating in different directions. Each wheel has its own unequal thrust, but when running together they cancel each other out and there is even forward and reverse thrust with no swinging to the left or right.

The uneven thrust of each individual propeller is actually useful in handling the boat. With the port engine in forward gear, the bow swings right; in reverse gear the stern moves right.

With the starboard engine in forward gear, the bow swings left; in reverse gear the stern swings left.

Knowing this, and *using* it, is what gives the skipper unlimited control of his boat in any situation. With two hands touching only the reverse levers, the skipper can back out of his slip in any direction. With just the starboard engine he will move left. With just the port engine he will move right.

When clear of the dock, the skipper can pivot his boat in any direction by using both engines, one forward and one reverse. The direction the boat pivots depends on how the engines are run. With the port engine forward, starboard reverse, the boat will pivot in a tight right hand turn. Reverse the sequence and it will pivot in a left turn.

All this is done with the rudder kept dead ahead and not used. However, in tight quarters and high winds, the rudder can be used to speed up a left or right pivot to get out of a crowded or dangerous situation. But, normally, you don't have to use the rudder. If you have Morse single lever engine controls, like I do, you need never take your hands off the two levers.

Once you get hooked on the ease and convenience of twin-screw boat handling, you're trapped for life. I know in my heart and mind that I don't need those two engines. I know I'm a good enough skipper to do anything with one engine that I do so easily with two, but how do you get out of a fiberglass trap with two engines that sleeps eight?

Why Twin Engines Last Longer, Use Less Gas

There is another bonus feature with twin engines: they have a greater life expectancy. Why? They don't work as hard because one engine helps the other. This is also why individually they use less gas, collectively they will use about 50 percent more gas then the one engine alone, not twice as much as some people imagine.

Single marine engines (Fig. 7-18) have a short life expectancy if pushed too hard or swing the wrong size wheels. The marine engine operates under 100% load conditions *all* the time. It never gets a chance to coast. To create "100% load" conditions with an automobile engine you would have to drive up a steep hill in low gear at wide open throttle. How long do you think an automobile engine would last under those conditions? When you have two engines in a boat, they split the load equally (Fig. 7-19).

HOW TO RUIN A MARINE ENGINE

Pushing a single engine too hard with the wrong size wheel can burn out the exhaust valves in one season of 100 hours use. I can attest to the truth of this statement because I've done it.

An engine must be wheeled to develop its full horsepower at the design rpm, whatever it may be. For example, if an engine

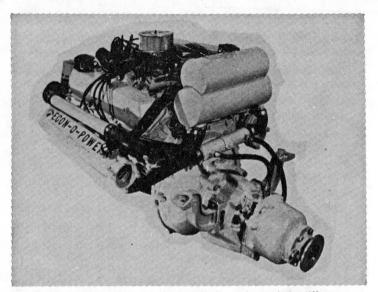

Fig. 7-18. The inboard marine engine works under entirely different conditions then the automobile engine, which loafs about 90 percent of the time and rarely is pushed to develop full horsepower. By contrast, a marine engine operates under 100% load ALL the time because there is no coasting or freewheeling downhill on the water.

develops 100 h.p. at 3600 rpm, it must be wheeled so it will freely turn that RPM with the throttle wide open.

If the engine only winds up to 2800 rpm, it is building up pressures in the combustion chamber which go beyond design limits. At 2800 rpm, the engine is not developing 100 h.p., but more like 75 h.p. But yet, with the throttle wide open, the pistons are sucking in more gas then needed to develop 75 h.p. As a result, more pressure and more heat is developed. The excess pressure causes faster bearing wear, the excess heat burns up the exhaust valves.

The solution: change propeller to either less pitch or smaller diameter to bring engine rpm up to 3600.

DON'T BECOME A PROPELLER FREAK

Propeller manufacturers provide a free consultation service to help boatmen with their propeller problems, and *everybody* today has problems with propellers. Everybody wants better efficiency and gas economy.

Warning! It's very easy to go overboard on propellers and become a nut on the subject. It's like a disease. I know a man who has one wall of his big garage covered with propellers.

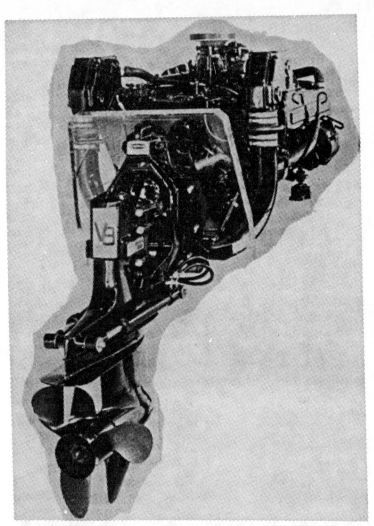

Fig. 7-19. This centaur-like mechanical beast is a conventional 4-cycle marine engine combined with the outboard motor's lower drive unit to form what is called a "stern-drive" power package. It is the only kind of power you can get in a powerboat built for today's fiberglass market.

They call him "Propeller Pete."

When you write to a manufacturer, give them all the details about your boat, including your engines and the propellers you are currently using. They will recommend two or three different types to correct your problem. Follow their recommendations, and then forget about propellers. If you don't you are in mortal danger of becoming a propeller freak.

STERN-DRIVES

Small fiberglass boats and stern-drives really should get married because they're meant for each other. And besides, they've been going together for a long time. But what these two have done to wood boats with single engine inboards is an entirely different story.

If you wanted to buy a fiberglass boat today with single-engine inboard power, you would have a few choices. One of the few major boat manufacturers still making one-engine in-boards is Thompson Boats. However, Thompson has developed something new with their "Tunnel Drive" hull. The shaft, strut and propeller are in a tunnel, protected from groundings and floating debris. The old wood boat with one in-board engine is joining the dinosaurs. You can see thousands of them all over the country rotting away in marina boat graveyards (Fig. 7-20).

Most single-engine fiberglass boats today are outboards or a combination of inboard-outboard, also called stern-drives. They remind me of centaurs, the fabled half horse/half man of ancient mythology. They even look like centaurs.

Fig. 7-20. The old-fashioned inboard-powered cruiser built of wood, with an engine connected to the propeller by a long bronze shaft, has joined the dinosaurs. If you still want one, you must go looking back in the weeds and bushes of boatyards where they are rotting away like this one.

242

If you have even handled a small outboard engine (and who hasn't?), then you already know how to handle any stern-drive cruiser. The boat is bigger, but the handling is basically the same. The only thing you must be careful about at first is *stern swing* when turning. The larger boat won't turn in as tight a circle as a small outboard. This will scare you at first when you see your stern getting close to somebody else's stern-drive sticking out beyond his dock.

Most small boat skippers with stern-drives are new to boating, especially cruiser-type boating. This fact is based on another fact: no seasoned skipper has been known to sell his twin-engine cruiser so he could get something smaller with a stern-drive. When an old seasoned skipper sells his boat, he does one of three things: Either he buys a bigger boat and lives on it, or he buys a sailboat and lives and sails on it, or he buys a condominium in Florida and plays around with a Cal 20. But he never, never buys a smaller boat with stern-drive. It must follow then that the owners of all those gleaming white fiberglass cruisers with stern-drives are new to boating.

None of the single-engine inboard problems with unequal propeller thrust applies to stern-drives or outboard engines. When you reverse, they move in whatever direction you point the propeller. The same is true for forward. Plain and simple—no adjustments and no wrestling with reverse gears. This is what accounts for the great popularity of inboard-outboards, which is a hybrid comprising the best of two worlds. You have the dependability and economy of the 4-cycle inboard engine, and the better maneuverability of the outboard drive.

So why isn't everybody happy?

So why isn't somebody crying?

Because nothing's perfect.

Handling Stern-Drive Problems

In spite of the fact that stern-drives are more maneuverable, small cruisers are often more difficult to handle then much larger boats with conventional power maneuvering in more confined areas. And a lot of these boats are getting their shiny glass hulls chipped, scratched and gouged because they keep hitting things. That's why there is crying in fiberglass Wonderland.

Why do they hit things?

Stern-drive skippers seem slow to learn that they must plan maneuvers ahead of time and not handle their boats like they do an automobile. They come rooster-tailing into a strange boating area, and then come to a dead stop to look over the scene.

You can do that with an automobile because it stays put when you stop. But a boat never stops moving until you rope it and tie it down like a wild mustang. And the smaller they are, the more they move. Stern-drive cruisers, up to 30 feet, are designed to be trailerable. That means no keels, no skegs, and nothing on the bottom that might interfere with pulling the hull up on a trailer. With only six inches of hull in the water and all that super structure above the water to act as a sail in the wind, the lightest gust of air sends them skittering sideways to bang into somebody's outboard drive raised up out of the water.

In light shallow-draft hulls, everything happens quickly. This offsets the stern-drives greater maneuverability because what good is superior maneuverability when the wind can cancel out every maneuver you make. There are many instances where an experienced skipper can actually be far more maneuverable in an old 40-foot single-screw displacement hull then in a light 30-foot stern-drive cruiser.

Twin-Screw Stern-Drives

Two outboard motors, or two outboard drives, on a boat transom gives you the same maneuverability that you get with one engine. Then why have two? I don't know. It is a proven engineering fact that one outboard motor on a boat transom will operate more efficiently then two. The outboard motor manufacturers themselves are the source for that statement.

You gain nothing in ease of handling, like the one-engine-forward-one-engine-reverse maneuver on twin-screw inboards. You can do it, but it just doesn't work as well. Why? There are two reasons: First, the outboard drives are too close together, and second, outboard propellers are not at an angle in the water like inboard wheels, therefore do not have the unequal thrust that makes twin-screw inboards so maneuverable. That unequal thrust, which is a problem on single screw boats, becomes a big asset when you have two of them turning in different directions. But you don't get that "asset" with two outboard propellers. All you get is an extra propeller pushing your hull, but less efficiently then one propeller doing the job.

Safety Factor With Twin Stern-Drives

With 2-cycle outboards, twin engines on the transom are an insurance policy and nothing else, for those skippers who frequently go out on Big Waters, especially offshore and near the Gulf Stream. No matter what the important advertising messages say, 2-cycle outboard power is not as reliable as 4-cycle inboard power. And those big beasts hung out there on a transom, with the boat bouncing around in rough water, are not something to tinker with (Fig. 7-21) until you get safely back home.

The big new outboards are monstrously complicated pieces of machinery that you don't service with a screwdriver and some sockets that you picked up at K-Mart. Everything you touch on these big animals requires a specialized and very expensive tool costing hundreds of dollars. And learning how to use those specialized tools means a training course at some manufacturers school for dealer mechanics.

Fig. 7-21. The big new powerful outboard motors are not meant to be serviced hung on a transom out on rough water somewhere bouncing around like the ball in a pinball machine. Servicing them requires special tools which only a dealer can afford to buy.

SERVICE MANUALS

Yes, there's a service manual available to you from the manufacturer to guide you in do-it-yourself servicing—if you can lift the manual after you buy one, for a considerable price. The Service Manual for one Big Name motor looks like the Manhattan yellow pages telephone directory.

I have before me the Owner's Manual for an inboard engine. It contains all the information needed to service and even repair that engine. And this booklet contains only 20 pages and can be read in 15 minutes.

Does that tell you anything?

With an inboard engine powering your outboard drive, you have a piece of machinery right there in the boat with you with everything easy to reach. And these engines are so simple—far, far more so then the engine in your automobile because you don't have all the extra clutter and plumbing of air-conditioning, power steering, power breaks, big air cleaners and pollution controls. The four or six cylinder inboard is a delightfully simple piece of machinery that is easy to service.

If you hate even the thought of being stranded with one inoperative outboard and having to go through the embarrassment of calling the Coast Guard for a tow, then you most certainly should have two motors hung on your transom. That's the only way you'll get home safely and quietly without going on the air and telling the whole world about your lousy seamanship. And that is really why you see so many dual outboard motor installations.

OUTBOARD DRIVE TORQUE

Since outboard propellers turn on a horizontal plane, rather then at an angle like inboard wheels, there is no uneven thrust, but there is a *torque effect* due to their high revolutions, something like 4000 RPM. This torque creates a pull to one side which must be corrected in steering. There is a tiny little "rudder" on the lower exhaust housing, also called a trim tab, which must be adjusted to compensate for the side thrust caused by torque. If you adjust this properly, you will not need to adjust the steering.

True Twin Outboards

Hanging an extra outboard motor on a transom doesn't suddenly make them "twin-outboards." They are more correctly just two outboards with both propellers rotating in the same direction to create twice as much torque effect.

True twin-outboards, like twin-inboards, are a matched set of engines with propellers rotating in different directions. This eliminates torque and the boat will steer a straight course with no trimming necessary.

Twin-outboard motors are available on order just like longer shaft lengths; even extra long shafts can be ordered for sailboats.

IMPROVING STERN-DRIVE EFFICIENCY

This is the Day of the Propeller. The gas crunch has everybody looking for a propeller that will give them greater operating efficiency and gas economy. The man who really knows something about outboard drive efficiency is Ralph Lambrecht, head of OMC's Stern Drive Engineering Department.

According to Lambrecht, most skippers make the common mistake of selecting a propeller with too little pitch. Since the get-away is quick and the engine revs up faster, it creates a false illusion of speed when in reality you're just making more noise and flapping your wings like a rooster.

To Get More Speed. Lambrecht advises that you can get more speed by selecting a propeller pitch that will peak your engine out at 4000 rpm.

To Get More Acceleration. If you want quick acceleration to get skiers up out of the water before they get waterlogged, Lambrecht suggests less pitch so your engine will peak out at 4300 rpm.

To Get Gas Economy. If you want economy, forget about propellers. Back off on the throttle instead. An OMC 235 on a 24-foot cruiser will consume more than 18 gallons of gas per hour at full throttle, 4100 rpm and 42 mph. Cut the throttle back one third to about 3000 rpm and the speed will drop to 30 mph; gas consumption will be only 9 gallons per hour. If fuel economy is what you want, this is the way to get it.

To Get Long Engine Life. At full throttle, the life expectancy of a 2-cycle outboard engine is just about 200 hours. Cut the throttle back to 50 or 75 percent of full load and the life expectancy will increase several thousand hours. That gives you an extra bonus when you don't use all the horses in the engine and beat them to death.

To further increase engine life, Lambrecht advises that you use only a single-grade oil of SAE 30 weight and stay away from so-called "viscosity improvers." Stay away from unleaded gasoline, unless your engine was built within the last two years. The lead in gasoline acts as a valve lubricant, and protects them from burning out. Newer engines have new type hardened valves and valve seats so they can safely use unleaded gas. Use of unleaded gas in an older engine can ruin it in less then 100 hours of use.

Protecting Stern-Drives

After a season in warm salt water, outboard drives look like something scuba divers bring up from old sunken Spanish galleons off the Florida coast. Outboard drives are complex mechanisms that just don't thrive too well when permanently immersed in salt water, or even fresh water. It's good for their health if you can tilt them up out of the water and flush them out after every use. With outboard motors you can do that, but you can't with stern-drives.

Stern-drives are universally used on houseboats. Often, they are so deeply immersed in the water that you can just see the tops, and there is no way you can tilt the drive up high enough to even change a propeller. That means they are never out of the water until haul-out time, and by that time they are a mess and you wonder if they will survive another season.

The stern-drive is ideally suited for trailerable boats that never remain in the water very long. They get regularly scrubbed and flushed and they look good for years. But on houseboats, they age a hundred years in one season.

The only advice that you can get from manufacturers of stern-drives on how to protect them from corrosion in the "hostile sea environment" is this: "check them frequently for nicks and scratches" and "flush them out with fresh water after every use."

But I have been unable to get any suggestions from any manufacturer on exactly how you do all that on a houseboat that is permanently left in the water, with a year between haul-outs for scrubbing and painting.

The only advice, therefore, for protecting stern-drives is: don't leave them in the water. When you take them out, wash them, inside and out.

THE JET DRIVES

Jet drives have never caught on in this country because their usefulness is limited to pulling water skiers. If this is your main interest in boating, you will love the jet drives, and so will the skiers you are pulling. Jet drive boats respond so quickly to the throttle that there is a danger of yanking the tow rope out of the skier's hands. With conventionally powered tow boats there is always a wobble period, the five or ten seconds it takes to get the skiers up out of the water and on plane. Jet drives, with their jackrabbit acceleration, have to be handled with a light touch on the throttle or you will find yourself pulling a tow rope with no skiers attached.

The jet drive has no propeller, shaft or rudder, just a water expelling device on the boat bottom shaped like a clam shell. The clam shell is rotated in a complete circle so that the hull can be propelled in any direction. In fact, a boat can be pushed into a dock sideways. With jet water pressure reversed, a boat can be stopped within its own length and you have to be careful about making sudden changes of direction with passengers aboard, or somebody could wind up overboard or with a whiplash.

The jet drives are very popular in the Mediterranean resorts of pleasure for the idle rich where you often see them in spy movies towing skiers around big yachts. The jet principal is also used on many European yachts to produce a powerful side thrust so that the hull can be maneuvered into a dock sideways. The skipper has control of his ship in all directions and is no longer at the mercy of the wind in a crowded boat harbor.

Why isn't the jet drive more popular in this country?

There are disadvantages. The most serious disadvantage is poor maneuverability at slow speeds. If you throttle back on the engine, as you would normally do in a crowded marina, there is not enough water pressure to make the boat respond. To get response and water pressure, the engine must be winding up at high rpm. You can change direction without easing back on the throttle, but the response is so quick it snaps your head back. And people all around are staring as you come in to dock and asking quesitons like, "why is that clown racing his engine?"

You don't just install jet drive on any boat. The hull must be designed expressly for jet drive, which means you must tie up

Fig. 7-22. Getting four skiers up out of the water in a hurry requires a special wheel that you should use only when towing a heavy load. Since such a wheel has considerably less pitch, it will rev your engine excessively high without a heavy ski load.

a lot of money in a specialized off-beat type of boat which might prove to be a dog when you try to sell it, and all boats are sold eventually (Fig. 7-22).

Summing up: The jet drive is a delightful Fun Boat. It is not a practical boat for anyone who looks upon every major purchase as an "investment."

SOME FINAL ADVICE

✔ If you get caught in a dangerous situation with high wind blowing you around in a crowded boat harbor, do like the bison do in a blizzard, back your butt into the wind. With outboard drives, you can control the stern with the engines backed into the wind. You *cannot* control the bow on *any* powerboat. If you can't make it to your dock, back up to some stationary object, like a piling, another boat, *anything* that is tied down. Loop a line to this object, then ease off about 20 feet and drop your anchor. This may not be exactly where you wanted to go, but at least you're safe for the moment and you didn't cause any damage. I've used this trick many times to same my hide and my boat.

✔ When approaching or leaving a dock, use the midship springline cleat to make your first tieup, or the last line to let go. This cleat gives you instant control of your boat and keeps the bow or stern from swinging away before you are quite ready (like where there's heavy river traffic).

 ✔ When approaching a gas dock, or any other strange dock, never heave a line from the stern. If you miss on the first try (you always do), the line falls in the water and you risk getting it fouled in your propellers.

 ✔ When visiting a foreign marina, especially Canada, never back into a boat slip. I did this once and banged up my wheels. The water isn't always the same depth the entire length of the dock.

 ✔ When coming out of a storm into a crowded boat harbor, keep a spare lunch-hook type anchor ready for instant use in the cockpit. You might need it in a hurry if the wind blows you into a hazardous position. When you lose control, nothing will stop you quicker then a lunch hook over the stern, (except banging into some expensive fiberglass cruiser). As an old skipper advised me once, "If you lose control, look for something inexpensive to run into." I prefer the lunch hook over the stern.

HOW TO TRAIN THE CREW

If something happened to you miles off shore, who would take over? Skippers do have heart attacks, strokes and seizures; they fall on wet decks and crack their skulls, break their arms, and legs. These are just a few possible mishaps that happen at sea everyday. Good seamanship means being prepared for such a contingency. How? By seeing to it that every member of your family knows how to handle your boat, and especially how to operate the radiotelephone. What good is a radiotelephone if you are the only one who knows how to operate the thing?

There is only one proper way to train a family-type crew. *DON'T* (Fig. 7-23)!

What I mean is don't *train* them. The minute you use that dirty word "train" in front of your kids, a negative reaction sets in. You have to use the Tom Sawyer approach. He made his friends actually vie for the "privilege" of doing his work—the whitewashing of a fence.

When your teenage son asks to take the wheel, tell him he's too young for such a responsibility, tell him when he gets a little older you'll let him handle the boat by himself. That'll do it. He'll nag at you to let him prove that he can handle the boat. You take this for a while, then, acting exasperated, you break down and "let him" take the helm.

With wives you use a different approach. Tell your wife about a remarkable woman you met at the club who can handle a 40-foot twin screw better then a man. A few days later, tell her about another woman who can out-sail some of the best sailors at the club. Act like you envy the husbands of these "remarkable women." Act (but don't say it) like you wished you were married to such a "remarkable woman."

That'll do it. You'll have absolutely no trouble with her refusing to take charge. She might even turn out to be a better skipper then you. The same with your kids. I have seen the above Freudian trickery used by a clever friend and this man's wife and teenage kids passionately love boating, and their father. Every member of this family is a qualified skipper.

The quickest way to alienate a wife and children against everything connected with boating is for the skipper to act like a skipper. You just can't do that on a privately owned pleasure craft because your family, at first, just won't take you seriously. When you put on a yachting cap and start acting like Captain Bligh, they at first think it's a joke. Then when they find out you're serious, they're horrified. Then they're repelled. Then your children and your wife start drifting away from boating.

Forget about running "a tight ship." That went out with

Fig. 7-23. This is where many skippers (fathers) blow it, when they try to train their family into being a good crew.

Humphrey Bogart and the *Caine Mutiny*. Throw away your yachting cap. There are men who actually undergo a personality change the minute they put on a yachting cap, especially the fancy ones with the scrambled eggs on the visor and the two gold stars of a vice commodore. The pomp and circumstance that automatically goes with being a flag officer makes it hard for a decent kindly man to avoid that most deadly of boating traps: the run-a-tight-ship-Captain-Bligh-Syndrome.

I have known many men who fell into this trap. Their children have all acquired other "interests," like tennis, cycle racing, rock music and drugs. The wives of these men have also acquired other "interests," like tennis, golf, bridge and alcohol.

You can't force your family to be a "good crew." You can't fool your kids by telling them "this is your boat," and then in the next breath chewing them out for not coiling the lines properly, or yelling at them at the top of your voice for failing to "batten down the forward hatch" and letting the bunks get wet.

These 10 "do's and don'ts" for training a family crew were printed in a Toledo area yacht club house organ so long ago, nobody knows the source. It was printed in a day when sailing was the only kind of boating that nice people were involved in. Crew training was very important because the boats were large, the sails were large and the rigging was less refined then it is today. It took a lot of hands and muscle to sail.

- Don't shout commands to the highest yardarm.
- Don't reprimand.
- Don't "put on report."
- Don't dress like a ship's Master.
- Don't overdo the use of "sea language."
- Do let the crew practice and freely make mistakes.
- Do let them try things their own way first.
- Do let the crew know they have not enlisted for life and can jump ship at will.
- Do let the crew know that they will not be "hung by the thumbs" for stupid mistakes.
- Do let the crew know regularly how much you need them, how much you appreciate them, how much you love them.

The above 10 rules are all you need to know about how to train a crew.

Chapter 8

Seamanship At Sea

One of the most disturbing experiences a new boat owner ever goes through is the day he gets his first test under fire, his first look at the sea when it is rough and he is looking at it through the glass at the helm. The sea looks different from this view. It often looks terrifying.

ROUGH SEAS

Even more disturbing then the rough sea to the new skipper is the behavior of his boat which has suddenly been transformed into a wild, bucking bronco. He can hardly believe that it is actually his boat that is being so violently buffeted about by every wave. Then he begins to wonder: is his boat a lemon? Did he make a mistake and buy a bad seaboat?

The boat is probably not a lemon. Nor is it necessarily a bad seaboat. The boat is just doing what all boats do when they go out in rough seas—its taking a beating. And the skipper is also taking a beating. And so is the crew. That's the way it is and that's the way it has always been when the sea gets rough.

Boat Size And Rough Seas

The bigger the boat the bigger the seas it can handle before life aboard becomes uncomfortable or hazardous. On the Great Lakes, three-foot seas would be extremely uncomfortable for a

Fig. 8-1. Hulls with no flare in the forward sections can be very wet boats in even a mild chop and light winds. Every time the bow comes down on wave, water runs straight up the sides high in the air, and comes down in the boat. Swim suits or foul weather gear should be worn in these types of boats.

14-foot outboard. For a 35-foot cabin cruiser it would be just a bumpy ride. Increase those waves to six foot and the cruiser would be extremely uncomfortable.

There is a point where all boats, regardless of size, become "uncomfortable." Some boats more than others. Why? Because they have so little flare in the forward sections (Fig. 8-1) that they throw water up in the air as they plow through the seas, and this water is blown back on the boat. These are called *wet boats*. Not only is everyone extremely uncomfortable in them, but also extremely wet.

When To Batten Down

That first encounter with rough seas is a shattering, and traumatic experience to many boat wives, especially the ones who have spent so much time lovingly decorating and fixing the boat up to be more "homelike" with little gadgets scattered about, such as nautical lamps, books and magazines. These wives learn the hard way that at sea when they say "secure ship," they mean nothing must be left laying around loose. And when the First Officer says "all secured," he means everything aboard has been nailed down, tied down, chained down or bolted down. Any object not secured can become a lethal weapon in rough seas as a ship is violently tossed about.

Drawers, cupboard doors and refrigerator doors, if not secured, fly open and out come their contents, including dishes, cutlery, pop bottles, food and casseroles which creates an unbelieveable mess. You can't visualize this, you must actually see how horrible a mess can be.

What is the message here?

You never take a boat out in rough weather until you have done what you must do—batten down and secure every loose object on the boat. You don't store food in a boat refrigerator the way you do at home. Don't put any glass or round bottles in them and don't bring anything aboard ship that is round and breakable, like pop bottles, beer bottles or ketchup. Buy beer and soft drinks in six-packs which can be compactly stored in the refrigerator. Keep canned goods in carton boxes with lids on them, stored on bottom shelves in the galley. Use only unbreakable dishes and don't stack them like you do at home.

SURVIVAL AT SEA

Almost any boat can survive at sea if properly handled and if its water-tight integrity is not violated. What does this mean?

Your boat must not take on any more water then it can pump out with its automatic bilge pumps. Manual pumps do not figure in this because they are considered standby pumps only.

The spray, even solid water, coming over your bow is more sound and fury then a threat. It looks scary but most of it just rolls off or out your cockpit scuppers. A small amount will get into your bilge, but this is considered normal and easily handled by your automatic pumps. The water-tight integrity of your boat is not violated and you are still a seaworthy vessel, which is just another way of saying your boat is buoyant. As long as a ship remains buoyant, it will stay afloat no matter how rough the sea. The key word, therefore, is *buoyancy*. And buoyancy is possible so long as a vessel retains water-tight integrity.

The sea-expression *batten down* originally meant covering all hold hatch covers with canvas which are further secured to the deck with long strips of wood called battens. The purpose of this is to keep the sea from working *under* the hatch covers and getting into the hold.

The bottom of the Great Lakes, and all the oceans, are

strewn with the wreckage of ships whose water-tight integrity was violated when the sea got into their holds. In fact, the last lake freighter to sink on the Great Lakes, the *Edmund G. Fitzgerald*, was believed to have lost its buoyancy when seas washing over its decks in a severe Lake Superior storm got under the hatch covers and into the hold.

The expression "batten down" also means the closing and the sealing of all openings on a boat that could admit the sea. For you, specifically, that means all hatches, and particularly that vulnerable forward hatch on almost all pleasure craft (Fig. 8-2) which is used as an air scoop to ventilate the cabin on hot summer days. This hatch is often bad fitting and poorly secured. So many times this hatch will be closed but not secured. Solid water coming over the bow can lift it up and tear it loose.

In a split second you can lose water-tight integrity. Soon you are taking on water faster then your pumps can handle and you are losing buoyancy. This could put you in a disaster situation unless you can plug up that hatch opening with a mattress.

Fig. 8-2. The forward hatch, used as a ventilating scoop to bring air into a hot cabin, is basically an escape hatch required on all craft for safety reasons. Without it, you could be trapped up forward if a fire broke out in the galley. However, this hatch is also a source of much trouble on small boats since so many leak and are poorly designed for safety at sea. On rivers and inland waters they may be adequate, at sea most are vulnerable.

You as skipper are responsible for the seaworthiness, and the water-tight integrity of your ship. It is you who must see to it that everything is secured and battened down before you attempt a passage in rough weather because in the final accounting, only *you* will be held accountable if the ship loses buoyancy and flounders at sea.

UNSEAWORTHY BOATS

Boats come in all shapes and hull types and to go into the handling characteristics of all of them would fill a book twice this size. But yet, it really isn't all that important and necessary for you to know this information unless you plan on becoming a naval architect. It's like when the little old lady asked the zoo attendant how he could tell the male hippopotamus from the female, and he answered: "That information is of importance only to another hippopotamus."

The only thing you must know is that your boat, regardless of size, shape, design, construction materials and hull type, can

Fig. 8-3. Boats that go to sea do not have big windows in an area exposed to solid water. The windows they do have will be small, at least a ¼-inch thick and tempered. Many production powerboats have large expanses of glass which often will be no different than the window glass in homes. This glass will cave in under the first pressure of solid sea water and you'll have the ocean pouring into your cabin. A good sea boat is just any boat that can keep the sea out.

survive *anywhere* if handled properly and if the sea is kept out and you retain buoyancy. But once you lose buoyancy, no boat is big enough to survive, which is the lesson taught by the sinking of the *Titanic*.

How safe a boat is in rough seas often depends, not so much on the hull, but on the things *above* the hull, like hatches and glass windows. You will never see big picture windows (Fig. 8-3) on boats that regularly go to sea. Instead you will see portlights which are smaller but still give you all the view you really need. Portlights seal themselves into rubber gaskets with screw clamps, and the glass is a half-inch thick. When you batten down these "windows" you can relax knowing that the sea will never smash the glass and flood you with more water then your pumps can handle.

If your cruiser has large deckhouse windows (Fig. 8-3), you should devise some means of covering them before making a rough sea passage (like people living in Florida do to protect windows in their homes during a hurricane).

How about the glass in windshields?

Most stock boat manufacturers install glass in flybridge windshields that is considerably thicker and stronger then deckhouse windows.

HANDLING ROUGH SEAS

With your boat battened down and all secured, you are now ready to make your first run in rough seas with some degree of confidence. You have done what had to be done, the rest depends on what you do at the wheel and throttles. If things get too scary and you panic, just remember that your boat, like the cowboy's horse, will take care of itself if you just leave it alone.

Turn off the engines and go lay down on a bunk and your boat will quickly heave to and ride it out without any further help from you. That's what ocean liners frequently do in severe Atlantic gales, heave to and ride it out. There's a good reason for this. A large vessel, when hove to, is under considerably less damaging structural stress then when it is moving all that tonnage under power through mountainous seas.

Thousands of lifeboats and dinghies have drifted about on oceans for months, even years, without sinking and were eventually found with no water in them, and often the skeleton remains of a "survivor" of some past sea disaster.

When To Heave To

The only thing you have to fear at sea is yourself. If, after fighting the sea for a time, you decide you are not up to the test and are doing everything wrong, don't be ashamed to heave to. You are not the first or last skipper to do this. I have done it many times, and I will continue to do it whenever I get scared enough. And the sea scares me all the time.

Heaving to is the beaten skippers court of *last resort*, the ace hidden up his sleave. When the world seems to be coming to an end out there on the angry waters, the prudent skipper heaves to, goes down below and has a drink, if the bottle hasn't broken.

The type of beating you will take in rough seas depends on what direction you are headed, and on what waters you are on. For small boats, western Lake Erie is the vilest, and the meanest body of water on the face of the earth. Bucking head seas, going directly into them, is something only a masochist does with pleasure. Try whenever possible to avoid a direct confrontation with head seas on any of the smaller Great Lakes because it is too much like bucking heads with a ram during mating season.

Fig. 8-4. This is the boat size that you will most frequently see being actually used in today's high-priced oil economy. This is the boat size that takes the most savage beating when the seas run 3-feet and over.

I am, at this point, referring to small powerboats in the 20 to 35 foot class (Fig. 8-4). These are the boats which take the most savage beating in rough seas and they are the ones which are most frequently used, even in today's tight fuel economy Larger pleasure craft, 40 to 60 feet, with fuel-hungry engines, don't go out very much anymore, and are used mainly as floating summer cottages. Sailboats, which I will go into later, take the least punishment.

Shallow Water Head Seas

When heading into six-foot waves of shallow waters in the Great Lakes, you adjust speed to take the least punishment and the least water over your bow. This is one time when you *want* your stern to squatt and your bow to point at the sky, as they say in Power Squadron classes. You throttle just enough to lift your bow up, which will usually be around 1800 rpm. Under normal sea conditions, this is a very inefficient speed because you would be just dragging a big wave behind you, using up gas and making slow progress. But you don't throttle for gas economy in rough seas. You just want that bow up to take the waves, to not plow under the next wave and take solid water.

As long as you are taking just spray over the bow, you are doing nicely, you have nothing to worry about. Solid water is something else. If you have confidence in the glass thickness and strength of your windshield, solid water over the bow is nothing to panic about, it just makes your cockpit wetter. But if you have doubts about that glass (if your windshield is a big one with a large expanse of glass), solid water could break it.

Does this mean you should heave to.

Not yet.

Tacking Into Head Seas

Running head on into the waves is hard on the boat and hard on the crew and it opens up countless new leaks as the entire boat is twisted and pounded. You can reduce the solid water coming over the bow by altering course slightly and doing what sailboats do—tacking into the waves, and taking them at an angle rather then head on. You can even increase rpm slightly to bring the bow up higher.

By tacking, your motion will change to both a pitch and roll, which is even more uncomfortable. But you will take less water and you will be very tired at the end of your long passage, and all passages are endlessly long when you fight the sea.

Beam Seas

Running in the trough of beam seas is probably the most hated thing in boating, next to sanding and scraping boat bottoms. The violent and continuous rolling can make even professional seafaring men seasick. This is where motor sailors have the advantage. They can hoist short sail and stop the rolling. This is called a steadying sail and you will see them on many trawler-type yachts that have small masts. You will even see the short mast on conventional powerboats. That mast is not just a nautical decoration; it can be rigged to a boom to launch a dinghy and to hoist a small steadying sail.

The steadying sail does exactly that, it holds the boat on an even keel in the troughs and at a heel angle away from the oncoming waves so that no spray comes aboard. On long passages it is a wonderful thing to have. Without it you just suffer, or alter course slightly. This will reduce roll, but it will also considerably lengthen the passage, which could, in some instances, bring you perilously close to running out of fuel.

Following Seas

Running with the seas is my favorite way of traveling on the Great Lakes. With small craft warnings up, I once made a 200-mile passage on Lake Erie to Buffalo with 6-foot seas at my back all the way, and it was one of the most enjoyable trips I have ever made. My crew slept, played cards, and enjoyed every minute of it.

Ha! Then came the brass knuckles.

It was a different script coming back and heading *into* those same 6-foot waves. Nobody slept or played cards. Everybody just hung onto something while groaning, praying and sponging up the water that was leaking in everywhere.

That return trip was one of the most agonizing of my life, and yet the only thing different was the direction of travel on water.

Dangers In Following Seas

A following sea is not for everyone. In fact, for some types of hulls it can be downright dangerous. You can lose control going down hill on a big wave and broach, which means getting flipped over on your beam ends. That is not a nice situation.

Any planing type hull with one engine, a small rudder and no keel or skeg is going to be difficult to control in such sea conditions. But planing hulls with permanently installed wood "shingles" installed at the trailing hull edge aft (Fig. 8-5) are not only difficult, they are *impossible* to control in a following sea.

If you have such a boat, with permanently-installed "shingles," you are taking a serious and foolish risk when you take that hull into such hazardous sea conditions. Shingles even make it more difficult in head seas because they keep the bow down when you want it up, and the more up the better.

What I have written above applies only to *permanently* installed wood shingles. Adjustable trim tabs are an entirely different thing. They can be lowered and raised at will, which makes them the *only* type of hull trim device that is safe to use. Wood shingles are usable only where water conditions remain unchanged, like in rivers and very small inland lakes and fish ponds.

Deep-draft displacement hulls with keels and twin-screw powerboats with their two rudders are the safest and easiest to

Fig. 8-5. Before boat levelers, shingles attached to the bottom of boat sterns, as above, were quite popular. But under certain conditions, like following seas, shingles can be dangerous.

control in following seas. Planing hulls with only one rudder are the most difficult.

When a big wave comes up behind you, it doesn't always exert an even pressure on your stern. When there is more pressure on one side, you can get into serious trouble because one rudder with no keel doesn't give you enough equalizing pressure to hold your course. Your stern is pushed hard to one side and you find yourself going downhill *sideways*—which will, I guarantee, scare you into becoming religious again.

Wood shingles keep the stern up, which is the worst thing that can happen because this only makes it easier for a wave to push the stern to one side into a dangerous broach.

How To Prevent Broaching

The only thing you can do in such sea conditions is cut back considerably on engine rpm to where your hull becomes a displacement hull. With the hull's entire wetted surface *in* the water, it is not so easily pushed around. By experiment you will find that there is a certain engine rpm where you can move in a following sea without broaching, and there is also a certain engine rpm that will get you in trouble. It is very important that you learn exactly what your safe rpm is in following seas. Only you can find that out.

Everything written so far in this chapter has been on the handling of small boats in comparatively shallow inland waters where wave action is quite a bit different from ocean waves.

It will also be noted by many sharp-eyed readers that some of the actions I suggested previously do not conform to what is considered accepted practice by experts and authorities who write learned papers and articles on marine subjects.

I frankly know nothing about text book boat handling. Everything I know about boat handling I learned by doing through by trial and error. If something works for me, that's the way I do it. If it doesn't work, I never do it again.

Handling Ocean Waves

As the cliche goes, it's a whole new ballgame when you go to sea.

The best advice that can be given on the handling of small craft in rough ocean weather is: you don't really need it. When the sea is rough, avoid it like a heart-transplant.

Sometimes, for bread and butter reasons, you have to take a

chance and make that run through the Outer Santa Barbara Channel to Newport Beach on a late Sunday afternoon because you have to hit the Freeways early Monday morning and get to work. I understand. I've been there.

From San Clemente Island to Newport Beach is only about 40 miles when the weather is nice. It's over 400 miles when the wind blows out of the west and you're headed for the coast of California riding the back of enormous following seas. When I first saw them, I could only mutter to myself, "My gawd, Lake Erie was never like this!"

Yawing And Broaching

Modern powerboats, with their broad, flat transoms, are poorly designed to run before the sea. Ships built to go to sea have rounded sterns which greatly reduces the tendency to yaw when a swell passes under. *Yaw* means a sudden lurching of a boat stern to port or stern to starboard. It can lead to loss of control and broaching, which means you are being swung broadside on the downward side of a big wave. You almost certainly will be flipped over on your beam ends, or possibly even bottom-up, like the *Poseidon* was in the popular movie.

There is a news story, on record, of a 42-foot Matthews sedan cruiser that was broaching in the Bermuda Triangle area of the Caribbean. It was flipped over by a huge following sea, made a complete revolution rightside-up-again, and continued on its journey with no damage. Interviewed at a Nassau yacht club, the skipper was asked by a doubting reporter: "Come on now, did your really turn a complete circle when you broached?"

Possibly annoyed by the question, or the reporter's manner, the skipper answered: "Of course. Doesn't everybody?"

I love that, even though I don't believe it. It's so beautiful.

In a twin-screw boat, it is best to just leave the rudders dead ahead and control your boat with the engines. You only have two hands, and since you will be so busy manipulating the throttles, you will have no time for the wheel.

Pitchpoling

Too much throttle, at the wrong time, can be a hazard to your health. It not only can send you into a broach, but coming down a deep slope too fast could bury your bow in the trough with the following wave lifting your stern end-for-end. This is called pitchpoling. It's even worse then rolling over.

The trick to avoid all that is throttle control. You rev like crazy going up hill, and you back way off on the throttle going down hill. That roughly is about it. I might add, the best place to be in running seas is right *behind* the top of a big wave. The worst place to be is right on top of a wave when it breaks.

This makes it look easy. But it isn't. It's hard to know, all the time, when you are behind a wave or when it is going to break. Waves are worse then women when it comes to changing their minds, they even suddenly change directions. That's what keeps you busier then the proverbial one-armed paperhander as you juggle throttles, swinging your head around in all directions, while making decision after decision. You rev the engine to chase a big wave and you try to stay behind it, but suddenly it changes direction and another big wave is suddenly chasing you and your stern is up in the air and you're going downhill into a trough and you must quickly back off on the throttle to avoid pitchpoling.

It is very nerve-wracking because you can't relax for a second or turn the helm over to someone else so you can make a visit to the head.

The Drogue

You probably have heard about streaming a drogue off the stern to exert a steadying pull to hold your boat to the seas.

Before you dash off to buy a drogue, consider first that they are effective only on certain types of hulls. They are mostly for sailboats and double-enders. They will not work very well on cruisers with wide, flat transoms and are not worth the effort it takes to put one out, which is considerable, especially at a time when you're busy fighting for your life.

You also may have heard about dragging a heavy line aft to create a steadying drag. Don't! The risk is too great that you might foul that line in your propellers. It's always risky to throw lines off your stern when the propellers are turning.

Heaving To At Sea

If you become alarmed at the situation and how your boat is responding, you can always turn around and take the seas on your bow.

There are two ways to heave to. First, you turn off the engines and just drift, or secondly, you can run the engines just fast enough to maintain steerageway so you can hold the bow into the seas without actually making any further progress.

The latter statement is what *text books* advise, but it just never worked for me. In my opinion it takes so much engine thrust to maintain steerageway into the seas that you end up traveling in the opposite direction. If you reduce engine power to hold your position, you lose rudder control and can't hold the bow into the waves. But, if you cut engines and drift, you are at least making some progress in the direction you were originally going.

SEA ANCHORS

To heave to with a sea anchor you must have a lot of sea room, and you should preferably be away from shipping lanes if you use a sea anchor at night. Also, you better be sure that there are no lee shores in the direction you are drifting. For example, if you were to put out a sea anchor after leaving San Clemente in heavy following seas, you would slowly be moving towards the lee shore of Santa Catalina Island. Don't confuse *lee shore* with *in the lee*. Lee shore *faces* the wind. In the lee means the opposite, referring to the *protected* side of the island. It is potentially dangerous to drift towards a lee shore. It is also potentially dangerous to drift in the direction of busy shipping lanes. You could get run over at night.

Sea anchors are effective only if they are big enough, which they seldom are. To hold a 35-foot cruiser into the wind would

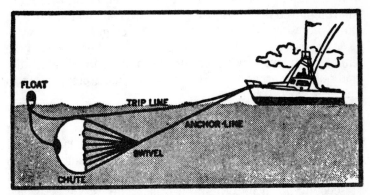

Fig. 8-6. When the sea anchor is big enough, like the small parachute type above, it really works. But many boaters are turned off when they learn about all the extra gear that must be used, like the trip line and float (courtesy of Manhattan Marine).

take a sea anchor almost the size of an old army pup tent. But they are effective at sea where there is pleanty of room, and they are almost a necessity for the single-handed sailor on a long sea passage. It gives the sailor a chance to get some much needed rest when the weather is unfit for sail.

Improvised Sea Anchors

Suppose you don't have a sea anchor, but need one desperately. You can always rig something up. I once used two plastic buckets secured to 150 feet of ¾ inch manila to hold a 22-foot cruiser into the wind. And it worked just as good as a conventional sea anchor. I know another instance where a big red Coca Cola ice chest was used in the same way on the end of 100 feet of ¾ inch manila secured to the two handles, and it held a 25-foot cruiser. Almost anything that will create a drag in water will work, especially at the end of a long line of ¾ inch manila.

Sea Anchors And Oil

It is an established fact that oil has proven value in calming the sea, so much so that "pouring oil on troubled waters" is not only a much used phrase but a part of the language. I have never personally used oil but I have seen how it works.

Some years ago I got caught in the Detroit River in bad weather. Strong easterly winds had 6-foot seas running but I just had to make that 50 mile run to Toledo. So I waited for a big empty coal freighter headed for the Chesapeake Coal Docks in Toledo for a refill, and followed her out into the angry lake on the lee side. I stayed close and well aft near an opening port where I could almost talk with the engine room crew.

As we passed the Detroit ship channel's last light, one of the engine room crew motioned for me to move up ahead. I did, and quickly learned why. Black oil was being pumped out in the area where I had been.

It was common practice, before the national concern for the environment, for freighters to pump their bilges, filled with dirty engine oil, into the lake after they passed the last channel light. Freighters even had tunnel-like steel tubes attached to the stern where the ship's cook could dump garbage and send it scooting down into the prop wash. This is why seasoned skippers always stayed clear of a freighter's wash after they cleared the ship channel.

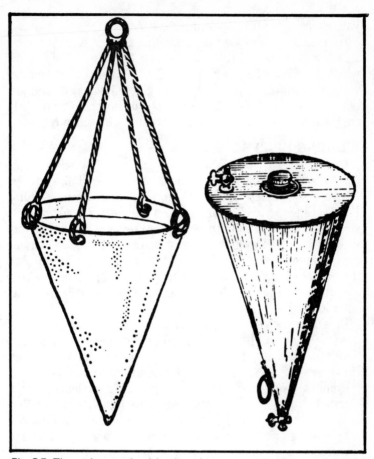

Fig. 8-7. The canister to the right above is a patented device for spreading oil on troubled waters, sold by Manhattan Marine, New York. It has a fill cap and two petcock valves, top and bottom, which when opened allow oil to slowly drip, it takes very little. The device to the left is a conventional canvas sea anchor. Always use the biggest size you can get (courtesy of Manhattan Marine).

A few minutes later, as I looked back, I could see white caps vanishing far behind me with the water becoming miraculously smooth. While up ahead, the lake looked mean and frothing with white caps.

Surprisingly, it takes very little oil to accomplish this miracle, about one or two gallons in a canvas bag will suffice. You prick a few holes in the bag with a small nail then, if you have a sea anchor out, feed the canvas bag out with another line, not too far. As the oil leaks out, it quickly disperses and almost instantly you will see a change in the turbulence behind you, especially in the breaking seas.

All it takes is a canvas bag, like those water bags you hang on a car door to cool the water, and a few cans of engine oil, which everybody has aboard (Fig. 8-7). Kerosene or diesel fuel will not work, however. Drained engine oil would do the job, but who saves it? Besides, why foul up the seas with dirty engine oil? You can do it so much better with clean oil.

RUNNING HEAD SEAS

On the ocean, running into the seas is not as painfully uncomfortable as it can be in some shallow Great Lakes waters where short, steep seas hammer small boats unmercifully. Even an inexperienced skipper can handle his craft credibly well after he catches onto alternately revving up the engines when going *up* a swell, backing off on the throttles when going *down* a swell, and just before reaching the trough, bringing up the bow again before hitting the next oncoming wave. There is a certain rhythm to this and after a while you do it unconsciously.

Diesel engines do not graciously accept, for long periods of time, this type of up-and-down acceleration because they function best at a steady laboring at 80 percent of full power. However, they'll survive, so don't be afraid to use them.

Running head seas is a lot like driving a big tandem rig in the Kentucky hills. You go 9-miles-an-hours uphill, and 90-miles-an-hour downhill. But if your try that in a boat on the downhill side of a big swell without using your engines to counter the waves, you'll torpedo your bow at the bottom and all your pistons will change holes.

Propeller Racing

Swells and rough seas differ in that the waves are shorter and things happen faster, and your throttle control rhythm gets screwed up. You often rev when you should de-rev, and a wave kicks your stern up out of the water, causing the racing propellers to bite at the air and make a terrible noise. This causes your boat to shake like crazy and everybody aboard panics, and then they all start putting on lifejackets and singing old religious songs.

The "Secret" Of Being A Good Skipper

Reduce speed, especially at the top, or near the top of a wave. And soothe your passengers and crew. Tell them the noise is just sound and fury with no bite (lie a lot). Tell them everything is under control, which will be partly true, if the racing propellers don't come out of the water too often.

Revving the wheels too fast when they are out of the water *can* be damaging, both to the engines and hull. So take it easy, watch those throttles. Change course if necessary, or try tacking. Something will work. It always does. Never let your passengers and crew know how scared you are and that you don't really know what the heck you're doing.

And *that* is the secret of being a good skipper.

RUNNING IN THE TROUGH

The bottom between two large ocean waves is quite a bit different from the trough of a shallow water waves, where you never lose sight of the world around you. In the ocean all you see in the *trough* is two menacing mountains of water on each side of you. It is a fearful and intimidating sight, especially to your crew and passengers who have more time to look around and contemplate upon what you are doing to them.

The motion of your craft as it moves in the trough is a combination of up, down, rock and roll. This will all happen at such a sickening extreme that you will be perilously close to having a mutiny on your hands, when everybody stops vomiting, that is.

The experts say you should change course and try tacking across the troughs, taking the waves at a 45 degree angle, first broad on your bow, then broad on your quarter.

This all reads well, but when I actually did this, I found no improvement in the situation. In fact, I found the motion of my boat even more disturbing to my crew.

What I am trying to tell you, gently as possible, is that running in the trough stinks and that there is nothing much you can do about it except buy a sailboat, a motor sailor or a trawler, with a steadying sail.

ENTERING AN INLET

There is another thing you can do when the sea makes your crew rebellious and near mutiny, and that is you can run for shore and wait for better weather. However, this usually means running in a strange, inlet, which is the worst kind.

Running an inlet can be tricky even when you know the waters because waves take on a new configuration as they run into the shallower waters of sandy beaches. Coming in from the sea this is not noticeable until you get fairly close. You should stop for a while, study the inlet through your binoculars, and observe how the waves are breaking.

Being a skipper means making decisions, and often the kind that affect the lives of other people. You have a few decisions to make before running that inlet, like should you risk running the inlet at ebb tide, or should you stay out in the weather and wait for the flood tide, or should you wait for a local boat to come along and then follow them in.

My choice would be the last one mentioned.

The worst time to enter a strange inlet is when the tide is *ebbing*. The incoming seas and ebbing waters collide in the channel to produce even steeper waves. At *flood* there is no opposing force to the waves and they just roll right in.

Inlet channels are always marked by buoys, but you can't always depend on them because sands are constantly shifting and changing the bottom. You can tell this by watching the waves. They always crest and break as they reach the shallowest areas, which are usually sand bars. The locals know this, and they also know where all the uncharted obstructions are. This is why I prefer always to follow another boat into a strange inlet.

I usually wait outside until I see another boat approaching. If I see an antenna waving, I try to make contact with the skipper by radiotelephone, saying, "Tempest III to the gray trawler approaching Sandy Hook inlet from the north."

I'll repeat this three times, then wait. I have never failed to get a prompt answer. I explain to the trawler skipper that I am a stranger and would like to follow him in.

Good seamanship is always standing ready to help another skipper. One particular skipper, replying to a call of mine, said, "I'll wait for you to get behind me. But don't get too close. The waves here run in groups of at least three. The last one will be the biggest. Watch me carefully. I'll wait for that big one to break itself on the bar, then shoot in right behind it. You do the same. Remember, wait for the big one to break its force, then run like mad."

And this is exactly how I took her in.

HELMSMANSHIP

The mark of a good farmer was once determined by how

straight a furrow he could plow behind a horse.

The mark of a helmsman and good seaman is how straight a course he steers when on a compass heading, and it's not as easy as you might think.

The first time you assigned the First Mate, or one of your crew, to helm duty, did you notice your wake? Was it straight? Or did it swing back and forth in a snake-like weave?

It takes time to learn the feel of a boat's steering characteristics, and no two boats steer alike. Some are more difficult to hold on a compass course then others. Single-screw inboards steer different then twin-screws. Deep keel displacement hulls have their special characteristics, and so do all the outboard drives and sailboats with their big rudders, centerboards and keels.

The single-screw inboard planing hull is the most difficult to hold on a compass heading, especially at slow speeds in rough water. The twin-screw displacement hull with keel and skeg is the easiest.

Steering by compass for long periods is very tiring because you must keep your eyes glued to the compass lubber line. If you turn to look at something else, you will be off course 5 degrees. This is the reason for the great popularity of auto-pilots. They never tire or get bored, which is why no human helmsman can match the auto-pilot for maintaining a perfectly straight course.

I refuse to go into the fine nuances of helmsmanship when on a compass heading. What I have read on the subject in learned tomes reminds me of an Instruction Manual in the old SeaBees of World War II which had 40 pages of detailed instructions on how to drive a nail into a piece of wood. After you read those 40 pages, you were so confused and benumbed by all the verbiage that you smashed a finger driving your first nail.

You don't learn how to steer a boat by reading 40 pages of instructions. You learn by doing it.

Effects Of Wind On Steering

There are still old boats around with wheel-drum and rope steering, a system of wire rope pulleys ending up on a quadrant tiller attached to the rudder post. With this type steering, you never dared take your hands off the wheel because, like the tiller on a sailboat, it was only your effort on the helm that physically held the rudder.

With a strong wind off the quarter bow, it took a lot of muscle to hold these boats on a course. This is why pedestal steerers have become so popular on sailboats and also why more women have taken to sailing (Fig. 8-8).

With the types of geared steering systems used on powerboats today, you don't notice the effect the wind and sea have on steering, but it's there and the strain is unbelievable. I have seen broken pins on 4-inch galvanized rope pulleys after a hard day of steering into a beam wind.

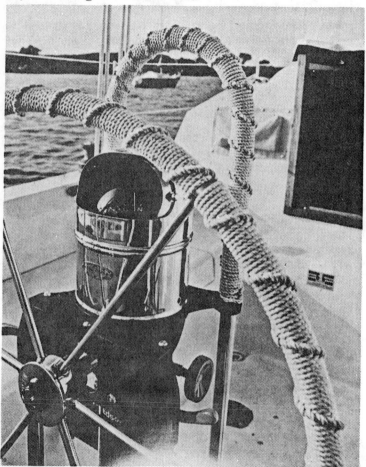

Fig. 8-8. Wheel steerers, with their easy effortless control of the rudder, are much loved by women, which is probably why there are so popular right now. Men like them, too (courtesy of Danforth).

Hydraulic systems, much used today, can also break down when you maintain high speeds, which puts more strain on the rudder and steering system. If you have any doubts about your steering system, or if you've had any trouble with it, take it slow and easy when heading into quartering and beam winds.

BOAT HANDLING IN FOG

Fog can be a frightening thing. On Lake Huron it comes in on you like a big white wall. The first time I saw that "white wall" approaching out of the north, I was so terrified I turned 180 degrees and raced 10 miles back to Sarnia, Ontario at wide open throttle. And I just made it. Sarnia and Port Huron weres souped in by a fog so thick you couldn't see your outstretched hand.

There is two types or seamanship in fog: open water where you have plenty of sea room and no traffic, and confined water where there is traffic. The second type will be covered extensively in a later chapter on piloting.

Fog on open water, free of boat traffic, is nothing to panic over, the way I did on Lake Huron, if you can *stay* there until the fog clears. But I was on the way to a tiny little Canadian village where I had never been before, but I had been warned what to expect. To have continued in that fog meant that I would have had to make a 40 mile run and pinpoint a coastal inlet whose entrance was marked only by big boulders sticking out of the water with numbers painted on them. And all I had was a compass.

But I would have been just as scared with all the electronics that I have today because that inlet, I had been told, was difficult to find even when visibility was good. The shoreline had no distinguishable object you could pick up with binoculars like a church steeple, water tower or smokestack. You couldn't see the inlet until you were almost in it.

The mark of a good seaman is knowing when to be scared, and when to avoid unnecessary confrontations with ugly sea conditions. When you are on vacation, taking dangerous chances just because you filed a Float Plan and ETA (estimated time of arrival) with friends at the next port of call is no reason for you to prove to them you can do it (Fig. 8-9 top). You can always make a telephone call. You'll get a chance again someday when you may have to prove that you are capable of handling your boat in fog.

275

Float Plan

Before going boating, complete this card and leave it with a reliable person who can be depended upon to notify the Coast Guard, or other rescue organization, should you not return as scheduled. Do not file this card with the Coast Guard.

1. Owner _____ Name of Boat _____

2. Description of Boat: Type _____

    Number _____

    Color: Hull _____ Deck _____ Cabin _____

    Sail: Color _____ Number _____

    Other Info: _____

3. Number of Persons Aboard: _____

4. Engine Type: _____ -rsepower _____

    Fuel Capacity _____

5. Survival Equipment: (indicate as appropriate)

    PFDs ____ Flares ____ Mirror ____ Smoke Signals ____

    Distress light _____ Flashlight _____ Anchor _____

    Paddles ____ Raft or Dingy ____ Food ____ Water ____

6. Radio: Yes / No Type _____ Frequency _____

7. Trip Expectations: Leave at _____ (time)

    from _____. Going to _____.

    Expect to return by _____ (time), and in

    no event later than _____ (time).

8. If trailer boat: Color and make of auto _____ .

    License Plate _____ Trailer Plate _____ .

    Launching from _____

9. Other Info: _____

10. Telephone numbers of persons to call if not returned by time indicated in item 7.

    Harbor police _____ Air/Sea Rescue _____

    Coast Guard _____ Other _____

Fig. 8-9. (top) It is wise to file a float plan if you are taking a long cruise. However, if for some reason you do not stick to your float plan, call your waiting family or friends and let them know. (Bottom) Coast Guard rescue boats have steel posts that are designed for towing. Let the Coast Guard do the towing (courtesy of the U.S. Coast Guard).

AIDING A VESSEL IN DISTRESS

Consider for a moment what you would do if you ever have to go to the assistance of a vessel in distress.

It will happen! If you are an average boatman (100) hours of cruising per year), the mathematical laws of probability indicate that the chances are 50-50 that you will be involved this season in some sort of assistance-to-a-disabled-craft, even if it's just radiophoning the Coast Guard to tell them about a sailboat stranded on a sandbar off the ship channel who is signaling for help.

I have gone three seasons without making a single assist. Then one year I made four. It all averages out.

There is a so-called unwritten law of the sea that obliges you to help anyone in trouble. However, when I say "help," I don't mean that it is your duty to get out the tackle and prepare to tow every disabled boat that you see. Start this and you'll be doing it all weekend, especially if you live in Southern California, Florida or the St. Clair River area in Detroit.

First, pleasure boats are not designed or equipped for towing. Second, you are obliged to "assist" a disabled vessel, but not to give them a free tow, usually to a gas dock.

You are obliged to do whatever is necessary to protect human lives on board a disabled vessel. But, if human life aboard the disabled vessel is not in imminent danger, you are not obliged to risk your own property and neck to salvage another skipper's insured private property, or give him a tow at your own risk, and it *is* a risk.

As stated before, pleasure boats are poorly equipped for towing, in fact, you are placing your own boat in a hazardous situation by even trying. Coast Guard rescue boats are equipped with the same type of steel samson post that you see on tug boats (Fig. 8-9 bottom). They are installed almost amidship and they are well braced and welded to the keel. When a tow line is secured to a samson post, there is no interference with the towing boat's steering capabilities.

On a pleasure boat, when you secure the tow line to a stern cleat, you lose all steering control. You can pull the disabled craft, but *where?* You have placed not only your own boat in jeopardy, but the disabled boat you *volunteered* to rescue. When you volunteer a tow, you place yourself in a position of double jeopardy. I am referring to damage suits you will face if more damage should occur to the boat you are towing, or if someone is injured. It will be argued in court, by contingency fee lawyers, that it was your *interference*, along with your lack of seamanship, bad judgment and negligence that was responsible.

Do what is necessary to protect human life, but forget the

private property. Never tow anybody unless it is requested in front of witnesses. Never volunteer a tow.

When you respond to a boat signal for help, if it's engine trouble or no fuel, inform them you will radio for help, and then standby until it comes. Never leave a disabled boat until the Coast Guard reaches the scene and releases you. It is your duty to remain on the scene, to make certain that all people aboard the disabled craft continue to remain in no imminent danger. Concern yourself only with *them*. Let the skipper worry about his private property.

What I have just stated above may appear calloused, and it may even be in direct disagreement with what has been written on towing in older books on boating, where the subject is handled in considerable volume and detail. However, all this was written 30 to 40 years ago when hardly anybody had a radiotelephone. Today everybody has a radiotelephone and you will rarely hear of a modern cruising boat seeking help from another cruising boat for the simple reason that the skipper of the boat in trouble has his own private Hot Line to Coast Guard. And if he doesn't want to call the Coast Guard, he can directly contact some Yard that maintains a tow vessel just for such contingencies. They'll even bring you some ice, gas and beer.

The people who chronically run out of gas or have engine problems are the owners of outboards in all categories, including cruisers. They usually have 1956 Mercury outboard engines for main propulsion and a 1950 Neptune 1 h.p. hung on the side for trolling (when they can get it started). When you pull alongside, they always ask you: "Got any spare gas, bud?" They look so surprised when you shake your head no, as if they expected you to unveil a Gulf Oil gas pump in your cockpit.

The bigger boats that spring leaks and then frantically wave a white T-shirt on the end of a fishing rod are the vintage hulls that were resurrected from some Yard's burial section for owner-abandoned boats with attached leins for unpaid bills. These old hulks are almost always bought in partnership by three bowling buddies who work the night shift on some auto assembly line. They load up every weekend with three cases of Strohs, potato chips, ice and bait.

If you ever volunteer to tow one of these flooded hulls, you do so at your peril (Fig. 8-10). Make one little mistake, or if

Fig. 8-10. The saving of human life should be your only concern in a sea rescue. You are not obligated to save anybody's mortgaged and insured property. If all they need is a tow, call the Coast Guard.

they sink just as you get them to their marina dock, they will threaten to sue you, claiming your negligence was responsible for their mishap.

If you think I'm reaching too far or if you think I made this all up, the news stories on which I based these illustrative examples are in the July 1978 files of the *Detroit News*.

Saving human lives at sea is everybody's business. Towing boats is business for the professional who know how, and who have the proper equipment to do it.

EMERGENCY AT SEA

The skipper who anticipates trouble and prepares for it rarely has any.

I am constantly hitting things floating in the water. For years I have kept an improvised "damage control kit" on my boat in anticipation of the day when I would hit a railroad tie with protruding spikes and get holed. My kit is made up of many odd sizes of boat lumber and plywood, especially the ¼ inch size of which I carry six pieces suitable for "patches."

All the pieces of plywood are pre-drilled with screw holds along the outer edges so they can be quickly slapped against a hole from the inside, held there temporarily with a special type of sheetmetal self-tapping screw. Using a cordless screwdriver, I can zap that plywood patch over a hole in less then a minute because the screws have a hex-washer head and drill their own hole.

So what happens?

Nothing! My damage control kit sits below decks year after year and will very likely never be needed, but I'm not complaining because it pleases me not to have a hole in my hull just like it pleases me that I never have occasion to use my lifejackets, ring buoys and fire extinguishers. You don't invest money in these things because you want to use them. You pray to God you will never need them. But you better have them around anyway.

Taking On Water!

The most frightening emergency at sea is *taking on water*. You look down into the cabin and the rug is under water. Your first thought is "My God, we're sinking!"

Not necessarily so. Have everybody put on lifejackets, yes, but do *not* abandon ship.

There has to be a reason for that water in the cabin. Find it! Power boats with inboard engines have many through-hull openings, any one of which could be the source of that water, and it doesn't take too long to check them. Raise the engine hatch and check the following:

— Engine cooling water through-hull intake. Hookup to the engine is usually with rubber hose. There is a seacock here (shutoff); if leaking, close it.
— Check the propeller shaft and stuffing box. Tighten gland nut if necessary.
— Check through-hull water intake for AC generator; close seacock if leaking.
— Check water intake for water-cooled refrigerator or air conditioning condensers.
— Check water-cooled exhaust system for leaks.
— Some marine engines have 13 plugs for draining water during winter storage. One could be leaking. Look around the engine while it is running. There are many cooling water lines around engine which might also be leaking. This is a common occurrence.
— Head intake and discharge through-hull fittings.
— Galley drain.

— Bait box pump and water intake fittings.
— The garboard drain plug in the lowest part of the bilge under that cabin rug.

Any of the above fittings could be the source of that water getting into your boat. If all that water got into your boat after you had left the dock and were underway, then I would immediately suspect and check the engine. With a leaking waterline, the engine can pump an enormous amount of water into your boat in a very short time, but only while it is *running*.

If you have two engines, you can get home on the other one. If you have only one, then the leaking waterline will have to be temporarily patched with whatever is available (Fig. 8-11). Improvise! The same with a hull leak. If you have an old wood boat with carvel planking, screw fastenings often loosen and planks at the stem can spring away leaving quite an opening.

But the flood can still be stemmed. Improvise! Use common sense! Stuff something into the opening, a wadded T-shirt, pillow slip or anything else you can find that will hold back the water until you get home.

Fig. 8-11. Almost any kind of leak can be at least stemmed, if not completely stopped, by just utilizing materials that can be found on any boat. Small boats have made it home safely with two feet of water in their bilges (courtesy of the U.S. Coast Guard).

Emergency Bilge Pumping

The one small bilge pump customarily installed by manufacturers on their stock boats is not designed to handle emergency flooding where a large volume of water must be moved. This is why seasoned skippers always have a second standby pump of large capacity, like the Par extra heavy duty Model 34600 which pumps 10 gallons per minute at a lift of 13 feet and can be installed high up out of the bilge where there is no danger of it drowning out or short circuiting. The only thing in the water is the pick-up hose and strainer.

To increase emergency pumping capacity every boat should have a standby manual pump on board. I like the "Guzzler 600" which can pump 30 gallons per minute at only three strokes per gallon.

How To Get More Pumping Capacity

If you don't happen to have anything on board but the standard equipment bilge pump, you can still rig up additional pumping capacity by using one of your engines. Close the water intake seacock, loosen the hose clamp, twist off the hose, drop it into the bilge water and start the engine. Marine engines suck in an enormous amount of cooling water, and in an emergency they make excellent bilge pumps.

However, be *careful*. This could backfire into a disaster if you leave the engine unattended. It could pump the bilge dry and the engine would then over-heat. It could pick up a lot of garbage and debris floating around in the bilge, also causing the engine to over-heat. Have someone monitoring the situation constantly and keeping the intake free of debris. When the bilge water is almost gone, stop the engine, transfer the pick-up hose back to where it belongs and then run the engine again. You may have to switch back and forth many times before you get home, but at least you *will* get home.

How To Signal Distress

If you don't have a radiotelephone, how do you signal for help (Fig. 8-12)?

I have already referred to the T-shirt-on-a-fishing-rod signal which, although not specifically mentioned in Rules of the Road or Pilot Rules, is effective. In fact, anything that attracts attention is good. But there are certain accepted procedures to follow, such as:

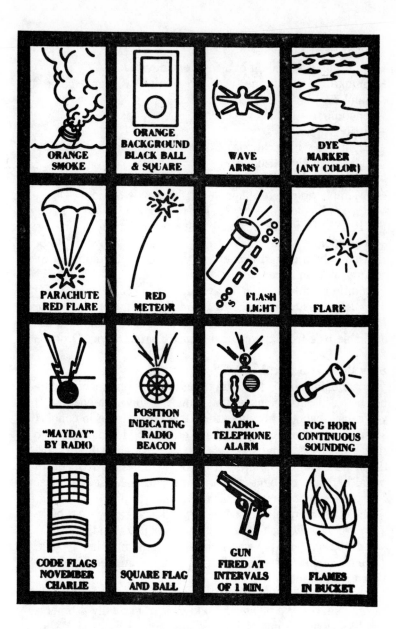

Fig. 8-12. Listing these types of distress signals for disabled craft may seem, to some readers of this book, antiquated and unnecessary because everybody has CB. That is a myth. Most of the boats using American waterways are small non-cruising craft who have little need for radio communications. They're too busy fishing (courtesy of the U.S. Coast Guard).

- Slowly and repeatedly raising and lowering both outstretched arms at the side.
- Continuous sounding of a fog horn device.
- Smoke signal, marine types which give off orange-colored smoke.
- Shooting off flares or rockets.
- Firing a gun.
- Flying the International Code signal flags of distress, a checkered and striped flag.
- Flying boat's ensign upside down.
- A simple orange-red flag waved from side to side.
- For radiotelephone owners, the spoken word "Pan," "Pan," "Pan," for disabled boats not in danger of sinking.
- The spoken word "Mayday," "Mayday," "Mayday" to be used only in extreme emergency, boat afire, sinking, or injured person aboard.

Additional information is available in a *Pocket Guide For Visual Distress Signals, CG-152,* and *Federal Requirements For Recreational Boats, CG-290.* Both of the above pamphlets are available free from the nearest Coast Guard District Office.

Stay With The Boat!

Abandoning ship is a painful thing to contemplate, but it cannot be ruled out so long as you remain involved in boating. If you must abandon, stay together, even use a rope to connect all survivors together, facing each other, and huddled close to reduce heat loss. And *stay with the boat!* Rarely will a recreational boat sink completely (Fig. 8-13), unless it is made of metal and has no built-in flotation devices. Most fiberglass boats have some form of built-in flotation to prevent sinking.

The old forgotten, and scorned, wood boat already *has* built-in emergency *flotation.* Take 10 pounds of metal and fiberglass and drop them into the water and they both immediately sink. Take 10 pounds of wood, drop it in the water and it *floats.* Wood is buoyant.

When a wood boat is swamped, even with two engines it still has enough reserve buoyancy to keep it from totally submerging. I know of boating mishaps where cabin cruisers sank with just the flybridge and trunk cabin visible above water. Yet there was enough reserve buoyancy to keep six survivors out of the cold water for hours until they were finally rescued. Had they left the boat, all of them would have perished, not from

Fig. 8-13. Very rarely does it become necessary to abandon ship. The above craft, holed and completely flooded, still kept four adults afloat until rescued. Even if you are in the water, stay with the boat. It is your best chance for survival.

drowning, but from cold water hypothermia (Fig. 8-14).

The lesson is: *stay with the boat!* You will be much easier to find. It is very difficult to spot a survivor in the water, but a partially submerged boat is easily spotted by a helicopter.

Personal Flotation Devices

You are breaking the law when you take aboard a vessel less then 18 feet in length any child under 10 years of age who is not wearing a personal flotation device (PFD) of appropriate size and approved by the Coast Guard.

Boats 16 feet or more in length must have one Type I, II or III PFD on boats for each person and one Type IV, a throwable device (Fig. 8-15).

Ring buoys are the best of the *throwable* devices (Fig. 8-16), but you don't see too many of them around anymore because there just isn't anyplace to put them on the modern fiberglass hulls, where they look out of place. Ring buoys look more natural and more at home hanging on the varnished mahogany of a wood boat.

To be of any value, the ring buoy must be instantly available, and preferably with a light coiled line attached that will not tangle when the ring is thrown (Fig. 8-17). If the line tangles in midair, valuable time is wasted and a man could drown. If you can just find someplace to keep the ring on a small cruiser, it is the best "throwable" device to have aboard for man-in-the-water situations.

In place of ring buoys, you can use life preserve cushions, which are also "throwable." But cushions have two drawbacks: first people sit on them and the kapok is crushed and buoyancy is reduced. Second, cushions are never instantly available with a coiled line attached. That means, valuable time is lost while you scrounge around for a line to secure to one of the straps.

I don't remember ever seeing a life preserver cushion hanging on a bulkhead with a neatly coiled line and sign reading: For Emergency Use Only. That is why the ring buoy is preferable, not because it is any better then a cushion, but because people don't sit on them and the ring is more likely to be treated for what it is—emergency life saving gear.

Man Overboard

The *throwable* flotation device required by law to be on all boats over 16 feet in length is supposed to be available if someone falls off your boat.

Fig. 8-14. The Coast Guard says, "STAY WITH YOUR BOAT" (courtesy of the U.S. Coast Guard).

	TYPE I Personal Flotation Device is designed to turn an unconscious person from a face down position in the water to a vertical or slightly backward position, and to have more than 20 pounds of buoyancy. Recommended for offshore cruising. Acceptable for all size boats.
TYPE 1 Example Life Preserver	
	TYPE II Personal Flotation Device is designed to turn an unconscious person from a face down position to a face up vertical or slightly backward position and to have at least 15.5 pounds of buoyancy. Recommended for closer, inshore cruising. Acceptable for all size boats.
TYPE 11 Example Buoyant Vest	
	TYPE III Personal Flotation Device is the most wearable type. It is designed to keep a conscious person in a vertical or slightly backward position and to have a minimum of 15.5 pounds of buoyancy. While it has the same buoyancy as a Type II device, a lesser requirement for turning movement makes it possible to design a comfortable and wearable device for activities where it is especially desirable to wear a device because of the likelihood that the wearer will enter the water. Recommended on lakes, empoundments and close inshore operation. Acceptable for all size boats.
TYPE 111 Example: Special Purpose Device	
	TYPE IV Personal Flotation Device is designed to be thrown to a person in the water and not to be worn. It is designed to have at least 16.5 pounds of buoyancy. All presently approved lifesaving devices that are acceptable as required lifesaving devices fall into one of the first four performance categories.
TYPE IV Example: A. Buoyant Cushion B. Ring Buoys	

Fig. 8-15. Here are some examples of PFD's.

If it is a child under 10-years-of-age, the throwable will not be necessary because the child will already be *wearing* a PFD. The child *better* be wearing one or you will spend the next few years of your life dodging process servers and talking to lawyers.

It is difficult to persuade a grown man to wear a PFD when he comes on your boat. He suspects you are questioning or have doubts as to his virility. I have seen guests recoil as if I had insulted them when I offered a life vest, which I only did when I knew the guest could not swim.

If you are the social type who likes people around when he boats, you must be prepared for man-over-board situations, even more so if you are a sailor. Sailboats heel, which make falling overboard much easier.

A well equipped powerboat should carry two Type IV throwables, one with a short floating line attached, 10-20 feet, and the second with a 50-100 foot line. If the crew member, or guest, falls overboard while your boat is moving slowly, you can throw him the ring buoy (also called life ring) with the long line while he is still in range and pull him in. If you are moving fast, you want maximum distance when you heave, so you

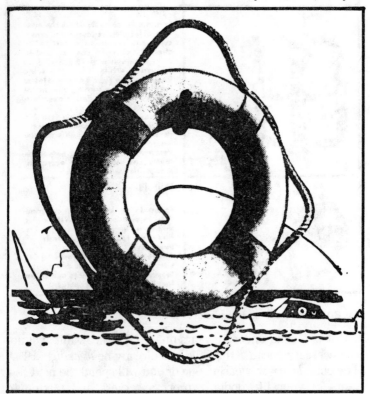

Fig. 8-16. Ring buoys, also called liferings, were once almost standard equipment on all boats over 18 feet because there was someplace to hang them. There is no point in having one unless it is hanging on the bulkhead, instantly available (courtesy of Manhattan Marine).

Fig. 8-17. The ring buoy, or life ring, must be handy with a line attached that will not foul up and tangle in mid-air when thrown (courtesy of the U.S. Coast Guard).

throw him the ring with the short line and he can swim to it. Figure 8-18 illustrates an alternative to the conventional ring buoy.

The Rescue

This is where you can blow it. Many attempted rescues of someone in the water end in tragedy, not because the victim drowned before being reached, but because the victim *was* reached, but the wrong way.

There were over 300 severe injuries and fatalities recorded in 1979 that were caused by boat propellers chewing up people in the water. Of course, only a small handful of the total were the result of botched rescue attempts of a man overboard, but it does point to the dangers present when you go looking for someone in the water. You must remember, the stern end of your boat is a lethal weapon.

However, swim platforms are located at the stern, so are swim ladders. The stern is where the man in the water will be the easiest to reach and bring aboard if he is injured or in-capacitated.

What do you DO?

MAYDAY
MAN OVERBOARD LOCATING DEVICE

MANHATTAN MARINE

Fig. A2912

The Mayday unit is no bigger than a small can of beans and weighs less than 120 grams. It attaches to a belt, lifejacket, or around the wrist by a universal strap on the can which carries diagramatic instructions.

Fig. 8-18. If you sail at night, you must be prepared for the unhappy contingency that you might have to search for a man overboard in the dark. Manhattan Marine has a device for you this purpose (courtesy of Manhattan Marine).

Make the wind work for you.

When you find the victim, go up wind from him, turn your starboard quarter to him and switch off the engine. The wind will blow you to him, swing the bow around so that when you reach him, he will be near the stern and can be pulled back to the swim platform with a boat hook.

This approach is the one recommended by the Coast Guard, and it's a good one, up to a point. There are times when it won't work. Suppose there's no wind or suppose there's a current or tide pulling the victim one way while the wind takes your boat in another direction?

You have some quick decisions to make and everybody on board will be looking at you. Being a skipper is more then just wearing a yachting cap. Some questions you must answer are:

Do you have a strong swimmer aboard?

Should you send the swimmer with a flotation device to the victim?

Consider this: when the swimmer reaches the victim, he may have to contend with panic and violent struggling. You could wind up with *two* victims in the water instead of one.

There is no need for haste or unnecessary risk if the victim is wearing a PFD, but if he isn't, you can't always go by the book. With lookouts posted up at the bow, you can approach the victim under slow power from *downwind* and have a PFD thrown to him. The instant he has it, switch off the engine and have him pulled around aft to be picked up at the stern.

Sending a swimmer is not recommended practice, except when all approved procedures fail. For example, if the victim is injured or incapacitated, it may be necessary to send a swimmer. However, the swimmer himself must be wearing a PFD and towing another one to the victim with a line attached back to the boat.

Do not put a swimmer in the water until the victim is sighted and you can guide him.

The skipper himself should never leave the boat to help a victim in the water. Somebody must be on board who can operate the rescue craft.

Rescue At Night

Most man-overboard accidents occur at night and in times of poor visibility, like fog. If you persist in boating at night, and taking people with you, then you have the added responsibility to provide some form of light along with the PFD so the victim can be found easily at night. On commercial vessels, lights are affixed to all throwable PFD's by short lanyards and they come on automatically. There are also other lights available which the victim must activate.

Devices That Aid Rescue At Night

A man-overboard locating device (Fig. 8-18) is available from Manhattan Marine in New York which releases a large high-visibility orange-colored balloon at the end of a 100 foot nylon line. This device is packaged in a small can no larger then those mini-cans of noodle soup. It attaches to a belt, a life jacket or wrist. To activate it, you pull a beer-can type ring. The rest is all automatic.

The highly visible balloon, four times the size of a man's head, and 100 feet up in the air, can be easily spotted at night when you sweep the horizon with a flashlight or your boat's searchlight.

Another life-saving device worthy of consideration to owners of small fiberglass cruisers, where there is no bulkhead space to hang conventional ring buoys, is the *Hiloat Buoy*, also available from Manhattan Marine. This device is easily stowed on even the smallest of boats (Fig. 8-19). When thrown to a victim in the water, a 20-inch ring buoy pops out automatically and inflates. It will hold two adults afloat for about 24 hours.

Finding A Missing Guest

Sometimes a guest or crewman will fall overboard and not be missed for quite some time. How do you find this missing guest?

Do what big ships do when a passenger is missed and considered to have fallen overboard, you execute *The Williamson Turn* , (Fig. 8-20).

This is a maneuver designed to bring your boat about 180 degrees, returning to its original line of wake. You now proceed precisely on this course until you find your missing guest or crewman. If he can swim, he'll be treading water and he'll be glad to see you. If he can't swim, and you didn't order him to wear a PFD, lots of luck with the lawyers.

If you had ordered your crew, or guests, into PFD's that had a Mayday Locating Device attached, you would be able to spot that big orange-colored balloon, without binoculars, at 500 yards. With binoculars you could scan a 40 degree angle of the

Fig. 8-19. If you have no suitable location to stow a lifering with instant availability, there are alternatives, like this small device marketed by Manhattan Marine. It is easily thrown and it automatically pops open to become a 20-inche lifering that will support two adults for 24-hours (courtesy of Manhattan Marines).

horizon to get maximum search coverage. At night you could do the same with your searchlight until you spotted that highly-visible speck of orange over the water.

Finding a needle in a haystack is actually easy when compared to finding a man overboard at night. There is nothing on the market today that makes the search easier then Manhattan Marine's Mayday Locating Device. And at $17.95, it's a bargain.

EMERGENCY REPAIRS AFLOAT

The Coast Guard answers thousands of unnecessary pleas for help each year from stranded boatmen whose engines will not start. I say "unnecessary" because nearly all causes of engine trouble are simple and can easily be fixed.

Very rarely will there be a major breakdown on a marine engine which will require the replacement of a major component. Marine engine components, like starters, fuel pumps,

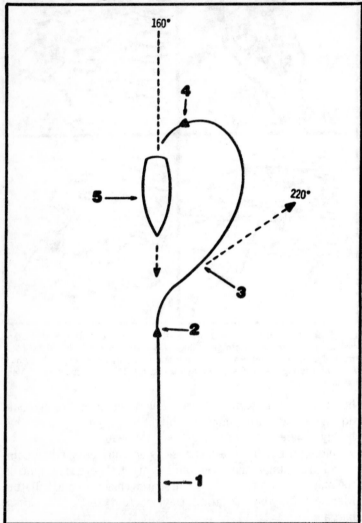

Fig. 8-20. The instant you discover a passenger is missing (1), check compass heading. (2) Have somebody throw a marker buoy overboard. (3) Change course 60° either port or starboard. If starboard you will change to 220° for about 30 seconds, then swing helm hard over to port until at (4) you will start to level off at a heading 180° opposite of your original 160° course. At (5) you will be on a heading of 340° going in the opposite direction and in the same lane of travel. Somewhere in this lane you will find your missing passenger, hopefully treading water and waiting for you.

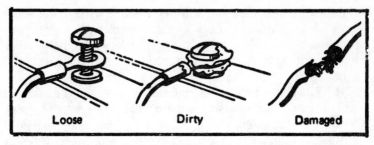

Loose   **Dirty**   **Damaged**

Fig. 8-21. Electrical terminals on boats that are winter stored under canvas are subject to much corrosion. Just one hard winter can foul up some electrical circuits. The ground battery post is always smaller in diameter then the positive post. But battery terminals are all alike with the same size post hold for both positive and ground. Frequently the ground terminal won't draw together enough for good contact with the battery negative or ground post. You may have to cut or file away some metal in the bolt gap (courtesy of the U.S. Coast Guard).

carburetors and distributors, don't get the same heavy use as an automobile engine, which can be cranked by the starter motor 20 times a day, every day of the year. So many times these components are not broken down, but merely dirty and corroded. And quite often to get a cranky starter motor to work will require nothing more then cleaning some electrical connections.

Starter Will Not Work

If the starter will not work, check the following areas:

● Check battery first with a hydrometer.

● Check for corroded terminals, acid-eaten cables (Fig. 8-21). Disconnect both battery cables and clean them thoroughly inside. Run emery cloth over the battery terminals until you see clean lead. Reconnect cables and tighten them hard to get good, solid contact. This is very important. Sometimes the battery clamps won't draw together enough to get good contact. Remove the bolt, spread the clamp with a screwdriver and file away some of the metal in the gap. I have had to hacksaw off ⅛ inch of metal here to enable the clamp to be drawn tightly over a battery post. Because of the enormous amount of current required to crank the engine, you cannot get this 300-500 amps until you have solid contact with the battery post.

● Turn the key in the ignition switch. If all the gauges work, the switch is probably all right. If the gauges do not work, check the two terminals on the back of the switch for tightness. Sometimes you will find a lot of wires here, some with spade terminals. If one of these wires with a spade terminal falls off, it creates a gap which loosens all the other wires. Check both terminals for tightness, then check the other end for tightness.

● A bad connection from the starter switch to the solenoid will create so much resistance there will not be enough current to activate the solenoid (Fig 8.22). If all the connections are clean and tight at both ends, make one more test. Using a heavy screwdriver with insulated handles, touch both the large and small terminals on the solenoid. If the starter jumps to life, you have a bad starter switch which will have to be replaced. However, do not despair, you can still start your engine by repeating what you just did with the screwdriver. You are simply doing with the screwdriver what the starter switch was supposed to do. Since it can't, you bypass the switch.

● If the starter spins, but does not engage the engine, the bendix pinion gear is probably stuck. Loosen the attaching bolts and remove the starting motor from the engine. Check the pinion gear to see if it is stuck on the shaft. If it is, give it a wack with a hammer. Squirt some oil on it, work it around until the gear slides freely on the shaft, and then stick her back in the engine. It should work now.

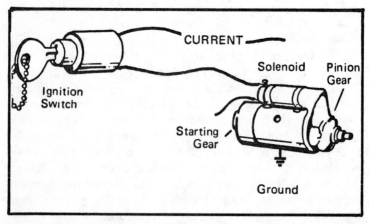

Fig. 8-22. On a marine engine, rarely will the starter itself be at fault if nothing happens when you turn the switch or push the button. Usually it's the switch at the helm. Sometimes, but not often, the solenoid on the starter will be the source of your trouble. In either case, don't despair. You can still get it started (courtesy of the U.S. Coast Guard).

● If starter works but engine does not start, start checking the primary electrical circuit including the small wires from the junction box to the ignition switch, the wire to the coil and the wire to the distributor. Look for corroded, damaged or loose connections which are quite common with marine engines which are stored outside for the winter under canvas. Changes of temperature under the canvas causes condensation on all metal surfaces and electrical connections badly corrode. This is the reason for all the checking of terminals.

● Next step is the secondary electrical circuit: those big fat wires from the distributor to the spark plugs. These wires carry very high voltage, up to 20,000 volts, which is not easy to contain or control. It's like trying to move water through pipes under very high pressure. One little flaw in the pipe, or one bad connection, and the water comes squirting out. High voltage electricity does the same thing. A bad connection or an invisible pinhole or crack in the insulation and 20,000 volts leaks out (arcs out) to negative ground. Since the entire engine itself is ground, all it has to do is arc out. Sometimes you can actually see this arcing, or even hear it. Most of the time you can't. A spark wire can look perfectly good, and yet be "leaking" where it touches something. Moisture on wires and plugs can cause leaking. The high voltage will follow the path of least resistance. It will follow the moisture on the wire insulation and plugs until it reaches ground. Until you make that high voltage jump to the gap across the terminals in the spark plugs, you will never get an engine to start.

First, you must have high voltage from the coil. You can make a quick easy spark test by using a pair of insulated pliers as shown in Fig 8-23. Pull that center wire in the distributor, hold it with the pliers about a ¼ inch from the engine while you crank the engine with the ignition switch *on*. You should be able to see and hear a spark arcing to the metal. *Caution!* Do *not* hold that coil wire in your bare hands. You could get quite a jolt. Better still, make yourself a simple little spark tester as shown in Fig. 8-23. All it takes is two lengths of wire with an alligator clip on each end. Staple bare ends of the wire to a board as shown. You can use this "tester" to now check each of your individual spark plug wires to see if they are delivering a hot spark to the plugs. If all your plugs are getting voltage, then your starting problem is not electrical.

If the plugs are not getting voltage, then our final check is

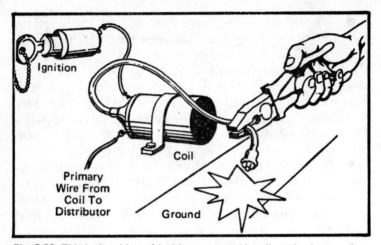

Fig. 8-23. This is the oldest of ignition tests used by all mechanics to make a quick check on secondary electrical output. If there is a big spark here, and none at the spark plugs themselves, then the trouble is narrowed down to the distributor (courtesy of the U.S. Coast Guard).

the distributor from whence all that voltage comes at the precise moment it is needed. Remove the distributor cap and pull off the rotor. Pull that center wire from the distributor cap and ground it to the engine. You must never crank the engine with that cap removed unless you ground that wire because turning over the engine generates high voltage in the coil, and that voltage must be released or it will arc inside the coil and damage it.

Crank the engine to see if the points are opening and closing properly with a noticeable gap (Fig. 8-24). If the gap looks small, you better check it. Turn the engine, and stop it alternately until you get those points at the maximum open position. Now check that opening. It should be about .020 inches. If you don't have a thickness gauge, a matchbook cover can be used in an emergency because it's reasonably close. There is an adjusting screw that must be loosened so that the point gap can be opened or closed. When you get the right gap, tighten the screw.

Check the distributor cap to see if that contact button is free to move up and down. That button must make good contact with the rotor. Don't forget to replace the rotor before you put the distributor back in position, and don't forget that center wire from the coil.

Fuel Checks

Two things are necessary to make an internal combustion engine run, electricity and gasoline. If your engine still will not start, then it has to be gas. It's as simple as that.

Are you *sure* you have gas? Did you check it before leaving port? A good rule to follow is never use more then one third of your fuel supply. Save two thirds for the return trip. If you still have gas, then something is keeping it from going to where it is needed—the combustion chamber.

We start at the beginning and go right down the line.

> *Warning:* Before you start making checks where gasoline might be spilled, be sure nobody smokes, turn off all electrical equipment, and have something handy and small, to catch the gas. Have someone handy with a fire extinguisher.

When gas leaves your tank, it goes through a main shut-off valve, through a main filter and then to the fuel pump. Is there

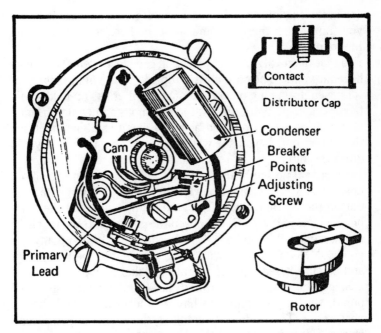

Fig. 8-24. That space, or "gap", in the breaker points, which open and close thousands of times per minute, breaks the flow of current, which, in turn makes the coil function as a transformer, stepping up the 12 volts to 20,000 volts so that it will have the driving force to jump that gap in the spark plugs. The breaker point gap is a critical .020 (courtesy of the U.S. Coast Guard).

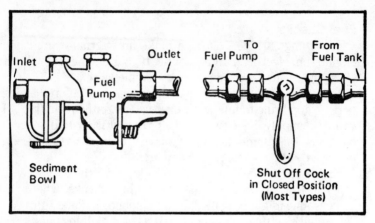

Fig. 8-25. Some fuel pump sediment bowls have porous porcelain-like filter elements which can plug up and cut off gas supply to the carburetor. In the construction of gas tanks, a welding flux is used which leaves a white sand-like residue which plugs up the filter elements, stopping you dead in the water. If gas is not getting to your carburetors, check that sediment bowl and filter element (courtesy of the U.S. Coast Guard).

gas in the fuel pump sediment bowl? If not, and there is gas in your tank, then there is some stoppage between the tank and fuel pump.

Is that main valve open? Vibration can close them. Gas tanks have air vents. They are always topside on the hull. Is it open?

Loosen drain plug on bottom of main filter as you hold a container under it. Watch for water, it is not an uncommon thing with marine gas purchased at many small establishments on the waterfront. If you see water, remove plug completely and drain the filter.

There will probably also be water in the fuel pump sediment bowl (Fig. 8-25). Remove bowl by loosening that large knurled nut on the bottom. Swing the wire clamp aside and the glass bowl will drop down. Don't loosen the gasket at the top. There is a screen at the top here. Check it for dirt. Wipe up any gas you spill, clean the bowl with a rag, return it to the fuel pump, and be sure it seats properly in the gasket above.

Since you drained water and gas from the filter and fuel pump, the fuel system will have to be primed, and the air pushed out. This is done by cranking the engine in five second bursts. But before you do this, disconnect the outlet line from the fuel pump to the carburetor, at the carburetor end. Wipe up all the gas spillage, and get rid of the gas you drained. Then run the bilge blower for a few minutes.

Put a container under that gas line at the carburetor, and then crank the engine while you watch the sediment bowl. Soon you should see it filling with gas. Shortly after that you should see gas coming out of the gas line at the carburetor.

Stop cranking. Your fuel system is primed, and the air has been blown out. Refasten the fuel line to the carburetor. The engine should start.

If the engine *still* will not start, check the carburetor (Fig. 8-26). Normally this is where I start when working on my own engine. Then I work backwards. But for purposes of illustration, I have taken each segment of the fuel system in sequence from gas tank to carburetor.

When an engine won't start, the professional always checks the carburetor first by looking down the throat and working the throttle valve. Working the throttle activates a pump

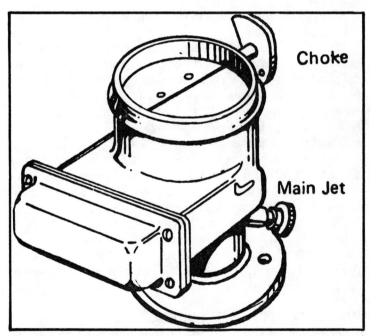

Fig. 8-26. A great deal of time, and swearing, can be saved if you check the carburetor first. This is what mechanics do. If gas squirts down in the throat when you jiggle the throttle, you eliminate a lot checking and can concentrate on electrical and ignition checks. The above choke is in the closed position, which is where it should be with a cold engine. You will never start a cold engine if that choke valve is in the open position (courtesy of the U.S. Coast Guard).

which shoots a stream of gas deep into the throat of the carburetor. When you look down, you can see that stream of raw gas. This immediately tells the professional that since the engine won't start, the reason *has* to be electrical. So he next checks to see if the plugs are getting a spark.

But since you are probably not a professional, the easiest way to explain all that to you was to start at the beginning.

If gas is reaching the carburetor, why won't the engine start? By a simple process of elimination, what is left?

The *choke!*

Remove the flame arrester. You will find the choke *open.*

You will never get a cold engine started with the choke open. Jiggle the choke linkage. It will instantly snap closed with a "clunk." If you have two carburetors, both will snap closed because they are linked together. If one sticks open, they both stay open.

Why did the choke stick in the open position?

I wish I knew!

My port engine gave me that trouble one entire season. The engine would never start and I would have to lift up the steps, crawl up into the engine compartment in my clean clothes and touch the choke linkage; that's all, just touch it. Then I would crawl back, drop the steps, and start the engine. I had to do that every time I started a cold engine, which was at least a hundred times that season.

There was nothing mechanically wrong, there was no reason for it to stick, but it did, even after I tried every type of no-stick lubricant on the market. I almost went out of my mind trying to fix the darn thing.

The next season it worked perfectly.

I can only conclude that some mysterious force is at work in the general scheme of things to test mens' souls, and prepare them for eternity. If your choke sticks open without cause, you are eligible to join the club.

IMPROVISING IN AN EMERGENCY

Survival at sea often hinges on improvising in an emergency, or put more simply, using plain common sense (like the boatman's wife who suggested he use one of her bobby pins in place of a cotter pin, which he needed desperately but didn't have; as a matter of fact, bobby pins make excellent cotter pins).

Fig. 8-27. There are still a great many automobile engines around in old boats that were converted to marine service with special conversion "kits." These engines have V-belts that operate both the alternator and water pump. Sometimes V-belts break, and boatmen who can't afford a conventional marine engine rarely carry spare parts, like V-belts.

Many emergency repairs can be made with what you have on board. Just use your wits.

Broken Fan Belt. Marine engines don't have "fans" but they still have that V-belt running off the crankshaft pully which, on some older engines, operates the water pump and alternator (Fig. 8-27). You can get home without the alternator, but not without the water pump.

Fan belts last a long time and rarely break, which is why a spare is seldom carried on board. In an emergency you make a temporary replacement from ¼ or ⅜ line. Just loosen the movable pulley, tie the line around the pulley, secure the ends with a simple square knot, tighen the movable pulley until you have tension again and you're on the way home, but take it slow and easy.

Broken Pipe Or Hose. Bandage the leak with rags, canvas or bobby sox and tie down with line or your belt.

Engine Oil Leak. Catch the leaking oil in whatever you have available on board, and pour it back into the engine. You can do this indefinitely until you get home.

Lost Rudder Control. Twin-screw boats can be steered without the rudder. In an emergency you can also steer a single screw without rudder control (Fig. 8-28). A sea anchor is perfect for this, but if you don't have one, you can use a bucket, an ice cooler, or anything available that can be tied to a line and towed behind your boat to create a heavy drag. By shifting the drag from one side to the other, you can control direction. It will not work perfectly, but it will get you home.

Complete Electrical Failure. When your ignition switch and starter switch are dead, how do you start the engine?

Disconnect all electrical equipment from the battery except that big fat wire to the starter solenoid, and the ground wire to the engine. You will need a short length of wire to make a connection from the positive terminal on the battery to the coil where that thin small gauge wire is connected from the ignition switch. To start the engine, you do the same thing that you do with a defective starter switch, as previously explained. You ground the small terminal on the starter solenoid with a screwdriver. This will start the engine. To stop the engine when you get home, disconnect that coil wire.

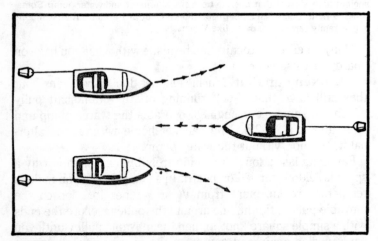

Fig. 8-28. This is best done with two people aboard, one at the helm, one aft moving the "drag" back and forth. But it could be done with one aboard, only moving more slowly (courtesy of the U.S. Coast Guard).

Repairing a "Holed" Hull. I am constantly hitting things floating in the water and I am almost paranoid about getting "holed" some day by a sharp object. In anticipation of this, I keep my own damage control kit aboard made up of many odd sizes of boat lumber and ¼ inch plywood. All the various sizes of plywood are pre-drilled with screw holes along the outer edge so they can be quickly slapped against a hole from the inside of the hull, and held there temporarily with a special type of sheetmetal self-tapping screw. This screw has a hex-washer head and drills its own hole. Using a cordless screwdriver and socket drives that are magnetized, I can zap that plywood patch over a hole in 30 seconds.

The skipper who anticipates trouble and prepares for it rarely has any. My damage control kit is stored below decks and will likely never be used. But you don't invest money in these things because you hope to use them. You don't ever want to use them. You just want the peace of mind they give you in being around.

TROUBLE-SHOOTING DIESEL ENGINES

Diesel engines do not have ignition systems. That automatically eliminates 90 percent of the things that can go wrong and screw you up out there on the water.

The gasoline engines electrical system, with its low/high voltages, coils, distributors, spark plugs and high tension wires, is so vulnerable in the corrosive atmosphere of the sea which eats up and spits out electronic circuitry faster then the Japanese can make them.

The diesel engine is relatively trouble free. There's only two things that stops a diesel from running: No air or no fuel!

When air is compressed, it gets hot. In the diesel, air compressed at a ratio of 19 to 1, is the "spark plug" that ignites the fuel. Air is actually a major part of the fuel on which diesels run, so much so that some diesel engines are equipped with turbines which force even more air into the combustion chamber to increase power.

Diesels are easy to start in hot summer months, but difficult in the winter, and impossible in sub-zero temperatures. When the Alaskan pipeline was being built, diesel truck engines were never turned off for months until they went inside to be serviced. Diesels can be easily started in sub-zero if pre-heated air is forced into the air inlets

Air Supply. When a diesel will not start, your first check is the air supply. Some engines are equipped with an automatic air shut-off device when the engine overheats or loses oil pressure. Check the air cleaner and screen to see if that passage to the intake manifold is open.

Fuel Supply. There's not too many things that can go wrong in the fuel system. You have fuel, or you don't have fuel. If you do have fuel, then why isn't it getting to the engine? Check the following.

— The shut off valve may have vibrated closed.
— There could be water in the fuel. Open that drain cock in the bottom of the fuel filter (Fig. 8-29), and watch for water. If you see water, drain the filter. Prime the fuel system by cranking the engine in short spurts for about a minute.

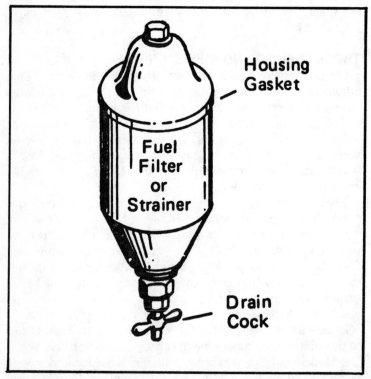

Fig. 8-29. If there is water in your fuel tanks, it will first show up in the fuel filter where it accumulates in the bottom. That's what that drain cock is for, to drain off water.

- Diesel fuel clogs up filters much faster than gasoline. Change the filter element.
- Air in fuel line. Disconnect the fuel line at engine, crank engine for a short period to bleed the lines.
- Some diesel engines have a safety feature which shuts off the fuel supply when the engine stops running. This is an electric switch or solenoid which you will find near the fuel pump. This switch may be defective or the solenoid may be closed by a short circuit. Disconnect the wires. The shut off valve, if it is closed, will open and the engine should start.

To find out definitely if this valve is closed, disconnect the outlet fuel line at the fuel pump and crank the engine. If no fuel comes out instantly, the valve is closed, Disconnecting the wires at the solenoid will open this valve. Crank the engine again, fuel should spurt out. The engine will start now.

BASIC TOOLS AND PARTS

Very few car owners carry tools in their car trunks. They have CB radios, or they have tow insurance. Most people can't be bothered with making emergency repairs.

This carries over when they buy boats. This past weekend the Belle Isle Coast Guard in Detroit towed the owner of a 27-foot cruiser who developed engine trouble the second time he used the boat. His engine had over-heated to the point where he had thought something was burning. On investigating, he found the fan belt was so loose that it was slipping and not turning the water pump.

When asked why he hadn't tightened that one simple nut with a ½ inch box wrench, or even an adjustable wrench, he replied: "I don't have a wrench."

But he did have a radiotelephone, which brought the Coast Guard and a free tow to his yacht club. This is a dangerous attitude which, unfortunately, is growing as a new breed of boatman takes to the water today with CB and radiotelephones which they feel is their own private Hot Line to the Coast Guard if they get into trouble and need a free tow.

When friends kidded one of these new boatmen about being brought in by the Coast Guard with engine trouble, he angrily defended himself by saying, "The Coast Guard spends millions of our taxes during the winter on ice breaking duty,

Fig. 8-30. The Coast Guard is responsible for keeping America's navigable waters open. This is the Coast Guard cutter Mackinaw clearing the ice from a shipping lane (courtesy of the U.S. Coast Guard).

and keeping the shipping lanes open so the big corporations can make more money. If the Coast Guard can do all that for free for the big conglomerates, why can't they burn up ten gallons of diesel fuel to help me? And when they do help me, why must I kiss their hand and thank them?"

Is there an answer to that?

Yes.

It is dangerous to assume that the Coast Guard is as near as your radiotelephone ALL the time (Fig. 8-30). Yes, you can reach them instantly on the radio, but they can't always reach you instantly. Sometimes 10 miles on the water can equal 100 miles on land. Sometimes you wait a long, long time before they can get to you, and not because they don't try. The Coast Guard does a magnificent job, but the sea is impersonal, it treats their little rescue boats no differently then it treats yours, and sometimes they have to fight the sea a long time to reach you, or even *find* you.

And while the Coast Guard is struggling desperately to reach the possibly inaccurate position you gave them, you will be down on your knees praying to God to send you a little screwdriver so you can fix a bilge pump.

For want of a nail, a battle was lost. For want of a screwdriver, your boat could swamp before the Coast Guard finds you.

You should have a minimum tool kit on your powerboat if you go out on big water (Fig. 8-31). When I say "big water" I am referring to any body of water so big that you need a compass to proceed from point "A" to point "B". You need a compass even on Lake St. Clair, the tiniest of all the Great Lakes. And the same with Lake Pontchartrain in Louisiana. Even some sections of the Mississippi River require a compass because it is so wide the shoreline cannot be seen when visibility is poor.

Here is a list of *hand tools* you should have on your boat:
- Adjustable end wrench
- Slip joint pliers

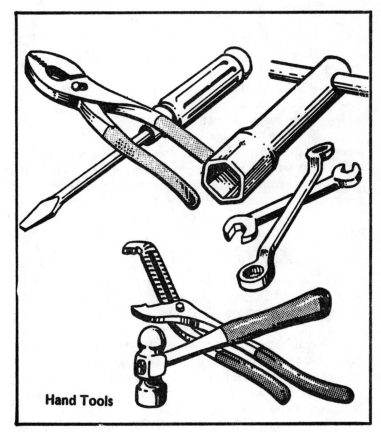

Hand Tools

Fig. 8-31. Every boatman should have tools such as these on board so that emergency repairs can be made.

- Pipe wrench
- Vice grip pliers
- Screw drivers (various sizes and types)
- Box end wrench set (all sizes)
- Hammer
- Spark plug wrench

Here is a list of *spare parts* you should have on your boat:

- Fan belt
- Spare distributor cap
- Spare rotor
- Points for distributor
- Condenser
- Coil
- Spark plugs
- Fuel pump
- Fuel filter for diesel engine
- Element for gasoline filter
- Engine oil
- Wire stripping/crimping tool
- Assortment of teminals
- Extra spark plug wires.
- Spool of 10-ga. ignition wire

Some of the above spare parts may be unnecessary; like the coil, rotor, spark plugs, points, condenser; and to a degree this is quite true because coils, which have no moving parts, never wear out. But coils can be accidently ruined in a matter of seconds if you crank the engine with the distributor cap off and forget to ground the center wire, which even trained mechanics occasionally do.

Rotors can be easily broken if the distributor cap is not replaced in proper alignment. Spark plug porcelain can be cracked if you accidently drop a plug. Points can be ruined if you do a bad fitting job. When replacing points, you should always replace the condenser because they work together as a team. Metal terminals on the end of radio-suppression type spark plug wires can be easily torn off when you pull a wire. That is why you should carry all the above spare parts, not because they will wear out, but because you may screw up and damage them accidentally.

Try to visualize in your mind the Doomsday feeling you would get if you put a distributor cap on crooked, and then hear a loud "clunk" noise when you cranked the engine, discovering that you had broken the rotor. Then you are anchored in some cove in the Georgian Bay with a bull moose feeding just two hundred yards away, and you need a new rotor.

You get even sicker when you remember that Canada does not maintain a coast guard such as the United States does—in fact, no other country does. Other countries have coastal patrols, yes, but their function is mainly policing and guarding rather than serving at the beck and call of their boating citizens who might get into trouble on the high seas. Spare parts are a necessity when boating in foreign waters.

Chapter 9
Sailboat Seamanship

Sailors are good seaman. They have to be because sailing is not easy. It takes brains to be a sailor, and brains are not too plentiful on popular boating waters today, according to Coast Guard and marine insurance statistics.

Sailing is not for dummies I was once told by a race committee member when I asked a stupid question on the morning of a big race. What made his remark even more painful was that he was so right.

Put another way, you don't buy a sailboat, drop it in the water and go sailing off in the breeze with a sexy little lady beside you like they show in the four-color magazine ads. First, you must learn *how* to sail, and you won't do that in 10 easy lessons. It may take a season, or it may take years. I know a man who has been sailing for 20 years and he told me recently that he is still learning new things. I sailed an old 42-foot ketch eight years and still consider myself a learner, even though I am quite proficient in textbook theory. But anybody can be proficient in theory, but not everybody can be a "proficient" sailor. There's a difference.

Sailing and seamanship go together like Scotch and soda. You can't be a good sailor without also being a good seaman. This explains why sailors are usually the best skippers.

SAILBOATS VERSUS POWERBOATS

As any fool can plainly see, sailboats and powerboats are different, and the difference goes much deeper then the appearance (like, for example, that big stick with a rag handing on it). It took thousands of years for sailboats to evolve into what they are today—layed-up layers of fiberglass, cloth, aluminum, stainless steel and synthetic cordage.

Recreational powerboats have been around less then 60 years. Today's new breed of fiberglass powerboat hulls haven't even been around long enough for judgements to be made on their life expectancy or stability as time and the sea take their toll. Many wood boats built over a century ago are still afloat and seaworthy. Nobody really knows if boats built of fiberglass will still be around in the Year 2000.

One of the major builders of fiberglass yachts recently came out with a 50-foot model that had a cruising capability of 3000 miles on its 2500 gallon fuel load. This yacht, the builder claims, can go anywhere. It this means going up and down the coastline offshore, or up the Intercoastal Waterway from Florida to the Great Lakes region, the skipper would never have to make fuel stops along the way, and that would be nice. But if "anywhere" means long open sea passages, I would not care to make such a voyage in such a boat.

This is because diesel fuel weighs about eight pounds a gallon. A fuel load or 2500 gallons would weigh 20,000 pounds, or 10 tons. Near the end of a long sea passage, this yacht would lose almost 10 tons of ballast. On the open sea this is a serious matter. Ships in the merchant marine and passenger service also use fuel oil as ballast, but as the fuel is used, they replace it with sea water to maintain ballast.

In the movie about the passenger liner *Poseidon*, which rolled over upside down when hit by a tidal wave, the captain was much concerned about the ship being topheavy because she was so low in ballast. He had an argument with a ship-owner representative about pumping sea water into empty fuel tanks for ballast.

Small pleasure yachts, powered by diesels, cannot do this because they already have enough troubles with water in the fuel without pumping more into the tanks. Large vessels use fuel oil to fire up their boilers where water is not the problem it is with diesel engines.

What this means is that diesel-powered yachts, regardless of size, are not suited for long open sea passages because they must carry such an enormous fuel load.

Fig. 9-1. This is the only safe way to cross an ocean in a small pleasure craft without having to carry 10 tons of fuel. I would not hesitate to sail anywhere in the world in this "Freedom 40" centerboard cat ketch with wishbone boom and unstayed masts (courtesy of Carnov Corp.).

SAILBOATS AND THE SEA

There is only one safe way to cross an ocean in a pleasure craft—*sail!*

At sea the sailboat (Fig. 9-1) is in its element and there is no limit to where it can go. There is also no limit on the size of the craft. After all, if Gerry Spiess can cross the Atlantic in *Yankee Girl*, which is only 10-feet in length, how can anybody say that such and such a sailboat is too small? If there are limitations to sailing, they are not in the boat, they are in the hands on the tiller.

There is no limit on what a sailboat can do or take at sea when skippered by a real seaman, like the 97 skippers who finished the calamitous Fastnet Race off Cowes in Britain's Isle of Wight, August 11th, 1979, in a freak storm that had boats tacking into winds of 70 knots and seas averaging 20 to 30 feet.

Although 306 yachts started the race, only 97 finished. The remaining 209 either retired, abandoned ship, or sank. Fifteen people died and over 136 were picked out of the raging seas by helicopter. And yet, in spite of the almost insurmountable difficulties facing each skipper, the race went on.

These sailing vessels were not out on a casual weekend cruise, they were *racing.* These people were driving and pushing their boats to move under sail through mountainous seas when under normal conditions they would hove to under storm trysail and spitfire.

What is most remarkable about this race is that 97 boats continued on and *finished.* When all the foam and spray had settled, Ted Turner's *Tenacious* emerged as the corrected time winner in this most impossible of sea epics.

In an interview later, Turner, winner of the America's Cup Race, said: "When you go to sea, you have to expect these things, you have to be ready and prepared."

Around The World Singlehanded

Few men have solo circumnavigated the earth in a sailboat. One of the first to do it in this century was Harry Pidgeon who, in November 1921, at the age of 52, cast off from Los Angeles in a 34-foot yawl that he built himself, and cruised through the South Seas and the Indian Ocean. He survived the violent storms around the Cape of Good Hope, and completely circled the globe in four years and 27,000 miles. And to prove it was

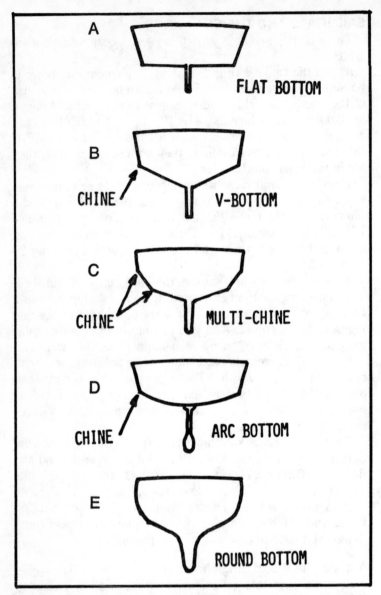

Fig. 9-2. Here are five basic hull forms, but each has dozens of variations and types of keels.

no fluke, Harry did it again in the early '30s.

During those nine long years of sailing on all the oceans and seas of the earth, Harry Pidgeon missed nothing that the sea can do to a man and his boat. And yet he survived.

SAILBOAT HULL FORMS

There are so many different sailboat hull forms (Figs. 9-2 and 9-3) that many would-be sailors often get discouraged, throw up their hands and take up another hobby, like collecting old cars. I have seen this happen.

Sailboating is complicated and confusing only if you try to absorb it all in one shot. There is no need to know everything about all hull forms since your involvement will only be with one—the hull you buy. And the hull type you buy will depend on what you want to do.

Fig. 9-3. This is only one of the many types of hulls that can be found on a sailboat.

There are many ways of sailing, like just fooling around on a nice Sunday afternoon with a six-pack, or going back and forth on a small lake. This is called *day sailing*.

Do you want sleeping and living accomodations so that you can sail to strange places and stay overnight? This is called *cruising*. It is also called "very expensive" (Fig. 9-5).

Are you interested in competitve sailing, or racing? Then you want a One Design or Meter boat, all of which are designed for Class Boat racing.

When you go into the sport of racing, you race only with other boats identical to yours. If you buy a Lightning, you race with other Lightning. If you buy a Dragon, you race with Dragons. There is a reason for all this—all the boats are equal.

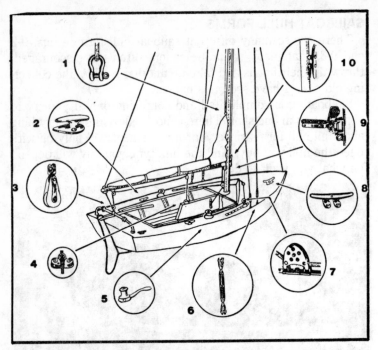

Fig. 9-4. Day sailing, just running back and forth, is usually done in small sailors of this type on the smallest of waters and rivers, sometimes no larger then a fishpond. The hardware used is universal. (1) shackle, (2) bumper or spring cleat, (3) single swivel block, (4) cam-action cleat, (5) winch, (6) turnbuckle, (7) adjustable lead block on traveler, (8) mooring cleat, (9) sliding gooseneck, (10) open base jam cleat.

The only edge you have is in your head. You can take your Thistle, your Lightning, or your Dragon to race anywhere in the world, and all the other boats will be exactly like yours. You can only win by being a better skipper.

Do you want versatility? Would you like to be able to do all things, like race, cruise and day sail? There is a hull form for that—in fact, it's the most popular of all hull forms today. These hulls are called *Cruiser-Racer* (Fig. 9-6). You can fool around on a Sunday afternoon just sailing or you can enter into the Club-sponsored race. You can cruise to San Clemente Island or down the coast of Mexico.

Cruiser-racers come in all sizes and shapes, and most do not conform to a specific class. Therefore, if you buy such a hull type you will not race with Class boats, you will race with the Big Bad Boys who will kick your brains out. These barracudas in yacht caps use every trick in the book to fool the rules committee and get an edge on the competition.

Although you will be racing with boats twice your size and sail area, and crewed by skilled sailors, things are still supposed to be even and there is a lot of slide rule correcting at the end of the race to make it so. If this wasn't done, boats with the largest sail area and the biggest spinnakers, would always win. In theory it sounds good, but this is cutthroat competition, and you still can get your eyeballs gouged before you get all your sails up.

The Most Popular Hull Type

The cruiser-racer is the most popular sailing hull type on the market today. It is especially big with the yacht club crowd where members like to both cruise with their families and compete in club-sponsored races.

When you go visiting the dealership to look at boats, you will see very little of anything but cruiser-racers, and if you are a man with a cardiac condition, it is best that you avoid looking

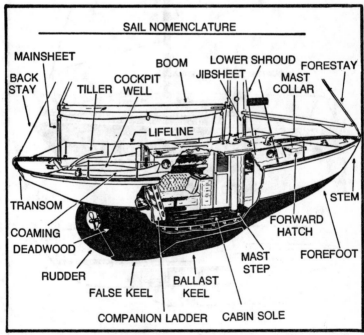

Fig. 9-5. Cruising is done in boats like this with a galley, head and sleeping accommodations. The new ones today are all made of fiberglass with aluminum masts and stainless rigging. However, the names for everything, the nomenclature, is still the same as it has been for centuries.

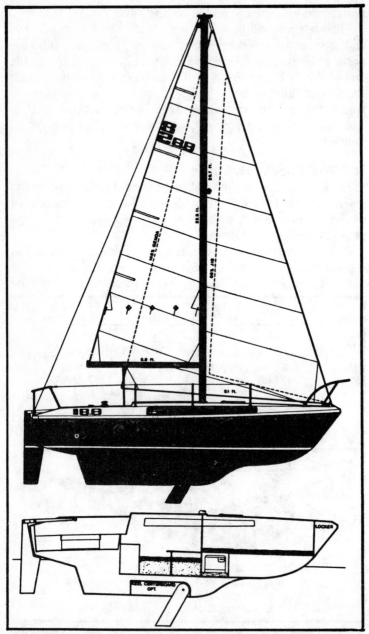

Fig. 9-6. This is the most popular cruiser-racing hull, and you will see very little of anything else in dealer showrooms today because everybody wants to race, but they also want to cruise in comfort. This hull is a combination of both centerboard and a weighted lead keel.

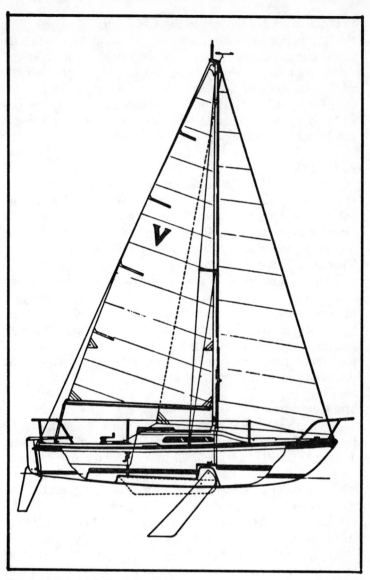

Fig. 9-7. Almost all One-Design racing Class boats are centerboards. You do not go to sea in a centerboard. The above boat, although strictly a centerboard hull, will carry some lead pigs in the bilge for trim purposes and increased stability.

at the manufacturer's suggested list prices.

You will get no discounts in April; maybe 5% after the Fourth of July holidays; and maybe 10% after Labor Day. But don't count on a discount. Sailboats are the biggest selling item in the industry right now and there is no sign of a slack off in the future. In some boating areas of California, Florida and the Great Lakes, dealers can't get delivery on all their orders.

I visited a big dealership in Detroit late in July and they had 14 big sailboats in their showrooms, ranging in price from $90,000 to $175,000. I went back there again on Labor Day and only one boat was still on the showroom floor, and it was in a hold pattern pending approval of a bank.

KEEL TYPES

Almost as baffling as hull forms are keels. When you look at them in the yards at haul-out time, no two will look alike. But yet, in essence, they all are alike in what they do, which is provide the necessary lateral resistance under water to keep the hull from going sideways when wind fills the sails from abeam. That lateral resistance is what makes sailing possible.

To understand what makes a boat sail, and move in any direction you wish, hold a small bar of soap between your fingers and squeeze it, applying pressure to both sides. What happens? The bar of soap will shoot out from between your two fingers. Those two opposing pressures, one on the sail and the other on the keel, are what makes a sailboat move in the direction you wish, guided, of course, by the rudder.

The Centerboard

There are two basic keel types—one is fixed and one is adjustable. Each has advantages and each has disadvantages. The *centerboard* type keel is *adjustable* in that it can be raised or lowered (Fig. 9-7). This is an advantage in areas of shoal (shallow) waters, like western Lake Erie and many sections of the Chesapeake Bay. It is also an advantage in Class boat racing because the centerboard can be adjusted to get additional speed on certain points of sailing.

Centerboard racing hulls are easily tipped over on their beam ends in sudden summer squalls. This is the major disadvantage of the centerboard hull. Also the centerboard trunk can be a nuisance in cruising boats with cabins because it sticks up in the middle of the cabin and limits interior design.

Although centerboards are easily tipped over by unexpected wind gusts, they will not sink, and they can be easily righted by one person. This one big advantage of the centerboard racing hull has saved many kids from drowning when, as so frequently happens during a summer race, a thunder squall flips over dozens of boats. The only casualty is pride. Everybody gets wet, but they all hang on to their capsized boats until help comes. After the water is bailed out, they can resume sailing to dry out.

The Deep Keel

The biggest advantage of the *deep* keel is *stability*, which is why they are considered the most seaworthy of boats (Fig. 9-8). They are almost impossible to tip over and when, on very rare occasions they do, if watertight integrity is maintained, they will eventually right themselves.

In a hurricane some years ago, a 42-foot yawl from Toledo was flipped over on its beam ends in Caribbean waters north of Cuba and it just layed there on its side for about fifteen minutes with both sticks in the water until the wind subsided slightly, and then she slowly righted herself. She picked up a foot of water in the bilge, but suffered no damage. Fortunately, they had been hove to with all canvas down. The boat had been secured and battened down, and everybody was down in the cabin. The companionway hatch and door had been tightly secured so very little water got in.

If buoyancy can be maintained, a deep keeled boat will always right herself. But if the sea gets in, it will sink quickly because bolted to the bottom of that deep protuberance under the hull is a big slug of lead or iron weighing thousands of pounds. It is that massive ballast weight which sinks the keeled boat in a hurry. A 35-foot sailboat is often ballasted with three to four tons of lead. Iron is not used much anymore because it requires too much mass for the weight needed. Lead gives the needed weight in a much smaller package.

Sailboats that go to sea have deep keels. They also have small *portlights* with ½ inch glass instead of big windows for the seas to break. The portlights seal watertight with screw clamps and the hatches are strong, tightly close and cannot be torn off. The cockpits are self-bailing with large scuppers. This is all designed to keep the sea out. The deep keeled boat is almost impossible to sink.

Keel-Centerboard

A type of hull form which captures the best of two worlds is the *keel and centerboard* (Fig. 9-6). There is no centerboard

Fig. 9-8. The weighted deep keel is the safest boat for long ocean passages, like that trip to Tahiti. Because of its low profile and small portlights instead of big picture windows, it is easy to maintain buoyancy by keeping the sea out. It can be flipped over on it's beam ends in a hurricane, but it will always right itself.

trunk in the cabin because the board swings up into the keel itself rather then into the cabin. You will find this on many motor sailers, which is another attempt to capture the best of two worlds.

The keel-centerboard will be found mostly on very large sail boats, usually over 60 feet, and they will usually have two centerboards which are often dropped in shallow waters as temporary anchors. When they come into crowded marinas or mooring areas where there is no room to maneuver, if strong winds start them drifting dangerously, they can drop those two centerboards and stop dead in the water.

This, of course, is not the primary purpose of the centerboards, but just a little bonus feature. Having the centerboards down reduces heel on certain points of sailing while having the centerboards up increases speed on other points. The weighted keel provides better stability then just ballast pig iron distributed around the bilges, and these hulls are almost as uncapsizable as a deep keel boat.

Fin Keels

The *fin keel* is strictly a racing hull and is not considered as seaworthy as the deep keel boat. Because the fin is thinner, it offers less resistance to forward movement, and thus makes the hull slightly faster. The fin, however, is not an integral part of the hull like the deep keel is, but instead is merely bolted onto the bottom. It is usually made of iron and it is flat with a heavy round cast on the bottom for weight.

You will find the fin keel on many racing Class boats like the Star and International 110's.

Daggerboards

The *daggerboard* is just a variation of the centerboard. Instead of swinging up and down on a hinge or pivot pin, the daggerboard just slides up and down. It can even be pulled completely out of the well. Its biggest drawback is that when the board is all the way up, the top is protruding right into the path of the boom swing. But when the board is down, it takes less of a shock if the boat runs aground.

Lee-Boards

Like Chinese Junks, the lee-board is an oddball curiosity in this country which attracts a lot of attention wherever it appears. Lee boards are used with great success in Holland where boats are designed to sit on the bottom because of shallow waters and extreme tides.

When these boats heel under sail, only one lee board is deep enough in the water to offer any reistance. Only that part of the board which extends below the keel line (not the waterline) offers effective resistance. Lee boards just don't have enough board extending below the keel by American standards, which is why you see them only on sailing canoes in this country.

SAILING RIGS

Sailing rigs can be divided into two general classes, the square rig and the fore and aft rig. From each there are endless variations, but there is no need for the new boatman reading this to get discouraged because he will not have too many sail options or decisions to make when he goes into the market place to buy a boat.

American boat builders have pretty well narrowed down your choices to the rigs that are best for the types of boats they build. If you want something offbeat for the times, life for example a schooner rig, it will have to be specially ordered because nobody stocks this old rig today.

The Square Rig

The only place you will ever see a *square rig* sail today is in the funny papers when comic strip character, *Haggar the Horrible,* sails off on his Viking ship to loot and sack Rome.

Nobody knows how long ago Man first used the wind's energy, but when he did it very likely was used with a square sail to move his raft made of reeds.

The square sail is most efficient when the wind is behind or abaft the beam. Old Yankee Clippers and merchant sailing ships of the past (Fig. 9-9) were all square-rigged to make use of the trade winds at their backs. Before they disappeared into history, square-riggers had developed into an extremely complex and efficient system of wind propulsion for ships of the day. Today they are used by many nations mainly as training ships for naval cadets.

Fore And Aft Rigs

In *fore and aft* rigs, the forward edge of the mainsail (pronounced mains'l) is attached to a mast, while the bottom edge

Fig. 9-9. The old square-riggers had reached the ultimate degree of efficiency just at that point in history when steel hulls and machinery were starting to compete for shipping cargo. The wind was free but time was not. Machinery was faster than canvas and wind.

is attached to a boom. The mainsail is controlled by a line called a *sheet.* The sail can be trimmed much closer this way, running almost straight fore and aft, so that the most desirable point of sailing, running close to the wind, is attained.

In racing, close windedness is important because every race has one windward leg (into the wind) and if you can't keep heading into the wind, you might as well give up racing.

There six common fore and aft rigs are: the cat, the schooner, the katch, the yawl, the cutter and the sloop.

The three most popular rigs today, mainly because of the new popular interest in racing, are: the yawl, the sloop, and the cutter. When you go to the dealer showrooms, these three are all you will find immediately available. If you want a ketch or schooner, it will have to be specially ordered, and if it is April, you can forget about sailing for the current season because you will be lucky to get delivery by Christmas.

The Cat Rig
New sailors are attracted to the cat rig because they look

disarmingly simple. There's just that one sail to handle. However, cats can have a mean weather helm, which is why it is not a good rig on which to learn.

Because the mast is located in the extreme bow section, the cat rig is difficult to stay properly. It could be forestayed if it had a bowsprit, but who ever heard of a cat with a bowsprit?

The cat rig is used mostly on very small boats.

The Schooner

The schooner was once the most popular sail rig in America and you will still see old schooners around in the Chesapeake Bay and New England coastal waters. They are all built of wood and they are all very old. Some are treated like national monuments, which they are, being links to our past. But you will see very few schooner rigs on hulls built of fiberglass. I have seen only one schooner recently and it was on a steel hull built 30 years ago in Wisconsin.

Why are schooner rigs in the doghouse? Because of the current preoccupation with *spinnakers*, which has reached almost mania proportions. Everyboday wants to compete, and you haven't got a prayer in competitive sailing today unless you have a crew who can handle that big balloon billowing out ahead so dramatically when running before the wind.

Schooner rigs are at their best when the wind is on their beam. But that short foremast prevents them from putting out a large spinnaker (and unless you can put out that big balloon when running, forget it, watch the race from a spectator boat).

However, sailboat racing is not a spectator sport. As the late Damon Runyan once said, after covering an America's Cup Race, "It's like watching grass grow."

The Ketch Rig

Schooners and ketches are the ideal rigs for long-range cruising. The ketch is especially good because you can reduce sail with maximum ease and because you have so many sail options. It is one of the most versatile rigs providing many sail combinations, and someday when you get fed up with the rat race decide to chuck it all, buy a boat, sail for Pango Pango in the Society Islands of the South Pacific, you're going to NEED variety is sail combinations.

The Yawl Rig

Yawls and ketches look so much alike it is sometimes hard to

328

tell them apart. But there is a difference and it is in the size and position of that smaller aft mast, which is called the *mizzen-mast*. In the ketch, the mizzen is forward of the rudder head. In the yawl, the mizzen is aft of the rudder.

Some boats, however, have *outboard rudders*. This makes for confusion because, on a technical point, this can make the yawl a ketch. But this is not necessarily so. Sail area makes for the final distinction. The ketch mizzen sail is usually two-thirds the size of the main. The yawl mizzen is only one fourth. Even with the sails down, just looking at the mast heights will tell you the difference between the two.

The yawl is a popular racing rig because it can be held close to the wind.

The Cutter

The cutter and the sloop are the two favorites of the long distance racers with their seasoned crews handling those huge spinnakers and genoas. There is nothing more embarrassing to a skipper then having his crew foul up getting the spinnaker up, and then having to watch it flop around until it finally lands in the water.

There is nothing more beautiful then watching Ted Turner's skilled crew handle the spinnaker, getting it up the instant they come downwind. *That* is what wins races.

The cutter has one mainsail, a fore staysail and a jib. A divided rig is always an advantage because the sail can easliy be reduced without *reefing*. Reefing is an old-fashioned way of reducing sail by dropping it a few feet and then trying the reduced sail to the boom. Eliminating one of the sails accomplishes the same thing, and none of the sails are so big that it cannot be easily handled by one man.

The Sloop

The racing sloop can be handled with a smaller crew since there are only two sails, in fact, it is the ideal single-hander. With a self-reefing main and jib (Fig. 9-10), one man can control the sails without leaving the cockpit. With a *genoa* up on the windward leg, this is a fast boat and a tough one to beat. The genoa is just a big oversized jib, but in overall sail area, it can be as large, or even larger then the main.

It was at a 1927 race in Genoa that the Swedish boat entry first introduced this sail. It created a sensation and became known afterwards as the *Jenny*, or genoa.

It is the Jenny that wins races when the winds are light on the windward leg.

Fig. 9-10. The sloop, with just two sails, is the favorite of many sailors who like to sail alone. With jib reefing, as above, you can handle the sails yourself without leaving the cockpit. This makes for more sailing and more fun because you are not dependant on others to crew for you.

HELM BALANCE

Most of the new boats hitting the water today have pedestal steerers. They are a big thing in sailing right now and you aren't *in* unless you have one. However, these wheel steerers are both good and bad, especially for the sailors who will miss something important in their education.

The old-fashioned hand tiller gives the helmsman a *feel,* a communication with his boat. It tells him how his boat is responding to wind and water, whether the rigging is properly tuned or whether the sails are trimmed for helm ballance.

The hand tiller also has a built-in safety feature. If the tiller should slip off the auto-pilot while the helmsman is using the head, of if he should have a heart attack, the sails would immediately luff up, and the boat would head into the wind as if hove to, the boat would be stable and safe. A boat's tendency to do this is called a *weather helm.* This is highly desirable.

If the rigging is not tuned or if the sails are not trimmed properly, when the tiller is let go, the boat will sometimes head off (away) from the wind. This is called a *lee helm.* This is not desirable.

Sailing with the tiller in your hand you *feel* this, so you know when your sails are not properly trimmed and you know when your rigging is not tuned.

When you sail with your hand on a big metal wheel, you feel nothing. Take your hand off that wheel and nothing happens. The boat stays right on course because the pedestal steerer is hooked up to the rudder through a worm and pinion gear. Turning the steering wheel moves the rudder. But, pressure on the rudder will not turn the steering wheel.

This is a convenience for the helmsman who doesn't have to sit there with his hand constantly on that wheel. He can relax and he can even go down below for a can of beer.

With the pedestal steerer your rigging can be out of tune and, unless you have a lot of experience at sailing, you will never know it.

A weather helm is desirable, but only in the right amount. Some boats have too much and some too little. In light breezes, there should be a light pull on the tiller. If the pull is heavy when the winds are light, when the winds freshen, the angle of heel will increase and effort to hold the tiller will be very tiring.

Too Much Weather Helm

In small boats, too much weather helm can be corrected by doing the following:

- Move weight or ballast aft
- Raise centerboard
- Trim jib sheet or set larger jib
- Prevent heeling to leeward
- If none of the above works, rigging is out of tune and mast will have to raded forward slightly by loosening the backstay, and tightening the forestay.

Too Much Lee Helm

Too much lee helm can be corrected by doing the following:

- Move weight or ballast forward
- Lower centerboard
- Ease jib or set a smaller one
- Heel to leeward
- If none of the above works, the mast will have to be raked aft by loosening the forestay, and tightening the backstay.

SAILS

There are only two types of sail in use today, the *gaff* sail and the *Marconi* sail.

The Gaff Sail

The chief advantage of the gaff sail is that you can use a shorter mast without sacrificing sail area. This is an advantage, even a necessity, in some areas where a boat must travel up rivers and under bridges where a taller Marconi mast would not clear.

In the days before aluminum masts, a shorter wood mast was often preferred to a tall one because it was easier to step, easier to stay, easier to trim and less apt to break. Wood masts are now just another relic of the past.

The gaff sail is more difficult to handle: it is heavier and there is more windage aloft with that extra piece of lumber up there.

The Marconi Sail

The most common and the most popular sail on the water today is the Marconi. It requires a tall mast. But this is one of its advantages because, by being up there so high, it can pick up those high breezes which are often missed by a lower sail. The Marconi sail is lighter and easier to handle and it creates less windage aloft.

Working Sails

Many new sailboats are delivered fully equipped with a set of *working sails*. These are the sails that a boat carries for just average day-to-day sailing. They are no good for racing or severe weather conditions.

Experienced sailors usually buy a boat without sails, especially if they plan to race. For the new sailor, it is best to just start out with working sails. Try to get sails made of heavier material, even though it will cost a little more, because your sails will take quite a beating that first year of learning. By the second year, you will know what you want, and whether or not you want to race. And if you think the business world is a rat race, wait until you've been through a few week-ends of yacht club competitive "racing."

I have crewed in a dozen races. I have been punched in the face twice (and I wear glasses), kicked in the shins by a lady skipper, and hit on the head by an empty beer can. I have fallen overboard twice and lost two fingers on my left hand.

So you want to race.

Lots of luck.

Not too many years ago, all the best sails were made of Egyptian cotton. Today everyting is synthetics like nylon, orlon and Dacron.

If you are a beginner, be advised that cotton sails must go through a long painstaking ritual of being broken in. This may be too much to throw at a begining sailor who will have enough to do and remember without being put through an antiquated ritual that is almost as bad as running cotton into seams, which dates back to the Stone Age of wood boats.

It is best to start right out from the beginning with the type of sail you will be using all the them, which will almost certainly be Dacron. Sails of this synthetic material require no "breaking in," and they are far more resistant to mildew, which is an Egyptian curse on all boaters. Dacron will not rot, stretch or shrink, and it is not porous like cotton, which absorbs moisture and has to be thoroughly dried out before being stowed away in sail bags.

Dacron working sails are best for learning the fundamentals.

But experienced sailors use a combination of both Dacron and nylon. The lighter weight of nylon is preferred for spinnakers and some small jibs. Nylon stretches considerably, but this does not affect the performance of a spinnaker—weight does, which is why nylon is preferred. They fill out more easlily in light airs, which is when spinnakers are used the most. In fresh breezes that big balloon billowing out ahead of you can become an unmanagable beast as it did in the Fastnet Race when boats with small spinnakers out broached, somersaulted and cart-wheeled. One 47-footer did a complete 360 degree roll after broaching.

Bending On Sails

Getting the most out of a new sailboat comes only by having the right equipment when you take delivery. Although it adds a few thousand dollars to the cost, buying a sail-away "package" from the manufacturer is the best way to buy a sailboat. Otherwise you will be spending months, perhaps the entire first season just buying and installing all the gear you will need, and in the end you will spend twice as much. Marine equipment bought piecemeal is priced as if all boatmen were rich.

The "packaged" boat is ready to sail when you *bend on* the sails. That's sailor talk for getting the sails "installed."

It is important that you learn the "language," or you will be forever saying "huh" and "what's that again" when somebody talks about "bending on the gaff sail." In the everyday world of commerce and high finance chicanery, you can conceal your ignorance by just smiling in a knowing fashion, but keeping your mouth shut. But that won't work around sailors. They're just too smart. To avoid looking like a dedicated lubber, learn the language.

All Marconi sails are held to the mast and boom by little slides, also called cars, which attach and ride on a track that is permanently secured to both the mast and the boom. When bending on the main, or mizzen, you start at the *headboard,* which is a plate of metal or wood that is sewn into the top point of a Marconi sail. This point is called the *head.* The halyard, a line or wire rope that raises the sail, is fastened to the *head-board* with a screw shackle. Make sure that screw cannot loosen because if it does and the sail head becomes disengaged from the shackle while the sail is hoisted, you will have to go up that mast to retrieve the shackle and halyard.

The Bosun's Chair

I am interrupting this segment on sail bending to explain how lost halyards 75 feet up in the air are retrieved. The hard way is to shinny up. I have seen this done and I find nothing in this method to recommend. There is a better way. Go up in a *bosun's chair.* But you don't have a bosun's chair. The marina will loan you one. Ask around. Somebody always has a bosun's chair.

Since the halyard is already up there, what do you use in its place to haul up the bosun's chair. The jib halyard. A few turns around a winch and up you go. Be sure you have an experienced hand at the winch.

Now that the halyard and shackle have been retrieved, and attached to the *headboard*, the first *car* or *slide* is slipped on the track. A pull on the halyard will hoist the sail to the next car, and the next and the next until all of them are finally on the track.

There is a little gadget at the bottom of the track, called a *slide stop,* which is turned or adjusted to keep all the cars from sliding down and off the track when the sail is dropped.

The *foot* of the sail, has the same cars attached to that line of grommets. The entire *foot* of the sail, from *clew* to *tack*, is now folded up in your hands until you get to that first car at the clew. After you make sure it is not twisted, you slip it on the *boom* track. Do the same with the next, and the next, and the next until the entire sail foot is on the boom. It is now pulled tight and the end clew *grommet* is secured to the *outhaul slide* with a clew pin. The outhaul slide has a small line attached to it, which runs through a *cheek block.* This is for the purpose of making proper foot adjustments. The foot of the sail on the boom mast must not be too loose or too tight, and the same with the luff of the sail up against the mast. These two tension adjustments are extremely important because they determine how the sail will perform when it fills with air.

Sail Draft

Adjusting the luff and foot of a sail for the best draft is a subject I do not want to get into at this time because of space limitations. This is a complex subject on which many books have been written, and I will write one myself some day if I survive racing and don't lose any more fingers.

For the beginning sailor, it is enough to just learn the fundamentals. Later, if you go into racing, you can then take up the fine nuances of sail handling that help you win races. It's like tennis. First you learn how to hit the ball over the net. Then, if you decide to enter competition and become a seeded player, you learn how to put spin on the ball.

In Class boat racing, everybody starts out equal, but some skippers are always just a little more equal. They have an edge concealed in their heads. They know all the tricks, like the minutiae, the infinite variety of adjustments and trimmings of the sails which will collect that extra ounce of energy from of the wind.

For the average weekend sailor, all this seems like a lot of trivia, much like making mountains out of molehills. And for the Sunday afternoon sailor it *is* "trivia." But, for the competitive racer, it's *winning*.

For this reason I will not go into "trivia" at this time, instead I will save it for another book. I will just say that you put moderate tension on the main halyard or downhaul so that the luff of the sail has no horizontal or vertical wrinkles. You do the same thing at the boom to the foot of the sail, pulling on that short line attached to the outhaul and running it through a cheek block. Remember, not too much tension. You draw just enough to smooth out the vertical wrinkles. Too much tension will only create horizontal wrinkles and distort the sail.

This will get you through a Sunday afternoon of sailing. You won't win any races, but you won't lose any fingers either.

The mizzen is handled in exactly the same way as the main, so I will skip the details.

Jibs and staysails do not run on tracks. The jib is attached to the forward stay with a special types of shackles called *hanks*, which are tied to all the grommets on the forward edge of the jib.

But first the bottom forward corner of the jib, called the *tack* must be secured. Then the hanks are snapped over the stay. The jib halyard is shakled to the *head* of the jib. Then, the jib is hoisted. The final step is shackling the jib *sheets* to the *clew*, which is the after bottom corner of the jib. The main and jib are now ready for sailing.

On many small day sailers, there will not be any tracks or

slide cars on the boom. The boom will be grooved instead to make the sail's *boat ropes*. These are the ropes that are sewn on the outer edge of all sails. You will also find these grooves on the masts of some very small boats.

Gaffs And Other "Oddities"

Gaff sails have become so rare today that you will probably never even see one let alone ever handle one. For this reason I see no great need to go into the complexities of bending on a gaff sail. You would get such a rig from only a custom builder, and even he would question your reasons.

To commission the building of a custom sailboat in the larger sizes today is an enormously expensive project to finance and for a simple pragmatic reason. The builder himself will tell you the reason and that is—every boat must be built with the thought in mind that someday it must be sold, if not by you, then your widow and executors of your estate. It is always a mistake to invest a large amount of money in anything that will be hard to sell. Oddball boats with old-fashioned gaff sails will be hard to sell at a fair market price.

This is the reason why all American sailboats look so much alike with the same Marconi sails and hulls. Buy something different and it will attract attention like all oddities do, like an incredibly expensive replica of a Chinese junk that could only be owned by a very rich man who can afford to indulge himself. But when this man tires of his expensive toy, who will take it off his hands?

If you were to ask any experienced racing yachtsman what was the one factor that contributed the most to winning, he would immediately say "sails." Then he might add "skipper know-how." But he would mention hull design last or maybe not at all.

The building of racing hulls long ago reached the ultimate in design. There are no new places to go, as countless designers of new America's Cup contenders and challengers have found out after spending millions. No matter how they redesign the hull, in the end it is always the sails and the skippers who win, not the hulls.

Sail Care

Your sails are the engines of your boat. Treat them like emeralds if you race and treat them like a woman you love if you don't race. That means you must unbend the sails after every race and store them in sail bags. Working sails, and the ones on bigger boats which are too big to unbend after every use, can be left furled on the boom. But never leave the sail furled still in tension on the boom. Always release the outhaul tension.

Halyard winches on masts cause a lot of damage to sails by pulling them out of shape. New sailors, unfamiliar with sailboat winches, don't realize how much power they have in their hands. This is why sails are usually stretched out of shape in the luff, which is that forward edge of the sail against the mast that takes the strain when the winch handle goes a quarter turn too far.

Cotton sails, which shrink when wet, are especially vulnerable to stretch damage. If you don't slack off on the halyard, and especially the boom outhaul, the sail will get stretched out of shape. You must make these adjustments while you are sailing. Even though it might not be raining, sails get very wet just from spray. This is the big reason why I

Fig. 9-11. Waterfront property is where much industry is located, and so are yacht clubs and marinas. As a result, boats are often the unhappy recipients of many by-products of industry, like cinders, coal dust and chemical residue. Then there's the gull droppings, another by-product. Here is how one yachtsman copes with this problem. He is docked on waterfront property his yacht club leases from a big chemical company, which means nobody dares complain about the crap they get from the smokestacks.

dislike cotton sails. They require a lot of attention *all* the time. Cotton sails must be hosed down when you return to your dock to remove all the salt. Then they must be hoisted again to thoroughly dry out before being stowed in their bags, or left furled on the boom under a canvas cover.

Never hoist a sail to dry if there is a breeze blowing. The constant flapping will damage, and may even break, the threads. Only dry them in this manner when the air is light or the wind comes from a direction that will fill the sail, and not flap it.

Cotton sails left furled on the boom should be protected with a sail cover. Synthetic sails don't really have to be covered, but they should be anyway, just to protect them from gull droppings and the unbelievable amount of dirt that can fall on a boat in just 24 hours (Fig. 9-11).

When putting sail covers on furled cottonsails, run the halyards *outside* the cover or you'll never get a tight fit around the cover's *collar* which goes around the mast (Fig. 9-12). Water will run down the mast and soak the sail. There should be some air openings underneath the cover so that the cotton sail can breathe or it will mildew.

Sails can be washed, but *not* in a washing machine like bedsheets and *not* with detergent. After washing, spread the sail out on your lawn in the sun until it dries.

PRINCIPALS OF SAILING

Sailing is not a science like computing the trajectory of a satellite in space or splitting an atom. Sailing is not a learned skill like golf or tennis. Sailing is an *art*. You either have it or you don't. If you do have it, you win races, and you become a champion like Ted Turner.

You can learn the theory of sailing and become a credibly good sailor, but you cannot learn the *art* of sailing. If theory and practice were all that were needed to sail and win races, I would be a champion. But I'm just another loser, and I've got the scars and missing fingers to prove it. I know everything about sailing except for the art of winning races.

To completely cover everything there is to learn about sailing would take about two books this size. I can only devote one chapter specifically to sailing, which severely limits me to touching briefly on basics and fundamentals. If I survive the

Fig. 9-12. If you put the sail cover over the halyard, you'll have a big leak around the collar and water running down the mast will wet the sails. Note the opening for ventilation.

racing wars and don't lose any more fingers, I will write another book entirely on sailing.

The Wind

You must always know what the wind is doing, and in which direction it is blowing, and you will not learn this by wetting a finger in your mouth and holding it up. I've tried that but it doesn't work for me like it did for Spencer Tracy in an old movie.

There are all sorts of wind indicators available, some even tell you the wind's velocity. You don't really need all that for sailing and the winning skippers don't need it for racing because they can determine wind velocity by how their boat is behaving, or how fast it is moving on a certain point of sail. For example, a skipper knows that on a broad reach in 10 knot winds he will do 4 knots; in 15 knot winds he will do 6 knots, and so on. All these figures are stored away in the memory computer bank that all winning skippers have stored in their heads. That's why they don't need fancy revolving gadgets on their mast heads. All you really need is a simple wind indicator (Fig. 9-13) that works through an entire season without you having to go up the mast in a bosun's chair. I hate the bosun's chair, which is why I am so fuss budgetty about halyards and shackles that can screw up and necessitate a trip up the mast.

This is why I prefer *telltales* to monitor wind direction. These are nothing more then ribbons or threads that are easily attached about six feet up the shrouds. Also, with the current practice of installing the UHF antenna on masts, it can get a little crowded up there on the *masthead.*

There are other ways to determine wind direction. If you keep your boat at a mooring (secured to a permanent cement weight or mushroom anchor), you can tell wind direction by how the boats are resting with their bows all pointing into the wind. In light breezes, ripples on the water's surface move with the wind, as do flags and smoke from passing ships.

POINTS OF SAILING

There are three points of sailing. You are always running, reaching or beating. No matter in what direction the wind blows, one of these three points will enable you to position and trip sails in a manner that moves your vessel on a course you

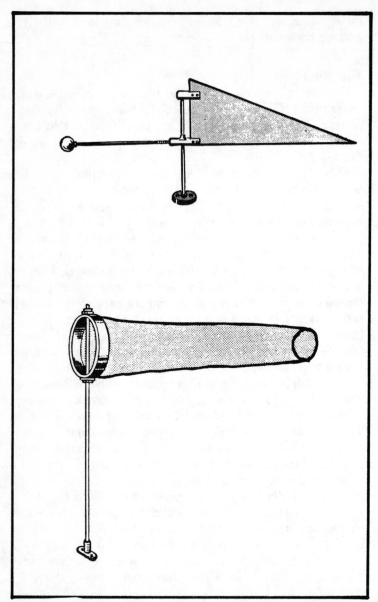

Fig. 9-13. You can spend a lot of money on electronic wind indicators, but they won't work any better than these thin strips of cloth material tied to the rigging or shrouds as high as you can reach (courtesy of Manhattan Marine).

wish to travel. That course is not always a straight life from position A to position B, but it does eventually get you there.

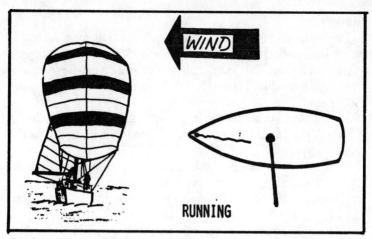

Fig. 9-14. It is not good to let a sail flap uselessly in the wind for long periods, like running down wind for a half hour. This is where a jib furling device, as in Figure 9-10, comes in handy because you can just roll up the jib like a window blind.

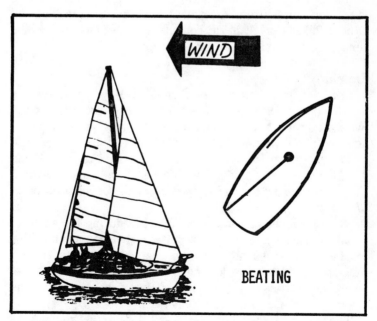

Fig. 9-15. Beating is a very important point of sailing if you plan to race because how close you can, or cannot, trim sail into the wind gives you an edge or a handicap.

Running

I especially like the term *running* because it means exactly what it says. With the wind at your back you are in fact running away from the wind which is chasing you. This is also called *off the wind, before the wind, sailing downwind and sailing free.*

In this point of sailing the jib is useless. It will just flap in the wind (Fig. 9-14) and sometimes, to avoid damaging the sail, it is best to drop the jib.

This is where the spinnaker comes into play to gain speed. Without a spinnaker, and a crew who can handle it easily, you can forget about racing. Downwind you'd fall so far behind they'd be sending search vessels out to look for you. This is why long distance ocean and freshwater racing is so hard on boats and crews. This is brass knuckles competition where everybody has spinnakers available in different sizes for that important downwind run where there is a chance to really fly and beat the competition.

That's what many boats were doing at Fastnet in England, running with small spinnakers at full speed ahead. Engines were torn loose from their beds and crews were bounced around like gravel in a cement mixer—cracking skulls, smashing ribs and breaking assorted bones.

Beating

Beating is just the opposite of running. However, there is a small difference. Although you can run directly *before* the wind, you cannot run directly *into* the wind (Fig. 9-15). Try it and you'll find yourself hove to with sails flapping in the wind.

To make progress against the wind, you have to bear off and take the wind at an angle. This is called *tacking* into the wind. It is also referred to as *close hauled, sailing to windward* or *on the wind.*

The closer you can sail to the wind (reducing the angle of wind on the sails), the better because the boats that can do this reach the finish sooner then the boats that take the longer route with tacks at a wider angle. It's just like in a horse race, every jockey tries to get his horse on the rail because that's the shortest distance to the finish line.

The cutter with a genoa up can sail close to the wind and on the windward leg of the race cannot be beaten (except by another cutter with a genoa and a smarter skipper).

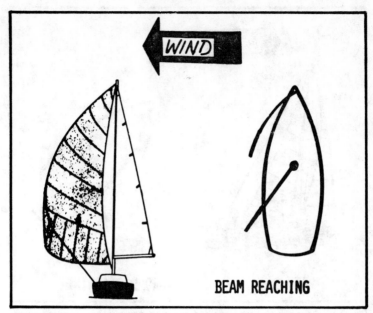

Fig. 9-16. Beam reaching, with regular running sails, is the fastest point of sailing because the jib is at its best. In running, the jib is useless and is either furled or rolled up on the forestay.

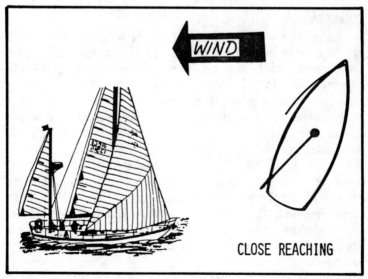

Fig. 9-17. The close reach in strong winds is where you can get your butt wet because heel is considerable, even with the board down, and a sudden strong puff of wind can flip you over if you're slow slacking off on the main sheet.

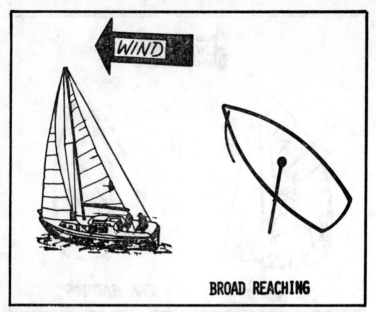

Fig. 9-18. On a broad reach your boom will be way out there and unless you are careful it will dip in the water if you heel excessively. This is a fast point of sailing with a genoa up. If you race, this is where the club champion and contenders kick your teeth out.

Beam Reach

The *beam reach* (Fig. 9-16) is sailing with the wind right smack on your side. If you bear off a little and take the wind a little forward of the beam, you are *close reaching* (Fig. 9-17) If you take the wind aft of the beam, or on the quarter, you are *broad reaching* (Fig. 9-18). Ketches and schooners sail very well in beam reaches. But in racing you must sail well on *all* points, and you must be able to use a spinnaker, which the ketch and schooner cannot do as well as sloops and cutters.

Using regular sails, reaching is the fastest point of sailing. This may come as a surprise because it would seem that running would be the fastest. Look at Fig. 9-14 again. Note how, in running, only the mainsail is pushing the boat. The jib is in the *wind shadow* of the mainsail. In running, with working sail up, you get nothing from the jib. But in reaching the jib is very effective.

In racing you don't use normal working sails. And spinnakers, which are not part of a boats's normal complement of sail, change everything downwind. That is why the spinnaker is so important in racing.

On a broad reach, the main sheet (line that controls the boom) is trimmed so that the mainsail is as far out over the water as it will ever go. The jib sheet is also trimmed in the same manner. If your sails are trimmed this way, your boat will really move. In fact, your boat may move so fast that you may have to trim in a little closer because of something called *apparent wind.*

Apparent Wind

There are always two wind forces acting on your sails, the true wind and the apparent wind. If your boat is moving at a speed of 5 knots and the true wind is 10 knots, then the apparent wind will be closer to 13 knots. This is due to boat movement. True wind is 10 knots only if you are motionless in the water, which you are not since you are moving at a speed of 5 knots. This difference must be allowed for when trimming sails.

The aerodynamics involved here is very technical and complicated and of little interest to Sunday sailors. But to racing skippers it is a subject of intense interest and much study with many books avaialble on the subject. To be a winning skipper you must be familiar with the aerodynamics of sail. You must know about many things, like the jib slot *venturi effect* of that low pressure area on the lee side of a sail. You must learn many "Dirty Tricks," like how to use *backwind* as a tactic to douse your competitors with turbulent air. In alley fighting, this would be equivalent to kneeing in the groin, and racing is a form of alley fighting. I have the scars to prove it.

On a beam reach, the sails are trimmed about half way out. On a close reach, the boom and jib are getting in quite close.

Turning

You don't turn a sailboat. You *tack* or you *jibe* or you *come about.* As mentioned previously, you cannot sail directly *into* the wind. You zig zag into the wind at an angle of about 45 degrees first broad on the port bow, then broad on the starboard bow. This is called tacking.

Some boats can sail closer then 45 degrees into the wind. That is a much desired trait. Some boats sail more then 45 degrees. That is NOT a desired trait in racing. On a Sunday afternoon sail, you won't even notice.

When you do all the above things running *WITH* the wind, it is called *jibing.*

SAILING FOR THE FIRST TIME

If your boat is in the water, the time has come to *sail.*

A nice way to start is with the wind on your starboard beam. Hold the mainsheet in your right hand, and the tiller in your left. Don't worry about the jib. Your crew always handles the jib. Let the boom swing way out until the sail flaps, then pull on the mainsheet, slowly bring the boom back towards you. Watch the sail carefully. You must learn to *see* the wind. Note how the downward edge of the sail fills first, gradually working out to the luff. The sail fills out smoothly and you are *moving* in the water and you hear it slapping against the hull. It's a beautiful sound that first time you hear it.

Practice, experiment, and play around with the sheet. Let it go, pull it back, and note how your boat slows down, or picks up speed as you trim the sail.

At this point in your education, it is important that you hold the mainsheet in your hand all the time. There are reasons for this. First, you are getting the *feel* of the rudder and sails as you trim; second, you have instant response in case something goes wrong.

What can go wrong?

With a inexperienced sailor at the tiller, if you are hard heeled in a small centerboard, you might capsize if hit by a sudden wind gust. With the mainsheet constantly in your hand, you can respond more quickly. Let the sheet go and the boom will swing out. The sail will flap and you will regain stability. No harm is done. You just start over again.

Later, when you gain experience, the mainsheet can be held in a cam action jam cleat. If holding the sheet becomes tiring, and it will, you can let the jam cleat take the strain while you just hold the loose end.

The Tiller

On sailboats, the rudder does more then just steer, it holds sails at the proper angle to take the wind. Unless this position to the wind is reached and held, you cannot sail; you just lay dead in the water with sails flapping.

You never sail with your rudder dead ahead as you do when moving under auxiliary power. The rudder is always being held off to port or starboard to keep the sails in a certain position in relation to the wind. This creates pressure on the rudder, and strain on the tiller, which is why pedestal wheel steerers are becoming so popular. It can be very tiring holding that tiller for long periods.

But it is still better, when possible, to learn sailing with a tiller in your hand. It's more work, but you learn the basics faster. Hand tillers were common on boats up to 35-feet. Now everybody wants those big metal wheels so they're currently putting them on boats under 30 feet.

The wheel steerer is a great convenience that you will appreciate later, but it gives you no "feel" and no communication with your boat. It's too much like steering an automobile—in fact, it IS like steering an automobile. Turn the wheel to port and that's where you go. With a tiller, it's just the opposite. Pull the tiller to port and your bow swings to starboard.

You will have no response to the tiller until you are *moving*. There must be water pressure on the rudder. Dead in the water means exactly that. To have control of your boat you must never stop moving.

In Stays

There will be many times, while learning to sail, that you will encounter a situation known as *in stays* or *in irons*. This frustrating condition develops when you loose steerageway and are dead in the water. It always happens when tacking or coming about to a new point of sailing. If you do not have sufficient way when making your move, or you do it too quickly, you will come to a dead stop, your sails will start to flap, and you will drift backwards helplessly waiting for your sails to fill. Often when they do fill, you will be right back on the same tack again.

You can be forgiven for this while learning, but it will be downright embarrassing later. You can avoid this by waiting for the right moment to come about. This moment is when you are trimmed for all the speed you can get. Be careful not to put your helm down too hard and too quickly. When you do, the rudder acts just like a brake and brings you to a stop.

When you find yourself in this awkward position, and you will, you can easily recover in one of the following ways: First, try backing your jib in the direction you wish to go, port or starboard, so that it acts like a weathervane. It will swing your bow in either direction. If you have no jib, you can accomplish the same thing by pushing the boom to windward. If your mainsail is pushed to port, and your rudder is to port, your stern will also move to port. You can also try setting your rudder hard to port, then wait. With your sails luffing, you will start drifting backwards, gaining steerageway. The rudder will now swing your stern to port.

Starboard And Port Tacks

New sailors are often confused by the terms "starboard tack" and "port tack." Their confusion is *direction*. When a boat is on a port tack, they assume it is moving left or to port. Not always, it depends on the wind.

For example, when sails are trimmed over the port side and the boat is moving to port, if the wind is blowing across the starboard side of the boat, then the boat is on a starboard tack even though it is actually moving left, or to port.

However, if sails are trimmed over the starboard side and the boat is moving to port, if the wind is blowing across the port side, the boat is on a port tack and it is also moving to port.

If you are still confused, just remember this: if wind is across the starboard side of the boat, you are on a starboard tack; if wind is on the port side, you are on a port tack *regardless* of which direction you are moving.

Tacking And Crew Training

Tacking is a basic and important maneuver. Until you learn to do this smoothly, and in harmony with your crew on all points of sailing, you are not a qualified Sunday afternoon sailor.

Tacking is part of a team play with the helmsman calling the signals. The skipper handles the helm and mainsail, while the crew (your family) handles the jib and fore staysail. In family boating, it is often best if the First Mate (the wife) handles the tiller, and the skipper (the husband) handles the jib and staysail.

In big boat racing, sail handling on tacks is a rehearsed precision. If it wasn't, you'd have the jib and staysail hands running into each other. With spinnakers, you could end up with something that looks like a Chinese fire drill. On really big racing hulls, like the America's Cup contenders, there is an expert for each sail and additional hands to relieve them.

The helmsman decides when it is time to tack and he always alerts the crew with: *"stand by to come about."* The crew must be given time to get ready, take their stations, get the sheets unbelayed and ready in their hands.

Just before making his move, the helmsman gives them another alert with: *"ready about."* He follows this with, *"hard-a-lee"* and then starts pushing the helm slowly leeward or into the wind.

As the boat heads into the wind, the crew slacks off on the jib and staysail sheets, and moves to the other side of the boat. There must be order in doing this. The jib goes first, and then the staysail follows. The crew should have completed this maneuver while the mainsail is still luffing into the wind. They should be in a crouched position to avoid getting hit when the boom swings over. This is why you and your crew should always be wearing some form of flotation device, in case somebody does get knocked overboard.

Reading stuff like this will never make you a sailor. You have to keep *practicing* these maneuvers over and over.

Jibing Downwind

Jibing is tacking as you run with the wind. It is best not to make your first attempt at tacking downwind when there is fresh breezes and high following seas. Pick a day when there is less wind.

You almost certainly will be warned about this back at the club and in small centerboards. Jibing in following seas can be dangerous because your boat is always on the verge of jibing by itself. There is no danger when you jibe intentionally and are prepared. The danger is when it happens accidently and you are *not* prepared and the boom swings unexpectedly and hits somebody in the head and knocks them overboard.

The wind does not blow in a perfectly straight direction like the airflow from an electric fan. The wind is constantly shifting and swirling. It will come at you from many angles and sometimes it hits you in gusts. If it catches you unexpectedly at the wrong time with a big rolling sea under your stern, it can jibe you into yawing and a broach. It can tangle your mainsheet around the tiller or your leg.

This is why in small centerboards it is best and safest to sail downwind in a slight zig zag course, with the wind on the quarter and the centerboard all the way down. Racing sailors don't like to do this because the board creates a drag, and reduces speed. But racing sailors have more experience running with the board up and can cope with it, well, most of the time. But sometimes even they get into trouble.

As far as sail handling goes, jibing is no different then tacking, you and your crew do the same things. The helmsman alerts the crew with "stand by to jibe." He waits for the crew to uncleat the jib and staysail sheets on the one side, and then cleat them on the other side. Then the helmsman shouts "jibe ho," and everybody ducks as the boom swings over, the crew trims the jib and staysail sheets, while the helmsman trims the mainsheet.

In jibing, the boom swings over faster and harder, so the helmsman must be prepared for this by having the sheet turned once around a cleat so it doesn't run through his hand too fast or get away from him.

Later, when you gain experience, you will learn to recognize certain signs that warn you of an approaching jibe. The helmsman must be especially alert when sailing downwind. He must be constantly watching for these warning signs, such as when the mainsail starts to fill on the fore side. When the helmsman sees this, he must immediately head more into the wind to fill the sail on the proper side.

Another warning sign: when the boat is approaching a jibe situation, the jib will always start to swing first. The helmsman, if he sees this, still has time to correct the situation with the tiller, by heading more into the wind.

The Kicking Strap

When the mainsheet is not properly shortened after a jibe, the boom will sometimes jump up or *goosewing*. This can be prevented with the *kicking strap,* which is a tackle attached to the boom up close to the mast. It is also called a *preventer*. This is because it holds the mast down, and prevents goosenecking.

The Spinnaker

The modern spinnaker is a powerful driving force on downwind sailing and without it you cannot even begin to think of racing in today's murderous competition. But the spinnaker is not new. It was first used over a hundred years ago on a British yacht named the *Sphinx* and was originally called the "Sphinxer."

Spinnakers are not easy to set and handle, and for that reason they are not for the beginning sailor; at least not until he has mastered the fundamentals of running, reaching, beating and jibing.

Although primarily used on downwind sailing, experienced sailors also use the spinnaker on other points of sailing. Since this book is not intended as a complete course on sailing, but merely to acquaint the reader with the basics, I will not go into detail on the spinnakers. If sailing really interests you, your appetite will be whetted and you will probably seek more information in books devoted entirely to sailing. If you are interested in racing, there are even books devoted entirely to racing.

Reefing, Shortening Sail

Wind and sea conditions determine how much sail you can safely carry. Except for hurricanes, there are no sea conditions in which you cannot keep some sail up, even if it is just a storm trysail, a spitfire or a reefed jib.

In the Fastnet Cup Race, winds reached 70 knots, and yet most of the boats kept right on racing under reduced sail; a few even had spinnakers outs. But the non-racing and prudent sailor takes no such chances, he reduces sail or he reefs when his boat heels excessively, buries her lee rail in the sea and solid water starts coming aboard.

Reducing sail is easy on some boats, like the cutter, which is my favorite rig. There's more to it then just eliminating one or two sails on a ketch or yawl. You must maintain helm and sail balance or you will heel excessively and find it hard to steer.

A cutter can sail with just the fore staysail alone. A ketch or yawl will sail with the main alone, or just the mizzen and the jib. A sloop can carry the jib, but you still must reef the main.

Reefing is reducing sail area by one of two methods; first, by rolling the sail up on the boom like a window shade, or secondly, by dropping the sail to a reef point, and then folding the excess foot of the sail into a neat roll over the boom where it is tied to the boom with reef points.

SAILING IN HEAVY WEATHER

There are special skills required for sailing in heavy weather and I know only one way to acquire those skills—*by sailing in heavy weather.*

The most important skill is knowing how to keep your boat *moving* at all times, which is not as easy as it seems. You must move so fast that your boat will be overburdened, hammer into head seas, bury her bow, and then *poop* in following seas with water over her stern.

On the other hand, if the boat moves too slow, she could be stalled by a big sea, become dead in the water *(in irons)* without steerageway and be at the mercy of the next big wave.

Sailboats do not roll in the troughs and the best place to be when beam reaching is right in those big valleys. The worst place to be is on a broad reach where following seas can hit you on the quarter and cause your boat to yaw and broach.

This means that you must often sail on a course that is not exactly to your liking, but is easier for sailing. If a certain point of sailing is hard on your boat and hard on you and your family, try something else. After all, sailing has never been considered as the shortest distance between two points, and Christopher Columbus, who thought he was sailing for Asia, saw his first landfall in the Bahamas, many thousands of miles short of where he wanted to go.

CAPSIZING

The small centerboard, on which most sailors learn the basics, is not designed for rough water sailing in open waters. It is strictly a Sunday afternoon fun boat for sailing in sheltered waters. Even though most of these boats have some form of built-in flotation for reserve buoyancy and are unsinkable, getting capsized is not one of the experiences a family that boats together wants to remember.

Sailboats capsize every day, and the accelleration rate continues to climb as more and more powerboaters take up sail, and begin learning the basics in small centerboards. Although capsizing is an ever present threat, it is not all that bad. It is bad only if the water is cold. And there is no danger if the sailor heeds that cardinal Law of Sunday sailing and racing—*always stay with the boat!*

There is almost a standard routine for handling a capsize where the boat is laying on its side with sails in the water.

— Leave the sails furled, they are needed for balancing when you climb back aboard.

— The biggest or heaviest man climbs up on the centerboard, the other man just hangs on.

— The man on the centerboard reaches over the side for the jib sheet, pulls on it until the knot stops at the fairlead.

— Then, holding on the jib sheet, he leans way back standing on the end of the centerboard and the boat will come right up.

— The man in the water climbs on the boat over her stern, uncleats all the sheets, and starts bailing out the water. Then he helps the other man in over the stern and they finish bailing and sorting out the gear. Later they resume sailing to dry out.

Not all boats are this easy to right. Some have too much built-in flotation while others have too little. Too much reserve buoyancy is bad, and could even be dangerous. This could make the capsized boat float too high in the water, causing the mast and sails to submerge until the boat would be floating upside down. In this position there is nothing for the crew in the water to hang onto, and it is extremely difficult for them to climb up on the smooth hull bottom, although it can be done by way of the rudder.

Boats with too little flotation sink with only the bow still above water. This type cannot be righted, but at least the crew has something to hang onto until help arrives.

Problems In Capsizing

A capsized boat, in high winds with half its hull sticking out of the water, gives the crew little time to get it righted properly on the windward side because the wind blows the hull around until the crew has to work from the lee side, which is *not* the proper position. When they finally do get the boat righted, the wind may hit the sail and capsize the boat again right on top of them. This could be a comedy of errors with the crew repeating this stunt all afternoon until they get very cold and tired (Fig. 9-19).

The proper way to handle this situation is for both men to stand on the centerboard, raising only the top of the sail out of the water just far enough so that the wind catches it. This will swing the sail around until it is in the lee. This will allow the crew to raise the boat with the wind at their backs so that it can't fall down on top of them.

A boat upside down in the water can be righted quite easily by two men. One man climbs up on the hull bottom with help of the rudder. The other man reaches around until he finds the jib sheet, which he hands to the man on the hull bottom. Then he swims around to the other side of the boat where both men put their weight on the line to bring the sail up to the surface.

Fig. 9-19. Righting a capsized boat in high winds often develops into a comedy of errors. When the boat is finally righted, it has swung around into the wind, which hits the sail and flips the boat right back on top of the two sailors in the water.

While one man holds the boat in this position, the other swims around to the opposite side again to push down the centerboard which has dropped into the trunk while the hull was upside down. The boat can now be righted in the usual way.

Sometimes with an upside down hull, the masthead will get stuck in the mud. It can still be righted, but first it will take the help of a powerboat.

Capsizing And Proper Clothes

How you dress for sailing can sometimes be a matter of life or death if you ever capsize.

Much boat racing is done at times of the year when the water is very cold, like the Frostbite Races in April and late October when frost is on the pumpkin. Up in the Great Lakes these little capsizable centerboarders are out on the water racing just days after the last ice left, and believe me, that water is cold!

If you go sailing in April on the Great Lakes, you should always dress with the thought in mind that you might wind up in the water. The clothes you wear could save your life.

Capsizing And Survival In Cold Water

When body temperature drops to subnormal limits, a condition called hypothermia results, which can kills in a very short time. When a body is immersed in cold water, the outer skin and tissues cool very fast. However, it takes longer, 10 to 15 minutes, before the temperature of the heart and brain begin to drop. When vital organ temperature (the core) reaches 90 degrees, unconsciousness may occur (Fig 9-20). When it reaches 85 degrees, the heart usually fails. However, a person in cold water (50 degrees or less) will usually drown before there is heart failure, sometimes even before there is loss of arm and leg movement and unconsciousness.

Temperature of the water itself is only one factor in survival. Whether you stay alive in cold water depends on many things, such as, big people cool slower then small people, fat people cool slower then thin people and children cool faster then adults.

Anything that helps you retain body heat increases your chances of surviving, which is why the clothes you wear is so important. Many sailors mistakenly assume that heavy clothing would impede their movements in the water and hasten drowning.

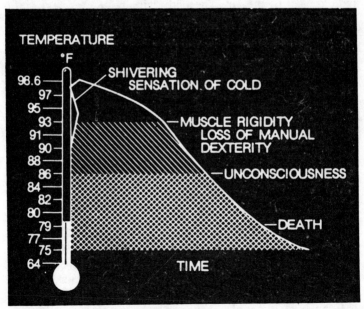

Fig. 9-20. Cold water will cause the body temperature to drop after a period of time causing various stages of hypothermia (courtesy of the U.S. Coast Guard).

On the contrary, movement in the water is what you definitely must *avoid* because it only hastens body heat loss. Since you will be, or should be, wearing a proper personal flotation device, there will be no need for you to tread water, which wastes body heat. Also, don't swim because this violates the Golden Rule of sailboat racing—*staying with the boat!*

Swimming and treading water cause the body to lose heat 34% faster then when you remain motionless.

Heavy clothing and head wear reduces heat dissipation from your body to the water. Water is the most efficient of heat dissipators, conducting heat many times faster then air. In an automobile cooling system, the water must circulate to remove heat. Wearing clothes next to the body keeps new water from circulating against the body to remove heat. This is what enables scuba divers, wearing wet suits, to work under the ice in winter.

You can buy special sailing wet suits for cold weather racing which do the same thing.

Warm head covering is also very important because we lose 50% of our body heat through our heads when it is uncovered and exposed to the air. The body will cool 82% faster if the head is submerged as in the *drownproof technique,* which is recommended for survival in the water without a personal flotation device. The so-called "drownproof technique", where the head is submerged between breaths, is all right for warm tropical waters but it simply will not work in cold water.

Recent research into hypothermia, supported by the U.S. Coast Guard, shows that there are certain critical areas of the body which are more susceptible to heat loss in cold water. They are the head, sides of the chest, neck and groin. Out of this research has come a new personal flotation device that is patented and marketed under the trade name of *UVic Thermofloat Jacket.* This device is essentially a miniature "wet suit" and tests have shown that it doubles survival time (Table 9-1)

There are also some things you can do to increase your chances of survival. Since most One Design racing centerboards are capable of remaining afloat when capsized, and since you will wisely remain with the boat, the more of your body you can get out of the water, the less heat you will lose.

If the boat is totally swamped with nothing much above water for ;you to climb onto, then you can assume the "fetal position, also called *HELP* (Fig. 9-21), the letters coming from

Table 9-1. Predicted Survival Time In 50°F Water (Courtesy of U.S. Coast Guard).

NO FLOTATION	Survival Time (Hours)
Drownproofing	1.5
Treading Water	2.0
WITH FLOTATION	
Swimming	2.0
Holding-still	2.7
H.E.L.P.	4.0
Huddle	4.0
UVic Thermofloat	9.5

*H*eat *E*scape *L*essening *P*osture. If there are several people in the water (Fig. 9-22), huddling together accomplishes the same thing.

If there is no help available within sight, what are your chances if you swim for shore?

Some swimmers have been avle to swim 8/10ths of a mile in 50 degree water before being overcome by hypothermia. There are other equally good swimmers who couldn't swim 100 yards. Remember, body weight and fat have much to do with how far you can swim before being overcome.

Distances are very deceptive on water. A shoreline may seem only a 100 yards away when it may actually be a mile. The general is: *do not swim* unless there is absolutely no chance of rescue and you are certain of the distance. If you do swim, wear a PFD.

And remember, a capsized boat is easier to sight in the water then a lone person.

FIRST AID FOR VICTIMS

When 1400 passengers of the *Titanic* were able to leave the sinking ship, some into the freezing waters wearing life-jackets, help didn't arrive until two hours later, and most of the people were dead and later listed as having drowned. But today it is believed that they died of hypothermia.

Many hypothermia victims are pulled out of the water alive, only to die later because of incorrect handling and proper treatment. There is a condition in hypothermia known as *After Drop*, which refers to the core temperature of the vital organs continuing to drop even after the victim is out of the water and in a warm room. After Drop occurs when cold stagnant blood

Fig. 9-21. The Heat Escape Lessening Posture can be used as a last resort to combat hypothermia (courtesy of the U.S. Coast Guard).

from the victim's extremities is allowed to return to the core of the body, which lowers the temperature there to a level that will not sustain life.

Mild cases of hypothermia are easily recognized. The victim will be hyperventilating and shivering, which is the body's way of increasing heat production. But advance stages of hypothermia are often mistakenly considered as dead. Never give up on a hypothermic. Shivering will cease. The victim then becomes semi-conscious, the skin turns blue, the pupils dilate, the muscles become stiff and the heart beat is irregular.

Do not handle unnecessarily or jostle a hypothermic in advance stages because the heart is in a critical and sensitive condition. After a sudden jolt, it could stop beating. The vicitm must be handled gently, and not allowed to walk.

Keep the victim face up on a flat hard surface. This will facilitate the administration of cardio-pulmonary resuscitation if it becomes necessary.

If the victim appears dead, mouth-to-mouth resuscitation should be administered. Heart massage can also be used if a doctor is present. If not, external heart massage can be administered.

360

The victim's wet clothing must be removed immediately, but do it very gently. Apply heat to the central core of the body in whatever form available, such as with an electric blanket, hot water bottles or towels soaked in hot water. The critical areas that must be warmed as quickly as possible are the victim's head, neck, chest sides and groin area. So vitally important is this that no desperate measure that might save the victim's life should be overlooked for reasons of modesty, such as two people removing all of their clothing and using their bodies to warm the victim's body. If the victim is aboard a rescue vessel without other alternatives to produce lifesaving heat, the do what must be done. Only *heat* will save the victim's life. No one will complain later about *how* this heat was produced.

Don't waste time warming extremities, like hands and feet. If they are warmed, it only increases circulation of cold blood back to the core.

Don't give the victim anything to drink, especially alcohol, which dilates the blood vessels and speeds circulation of cold blood from the extremities.

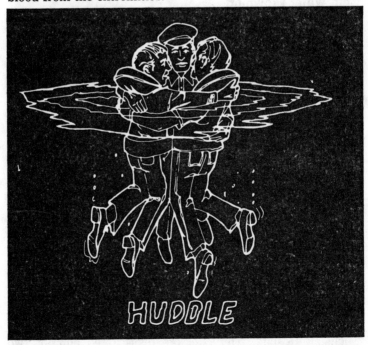

Fig. 9-22. When there are several people in the water, huddling can preserve precious body heat (courtesy of the U.S. Coast Guard).

Don't rub cold areas of the body.

Don't wrap the victim in a blanket, unless it is an electrically heated blanket, or unless it is to protect the victim from further heat loss.

Don't put an unconscious victim in a bathtub.

In mild cases of hypothermia, shelter and dry clothing may be all that is necessary.

How To Avoid Hypothermia

There is only one sure way of avoiding hypothermia, without giving up small boat sailing and racing—move to Florida, Southern California or the Gulf region of the United States.

If this is impossible for you to do, and you still don't want to give up sailing, then just shorten your season and confine your sailing activities to July and August. Or, better still, buy a bigger boat with a deep ballasted keel and when sailing during the cold months, always wear a safety harness like single-handers do on long ocean passages.

Cold Water Drowning

Not all sailors and Sunday boatmen pulled out of cold waters are hypothermia victims. Some are drowning victims. Every year approximately 8,000 people drown, making it the third leading cause of accidental death in the United States, according to the National Safety Council. This statistic is even more tragic because recent medical research has shown that many drowning victims, who in the past had been considered beyond help, could have been saved, in spite of long submergence and the absence of any life signs.

It was once believed that irreversible brain damage would occur to anyone deprived of oxygen for over four minutes. This belief, however, has been medically disproved many times. Only recently an 18-year-old Jackson, Michigan, college student skidded off the road and plunged into an ice-covered pond, with the car rolling over and eliminating all of the air bubbles. Rescuers pulled him out of the car 38 minutes later. He was declared deat at the scene.

While being loaded into an ambulance, the "dead" youth was heard to gasp. Ambulance paramedics immediately began revival efforts while he was being rushed to the University of Michigan Hospital. Here doctors resuscitated him for two hours. After 13 more hours of respiratory support, the young man woke up and immediately recognized his mother. In later months he made A-grades in college.

There have been many similar cases where "drowning" victims have been revived after being submerged in cold water (below 70 degrees) for up to an hour, and in one recorded case, even longer.

Why Drowning Victims Survive

How is it possible to survive after having drowned?

First, the term "drowned" is both misleading and premature

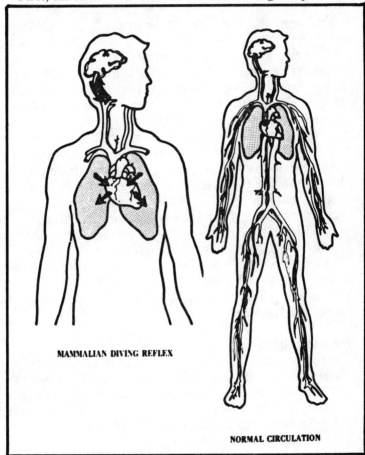

MAMMALIAN DIVING REFLEX

NORMAL CIRCULATION

Fig. 9-23. This is the reason why a drowning victim should never be considered dead, especially in cold waters. They are still getting oxygen to the heart, lungs and brain from residual oxygen in the body and bloodstream. In a state of suspended animation, which the drowning victim is in, the three vital organs can survive on little oxygen (courtesy of the U.S. Coast Guard).

because it presumes death. Just because a person has been submerged until they inhale water and lose consciousness for over four minutes does not mean that they are "dead." A better word then dead might be *suspended*, which more accurately describes what happens to vital life forces due to a phenomenon known as the *Diving Reflex.*

It is now known that sudden face contact with cold water touches off what scientists call the *mammalian diving reflex* (Fig. 9-23), which is a complex series of body responses that shut off blood and circulation to all parts of the body except heart, lungs and brain. The little oxygen left in the blood goes to the brain, and the cooled brain in this suspended state, requires much less oxygen then normal.

Although there is still much to be learned about the mammalian diving reflex, scientists believe that mammals like whales, porpoises and seals survive for long periods submerged though a similar mechanism.

Anyone involved very long in boating is inevitably going to find himself involved someday in a "drowning." The mathematical laws of probability just about guarantee this. With all the boats and people currently on the water, and with all the swim platforms and other gear attached to the sterns that make swimming so much easier anchored offshore in deep water (Fig. 9-24), how can you avoid getting involved? I have been involved six times without even trying.

Children and young people are the most frequent drowning victims. The young are also most likely to be saved by resuscitation because the Diving Reflex response is more pronounced in the young.

Resuscitation

Resuscitation is a blanket term covering all methods of restoring life to those who appear to be dead. Among these methods is artificial respiration, external heart massage, mouth-to-mouth breathing and mouth-to-nose breathing (Fig. 9-25). These methods are also referred to as "CPR", which is cardio-pulmonary resuscitation.

What To Do

All drowning victims *appear* dead. Their skin is blue, and they are cold to the touch. There is no heart beat and no breathing. The eyes are fixed and pupils are dilated. There is

Fig. 9-24. With more and more Americans taking to the water every year, and with powerboaters now doing less cruising and more anchoring offshore in deep waters where they swim and play, there inevitably is going to be more drownings.

not the slightest sign of life, bur *never* give up. If the water is cold (70°F or colder) and the victim is young, there is a good chance of reviving the person.

Mouth-To-Mouth Breathing

Follow these steps when using mouth-to-mouth resuscitation:

● With a finger, remove anything in the mouth, like chewing gum, dentures or seaweed (Fig. 9-26). Start mouth-to-mouth breathing. This is always done first. Don't worry about the water in the lungs because the body will quickly absorb it.

● Place the victim on back, and kneel beside shoulder.

● Place one hand under the victim's neck, other hand on forehead so forefinger can close the nose.

● Lift gently with hand under neck while pushing down with hand on forehead. This will extend neck and open air passages wider.

● Start off by giving the victim four quick breaths without interruption, then take a deep breath, place your mouth tightly *over* the victim's mouth and blow.

● Watch for chest rising. When it does, remove your mouth and allow the air to expire naturally from the victim's chest.

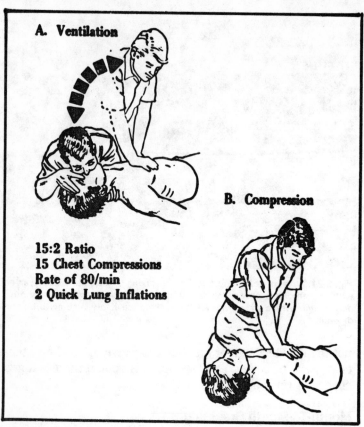

A. Ventilation

B. Compression

15:2 Ratio
15 Chest Compressions
Rate of 80/min
2 Quick Lung Inflations

Fig.9-25. Cardio-pulmonary resuscitation, also called CPR, is a combination of ventilation, forcing air into the victim's lungs by way of mouth-to-mouth blowing, and heart massge by compression as shown (courtesy of the U.S. Coast Guard).

● Repeat this once every five seconds (12 times a minute) for adults, once every three seconds (18 times a minute) for children.

✔ If the chest does not rise when you blow, do the following:

— Be sure there is an airtight seal between your mouth and the victim's, be sure nose is closed with your fingers.

— Check for possible air passage obstruction like vomit or bloodclots. Remove anything in mouth with finger.

— Straddle victim's pelvis, placing one hand over the other, and thrust forcefully into upper abdomen. This compresses lungs and expels any air in lungs. Also, any foreign object pre-

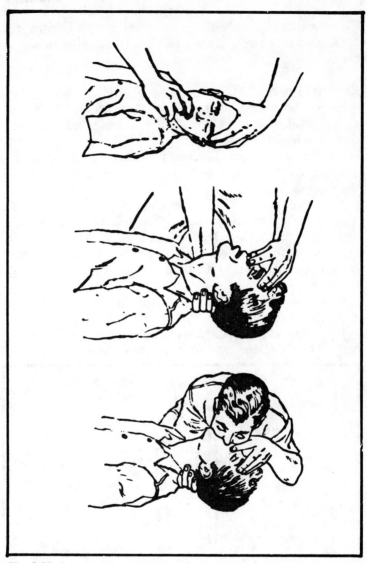

Fig. 9-26. In mouth-to-mouth resuscitation, remove any obstacles in the mouth, place victim on his back and kneel beside his shoulder, and then gently lift the back of the neck and begin resuscitation.

sent will pop right out like a cork from a bottle. If victim vomits, mouth should be cleaned out by turning head to one side, wiping out mouth with finger or cloth.

● With Children, a lesser amount of air is needed. With infants, it is sometimes easier to place your mouth over both the mouth and nose at the same time. Mouth-to-nose breathing is sometimes easier and less apt to leak. Use whichever works best.

External Heart Massage

In most cases, mouth-to-mouth breathing will be sufficient to cause resumption of heartbeat. If it doesn't, external hear massage should be considered.

Check first for pulse. The best pulse to check is the carotid artery in the neck lying close to the surface on either side of the Adam's Apple.

Also, check the pupils. They are a doctor's first check for life signs. Even though unconscious, the pupils react to light. On death, they do not react. If the pupils are dilated (large) and do not constrict (get smaller) when light strikes them, there is no blood to the brain. It is then time for the heart massage (Fig. 9-27).

● Victim must be on a firm surface, like the ground.

● Locate the lower end of the breastbone (Fig. 9-28).

● Measure up two fingers from the xiphoid process and place the heel of one hand over the breastbone *above* the two

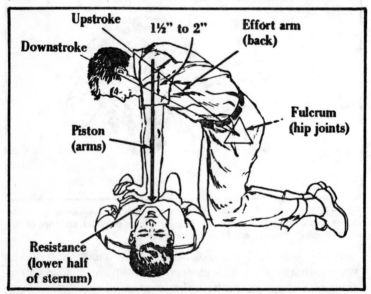

Fig. 9-27. In the external heart massage, bring your shoulders directly over victim's breastbone, keep arms straight and exert pressure downward on the lower breastbone.

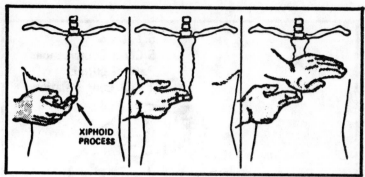

Fig. 9-28. In the external heart massage, it is very important to locate the victim's breastbone so that the technique can be carried out correctly.

fingers, place the other hand over the first hand. Do *NOT* cover the xiphoid process area with your hand. Heel of hand must be two fingers *above* the area.

● Bring shoulders directly over victim's breastbone, keep arms straight, and exert pressure downward on the lower breastbone. Release pressure immediately. Pressure and release must be of equal duration. Do not remove hands from victim's chest when pressure is released. Be sure to release pressure completely so breastbone returns to normal resting position between compressions.

Vital Tips:

The breastbone should be compressed about 2 inches for adults.

For small children only one hand is used.

For infants only the tips of two fingers are needed.

In small children and infants the heart is higher in the chest and external pressure should be applied slightly over the mid-breastbone area.

The compressions should be in a smooth rhythmatic fashion and repeated 60-80 times for adults (about one per second), and 80-100 times per minute (slightly faster then one per second) for children.

"CPR" By One Rescuer

If only one rescuer is present, both heart massage and ventilation can be accomplished in an alternating ratio of 15:2, which is 15 chest compressions to 2 quick lung inflations.

"CPR" By Two Rescuers

With two rescuers working together (Fig. 9-29), the ratio is

Fig. 9-29. With two people administering CPR, the correct ratio is five chest compressions at a rate of one per second to one full lung inflation.

5:1, which is five chest compressions at a rate of one per second to one full lung inflation.

During all this ventilation, the victim's stomach may become distended with air, which can interfere with lung inflation. This air can be expelled by applying pressure over the stomach with the heel of your hand. This will get rid of the air, but it may also regurgitate some stomach contents, which will have to be removed from victim's mouth.

Once you start "CPR", you cannot stop until breathing and heartbeat is restored, or the victim is turned over to a doctor or ambulance paramedic team. Under no circumstances should you stop what you are doing to save a life for more then a five second period. You are committed. You are *involved!*

Chapter 10
Anchoring And
Ground Tackle

A funny thing happened recently when America's newest attack submarine dropped its anchor outside New London harbor one night. They lost it!

The sleek 360-foot USS Philadelphia had completed its second sea trial and was returning to the navy's submarine base, but because the Thames River was foggy, it was decided that she should anchor for the night.

The anchor was dropped, and its long chain followed it to the bottom of the Long Island Sound. The sub spent the night circling in the sound (Fig. 10-1).

No harm done. The builder would replace the anchor and chain, write off the $50,000 cost as a tax loss, or make it up on the next sub they built for the navy.

If you or I did that, the Internal Revenue Service would disallow the deduction because only taxpayer losses due to accidents, thefts or acts of God are allowed. No losses due to stupidity can be deducted.

That makes me stupid. I lost an anchor the same way once a long time ago before I knew the difference between catenary and scope distance, and before I learned that a thimble was not something sailors used on a finger when sewing torn canvas.

371

Fig. 10-1. Only lubbers and dump stinkpotters are supposed to do stupid things like dropping an anchor without having the bitter end of the rode or chain first secured inside the hull. But when a U.S. Navy nuclear submarine does it, that's not stupid, that's a computer programming malfunction on the civilian level (courtesy of the U.S. Navy).

WHY ANCHORS ARE LITTLE USED

The last thing the new boat buyer today thinks about is an anchor. He knows what an anchor is but he doesn't quite understand how it relates to his needs, like how to get maximum use and enjoyment from his investment. He thinks the anchor is just a necessary piece of gear required by U.S. Coast Guard regulations, just like fire extinguishers, lifejackets, flame arrestors and horns.

The anchor is probably the most ignored piece of gear on the modern powerboat. This is because anchors are usually not designed with the thought in mind that the boat might have to be anchored in an emergency. The reverse sheer forward deck areas of so many of these new boats are sloped, curved or rounded in such a way that there is absolutely no place to store an anchor in chocks on the deck (Fig. 10-2). And if, in spite of this, the owner did store an anchor on the deck, it would look as incongruously misplaced on that sleek fiberglass surface as a pair of Texas steer horns on the radiator of a Corvette Stingray.

As a result, the anchor and 200 feet of rode must be stored aft, somewhere in the bilge or engine compartment. If the anchor is ever used, it is dropped over the stern since there is no way of getting it forward except through the cabin, or up the forward hatch while standing on a bunk mattress.

Later when the anchor is raised, 100 feet of wet rope must be hauled in, lowered down into the cabin onto the bunks, followed by six feet of wet muddy chain and an anchor with 20 pounds of clay or mud clinging to the flukes.

The whole anchoring experience is so painfully difficult and unpleasant that once tried by the new boatman, he forever after avoids it.

Even on larger yachts, where the anchor is still carried on the forward deck in the traditional manner, it is often ignored, and rarely used.

When I asked the owner of a 48-foot Hatteras how he liked his elaborate anchoring gear, including the fancy bow pulpit that held the anchor, the power winch and the chain rode instead of nylon, he just shrugged and said, "I don't know, it came with the boat. Ain't had a chance to use it yet."

He had owned that yacht for three years, yet he had never once used the anchor. In fact, he didn't even know how to operate the winch. When he ordered the boat, he wanted the

Fig. 10-2. Where do you keep the anchor on reverse-sheer fiberglass hulls. To be of any use, the anchor must be instantly available should an emergency arise, and they do.

best of everything, he said, and that is what they installed. He had some papers and manuals somewhere, he told me, but he'd been very busy, and besides, he didn't like to anchor. His wife complained that all of the rolling made her seasick, and "those damn flies got on the boat whenever you anchored."

"When we start up the diesels and pull out of our slip, we like to GO someplace," he said.

"Going someplace" usually means a 4-6 hour run down the coast, or across the lake, or bay, to another marina where overnight docking facilities are available.

The dock that the boatman will stay in overnight is by coincidence temporarily vacant because its occupant also likes "to go someplace" and is probably staying overnight in the vacant dock of the first boatman. What is happening here is that every weekend, thousands of cruising American boatmen "go someplace" and exchange docks with each other overnight. Under these circumstances, who needs an anchor?

INCREASED ANCHOR USAGE

That is the way it was. And then the gas crunch came into our lives. Almost overnight, everything changed.

This current season there have been few boats "cruising" to distant ports. More boatmen have taken to short rides to a lee shore or quiet bay where they anchor, swim and have a picnic lunch.

In some ways, the gas crunch is helping to bring American boating families closer together, which is a good thing. It is also helping to revive sales of anchors and related gear, which had slumped in recent years. When more anchors are used, more get lost.

Also, when boatmen start using their anchors, especially the one that come with the boat as "standard equipment," they find that this anchor is more for show then practicality. It is usually a modified version of the navy anchor and it looks very neat and nautical in its chocks on the deck, but it is often too heavy to do the job.

WHAT ANCHORS ARE NEEDED

Our new boatman often discovers that he needs a new anchor, a light one that can be easily handled (Fig. 10-3). Then he discovers that one anchor is not enough. He needs two anchors, maybe even three. One big storm anchor would be suffi-

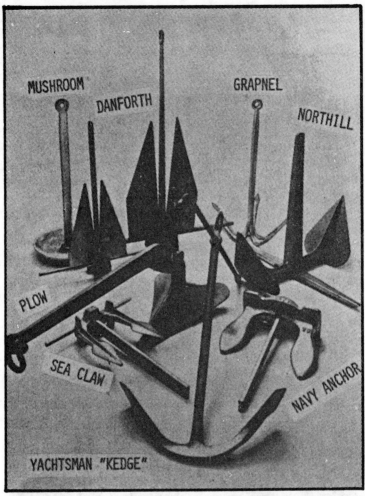

Fig. 10-3. All anchors are advertised as having "tremendous holding power," and most of these above really do. Even the mushroom has "holding power" if it's heavy enough and you allow a few months for it to bury itself. But instant holding power in all types of bottom is a different matter, and this is where the experts start hedging when you try to pin them down (courtesy of Danforth).

cient, but why drop a big 40 pound hook in a quiet bay just to have a swim and lunch when a four pound lunch hook would do just as well? There is really no reason to drop a 22 pound working anchor.

The storm anchor is usually stowed away below decks as an insurance policy. It can be a lifesaver when running aground or in a strange mooring basin with strong winds blowing you in the direction of a stone breakwall. You'll sleep a lot better with a big storm hook down.

The lunch hook is too small for all-around service, while the storm anchor is too big. You need a third anchor which should be your regular working hook, the one you keep secured in chocks on your deck instead of that "standard equipment" hunk of iron.

The Navy Anchor

The *navy* anchor, also called the *patent* anchor, supplanted the old kedge with its huge wooden stock, when iron ships began to develope in the 1800's. The kedge is not an easy anchor to stow and cannot be drawn up neatly into a hawsepipe like the navy anchor (Fig. 10-4).

The navy anchor's holding power comes from sheer mass and weight rather then its digging-in properties. To hold a 20 foot boat you would need at least a 100 pound anchor. To hold a 35-footer, you would need a 200 pound anchor.

The Navy Anchor On Big Ships

Why is the navy anchor used on all big ships?

On big ships, weight is no problem. On big aircraft carriers,

Fig. 10-4. The navy anchor requires no special handling by the crew and easily winches up into a hawsepipe by itself. Since weight presents no difficulties on big ships, the anchor and chain can be big enough to hold.

the anchor will weigh 20 tons. Each individual link in the chain will weigh about 2 tons. When they drop that hook and a hundred links of that chain to the bottom, you have about 220 tons sunk into the mud, which provides tremendous holding power. Also, this great weight holds equally well on any bottom, whether sand, mud, rock, grass or heavy weeds. This factor alone is why the navy anchor is universally used because it would be impractical for large vessels to carry a variety of anchors for different bottoms and weather conditions. Considering the size and weight, they could never change anchors at sea.

The Danforth

Small boats must have light anchors that are easily handled by one person on a rolling, or pitching boat, and yet they must have good holding power in all types of bottoms. That is a lot to ask of one anchor, but the Danforth, developed by R.S. Danforth just before World War II, comes fairly close to filling all those requirements.

The Danforth proved itself during the war when it was used by amphibious craft who, after disgorging men and equipment on enemy-held beaches, would pull themselves off those beaches by winching back on Danforth anchors they had dropped a few hundred yards astern.

The Danforth comes in two types, the Standard and the Hi-Tensile. Although both look pretty much alike, the Hi-Tensile, according to the manufacturer, is supposed to have 20% to 30% more holding power. I have used both and could never tell the difference because I have never had a Danforth drag on me. I honestly cannot say the Hi-Tensile is worth the extra cost (Tables 10-1 and 10-2).

However, I will say that the Danforth 5-H, weighing all of five pounds, is the finest lunch hook in the world. It is so light, you can heave it off your stern and pull yourself off a beach in an 18-20 foot outboard.

I have used this ridiculously small anchor to hold my heavy 42-foot double cabin in weather that called for my working 22-pounder, but yet it has never dragged. The 40-pound storm anchor I keep stowed below decks. It has never been used. I keep it for emergencies, like pulling myself off a mudbank.

Danforth Drawbacks

Considered by many as the finest American anchor, the Dan-

Table 10-1. Horizontal Holding Power of Danforth Anchors, In Pounds

Model	Soft Mud	Hard Sand
5-H	400	2,700
12-H	900	6,000
20-H	1,250	8,750
35-H	1,600	11,000
60-H	2,400	17,000
90-H	2,900	20,000
200-H	5,000	35,000
500-H	7,500	50,000
3000-H	21,000	140,000
2½-S	140	800
4-S	230	1,600
8-S	480	3,200
13-S	720	4,900
22-S	1,200	8,000
40-S	1,500	10,000
65-S	2,300	15,000
85-S	2,700	19,000
130-S	3,100	21,000
180-S	3,500	23,000
6-U	450	450
12-U	900	900
20-U	1,500	1,500
30-U	2,200	2,200
50-U	3,200	3,200
80-U	4,000	4,000
100-U	5,000	5,000

forth does have two drawbacks if you boat in quiet waters, like rivers where there are no swells or big waves. If the anchor ever buries itself in heavy Mississippi mud or clay, you will

Table 10-2. Suggested Working Anchor Sizes.

Boat Length	Danforth* Standard Anchor	Danforth* Hi-Tensile Anchor
0-9	2½-S	—
10-16	4-S / 4-SR	—
17-24	8-S / 9-SR	5-H
25-32	13-S / 16-SR	12-H
33-38	22-S	12-H
39-44	40-S	20-H
45-54	65-S	35-H
55-70	85-S	60-H
71-90	130-S	90-H

For storm anchor, use one anchor size larger.
For lunch hook, one size smaller.

have one terrible time breaking it out because you can't use the lifting power of a big wave to free the anchor.

Freeing An Anchor

Even the smallest wave action will free an anchor for you by just working yourself in directly over the anchor. Then, snub the rode on the mooring bitt at the bottom of a wave, when the bow rises on the next wave, it frees the anchor.

There is no wave action on river waters to help you do this. To break the Danforth loose in quiet waters, you have to swing around and pull in the opposite direction just enough to break loose, then haul directly up before it digs in again.

The Danforth does not hold too well in grassy, weedy bottoms, but neither does any other anchor that has to dig in to hold.

The Northill Anchor

This anchor was once made of stainless steel. It is now made of malleable iron hot-dipped galvanized and is called the Danforth Utility Anchor. It is considered about equal in holding power to the Danforth, but it is not as widely used on the new cruising boats because many of them have the new bow pulpits that hold and store the anchor. The Northill cannot be used or stored without first doing something to the anchor, like putting the stock into proper working position. For stowing, the stock is turned and rests along the shank or across the arms. This means the anchor is not instantly useable like the Danforth is when it is drawn up into hawsepipes or a pulpit.

Resting in chocks on a boat deck, the sharp edges of those big blukes on the Northill look a little menacing. You keep imagining one of your kids slipping on the wet deck and falling on the anchor, which has happened many times. I suspect a lot of family boatmen think of that, which is probably why the Northill is rarely seen in chocks on boat decks, even though it is one of the best anchors, pound for pound.

The Northill is a modified version of an anchor used on wooden boats in Malaysia thousands of years ago. It is a *hooking* anchor, digging in instantly on all bottoms, even grass, which is the most difficult of all bottoms in which to anchor. As the fluke buries itself, the stock provides additional holding power.

A bad feature of this anchor, which it shares with the kedge, is that unburied fluke which never totally disappears into the bottom mud or sand. It is always sticking up and when the boat

Fig. 10-5. The plow anchor, also called CQR (secure), was never too popular in this country until just recently, and all because of the growing popularity of bow pulpits. The plow is easily adaptable to many different methods of stowing it on the pulpit, as above, where it is instantly available.

swings in a changing wind, the rode can become entangled in that exposed fluke.

The Plow Anchor

This odd looking anchor, which has been around for a long time, is suddenly growing in popularity because, like the Danforth, it fits so neatly into those new bow pulpits that hold the anchor (Figs. 10-5 and 10-6). Plow is an apt name for this anchor because it looks exactly like an old-fashioned one horse

Fig. 10-6. The Danforth is also being stowed on bow pulpits in many different ways, as above, and also on pulpit platforms. Anchors somehow just don't look right chocked on fiberglass decks, so builders are getting the anchor off the decks and on the pulpit. The Danforth and Plow are both adaptable to this type of stowage.

plow. In England, where it was invented by a Professor named G.I. Taylor, it is called CQR (secure). There are several American versions, one called CQR and another called the Woolsey Plowright Anchor.

The shank of this anchor is pivoted so that as the boat swings back and forth, the plow itself remains buried. On a straight up pull, the plow, with that sharp point angled upward, releases easily.

This anchor holds very well for its weight, with a 10-pounder doing the job for a 20-foot boat, a 35-pounder for a 40-50-foot boat and a 60 pounder for a 65-100 foot boat.

There are differing opinions as to its digging in abilities in heavy weeded and grassy bottoms.

Other Types

There is an even lighter version of the Danforth called the *Viking*. This anchor is made of high-tensile marine aluminum. This could be the anchor for the sailor who wants extra holding power without more weight.

The Danforth, size 22-S, weighing 22 pounds, is considered the proper working anchor for 35-foot powerboats with 10-foot beams. The Viking version of this anchor is their size 40-ST which weighs slightly over 11 pounds, a weight reduction of 50%.

There is also a substantial difference in price. The Danforth Standard size 22-S costs $105. The Viking size 40-ST, with the same holding power, costs $79.

The Sure-Hold Claw anchor is a modified version of the Danforth. The Sea-Claw anchor, with stock added, is a considerably improved version of the navy anchor. There is a tripping eye in the lower shank for securing a trip line in the event the anchor becomes snagged in rock, coral or foul bottoms.

Folding Anchor

Manhattan Marine lists two folding type anchors in their current catalog, and one of them is a folding kedge, which has always been a beast to stow. They claim that the folding feature of the flukes does not sacrifice strength. When folded up, the 75-pound size of this anchor could be stored laying on the inner keel of a sailboat as an extra piece of inside ballast.

The other folding anchor (Fig. 10-7) is ideal for small boats, especially those new fiberglass fishing machines with no deck

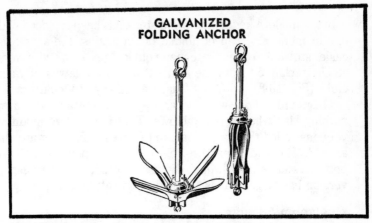

Fig. 10-7. Manhattan Marine of New York lists this folding anchor in their current catalog. This is an ideal anchor for many of the new fiberglass boats of today that have no forward deck space where a conventional anchor can be stowed in deck chocks.

space where an anchor can be stowed in chocks. When folded, this anchor can be stowed almost anywhere. In the opened position, two of the flukes are always in position to dig in.

The Kedge

The modern anchor is designed on principles laid down by the Vikings and Phoenicians. Nothing has happened in the centuries since to change those basic principles which produced a simple hooking device which, when dropped to the sea bottom and pulled by a connecting rope, is forced into a position where it hooks itself to the bottom. Basically very simple, but then, all great inventions look so simple in retrospect.

The kedge of today is one of our oldest links with the past. It has changed the least, and most of its changes have been in the stock. Older versions had huge wood stocks of stout oak. But other then that, they look exactly as they did hundreds of years ago on Admiral Nelson's flagship *Victory* at the great sea battle off Cape Trafalgar. Christopher Columbus had a kedge anchor on the *Santa Maria*. Kedges are constantly being found and salvaged by treasure hunters in the Caribbean area between the Bahamas and Florida coast where many a Spanish galleon foundered on the way home ladened with New World plunder. Scuba divers who systematically work these waters looking for those old wrecks always hope to find the anchor first, and frequently they do.

In the modern kedge, the wood stock has been replaced with one of metal that can be folded down against the shank for easier stowing. You will see many old kedges, some with wood stocks reclaimed from the sea, sitting on the lawns of yacht clubs (Fig. 10-8) and Coast Guard Auxiliary headquarters.

There are sailors who swear by the kedge and will drop nothing else when it really blows. That is why two modified versions called the Yachtsman and Herreshoff anchor are still around. The Yachtsman has sharp flukes for penetrating hard bottoms and getting through grass and weeds. The Herreshoff version has larger flukes for holding in soft bottoms.

Mushroom Anchors

In a weight and size that would be usable on small pleasure craft, the mushroom anchor is at the bottom of the scale in efficiency. However, when of sufficient size and weight, the mushroom is used in anchorages as permanent mooring anchors. To permanently moor a 25-foot power boat

Fig. 10-8. Old kedge anchors and ships wheels like these, some hundreds of years old, can be found on Yacht Club and Coast Guard Auxiliary lawns. But smaller versions of these same kedges are still being manufactured and sold to yachtsmen who will not trust anything else.

requires a mushroom anchor weighing 225 pounds. The weight proportionately increases and a 55-foot yacht will require a 500 pound mushroom anchor.

Compare this with the Viking aluminum anchor, the Hi-Density model 45-HD for boats of 45-55 feet, which only weighs 17¼ pounds and has horizontal holding power in hard sand of 12,000 pounds.

There are special small versions of the mushroom which are suitable as anchors for canoes, dinghies and small rowboats.

Grapnels

The U.S. Coast Guard is probably the biggest user of grapnels and for a rather mournful reason—dragging for drowning victims. The grapnel is also used to recover other objects lost in the water. Commercial fishermen are the next biggest users of this five-pronged hooking device.

For pleasure boatmen, the grapnel is not recommended.

The Sea Anchor

Any device or object secured to the end of a long line to keep a boat from drifting can be truthfully called an "anchor," even if it doesn't look like one. A popular "anchor" in Mississippi Delta country is the common cement building block, with the corner-type blocks preferred because they are heavier. A common anchor with boat liveries is discarded paint buckets filled with cement.

However the device called a "Sea Anchor" is not a true anchor and it would be folly to think of them as such because they do *not* hold a boat to a fixed position. They merely "anchor" the boat's bow into the wind and seas while it continues to drift. A sea anchor should never be used anywhere except far out at sea away from international shipping lanes, where there is plenty of room to drift in all directions.

Chapter 11
Piloting

The new boatman is often confused by piloting and navigation. "What's the difference?" he asks.

When you sail a boat thousands of miles across the Pacific Ocean to Tahiti in the Society Islands, that is *navigation.*

When you run a boat thousands of miles down the Intracoastal Waterway from New England to the Florida Keys, that is *piloting.*

Regardless of which you do, a course cannot be steered without reference points.

In basic celestial navigation, you get your reference points from the stars and the sun at precisely noon of each day with a sextant. When you determine longitude and latitude, you have a *reference* point on your chart from which to plot a course and to steer by with a compass. The following day you shoot the sun again with your sextant and establish another reference point. You keep doing this every day until you arrive at your destination.

This is elementary navigation, the way it has been practiced for centuries.

In piloting you do not use the stars or the sun to obtain a reference point because you are never too far beyond the sight of land, and the land itself is a reference point. And on the land, and close to the land there are thousands of other aids to navigation that help a pilot determine where he is at all times, and he has no need for a sextant.

FORGET ABOUT NAVIGATION

The owner of a pleasure craft should concern himself only with piloting, and forget about navigation. Leave it to the professionals on the high seas and those adventurers who can afford to cop out, blow the rat race and sail for Pago Pago in the South Seas. If you have such thoughts and plans, there are books written especially for you and devoted entirely to navigation and how to get to Pago Pago.

This is not to suggest that piloting is easier for you to learn then navigation. On the contrary, piloting is far more difficult with more things to learn, and more things to remember and forget. An error in piloting can mean instant disaster for your boat. An error of just a few yards can run you aground, while a wrong turn can have you run down by another vessel. CWO Donald Robinson, skipper of the ill-fated Coast Guard cutter *Cuyahoga,* will certainly agree. His error in piloting cost him his ship and 11 lives.

Make an error in navigation on the high seas and what happens? Nothing. You don't hit anybody. You don't run aground. You don't wreck you ship on the rocks. You just run off course a few hundred miles. But you have plenty of opportunities to catch the error when you shoot the sun each day or cross check with electronic navigational equipment.

The point is, a navigational error on the high seas does not instantly endanger your vessel as it would with even a small piloting error in Boston Harbor or the Chesapeake Bay.

The average boatman, who gets on the water only on weekends, has enough to do just learning as much as he can about piloting without confusing himself over something that he will never touch in his life, no matter how much he daydreams about Tahiti.

I, too, have dreamed about Tahiti. I even designed a sailboat, and layed down the lines and made the patterns. I even bought linotype metal for inside ballast. I even got a sextant for Christmas.

I still have the linotype pigs. I still have the sextant, which hangs on the wall over my typewriter. Instead of the sailboat I built a cabin cruiser.

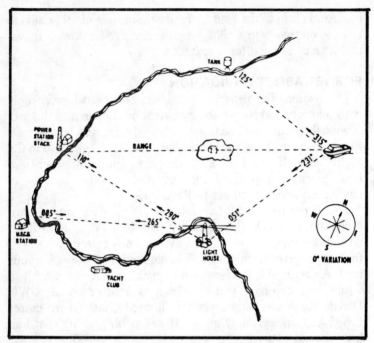

Fig. 11-1. When cruising offshore or on inland waters a boat is rarely beyond sight of some object on which a bearing can be taken, as above where there are five different landmarks, each of which is shown on charts for that area. By taking a compass sighting on these landmarks, a skipper can pinpoint his position (courtesy of Airguide Instrument Co.).

As somebody once said: "All men live out their lives in quiet desperation." Only a few of us make it to the South Seas in a sailboat—statistically, about one in 500,000.

DEAD RECKONING

Every time you take your boat offshore for a run down the coast, across the bay or across the lake, you are mentally keeping track of your position by what you think is a method of your own devising (Fig. 11-1). Most of the time you do this routinely because it just comes naturally. You pass the Harbor Light at 0800, change course to 84° magnetic. You pass Bay Point light at 0900. The distance between these two lights is 15 miles. So you calculate your speed at 15 MPH. Squaw Island light, according to your chart, is 30 miles away. By your calculations, the light should be on your port beam at 1100.

The above computations, using speed, time and visual bearings to determine where you are, is the oldest form of piloting and sailors have been doing it for years. It is called *dead reckoning*.

You dead reckon every time you go out in a boat, even for just an afternnon of fishing because you always have a favorite spot, like a reef, a deep hole or an old wreck where the fishing is good. To get to that precise spot you use the compass, your speed through the water, and visual bearings which can be navigational markers in the water, or on land as lights or beacons (Fig. 11-2). Then there are land bearings like smokestacks, church steeples and transmitting TV towers. All of these things help you determine where you are, and dead reckoning is mostly what piloting is all about.

When you graduate from outboards into larger boats and start cruising, you are more deeply involved in piloting, and it is piloting that will sustain your interest in boating. Just riding around in a boat soon gets to be a bore. But piloting never bores, it fascinates, so much so that boatmen spend millions every year on equipment and electronics to help them with their piloting. And soon they are so immersed in gear and the gadgetry of piloting that the boat itself becomes almost secondary, a means to an end, a place to keep all the equipment and

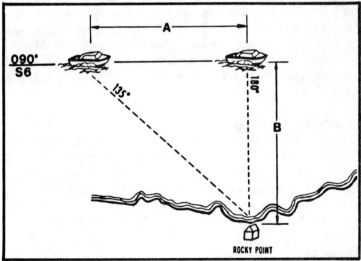

Fig. 11-2. In this drawing, the boat, on a heading 90°, reaches 135° at 12:30, it reaches 180° off Rocky Point at 12:40. The distance of "A", which is one mile, has been covered in 10 minutes. The distances of "A" and "B" are the same. So the boat is exactly 1 mile off Rocky Point. This is the most basic example of Dead Reckoning (courtesy of Airguide Instrument Co.).

electronics where they can plot new courses to get from anchorage A to island B. Piloting itself becomes a fascinating hobby in itself and many of these boatmen acquire a very high degree of proficiency at dead reckoning.

IMPORTANT ASPECTS OF PILOTING

There are four basic dimensions you must determine in piloting—*direction, distance, time, speed.* There are three compass directions used in piloting calculations—*true north, magnetic north, compass north.* When referring to compass directions, you always specify *which* one you are referring to, you never just say "heading on a course 082°."

When plotting a course, it is customary to use 3-digit figures for all points of the compass, like 008°, 080° and 180° instead of 8°, 80°. If your course is to be 082° you always add the word "true", "magnetic" or "compass," whichever applies.

When giving your position offshore, after getting two bearings with an RDF, you say: "I am 082° true, 3 miles from Bay Point light."

How did "true" and "3 miles" get in there, you wonder?

When you fixed your position with the RDF, you measured off your distance from this position to Bay Point light with a course protractor. This gave you both the true compass heading and distance, which you measured off with dividers against a scale on the chart. With this information, your friend can determine exactly where you are, and plot his own course for a rendezvous.

Reciprocal Headings

When plotting an extensive cruise, it will save time to make two compass readings for all headings—the regular heading going and the *reciprocal heading* returning. The reciprocal heading is just the opposite of the normal heading. There are 360° in the compass. Half of this is 180°. To get a reciprocal, just add 180° and 080° becomes 260° returning home.

Distance

The second dimension you must have in piloting is *distance,*. but distance is a relative thing because there are two different measurements used, both related to where you *are* when you do the measuring.

For example, on the ocean, offshore in tidal waters of the

United States you measure distance by nautical miles, which is 6076.1 feet. On inland waters, Great Lakes, rivers or Intracoastal Waterways, you measure by the statute mile, which is 5280 feet.

It is extremely important that you never forget this because serious miscalculations can be made, especially when you go from fresh water into salt water, as boatmen often do when cruising down the Intracoastal Waterway.

If you saw the John Wayne movie, *The High And The Mighty,* perhaps you remember how the navigator had to determine if they had enough gas to make the airport instead of ditching at sea. According to his calculations, they could just make it with a few drops to spare. Later, he discovered an error he made in calculating. He had used knots instead of miles. Knot speed is based on the nautical mile, which means he had figured more distance for a given amount of fuel.

If you are curious as to why the difference in miles, on the high seas a nautical mile is equal to one minute of latitude, which makes it an important factor in navigational calculations. On land you don't determine your position by longitude and latitude. You just look at the road signs.

Time

A third dimension you must have in piloting is *time.* This is where so many boatmen run into trouble because being essentially land oriented, they live by a clock that is divided into two 12-hour segments, designated as AM and PM.

In piloting the 24-hour clock system is used and there is no AM or PM. Time of day is measured always in 4-digits, and starting with 0000 which is midnight. The first two digits represent hours, the second two represent minutes.

The first 12 hours is fairly easy for strangers to the system to understand because you read the numbers and you have the time, like 0830 is 8:30 AM. When you see that zero you know it is the first 12-hour segment, or AM.

It's the second 12-hour segment that gives strangers to the system fits, like 1330 is 1:30 PM, 1800 is 6:00 PM. It's just a matter of doing some subtracting in your head, which is difficult for some to do, and I am one of them. On the second 12-hour segment, you must subtract 1200 from all time readings, thus 1940, with 1200 subtracted, becomes 7:40 PM, 2315 becomes 11:15 PM. It's easy once you get the hang of subtracting in your head without looking for a pencil and paper.

You always speak of time in hundreds, and you never say "hours." For example, 2000 is twenty hundred and not "two thousand hours," 0800 is zero eight hundred and not "800 hours."

This is the way it is done in the real navy and merchant marine. It is not the way it is done in Hollywood. In all the movies I have ever seen, they always say:"We counterattack at twenty three hundred hours," or "We shove off at O six hundred hours."

I do it the Hollywood way, even though I know it is wrong. I mention it only to keep the record straight, not to nit-pick.

Another thing that can screw up your calculations is passing through time zones and areas of daylight time. When you go from standard to daylight time, *add* one hour, *subtract* an hour going the other way.

Speed

A fourth very necessary dimension in piloting and course plotting is *speed*. The most common way of referring to speed is in *miles per hour*. Boatmen are also drivers of automobiles and they seem to be more comfortable with this terminology. But before the automobile replaced the horse, speed was always given in *knots*.

However, it doesn't really matter WHAT you call it because if you are calculating in nautical miles, it will still come out knots. For example, if you are working in nautical miles, then 10 miles-per-hour is actually 10 knots, which, in turn, figures out to almost 12 miles-per-hour in statute mile calculations.

One knot is 1.15 miles-per-hour. The unit knot indicates both *distance and time*. It stamps you as a lubber when you say "10 knots-per-hour" because you are only repeating yourself. Ten knots is "10 knots-per-hour."

Depth

The depth of water underneath your hull is an important factor in piloting and course setting. This is where you better not make any mistakes because many times an error of only a few yards can hang you up on a mud bank. I once made such a piloting error, which caused me to briefly skirt the edge of a shoal area where I hit something hard on the bottom and bent my starboard rudder so bad it got pushed up into the planking and I couldn't steer. I had to make it home, 44 miles in heavy weather, steering with the engines alone.

Reiterating, piloting is far more difficult, far more demanding and more nerve-wracking then navigating because there is so little margin of error before the roof falls in on you. Almost any day you can read in the newspapers about large vessels colliding in harbors, or running aground, or running into bridges. And the licensed pilots on these vessels are working with the latest and best electronic equipment. With all that sophisticated gear, they still get into trouble, which further supports my claim that in all phases of boating, there is nothing more difficult then piloting, nor more important. Your very life depends on how well you can pilot. Every licensed pilot in the world will say "Amen" to that.

The piloting of a large vessel in coastal, harbor and inland waterways is like walking on eggs. Every step must be carefully considered and planned ahead of time to make certain there is always sufficient water under your ship.

To a land person, looking out over a large bay, there is water everywhere, but not to a pilot. There is plenty of water all right, but not in the right places. If you were to drain all the water out of that bay, you would find remaining only a narrow little ditch still filled with water and looking like a winding river in all that vast space once filled with water. That ditch, better known as a "channel," is the only area in that large bay deep enough for boat traffic. Stray out of that ditch and you are in serious trouble.

This is how it is in almost every harbor, bay, river and inlet in the world. As a Great Lakes pilot told me: "Piloting is mainly a business of keeping vessels out of places where there ain't water, where there ain't bridges to hit and where there ain't ships to hit."

That is the best description of piloting I ever heard.

The depth of water on the oceans is always given in fathoms. A fathom is six feet. When you get into coast tidal waters, harbors and inland waters, depths are given in feet. In foreign waters, charts will use metric designations like meters and decimeters. Always check a new chart to learn what unit of measurement is used, and if you go into foreign waters, which is very easy to do off the coast of Florida, be sure to have a metric conversion slide rule on board because once you leave the United States, you are in a world of metrics.

The depths given on charts are not to be taken too literally on first glance. Because of tides in coastal waters, wind shifts on inland waters, depths are constantly going up and down. Always check the chart to see what reference plane, or what *tidal datum* was used for the depths indicated on the chart.

Coast and harbor charts carry tables with important tide information which show mean high water, mean low water and mean tide level. This is important information for licensed pilots of large vessels and skippers of sailboats who must accurately determine heights above Mean Low Water levels for clearance under bridges and other obstructions overhead. It is a heart-thumping sight taking a sailboat under a bridge at low tide and watching the mast just clear by inches, or seeing the VHF antenna bent over to get through. Minutes later, with the tide coming in, the mast will no longer clear the same bridge.

THE MAGNETIC COMPASS

The magnetic compass is still the basic navigational and piloting tool aboard pleasure craft and the variety of design, shape and size is downright tiresome when it comes to making a decision on what to buy. Figure 11-3 shows a few. They're all good. But some are exceptionally good. In the good range you can easily find something affordable and adequate.

In the exceptional range, your choice narrows down to a precious few (two brands), and they are not exactly affordable. For a small cruiser, $25 will buy a good compass. For the serious boatman who wants the best, it will take about $500 to get it. You can even spend $1,200 for a really good one.

What's the difference between a good compass and an exceptional one?

The more expensive ones are steadier.

In rough water, when your boat is bouncing around, the affordable good compass becomes a very "busy" compass. It never stops moving.

The non-affordable compass remains as steady as a church. When the boat heading changes, the compass card moves instantly, and then stops instantly. There is no over-shoot in any direction, and no unnecessary movement. These compasses are an absolute joy to steer by, but, oh, how you pay for that joy.

Fig. 11-3. This is just a small sampling of one manufacturer's line, which is Aqua Meter. These are all good compasses, and in a price range affordable by all boaters. But other manufacturers, like Airguide, Danforth, Ritchie have equally affordable compasses (courtesy of Aqua Meter).

Compass Deviation

Other then steadiness, there is absolutely no difference between any of the fine marine compasses that are available today. If your cheap $10 compass has a 6° deviation on an east heading, an $800 compass will have the same identical deviation if it is installed in precisely the same location on your boat.

Deviation is not a fault of the compass. But many boatmen

refuse to believe this and remain grimly determined to correct all the error out of their compass. This type of boatman often becomes what is known in boating circles as a "compass freak."

Compass Freaks

There is at least one compass freak in every yacht club, marina or mooring basin. He is a first cousin to the propeller freak, the bottom paint freak, the radiotelephone freak and the sail freak.

Boating does strange things to some men—like getting them hung up on one small part of boating to the exclusion of everything else. A compass is important, but not that important.

The compass freak is a man who buys a new compass at least twice a season. He never finishes a season with the same compass. If you ask him what was wrong with his old compass, he always has an answer, like: "The compensating magnets were no good."

Ask him what was wrong with them, he'll say: "They only corrected five degrees. I got a ten degree error on some headings."

This man is so obsessed with a fear of "compass error" that he spoils boating for his wife and kids who get bored spending every Sunday afternoon out on the lake going nowhere but back and forth and up and down on various known headings to adjust the compass.

I said this man was obsessed. That's not true. "Hooked" or "addicted" is a better word. I know because I was "hooked" myself once, and then I met this professional compass adjuster who worked the summer season in the Detroit area.

He had been working on two yachts at the Detroit Yacht Club, one of them was my dock neighbor. We got to talking and I invited him up to the club bar for a drink. This is an interviewing trick I learned working on newspapers. After a few drinks I told him what a difficult time I was having with the deviation in my compass. He just laughed. "You're wasting your time."

"Why?" I asked.

"You want perfection. There ain't no such thing as an accurate compass."

"Then what have you been doing all day here—"

"I adjusted the compasses, took most of the error out, then I made out a deviation card on which I recorded what small deviation remained. It is impossible to remove all error for the simple reason that is impossible to remove all magnetic influences that affect a compass and still have something left that can be called a boat. A compass will always have some error, but it's no big deal."

"Do you tell your customers that?" I asked.

He laughed again. "They wouldn't believe me if I did. That's human nature. That's why I made $20,000 last year adjusting compasses that didn't really need adjusting."

"Because they had so little error?"

"All compasses have a little error, but it doesn't really matter so long as you know exactly what the error is. That's the whole point, knowing. You don't have to fool around with the magnets, just find the error and record it on a compass deviation card. When you have a record of deviation on all 360°, you just make allowances for the deviation when you plot a course and you'll be able to pilot and navigate in complete confidence."

Compass "Error"

It is common practice to refer to compass deviation as *error*. This is grossly untrue and misleads many into thinking that their compass has an inherent weakness or defect. This is very likely the reason why some boatmen waste a great deal of money buying new compasses every year because they mistakenly believe that the so-called better, and more expensive, compass has less "error."

These are all myths. There is rarely error in any compass, regardless of price. But all compasses are subject to outside magnetic forces which cause them to *deviate* from proper headings (Fig. 11-4). Therefore, deviation is the proper term to use, but deviation is still interchangably used with error. However, there is no harm in this so long as you clearly understand the difference.

MAGNETIC INFLUENCES

If you have more then 005° of deviation on any heading, before you go about trying to correct this with the internal built-in compensating magnets in your compass, do some checking for sources of magnetic influence. You may not have

Fig. 11-4. This is a $500. compass which, because of that beer can, now has an error of 005°. Compasses do not have "errors." They just have things that affect their accuracy, like beer cans and a hundred other things. Beer can errors are easily corrected. But some other errors can never be corrected because even people are a magnetic influence.

to do any adjusting. Sometimes just moving something is all you need to do.

The biggest source of outside influences on compasses comes from radios, bullhorns, direction-finders, motors and radiotelephones. Small transistor radios, which also double as direction-finders, are often kept at the helm close to the compass. Speakers in radios have powerful magnets which can affect a compass even three feet away.

Remember this when installing your radiotelephone or direction finder. Fortunately, direction-finders are mobile, and can be shifted around. But radiotelephones are permanently secured, and most often right at the helmsman's fingertips as if he couldn't control the boat without it.

Most experienced boatmen will install their electronic gear on the opposite side of the helm, which is where it belongs. The First Mate, on her side of the boat, can play with the electronics. The skipper should concentrate on handling the boat, not playing with radiotelephones.

Windshield wipers on small windshields are a source of trouble because the compass will often be mounted right under the wiper motor. On a small boat, windshields are not very large and so the motor is usually close to the compass, and vertical magnetic influences are the worst.

Changing the compass location will often help. But before you do this, check out your present location. Unscrew the compass, lift it carefully and move it slowly in all directions without *turning*. Watch the compass card closely. If it moves ever so slightly, there is magnetism affecting it somewhere.

Large magnetic influences are more easily found, and more easily eliminated then small ones. You can easily move a radio, a bullhorn, or an RDF. It's the other kind, the accumulation of an endless variety of small influences like instruments, gauges, D.C.

Fig. 11-5. There are compasses now available with extra 45° lubber lines, plus the 180° line, which gives you a constant reciprocal heading. The 45° lines are useful in dead reckoning calculations and steering with the compass mounted on the boat's centerline rather than directly in front of the helm, where all the instruments and D.C. current flows (courtesy of Aqua Meter).

wiring and large hunks of iron, like worm gears in steering mechanisms, that will often be in an area right under the compass.

Each of these things, individually, will have only a small effect on the compass, but all bunched together behind the instrument panel (as they always are), they add up to enough magnetism to throw the compass off 005° or even more.

The ideal location for the compass is directly in front of the helmsman's line of sight sitting at the wheel. And invariably, on many small boats, this will turn out to be the worst possible place to install the compass (Fig. 11-5). Since you can't eliminate the instruments, or move the windshield wiper, you try to relocate the compass, but not so far that the helmsman will get a sore neck as he swivels back and forth steering the boat. For some strange reason designers and boat builders never take into consideration the fact that boats must have a suitable location to install a compass.

Recently, while visiting a new marina, I saw how one boatman solved the windshield wiper problem on his boat. His solution was an idea that also occurred to me, but I never tried it. This man replaced the wiper on the helmsman's side of the boat with a manual hand-operated windshield wiper. On the other side he installed a big heavy-duty motor-driven wiper mechanism. Then he connected the two together with a small diameter aluminum rod just as it is done on automobiles. The one motor swung both blades, but the motor was on the opposite side of the boat. I never got a chance to meet the owner and learn how it worked. But a system just like this works very well on my car.

D.C. Electrical Influences

When there is current flowing through D.C. wiring, a magnetic field is created. All the wiring to boat gauges and instruments is of this type, and they are all together there behind the instrument panel and *under* the compass.

If there are two wires to each instrument, the magnetic field can easily be neutralized. Remove all the wire terminaled ends at the instruments, turn and twist them around each other, and then refasten them to the instruments. Twisting the wires produces the same neutralizing effect that occurs in AC wiring where current flow in two directions develops opposing magnetic fields that cancel each other out.

Manufactured stock boats are built, fastened, bolted, screwed, and fitted out with non-magnetic metals like brass, copper, bronze, aluminum, chromium and stainless steel of the non-magnetic type. All boat hardware is made of non-magnetic metals and it is a very rare thing to find magnetic metal (iron, steel) on a boat. But I did. On a big Name Brand cruiser I owned, the towel rack on the head door was ordinary steel and it was in a position directly *under* where my compass was installed. It caused a compass deviation of 001°.

"EASY" COMPASS CORRECTING

Magnetism is everywhere. The sun, the human body, the earth and all other matter is magnetic to some degree and you can never eliminate all influences on your compass, so be satisfied doing what you can. Your next step is to correct remaining deviation as best you can with the built-in compensating magnets, and then live with the deviation that remains. If you fight it, you could become a compass freak.

Fig. 11-6. You cannot work with a sun corrector compass in an enclosed pilot house, like a sedan cruiser or under a hardtop because the pin shadow must be visible on all headings, and this is not possible if the bridge is covered, blocking off the sun.

I have headed this sub-chapter "Easy" Compass Correcting as a joke. I have read much on the subject in learned books. In popular boating magazines I have seen articles with headings like this, which is my reason for using it.

I have never read anything that explained, in a way I could understand, an easy way to correct a compass. The reason is there is just no easy way to correct a compass if you do it in the time-honored way of traditionalists. In fact, if you followed some of the instructions I have read, you would wind up killing the First Mate or getting killed yourself.

Adjusting a compass, like the books say, is frustrating and irritating and the less time you spend doing it, the more happy your marriage and family life will be. Remember, boating is supposed to be fun. Compass correcting is not fun.

There is an easy way to correct a compass. There are also many hard ways.

First I will tell you about the hard ways. I will tell you about the sun corrector compasses (Fig. 11-6). They were once advertised as being easy to use, fool-proof and accurate. And they are. But not for me. In all fairness, it was my fault. I tried to do the job under a hardtop, which is impossible. I also tried to do the job in rough water, which is stupid.

The sun corrector compass is just a compass card on gimballs for automatic leveling. There is an upright pin in the center of the card which casts a shadow on the compass, much like a sun dial clock. The sun corrector compass must be in the sun at all times. If you have an open boat, or a bimini soft top which can be folded down, you can use this device to correct your compass. If your boat is like mine, with a hardtop over the bridge, you are in and out of the sun and the corrector is useless.

This compass corrector was once advertised a lot and it was easily available and a great many were sold, including the one to me. It is necessary to have this device for my method of easy compass correcting, but since it is no longer readily available, here is the address where you can buy one. M & E Marine Supply Co., U.S. Route #130, Collingswood, New Jersey. Mailing address: P.O. Box 601, Camden NJ 08101.

Warning!

Don't try to correct your compass until you check and make certain that the fore and aft lubber lines of the compass are in a direct line *parallel* with the keel line of the boat (Fig. 11-7).

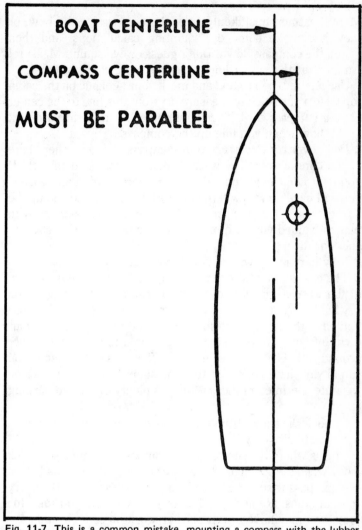

BOAT CENTERLINE

COMPASS CENTERLINE

MUST BE PARALLEL

Fig. 11-7. This is a common mistake, mounting a compass with the lubber line pointed directly at the bow, or almost as bad, lining it up parallel to the boat centerline by the aiming-down-the-gun-barrel-method (courtesy of Airguide Instruments).

Ideally the compass should be installed *on* the keel line of the boat, but boat helms are almost universally set up on the starboard side for a definite reason, it gives the helmsman a better view of approaching privileged vessels to whom he must yield.

However, it doesn't matter where the compass is installed so long as the lubber line is perfectly parallel to the keel line.

Many boatmen mistakenly *point* the compass at the bow, or they just make some eye-squinting calculations, and then fasten the compass down. Don't guess or eye-squint. Measure! An inch off the lubber line can cause a big compass error.

Use a plumb bob to find and mark your keel line on the cabin top. Use a yardstick to measure off from this line to the center of your compass card. Then have somebody hold the yardstick at the bow while you line up the compass.

Don't ever try to correct your compass on a day when there is wind and waves. The water should be fish-pond smooth. If you try to do the job on a day when there is wind and waves, you will have fits. So will the First Mate. You could end up the day getting hit in the face with a fire extinguisher, or with papers handed you by a process server when your First Mate sues for divorce.

Now here is my way of correcting a compass.

The easiest way to correct a compass is when the boat is *out* of the water. I mean with the boat resting in its cradle up on dry land. If your boat is kept on a trailer you are lucky because you have the perfect set-up. You can do the job right in your own driveway if you have enough room to swing the trailer around full 360° and the surface is fairly level. If it isn't, you can always haul your boat to some shopping center where on the outer perimeters there is always plenty of unused parking space.

Unhook the trailer from the car so you can swing it around in a complete circle by hand.

This is where the sun corrector compass pays for itself. Pick a day when the sun is bright to give you a good crisp shadow on the compass card. The sun moves across the sky 001° every four mintues. Remember this as you work. If you take too long, you may have to repeat your work on some headings.

This job takes two people, one in the boat and one to turn the boat. Set the sun compass down on a flat surface close to your boat compass. Have the boat turned until your boat compass is right on north or 000°. Then turn the sun compass until the pin shadow is right on north or 000°.

Have the boat turned around a full half circle until the pin shadow on the sun compass is precisely on south 180°. Quickly look at your boat compass. Theoretically, it should also read south or 180°, but it won't. Note the difference. That is your deviation, or error if you prefer. If the deviation is 006°, you will remove *half* of it with the compensating magnets. I will explain why later.

At the base of your compass, on two sides (facing you and to the right), there will be two slotted screws, one marked "E-W", the other "N-S" (Fig 11-8). The slots were set at the factory in the horizontal position (—). In this position the internal magnets are in what is called a *zeroed-in* position, which means they exert no magnetic influence on the compass.

The full range of adjustment with that slotted screw is only a quarter turn. This will make the slot vertical (l), up and down. You are wasting your time going beyond that quarter turn. The amount of adjustment you can make in that quarter turn of the magnets varies with different makes of compasses. It can be as little as 005°, or as much as 020°.

The adjustment screw must be touched only with a nonmagnetic screwdriver. One is usually supplied with the compass. At this point, be careful because the compass is very sensitive to *all* magnetic metals in close proximity (six inches).

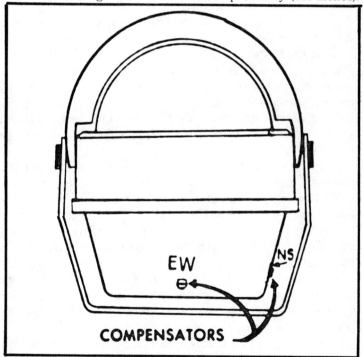

EW

NS

COMPENSATORS

Fig. 11-8. When the slot is horizontal, the compensator is neutral; when the slot is vertical, you have maximum compensation.

Remember to check for things on you for steel such as your eyeglass frames, your dentures, your wristwatch, the metal ornament on your yachting cap, the ring on your finger, the cuff links on your shirt sleeves or the pipe in your mouth.

If you found a deviation of 006°, slowly turn that slotted screw marked "N-S" until you remove *half*, which is 003°. Why only half? When you remove 003° south you at the same time remove 003° north. After removing 003° of the deviation go back and check your boat compass with your sun compass. They should now match exactly on north-south.

You now do the same thing on the east-west headings. Remove half of whatever deviation you find. Now you are finished. Your compass is corrected on the cardinal headings of north-south and east-west. You can do no more.

Wasn't that easy? It shouldn't have taken more then 15 minutes. In the water it would have taken a day, maybe even a week. It is very difficult to make compass adjustments on a boat that never stops moving.

How is the above done on a large boat that is not kept on a trailer?

All larger boats are stored on cradles when out of the water. It is becoming the custom today to winter-store boats in large enclosures with cement floors. A few years ago there were only two such storage facilities in my area. Today there are over 50 capable of storing thousands of boats. One large building stores small boats on four levels. This is happening all over the country.

Larger boats, in their cradles, are rolled around easily on big casters placed under the cradles. I have seen two men easily roll a 45-footer in and out of these buildings.

The boat owner can easily arrange with the marina to leave his boat on those casters a few days while he gets his compass corrected. They won't even charge you anything if they aren't busy.

Three members of my club had their boats sitting on casters out in the sun three days last May waiting for delivery and installation of new propellers. They had plenty of time and opportunity to work on their compasses.

It is a rare thing for a boat to be rolled out of a building and immediately launched. They always sit outside on casters for a few days waiting for bottoms to be painted or new equipment to be installed.

This is your opportunity to correct the compass the easy way. Or you can wait and do it in the water the hard way.

Using Ranges To Correct Compass

Many boatmen just don't care to get involved in compass correcting, which they consider a can of worms best left untouched. They have my understanding and sympathy.

It is possible to correct a compass, and put together a workable deviation chart in the normal course of events by just noting the magnetic bearings on the countless ranges that are encountered during an average season on the water (Fig. 11-9). Many times ranges will be on, or very close to a cardinal heading like east-west, or north-south. These range headings are all shown on navigational charts. If a heading is within 10° of a cardinal point of the compass, it can be used to adjust the compass.

After the compass is corrected on the cardinal points, there are countless other intercardinal bearings that you can find by just carefully studying your charts. These will help you make up a deviation chart. For example, the chart will show a smokestack, and then behind it, a watertank. Line the two up and you have established a new magnetic range to find deviation on an intercardinal point.

All navigational aids are shown on charts. If you want to check out your deviation on 045° and 225°, which is the reciprocal, pick out some navigational marker, line it up with something on land like a TV tower, a tall building, or some other landmark which will be shown on the chart. Use your course protractor to find the magnetic range when these two objects are lined up one behind the other.

There is not a point on the compass that you cannot easily check by this method, and you don't have to do it all in one day. Just two bearing checks a weekend, and you'll have a deviation chart completed in six weeks. I have done this myself many times, which only proves how easy it is.

When I said earlier that you were "finished," I meant only with making compensating adjustments with the built-in compass magnets. A compass can be "corrected" *only* on the cardinal headings—north-south and east-west. You still have deviation on all the intercardinal headings like NE, SE and the quarter points like NNE and SSE. These are called *residual errors*. They cannot be corrected. You just have to live with

Fig. 11-9. Range lights, like this one on a major ship channel, are set up and maintained by the Coast Guard. This is the rear light. Another one just like it, but on a much lower level, is about 200 yards forward. As you come down the channel, you see these two big red lights, one higher than the other. When you line them up, one directly over the other, you are right smack in the ship channel. The compass bearing of all ship channel is noted on all harbor charts. If the channel is 189°, that's close enough to be used to correct your compass on north-south.

them.

Once your compass is corrected on the cardinal headings, *do not touch the adjustment screws* to make any intercardinal corrections. It would even be a good idea to cover the N-S and

E-W screws with black tape.

Remember, you are *finished* with the magnets. But you are *not* finished working on the compass.

Although you cannot correct the remaining residual deviation on the intercardinal and quarter points, you still must determine *what* the error is and make a record of it. This record is called a *deviation chart.*

THE DEVIATION CHART

At marina stores you can buy a compass deviation card for about $3. It looks like a compass card. In fact, it is two compass roses—a small rose inside a large rose. On the outer rose you record, with pencil (so it can be erased), magnetic headings you plot from the chart. On the inner rose you record what your compass actually reads on that heading.

A compass deviation card looks nautical and impresses your guests, but you don't really need one. You can write the data down on a simple filing card in this manner:

Magnetic	Compass
000°	000°
015°	014°
030°	028°
045°	041°
055°	054°
070°	068°
090°	090°

You will note that there is no deviation on both 000° and 090°, which is north and south. It is only between the cardinal headings that you will find residual error.

Some boatmen like more information of their deviation charts and fill it out in this manner:

Magnetic	Compass	Deviation
000°	000°	—
015°	014°	1°E
030°	028°	2°E
045°	041°	4°E
055°	053°	2°E
070°	069°	2°E
090°	090°	—

If your compass reads less then magnetic, you have an easterly variation. If it reads more, you have a westerly variation.

All this extra bookkeeping and data recording really isn't necessary on small pleasure craft, but some skippers like everything shipshape.

You obtain the deviation data using the sun corrector compass in precisely the same manner that you used it to correct your compass on the cardinal headings.

Example: you start on the intercardinal heading of 045°. After turning 180° you end on the reciprocal heading of 225°. If your compass reads 231°, you record *half* of that on your deviation card. Since your compass reading is higher, you have a westerly variation and you record it 3°W. You keep repeating this until you have a record of the deviation on all the intercardinal and quarter points. You now have a compass that you can trust with your life.

COMPASS VARIATION

In plotting courses with charts, you must always remember that there are *two norths.* The *true* poles, the north and south, are the theoretical axis on which the earth revolves. But the true north pole, where all the lines of meridian converge, is not precisely where magnetic north is located. The difference between these two locations is what causes variation.

Billions of years ago the earth was a molten mass of iron, in fact some of it is still molten. As the outer surface cooled, this molton iron was trapped under the surface and became a big magnet. However, the two poles of this magnet did not line up directly with the earth's axis, but off to one side.

At the north axis, the pole of this magnet is on Canada's Bathurst Island about 850 miles south of the true north pole. The south pole of this magnet is on the coast of Wilkes Island in Antarctica about 1,600 miles from the true south pole.

The compass card on your boat compass always points to the pole of that big magnet on Bathurst Island in Canada. And that is where variation comes into the picture because all meridian lines meet at the earth's axis and all navigational calculations are based on those lines, like longitude and latitude.

When you plot courses on a chart, you use the above mentioned lines as reference points. The final figures you arrive at are based on *true* north. But the compass steers by magnetic north. The difference between the two is called *variation*, and it must be accounted for whenever you plot a course (see Appendix A for information on where you can obtain navigation charts).

The Compass Rose

On every large navigational chart there will be several compass roses and on each will be shown the variation on each section of the chart. Since magnetic north is 850 miles off to one side of the north pole, which is 76 north latitude, 101 west longitude, the degree of variation changes as you go around the earth from a point east or west, from zero variation. And you will note this on the compass roses as each one will have a different variation.

Zero variation runs on a line just off the coast of Florida up through the midwest around Indiana. Everything west of that line through the Gulf and Pacific coast is easterly variation. Everything east of that line, all of Lake Erie and the Atlantic coast, is westerly variation, in increasing degree, as you move east. On the western end of Lake Erie, it is 3°W. By the time you get to Buffalo it is about 6°W. Somewhere along the eastern shore of Lake Michigan is zero variation.

When the variation is westerly, you *add* the variation to your magnetic heading. When it is easterly, you *subtract*. When plotting a course, you always use the compass rose closest to where you are working, and then note the variation.

Variation/Deviation Corrections

To arrive at a proper compass heading when plotting courses, you always have two corrections to make—*variation and deviation.*

Example: If the heading you plotted off the chart is 100° and variation on the rose is 6°W, then $100° + 6° = 106°$. if the deviation is 3°W, then $106° + 3° = 109°$. The course to steer by is 109°.

COMPASS TYPES

Before the turn of the century, British Victorian physicist Lord Kelvin made three important contributions to help Britannia rule the Seven Seas. He devised a way to predict tides, he devised an apparatus for taking soundings in shallow and deep water and he reconstructed and improved the mariner's compass.

Kelvin's compass is still referred to as a Navy-type compass and when this second-hand model was given to me in payment

Fig. 11-10. This new Aqua Meter 5½ inch binnacle is easy to read sitting down, standing up or off to one side.

for sanding and painting the bottom of a sloop, it was considered a fine compass and I was very proud to own it. Today, compared to the modern spherical compasses with their internal gimbals, it is almost a museum piece. It sits today on my desk where I often use it as a paperweight.

The concave dome on spherical compasses magnify, make 2-inch cards look like 3-inch. On some compasses the card itself will be concave, which makes them easier to read from a lower angle (Fig. 11-10).

A new Aqua Meter compass has 45° grid lines and an aft line. The 45° lines make it easier to steer a course from either side of the helm. They also help in taking bearings and correcting the compass for deviation on intercardinal headings. The aft line provides an instant reciprocal heading.

Front reading compasses, with the lubber line on the near

side, are easy to read from any position—standing or sitting. This is something to remember when buying a compass. The compass has to fit the boat. On some modern boats there is just no place to install a big binnacle mount compass forward of the wheel because there is no space forward of the wheel. The front view "outboarder" compass (Fig. 11-11) may not be the ideal choice, but it can be installed anywhere and you can read it easily from any position.

COMPASS CARD SIZES

Regarding compass card size, a good rule of thumb is—the bigger the boat, the bigger the card. For an offshore cruising or fishing boat, a larger card makes for a more accurate course reading and a steadier performance. For just short runs and piloting in sheltered waters, a smaller card will suffice.

INTERNAL EXTERNAL MAGNETS

Many compasses are available with or without internal magnets for compensating purposes. One manufacturer advises that you can avoid having to compensate the compass if

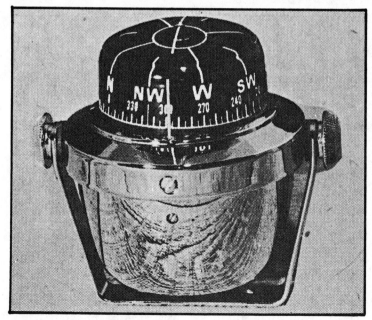

Fig. 11-11. The outboarder compass can be installed anywhere and you can read it easily from any position.

you don't install it near "large objects and electronics." How nice.

If compensations are necessary, and you don't have the internal magnets, you have no option left but to buy external compensating magnets which, on many boats, are impossible to use.

To compensate with external magnets, the compass must be installed in a flat area with plenty of room on all four sides to position and move the magnets. The magnets must all be on the same level, four magnets in all, on a north-south, east-west line.

You just won't find that kind of working space available on boats under 40-feet, or even 50-feet. The instrumentation and controls on smaller boats make things pretty crowded around the helm and places to install compasses are something boat builders aren't too concerned about. It is best to buy a compass with built-in internal magnets.

COMPASS MOUNTS

Compasses can be mounted in these four different ways:
- Deck/pedestal mount
- Flush mount
- Bracket mount
- Bulkhead mount

A marina owner advised me: "Never trust a man who flush-mounts TV sets, radiotelephones or compasses."

Technicians despise anything that is flush-mounted on boats because as one told me: "It's like performing brain surgery in a telephone booth with one arm tied behind you."

The flush-mount compass requires the cutting of a hole and once the compass in installed in that hole, you cannot reach the compensating adjustment screws without removing the compass.

Ideally, a compass should be deck-mounted in a way that it can be easily removed to take a bearing. Yes, the ordinary boat compass is excellent for taking hand bearings and there is no need to buy yet another compass expressly for that purpose.

Bracket mount compasses, when installed on a deck rather then a bulkhead, make it hard to reach the magnet adjustment screw on the right (Fig. 11-8) because the mounting bracket is in the way. You must tilt the compass to get at the screw. Turn the screw, let the compass swing back, and wait for the card to settle to see if you got it. Imagine doing all this out on the water where the boat is never still. You can understand why compass adjusting is so often a loathsome chore.

Compasses are available with cards calibrated in 5° marks with numerals every 20° or 30°. The 30° cards are preferred because the numerals are larger and can be easily read. You can also get cards calibrated in 1° marks, but this is not desirable on small pleasure boat compasses with their 4-inch cards because the 5° calibration marks are close enough (Fig. 11-12).

PILOTING TOOLS

The compass is the basic piloting tool, but to get around in coastal and inland waters, you need charts and these important

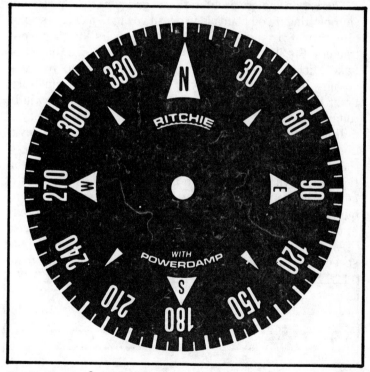

Fig. 11-12. The 5° calibration marks are best for small pleasure craft because the numbers, being further apart, are much larger and more easily seen. Numerals every 20° reduces the size of the numbers and makes the card look more crowded. Cards are available with 2° and 1° markings, but these are not recommended with cards smaller then 6 inches (courtesy of E.S. Ritchie & Sons).

navigational aids are of little use without a few simple tools—and the fewer and simpler the better.

It's easy to go overboard here and buy things you will never need or use. I have a garage full of boating gear I never use. A hand bearing compass, for example, is a fascinating little gadget that I enjoy playing with, but there is nothing it does my regular compass won't do as well.

An argument might be made that it is not wise to deprive the helmsman of his compass, while underway, so that somebody else can take a hand bearing. In some cases this might be true, but so many boats today have two steering stations, one in the flybridge and one in the deckhouse, with a compass at each station. The helmsman doesn't really have to be deprived of his compass. Just take the one that isn't being used.

There is an endless proliferation of gadgetry to help you with your plotting if you plan a long ocean voyage—like course plotters, drawing triangles, parallel rules, coursers and course protractors. But if you plan on just making an 80-mile run across Lake Michigan from Milwaukee to Grand Haven, you need nothing but a compass. If you set your course from North Point Light in Milwaukee to Grand Haven Light, you will be running a straight east-west course both ways and you can utilize the trip to check out your compass for east-west deviation.

About ninety-nine percent of small boat piloting is of this type—short runs between two navigational aids on a point of land or in the water. To pilot between these two points requires nothing more then a good course protractor and a pair of dividers, which are necessary for measuring off distances.

Another necessary tool in small boat piloting is a good speedometer and odometer, also called a *log*. Being able to ac-

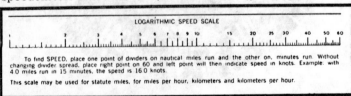

Fig. 11-13. Speed can be determined without a speedometer or log. With the logarithmic speed scale, you must know two things: distance and time. This is easy to determine in piloting and dead reckoning because you are never beyond sight of some charted object or aid to navigation. But at sea you can't dead reckon. You don't pilot, you navigate. So you use a log or speedometer (courtesy of Airguide Instruments).

curately record distance traveled is important information that is used in many ways (Fig. 11-13). Small boat pilots use this information to figure fuel consumption, to check propeller efficiency and to check boat trim.

When you know the exact distance you have traveled, you can quickly dead reckon your position by taking just one hand bearing with your boat compass. Draw a penciled line on your chart, then spread out the dividers to the mileage you have traveled. With one end of the dividers on the chart where the mileage began, swing the other end of the dividers until it intersects that magnetic compass line from the bearing you took. Where the two lines intersect is your dead reckoning position at the moment.

Without the log mileage reading, you can't use the above method for dead reckoning. But you can still determine position by taking *two* hand bearing readings. The only trouble is, sometimes you just can't find *two* suitable objects on which to take a reading. Remember, whatever objects you must be *on the chart*. You can't measure something that isn't on the chart. Most of the time there will be one charted object you can use. Which is why the log is so important—one is all you need.

There have been big improvements in marine speedometers, particularly in how the information is picked up in the water and under the boat by sending units with new type impellers. With older type logs, still much in use, the sending rotator is attached to a long line that is pulled along behind the boat. As the line rotates, it transmits this rotary motion to a registering device which is calibrated to tell speed and distance traveled. This type of log is still preferred by sailors on long ocean passages. If they ever have one of the modern types, with a hull attached sending unit or transducer, they will still have an old-fashioned log as a back-up unit.

Newer type sending units are even further improved in that they can be removed for cleaning or replacement while the boat is still in the water. The sending unit is the chief source of trouble with all modern speedometers because it is always in the water, and anything that is in the water for a long time is eventually going to foul up and cause trouble.

This is why ocean sailors prefer the log that is towed. When not in use, the rotator can be hauled in and stowed away. The log and speedometer are indispensible in dead reckoning, even for the small boat skipper.

Here again you can be seduced by the siren lure of gadgetry. There are all sorts of slide rule type devices to help the pilot solve navigation problems, conversions and measurements, like speed-time-distance. Most of these I have. Most of these I never use.

The Pelorus

The *pelorus* (Fig. 11-14) was once an important piloting tool on large merchant vessels that traveled at sea or on the Great Lakes only in clearly designated shipping lanes. You can see

Fig. 11-14. The pelorus was once an important piloting tool on large merchant vessels.

them on all large area charts and you will note that these lanes frequently change direction. How does the pilot know the precise moment when he must change course to stay in the lane?

Ship channels going out to sea are clearly marked by buoys. At the last buoy, the pilot knows that a turn to course 098° will put him in the shipping lane. But only for 56 miles when the lane changes to 085°. There will be no buoy there, no navigational marker of any kind, to tell the pilot he must change course; only the chart tells him this.

The chart will also show the pilot land objects on which he can take bearings. Using the sights on the pelorus, he can determine when his vessel is directly abeam of the land object, which is the precise moment when he must change compass heading to stay in the shipping lane.

The pelorus is also used to determine the direction of objects from the boat (Fig. 11-15). The peolrus has a rotating compass card which can be locked in any position. With the pelorus set up directly on the keel like with the card at 000°, it can be determined if an object is 10°, 20° or 30° off the starboard bow, or 90° off the starboard beam.

Things that the pelorus did are now being done by other more interesting piloting tools, like the hand bearing compass, for one. The boat owner who has invested money in a hand bearing compass is going to try to make use of it at every occasion, if for no other reason then to justify its purchase.

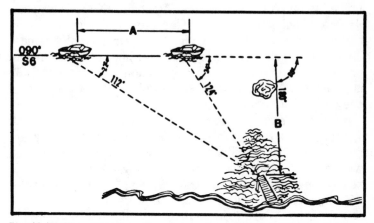

Fig. 11-15. The pelorous can be used to determine the direction of objects from your boat.

Also, modern compasses have been updated to handle other piloting duties besides being just something to steer by. Many compasses have additional lubber lines all around the compass for taking bearings.

Binoculars

Binoculars are another indispensible tool for the small boat pilot. Binoculars will help you pick out the numbers on buoys, names on boats, inlets and harbors that are just a dark smudge on the shoreline. Distances are deceiving on the water, everything is so far away and so small that at night you can't tell if a blinking light is a channel buoy or an anchored boat fishing off the channel. The human eye, unaided, sees very little at sea. This is why you *must* have binoculars if you cruise.

Once upon a time you could buy one of the best made binoculars in the world with an American name on it. The Bausch & Lomb 7X50, used by the U.S. Navy, was the equal of any German Zeiss glass. Some Kodak and Wollensak camera lenses were just as good as Zeiss Tessars.

After World War II, the Japanese moved in on the camera and optics field and American manufacturers just let them take over. Today, photographers like myself, have no choice but to use Japanese cameras and lenses. Boatmen, like myself, have no choice but to use Japanese binoculars.

The first Japanese binoculars after the war were just very bad imitations of the German Zeiss glass. Then they started imitating the American Bausch & Lomb 7X50 Navy glass. After a while, Japanese binoculars started getting better and better. Today some are excellent. The quality of Japanese binoculars depends on the importer. Bushnell of California imports only the best. Their super wide angle Rangemaster 7X35 is probably the best all-around binocular in the world. I own one and it is absolutely superb.

Bushnell's 7X35 Rangemaster is standard equipment with spotters at football games who assist the play-by-play announcers by identifying players quickly. The glass has such a wide angle of view that, without moving the glass, you can keep an eye on the quarterback without losing sight of the wide receivers as they run down the field.

Binoculars are so important to the boatman, and there seems to be so much ignorance on the subject, that I am going to go into the subject at considerably more detail and try to answer some of the questions that I have so often been asked.

One of the questions which makes me cringe, and which I am always being asked is: "How far can you see with binoculars?"

That is a silly question and it always annoys me. I try to control myself and always answer: "Just as far as you can see without binoculars."

They always look offended. But that was not a silly answer. It was the truth. You don't see any *farther* with binoculars, you just see the same area *better.*

How "far" you can see is relative. It is relative to where you are standing and what you are looking at. If you are looking at a building across the street, that is as far as you can see. If you are looking at the planet Jupiter, you can see millions of miles into space and actually count five of Jupiter's moons. But then, you can see Jupiter without binoculars. But with binoculars, you can see it better. That is the only reason you need binoculars, to see *better.*

All binoculars are rated with figures like: 6X30mm, 7X50mm, 8X40mm, 10X50mm, 16X60mm. The first figure is magnification. The object you look at is magnified to look 6 times bigger, or larger with more magnification. There are binoculars that go up to 20X magnification. Power, or magnification, is not important. But being able to clearly see what you are looking at is important. That is why the general purpose glass in the U.S. Navy is 7X50mm.

Magnification beyond 7 power only means more movement, and more difficulty holding the glass steady on a rolling boat. Through personal experience, I have been unable to read numbers on buoys with a 12X50mm glass, but I could easily read them with a 7X50mm.

That second figure, 50mm, is the diameter of the big objective lens . The bigger this lens , the more light it admits and the better you see, especially at night. The 7X50mm is often called a night glass because of that big 50mm (2-inch) objective lens .

Another important feature of prismatic binoculars, not generally understoood, is the stereoscopic effect which shows *depth* rather then just two-dimensional height and width, which is what you get looking through a telescope with one eye. In binoculars, because of the two prisms, the two objective lenses are farther apart then the two eye optics. Therefore, each eye sees from a different angle, which is what creates the steroscopic three-dimensional effect of depth.

Looking through a telescope, or ordinary field glasses, everything looks flat and two-dimensional; all objects appear to be side-by-side. You can't determine who is *behind* who. Looking at two ships at sea, both may appear to be the same size, and the same distance away. But actually one may be twice as big as the other, but since it is farther in the distance, both ships look the same size. You can appreciate how important this is in the military and navy. This is why, in World War I, German commanders, with the first prismatic binoculars, had a considerable advantage in the field. The German navy also had the same advantage at sea.

Prisms made possible higher magnification and, at the same time, reduced the length of the binocular. An old field glass or telescope, in 7 power, would be over two feet long and unmanageable. For this reason, field glasses were usually about 3 power. Telescopes in higher power would be three feet long and would have such a small width of field that you couldn't find what you wanted to see unless you aimed the glass like a rifle. Watching a football game with such a glass, all you could see would be the quarterback's head, if you could find it.

The short length of binoculars, and the result of light traveling in five different directions through those prisms, increases the field of view. To illustrate this, cut a small hole in a sheet of paper and look through it. The closer your eye is to the hole, the more you can see. In binoculars with prisms, you eye is closer to the objective lens.

Field of view is very important. A good navy type 7X50mm glass will have a field of view of 376 feet at 1,000 yards. The Bushnell Rangemaster 7X35 field is an amazing 578 feet at 1,000 yards.

Binoculars are available in center focus (C.F.) or individual eye focus (I.F.). Navy glasses are all I.F. because in this type the internal optics and prisms are sealed against entry of dirt, moisture, and, in the tropics, fungus. Only this type can be made waterproof. Each eye is focused separately, but there is a numbered scale to enable the user to quickly return to a certain focus without looking through the glass. Once the user becomes familiar with his glass, he knows instantly where to pre-set his focus.

With C.F. you must look through the glass to focus, you cannot pre-set. Where many people will be using a glass, C.F. is often preferred because each individual has to focus for his or her eyes. Where only one person will be using a glass, I.F. is preferred.

For eyeglass wearers, there is one more indispensible feature, retractible eye-cups to enable the user to see the entire field of view. If you have ever looked through binoculars wearing glasses, you know how the field of view narrows, and field of view is what you pay for in quality glasses like Bushnell's Rangemaster. Of course, you can always remove your glasses, but this is a bloody nuisance on a boat. And when myopia reaches a certain point, you can't focus some binoculars to see without your glasses. I know because I have finally reached that point. A few years ago, I could focus without wearing glasses. Not any more.

The 7X50mm binocular, with coated optics to reduce glare and foggy image, is generally considered the standard marine glass.

PILOTING WITH ELECTRONICS

The ultimate piloting tool is radar, which is covered in an earlier chapter. Radar does many things better, faster and more accurately.

On the radar scope, the pilot's vessel itself is the center of all scanning. All objects relative to the center are visible where their distance can be measured off, and their compass bearing noted. Within its range, radar makes all other piloting aids almost obsolete.

When visual bearings are obscured by fog, the radio direction finder (RDF), provides bearings at greater distances then might otherwise be available with radar.

Bottom characteristics are very useful in dead reckoning. The depthfinder can be an important piloting tool when used properly.

Most skippers turn on the depthfinder only when they get into shallow water so they won't "run aground." But the finder can be used to "home in" on deep water in channels and to keep a check on fathom lines when running along a coastline. Very often fathom lines will run parallel to a coastline and will guide the pilot like the white line in the center of a highway.

The depthfinder is almost indispensible in the Intracoastal Waterway. Through most of its route from New England to the Florida Keys, the Big Ditch, as it is sometimes called, provides craft with well-marked canals and channels at least 90 feet wide and a minimum of 12 feet deep. But there are many long stretches of water, such as open bays between canals and bordered to seaward, that are shallow. There are days when visibility is poor and you can't *see* the next navigational aid and, if you don't have radar, you must sound the bottom continuously to make sure you don't stray.

Inlets are a problem to all pilots, mainly because they are always changing and can't be accurately charted. You always approach inlets with caution, and continual sounding. Inlets do not abruptly shoal into one big sandbar. It will be more gradual. There will usually be a series of sandbars like ripples in the sand, but each one getting a little bigger. When they start getting too big, it's time to back off because that last one could hang you up. All this you can *see* with a depthsounder.

A piloting error made by many new boatmen is failing to allow for transducer differential. Transducer depth is not the same thing as actual water depth. Transducers are usually mounted about two feet below the waterline, from which point they record depth. If the water is 8 feet deep, the finder will show 6 feet. This is the depth from *transducer* to bottom.

Some depthfinders have a way of correcting transducer differential so that the actual depth is shown on the indicator dial. With most, however, you must remember to make a mental correction.

When piloting with a depthfinder, you must always know the *exact* depth, not transducer depth.

RIVER PILOTING

River piloting is a breed of dog I want as little to do with as possible. I have never personally piloted anything on a river, but I crewed for two weeks on a friend's 55-foot houseboat down the Ohio and Mississippi rivers, after which I became convinced that I was never cut out to be a river boat pilot, not on today's rivers.

The rivers didn't bother me. I could learn to live with floating debris, the snags, the trees, the roots, and all the other things that get washed into rivers. You get that same junk on the Great Lakes at certain times. It was the commercial traffic on the Mississippi that soured me on river boating.

Monstrous tows dominate that great river. Anything else is an interloper and a trespasser. There is no such thing as Rules of the Road. There is only one "Rule" on the river—the towboats. They *own* the river. you just get out of the way or they'll be fishing pieces of you out of the water all the way to the Gulf of Mexico.

The tows, consisting of an extremely powerful towboat and a long string of barges lashed together, are an irresistible force, a juggernaut that, when moving downstream at 10 knots, cannot be stopped in less then 10 lengths, and some of those tows are a quarter mile long.

What this means to a pleasure boatman is you never cross in *front* of a tow unless there is at least a mile between you and the tow (two would be better).

Why so much space?

You will need the time. If your engine should conk out in mid channel, with that juggernaut bearing down relentlessly, there would be a few minutes grace in which you could: a) try to get the engine started, b) jump overboard and swim like crazy, c) stay with the boat and write a will or d) if your family is with you, herd them all together and start praying and singing religious songs.

The pilot on the towboat will blast warnings when he sees you, but beyond making a lot of noise, there is nothing he can do to save you, except radio the lock tender ahead, who will send boats out to pick up the small pieces of you that will be following along in the wash of the tow.

This is what spoiled my two weeks on the Mississippi. We were always dodging tows, often getting into shallow water to do this.

The tows can easily be passed, since they travel at a steady 10 knots, but once you pass a tow you must move over and run down river in front of them, which is absolutely the last place in the world I want to be.

The only safe way to cruise down the Mississippi is at least a half mile behind a tow. And I don't think I like that either.

TIDES

Tides and tidal current are related, but not the same thing. Tide is a *vertical* change in the ocean level. Tide current is a *horizontal* flow of water from one place to another. Tides originate out in the ocean but their effect is felt only in coastal areas like bays, sounds, beaches, and rivers which empty into the sea. All such areas affected by tides are called *tide waters*.

425

Cause Of Tides

It is the gravitational pull of both the moon and sun that causes tides. The sun exerts a greater pull then the moon, but it is farther away—some 93 million miles, whereas the moon is only 238 thousand miles away. The moon's lesser gravitational attraction exerts more then twice the pull on the earth's large masses of water.

The earth rotates on its axis once every 24 hours, with one half of its total surface always exposed to the sun. Land masses are not affected by gravitational forces, but water masses are because water can be pushed around and moved from one area to another.

The water masses of the earth are commonly considered as being broken up and divided into many oceans and seas. This is not true. All these oceans and seas are actually a *single body of water.* Together they cover approximately 71 percent of the earth's surface. The earth's land masses merely separate this water into three major divisions, the Atlantic, the Pacific, the Indian.

Two forces act on the earth's mass of water—centrifugal and gravitational. As the earth rotates on its axis, a lot of water has to move. But because of Newton's Law of Inertia, we know the water masses resist being moved, standing still while the earth just revolves away. This means an awful lot of water builds up in other places, and were it not for the counter influence of the moon and sun, that water would go shooting off into space, and it would cover the land masses and destroy life. It is the perfect balance of opposing forces that holds the earth's mass of water in check. This is what makes life on the planet earth possible.

The effect of the tide-generating forces of the sun and moon cause the movement of water masses to accumulate at two diametrically opposite positions on the earth's surface. This causes the withdrawal of equal amounts of water from 90° around these tidal bulges. Land masses prevent total free movement of all this water, acting as dams and breakwalls.

In each lunar month there are two occasions when the moon and earth will be directly aligned with each other—the moon being between the earth and sun at "new moon" and on the opposite of the earth during "full moon." At these times, the moon exerts maximum force on the earth's water masses, resulting in higher high tides and lower low tides. These are called *spring tides.*

426

At two positions, 90° in between, the gravitational forces of the sun and moon tend to counteract each other. This reduces the range between low and high tides. These are called *neap* tides.

On most coastal areas throughout the world, two high tides and two low tides occur every lunar day of 24 hours, 50 minutes and 28 seconds. The *tidal* day is longer then the *civil* day. The actual amount of depth change in the deep waters of oceans may be only a foot or two, but in coastal areas tide effect is greatly increased, as in the Bay of Fundy where it has reached 53 feet.

In some areas, there are two equal high tides and two equal low tides each lunar day. These are known as *semidiurnal* tides and they are most common on the east coast of the United States. On the west coast, in the San Francisco area especially, they have a *mixed* type of tide where the highs and lows change twice daily.

In Pensacola, Florida they will have one high and one low water each lunar day. This is called a *diurnal* tide.

Tide Information

You cannot pilot safely in tidal waters anywhere, even hundreds of miles up rivers from the sea, unless you understand tides and carry with you, along with your charts, necessary tide information.

The mariner's Bible of tide information is the *Tide Tables* published by the National Ocean Survey of the U.S. Department of Commerce. In coastal areas and waterfront communities you can get tide information from local newspapers, radio and TV stations, but the information they provide all comes from those same Tide Tables. Why get this information second hand? However, if you do not have the Tide Tables, almost any place you stop for gas or supplies, or for an overnight stay, will have local tide information.

The Tide Tables give you information as to the predicted times and levels of high and low water at various locations called *reference stations.* The tables are available in four volumes covering the East and West Coasts of both North and South America. The price for each volume is, or was $3.75. You can buy them from any sales agent for the National Ocean Survey.

Tide Tables

Each volume of the tables provides different information. They are arranged in this manner:

Table 1. Here you will find the time and heights of tides for each day of the year for designated localities called *Reference Stations.*

Table 2. In hundreds of subordinate *Reference Stations* there will be tide differences. This table provides the information that enables you to modify local tidal information, as in San Francisco, for example, which uses a different low water datum then the East Coast.

Table 3. This table enables you to determine the height of the tide at any time and is necessary to calculate bridge clearances.

Table 4. This table tells you when the sun rises and sets in various latitudes for a full year.

Table 5. This is a time adjustment table for converting local mean time given in table 4 to zone or standard time.

Table 6. This is the table that gives you the zone time for when the moon rises and sets for every day of the year in certain areas.

The National Ocean Survey also publishes a supplement to the Tide Tables called Tidal Current Tables. This consists of 12 separate charts, one for each hour of the tidal cycle.

Tidal currents are of great interest to large vessels where very precise piloting is necessary in areas where there is limited space. The moving and turning characteristics of large vessls is a long, slow laborious operation, sometimes taking a half hour just to back out of a grain-loading facility and then turning to leave a port.

I watched the *Queen Elizabeth II* dock in New York during a tugboat strike. The crew did it without tugs, but it took almost two hours. But the wind, river and tide current did all the work. But it took a lot of computing with slide rules.

Current Tables

In addition to current charts, there are current tables which look and read like tide tables, but they don't provide as much extensive information. There are two volumes of these Tables and they are arranged as follows:

Table 1. This is a complete list of predictions for maximum currents and slack, with speeds given in knots.

Table 2. This table lists the differences and speed ratios at a large number of *Reference Stations.*

Table 3. This table shows you how to calculate the speed of the current at any time.

Table 4. Current speeds will sometimes exceed speeds given. This Table lists the number of minutes current will not exceed maximum speeds.

Table 5. This table provides information on rotary tidal currents.

You don't really need any instructions on how to read Tide Tables because they are self-explanatory. If you can read this book, you can read and understand the Tide Tables.

Reading A Tide Table

Here is what an entry in a tide table for one day looks like:

Table 1

TIMES AND HEIGHTS OF HIGH AND LOW WATER

JANUARY

DAY	TIME	HT.
	H.M.	FT.
1	0644	-0.6
W	1020	4.2
	1678	-1.8
	2323	5.1

These are tide predictions for Wednesday, January 1st. Time is given in the four-digit system. The letters "H.M." mean hours and minutes. Translating the above, on January 1 at 6:44 A.M. the tide at ebb was 6 inches below mean low water level. At flood tide, 10:20 A.M., mean high water was 4 feet 2 inches above mean low water. In the afternoon of that same day, 4:38 P.M., the tide ebbed to 1 foot 8 inches below mean low water. Later that evening at 11:23 P.M., the tide rose to 5 feet 1 inch above mean low water.

When there is a minus sign before a figure, you *subtract* this from water depths shown on charts. When there is nothing in front of the figure, you *add* this to charted depth. For example, if the chart shows 2 fathoms in the spot where you intend to anchor, at 1123 P.M., while you are asleep, the depth under your hull will increase 5 feet, 1 inch. When you add this to 2 fathoms (12 feet), you are now in slightly over 17 feet of water.

You should have allowed for this when you estimated your scope.

DETERMINING BRIDGE CLEARANCES

At the base of all bridges there will usually be clearance gauges, but in a tight situation where you are down a few inches, I would not trust any gauge. A foot, I would trust, but not two inches. Just tipping one inch of your masthead under a bridge can cause incalculable damage to a sailboat.

This is where piloting for the small boat skipper gets to be an aggravation—trying to determine the exact clearance under a bridge or overhead cable. You do it one way on the East Coast, and you do it a more complex way on the West Coast.

Normally, the heights for Mean High Water are measured from Mean Low Water, *except* when you are determining clearance under bridges, then you use the *Mean Range* as listed in Table 2 of the Tide Tables.

Are you confused?

On the West Coast it's even more confusing. Mean High Water is measured from Mean *Low* Water, which fluctuates. Then there are different *Mean* ranges, and so there are different tables. There is the sum total of one figure, plus half of another figure and you finally wind up with something that does not match what you get from the chart or the clearance gauge under the bridge. This happens because figures on both the chart and the clearance gauge will not always be right.

In a close situation at high tide, you would be wise to just wait a few hours for the tide to ebb. Even licensed pilots do this, and making sense out of gobbledegook tide information and instructions is their business. And even then, the professionals miss occasionally because every day, during every shipping season, ocean freighters scrape the tips of their masts going under bridges.

The pleasure boat pilot will confront a tight situation of clearing a bridge perhaps once in his lifetime. The professionals confront them every day. If occasionally they miss by inches it's because merchant vessels operate on tight time schedules with operating expenses of thousands of dollars per day. Pilots are pressured not to delay a vessel by waiting for lower tides. It's not that pilots make mistakes, it's that they have to keep the ship moving.

The pleasure boat skipper is not under these pressures. In a tight situation, it is better for him to wait a few hours, even another day, for lower water.

Running Through Drawbridges

Flooding, ebbing tides, current and wind cause hundreds of drawbridge accidents every year simply because inexperienced skippers fail to make allowances for tide currents.

Why so many bridge accidents?

Because there are so *many* drawbridges.

In New Jersey alone there are 38 state operated drawbridges, not including an equal number operated by railroads and counties. All of these bridges are on busy waterways used by pleasure craft, and on weekends during the summer, some of them look like freeways during rush hours.

On tidal waterways you will be encountering flooding and ebbing tide currents on an alternate schedule every day. Going out and coming back with those currents is where boatmen get into trouble. One a drawbridge over the Shrewsbury River in New Jersey averages about 10 bridge collisions a year due to skipper miscalculations of tide current.

Drawbridges raised provide vertical clearance for masted powerboats and sailboats, but they do not provide more clearance *horizontally.* It's a tight squeeze for two large boats to get through at the same time, and everybody's in a hurry to get through because bridge tenders don't like to hold up Sunday drivers too long.

Often when a large boat approaches the opened bridge and sees another boat already committed from the other direction, the skipper will try to turn around so he can go back and try again. This is the fatal mistake—trying to make a 180° turn with a strong tide current pushing them towards the bridge.

A boat moving slowly *with* a strong current has almost no steerageway, and then when you try to make a long 180° turn, it takes so much time that before you have swung 90° the current has you pinned up against the bridge.

Many accidents occurring at bridges are for this reason. When a boat turns broadside into a strong current, with no room to maneuver, it is in a vulnerable and dangerous position.

The only part of a boat that is controllable running *with* a strong current is the stern. If you must stop at a drawbridge with the current behind you, to wait for another boat to pass through from the opposite direction, reverse engines and back

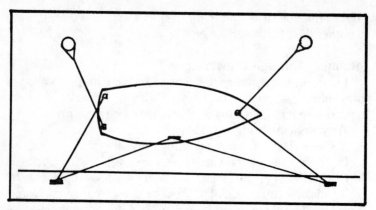

Fig. 11-16. Always use long runs in your dock lines when you tie up in tidal waters. Note how the two stern lines are criss-crossed to make them longer. The water level can go up 3-feet or down 3-feet without hanging the boat up on its dock lines.

into the current with all the power needed to make progress with twin screws, and outboard drives, thsi is easy. With single screw inboards, the rudder, being pushed against the current, will give steerage astern.

DOCKING IN TIDAL WATERS

Cruising fresh water boatmen, making their first trip through the New York canal system, and down the Hudson River to New York, often get some unpleasant surprises after laying fast to a visitor's dock at some marina or club. Unless they have been warned by friends, or if they are not too observant, they will tie up and handle their lines pretty much as they had been doing all through the canal system and back home on the Great Lakes.

Then they go downtown like typical tourists to window shop, looking for a good restaurant and a nice cocktail lounge with entertainment. If they do not get back to the boat until after the tide has ebbed, they will find their boat in a very strange position—the bow will be down, but the stern will be up and hanging on a cleat. On some fiberglass boats that stern cleat might be pulled right out, or the line will have broken and the stern will be swinging loose.

In tidal waters, boats are tied up differently at docks, piers or wharves. Figure 11-16 shows you the approved way to tie up to a dock in tidal waters. I personally use this method ALL the time regardless of where I am. We may not have tides on the Great Lakes but we do have *winds* that can have dramatic

432

effects on water levels.

On Western Lake Erie I have gone to sleep on my boat in eight feet of water, and woke up the next morning with my hull resting in the mud.

Chapter 12
American Aids
To Navigation

If you have done much cruising in foreign waters, then you probably are, like myself, a great admirer of the U.S. Coast Guard. Only after you have piloted a boat in *other* waters can you appreciate what we American boatmen have—the best aids to navigation.

U.S. COAST GUARD

There is more to the Coast Guard than their checking for inspection stickers on boat windshields every year (Fig. 12-1), or somebody to call on the radiotelephone for signal checks—or a free tow when you get hung up on a sandbar or run out of gas.

Playing Big Brother to millions of boatmen every year is not why the Coast Guard was created by a Congressional enactment in 1915. At that time yachting was only for the rich and, although the new service had the responsibility of enforcing Maritime Law and protecting American lives and property at sea, they had little contact with individual taxpayers.

The Coast Guard's primary function then and now is the setting up, operation and maintenance of aids to navigation on all navigable waters subject to Federal jurisdiction (Fig. 12-2). The words "Navigable" and "Federal jurisdiction" applies also to inland waters that have *access to the sea*. Those last four words, "access to the sea," are what determines whether waters are "navigable," and therefore under Coast Guard

Fig. 12-1. Inspections like this can be both embarrassing and, if you have been assisted after a radio call for help, quite painful. After all such rescues, the Coast Guard gives your craft a rigid inspection and if there are violations, issues a citation. However, under other circumstances, they will merely issue a warning and if you voluntarily submit to an inspection by the Coast Guard Auxiliary, you won't even get a warning, just friendly advice and suggestions (courtesy of the U.S. Coast Guard).

jurisdiction. Waters like lakes and rivers, which do not have access to the sea, are under the jurisdiction of the states in which they are located.

WHAT BUOYS DO

On land the driver of an automobile has clearly defined areas where he must stay. Streets and highways are to the auto driver what channels are to a ship pilot. Since the surface of a highway is visible, there is no need to mark it with guide signs that tell you where it is. You can see it.

On the water there are no visible highways to steer by, yet ships are just as limited as automobiles as to where they can go. That is what buoys are for, to keep ships "on the road."

Looking out over large expanses of water can be very deceptive. Almost always there is far less water out there than you think—that is, water of sufficient depth for ships to move through safely. Very often there is not enough depth, in which case depth is artificially created by dredging.

The U.S. Army Corps of Engineers has the responsibility of

435

maintaining proper depth in all navigable waters of the United States. Army Corps dredge ships (Fig. 12-3), huge monsters with suction devices extending from each side, work the year round to keep channels dredged to a depth of about 24 feet.

If you look at any harbor chart, you will see square areas marked off with the words "dumping ground." This is where dredges get rid of the silt and mud they suck up out of channels. After channels are dredged, they have to be marked because you can't see them. That is what buoys do. They show you *where* it is safe to take your boat.

THE AMERICAN BUOYAGE SYSTEM

The *lateral* buoyage system used in all American waters is both simple and complex, depending on who you are and what you are piloting. To the navigator of a foreign vessel entering American waters for the first time, our lateral system is confusing and very complicated, so much so that captains of foreign vessels are only too glad to take on American pilots.

The professional licensed pilot is a specialist in certain area

Fig. 12-2. When the Coast Guard Cutter Katmai Bay originally went into service it had little contact with ordinary taxpayers in their small boats. It was engaged mainly in ice breaking and protecting American lives and property at sea. Today that protection extends to thousands of pleasure craft, and cutters, like Katmai Bay, are called upon to stand watch over regattas and even search for missing boats (courtesy of the U.S. Coast Guard).

Fig. 12-3. It is dredge ships like the Hoffman, here working in Buffalo harbor, that made it possible for Houston, Texas, some 50 miles from the sea, to become the third largest shipping port in the United States. Dredges suck up the silt from channels to a depth of 24 feet, then take the silt to dumping grounds at sea (courtesy of the U.S. Coast Guard).

waters, like the Great Lakes, the Mississippi River, the New York Harbor, etc. Even with the water area narrowed down, there is much to know and remember, not only about buoys, but lights on ships. Many buoys are lighted, and all boats are lighted. And there are lights on the shoreline. At night you can blow your mind trying to distinguish which is which. It was confusion over lights that caused the collision between the Coast Guard Cutter *Cuyahoga* and the Argentine freighter *Santa Cruz II* that claimed 11 lives when the cutter sank.

Fortunately, for the private boat owner, things are a lot easier because your personal confrontation with the American buoyage system is going to be on a smaller, more digestable scale that will not overwhelm you with too many things to remember. It is very hard to remember things that you use for only a few weeks every year on short vacation cruises to new waters.

Buoy Systems

There are two buoy systems used by all maritime nations, the *lateral system* and the *cardinal system.* The lateral system, as used in all American waters, indicates danger *lateral* to the course you are traveling. The color and numbers on buoys tells you on which side of them is danger.

To illustrate this, entering a channel from seaward, to the left of you will be black buoys with odd numbers like 3, 5, and 7. To the right of you will be red buoys with even numbers like 2, 4, and 6. As long as you keep those black buoys on your left (port), you are on the safe passing side. The same applies with the red buoys, which must be on your right (starboard) as you pass. The two opposite areas, *lateral* to the buoys, is danger. The American buoyage system is based on this very simple principle, with only two things to remember: on one side of a buoy is safety, on the other side is danger.

In the cardinal system, used by many other countries, the color, shape, numbers and lighting on a buoy tells you the cardinal compass point of danger relative to the buoy itself. Are you confused?

When you approach such a buoy, it's type tells you that there is danger 180 degrees from the buoy itself, which is south, one of the four cardinal points on a compass. But this does not tell you on which *side* you pass the buoy. That is something you must figure out for yourself. All you know is that danger lies south and you must pass to north . But where is north? You have to figure that out for yourself.

The American system is simpler, and less prone to error. Even if you are color blind, you still know that even numbers are on red buoys and you keep them on your right as you pass entering from seaward. It is almost foolproof, but not quite.

Aids To Navigation

Two boating terms interchangeably used are *aids to navigation* and *navigational aids,* but they are not they same thing. "Navigational aids" can be anything that is used in piloting, like charts, depthfinders, radar, compasses, dividers, parallel rules and even pencils. But "aids" to navigation are only those devices the Coast Guard sets up on land and in the water as markers, guides and reference points to enable pilots and skippers to determine their positions and maneuver their vessels through dangerous waters.

Landmarks

Another point of confusion are those markings on charts to indicate TV towers, chimneys, water tanks and buildings. These are often referred to as aids to navigation. They are helpful in dead reckoning calculations, but they are not *aids* to navigation because they were not put there for that purpose. They are nothing more then recognizable *landmarks* which are useful in dead reckoning. The trouble with landmarks is they're not always there when you need them, but aids to navigation *are* there when you need them. Smokestacks and TV towers were not built as aids to mariners. They just happen to be there are are so noted on navigational charts so that they can be used as dead reckoning reference points.

Aids to navigation are that and nothing else. They are not meant to do double duty, like serving as anchors for fishermen. In fact, it is a serious criminal offense to tie up to or damage an aid to navigation. If you accidently hit one, you must immediately report this to the Coast Guard by radio, if you have one.

The Coast Guard will not set up aids to navigation for the sole convenience of private interests, like clubs or marinas so docking boatmen can avoid rocks and sandbars near the entrance to an anchorage. There must be compelling economic justification and a reasonable amount of general water traffic, which excludes special interest groups.

COAST GUARD DISTRICTS

There are ten Coast Guard Districts in the continental United States, plus one in Alaska and one in Hawaii. Each District operates as a self contained operation with its own commander, engineers, administration headquarters, supply depots and specially designed ships and rescue craft to properly service its area. Buoy tenders, cutters, icebreakers in District 17, which is Alaska, will be different from deep sea offshore cutters and rescue equipment designed for District 8, which takes in Texas, New Orleans and the Gulf of Mexico, all popular boating areas.

Last year the Coast Guard maintained over 21,000 unlighted buoys and 3,700 lighted buoys in all the navigable waters under its jurisdiction (Fig. 12-4).

TYPES OF AIDS TO NAVIGATION

Lighthouse is a word the Coast Guard no longer uses, except unofficially. The official name for lighthouse is *Primary Seacoast Light* and *Secondary Lights.*

These are the biggest and most important lights the Coast Guard maintains, and they are the first light the seagoing

Fig. 12-4. Cutters like the Mesquite, above, are the buoy tenders of the Coast Guard. They are responsible for some 24,700 buoys of all types in all navigable American waters, including the western rivers (courtesy of the U.S. Coast Guard).

sailor sees as he nears land. This is the light that gives him the biggest thrill when he identifies it by its phase characteristics. It is his landfall. He is home.

These lights can be on land, like the Split Rock Light in Lake Superior, which sits 178 feet above the water on a rock cliff. Its light is 1 million candlepower and can be seen about 24 miles.

The Dry Tortugas Light is way out in the Gulf of Mexico sitting on a white tower 157 feet above the water. It can be seen 20 miles.

The Detroit River Light (Fig. 12-5) sits about 10 miles out in Lake Erie marking the channel entrance into the Detroit River. This light is very similar to the Toledo Harbor Light, 10 miles out in Lake Erie, and the lower Lake Huron light which marks the channel entrance into the St. Clair River. These three are classified as *Secondary Lights*, 10,000 candlepower, visibility about 15 miles.

One of the most powerful lights in the world is the Charleston Light on Sullivans Island, South Carolina, with 28 million candlepower and a visibility of about 26 miles.

Identifying Lights

For navigational purposes, a light is useless unless it can be clearly seen and identified. The sailor coming in from a long sea voyage is extremely anxious to sight a charted object to determine his position. It is the Moment of Truth for all navigators. Finally he sees a pin-point of light on the horizon. To make sure the light is on the horizon, the navigator makes the *bobbing a light* test, reducing the height level of his eyes.

This test is made by standing on the toes, then dropping to the knees. If the navigator is in a pilot house, he can go down

Fig. 12-5. The Detroit River Light sits about 10 miles out in Lake Erie marking the channel entrance into the Detroit River.

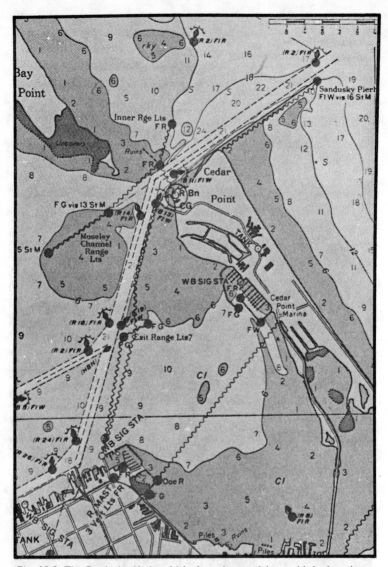

Fig. 12-6. The Sandusky Harbor Light is at the top right on this harbor chart. Note the great detail you get in a harbor chart, how you can even pick out the docks in the Cedar Point Marina. Note also the three sets of range lights, the Moseley Channel Range Lights, The Inner Range Lights and the Exit Range Lights. All of these can be used to correct a compass, preferably on a weekday when there is less boat traffic.

to a lower level. If the light disappears at a lower deck level, it *is* on the horizon. If the light does not disappear, then it is not on the horizon and has to be considered as just another boat. A small boat running in high swells will see the horizon light appear and disappear.

The navigator knows he *should* be about 20 miles from the Cape Henry light at the entrance to the Chesapeake Bay. He sees a light. Now it must be identified.

Information on the range and identifying characteristics of all navigational lights are in the *Light List*, published by the U.S. Coast Guard in five volumes covering different geographical areas. The *Light List* gives you more information than you get on charts.

The visibility range of all important lights is given on charts like this one for the Sandusky Harbor light on Lake Erie: "Fl W vis 16 St M (Fig. 12-6.)" This translates to: Flashing white, visibility 16 statute miles.

The visibility range on charts is calculated at Mean High Water and an eye height of 15 feet at the seeing end. Table 12-1 shows you the distance to horizon at different heights. As eye height is raised or lowered, visibility range of a light changes.

According to the table, a light 70 feet high would have a range of 11.0 miles to the horizon. With eye level at 15 feet, the horizon is pushed up another 5.1 feet, and added to the 11.0 miles of the light, visibility is increased to 16 miles.

In a small outboard boat, eyeheight is considerably less than 15 feet; more like 6 feet standing up. At 6 feet, according to the table, visibility is 3.2 miles to the horizon. Add this to 11.0 miles and the Sandusky Harbor light visibility is reduced to 14.2 miles.

On large freighters, eye height can be 150 feet atop a mast. At this eye level, visibility to the horizon is 14.0 miles. Add this to 11.0 miles and the Sandusky Harbor light range of visibility increases to 25 miles.

Now that the light is seen, it must be identified. This is done by watching it through binoculars. All *Primary Seacoast* and *Secondary Lights* go through sequences of blinking, flashing and changing patterns. This is called *Light Phase Characteristics.* Figure 12-7 shows 10 different light patterns. On charts, this will be printed in abbreviated form like:

Alt Fl	(alternate flashing) usually in two colors, like red-white or green-white.
F and Fl	(fixed and flashing) a fixed white light varying at regular intervals with short flashing.

Illustration	Symbols and meaning		Phase description
	Lights which do not change color	Lights which show color variations	
	F – Fixed	Alt – Alternating	A continuous steady light.
	F Fl – Fixed and flashing	Alt F· Fl – Alternating fixed and flashing	A fixed light varied at regular intervals by a flash of greater brilliance.
	F Gp Fl – Fixed and group flashing	Alt F Gp Fl – Alternating fixed and group flashing	A fixed light varied at regular intervals by groups of 2 or more flashes of greater brilliance.
	Fl – Flashing	Alt. Fl Alternating flashing.	Shows a single flash at regular intervals, the duration of light always being less than the duration of darkness. Shows not more than 30 flashes per minute.
	Gp Fl – Group flashing.	Alt. Gp Fl – Alternating group flashing.	Shows at regular intervals groups of 2 or more flashes.
	Qk Fl – Quick flashing.	. . . .	Shows not less than 60 flashes per minute.
	I. Qk Fl – Interrupted quick flashing.	. . . .	Shows quick flashes for about 4 seconds, followed by a dark period of about 4 seconds.
	S-L. Fl – Short-long flashing.	. . . .	Shows a short flash of about 0.4 second, followed by a long flash of 4 times that duration.
	Occ. – Occulting	Alt. Occ. – Alternating occulting.	A light totally eclipsed at regular intervals, the duration of light always equal to or greater than the duration of darkness.
	Gp. Occ. – Group occulting.	. . . .	A light with a group of 2 or more eclipses at regular intervals.

Light colors used and abbreviations: W – white, R – red, G – green.

Fig. 12-7. Shown are ten different light patterns that are used to identify lights.

F and Gp Fl	(fixed and group flashing) similar to above except that short flashes will be in varying groups.
Gp Fl	(group flashing) light flashes in spaced groups, followed by periods of darkness.
Occ	(occulting) the light just goes on and off, but the periods are longer.
Gp Occ	(group occulting) a light with a group of two or more eclipses spaced at regular intervals.
E. Int	(equal interval) the cycles of on and off being equal.

Identifying Lighted Buoys

Lighted buoys also have *Phase Characteristics* which identify them. Figure 12-8 shows these changing light patterns and how they are listed on charts:

Mo A   These are short-long flashes spelling out the letter "A" in Morse Code. This light is always white and is used only on vertical

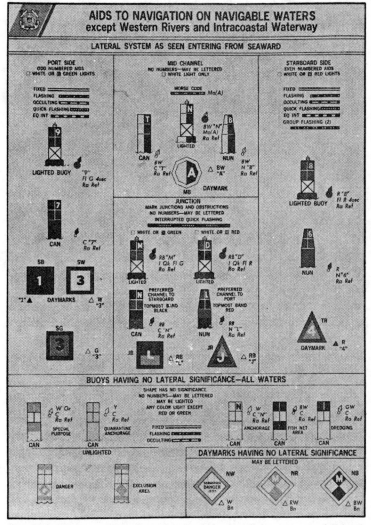

Fig. 12-8. Shown are the phase characteristics and light patterns of lighted buoys.

striped buoys that mark a mid-channel or fairway.

Qk Fl (quick flashing) this light is used to mark wrecks, dangerous obstructions and changes in the width of a channel.

I Qk Fl (interrupted quick flashing) this is used only at channel junctions and obstructions. This buoy will have horizontal red-black bands.

Fl l (flashing light) this light flashes at a rate not more than 30 times a minute and can be on either red or black buoys, or on buoys used for some special purpose.

Lightships are the floating equivalent of a lighthouse anchored or moored miles out at sea. However, lightships provide more information to mariners. Lighthouses, *Primary Seacoast Lights,* are unmanned and function automatically. Lightships on the other hand, are manned by crews who can be communicated with on the radiotelephone by approaching vessels who want information. Lightships also operate fog signals, submarine sound signals and radiobeacons.

The name of a lightship will be painted in large letters on the side and by day they will fly the International Code signal flags so approaching vessels will recognize them.

Beacons are sometimes confused with radiobeacons, which they are not. Also called *daybeacons* and *daymarks,* they are unlighted fixed markers in shallow waters providing some special guidance information or special warning.

Radiobeacons are little radio transmitters which broadcast a recognizable signal which is useful to mariners in plotting their position.

Electronic Aids, like Loran-A and Loran-C, transmit a special signal over much longer ranges than radiobeacons.

Types of Buoys

Buoys are the most common aids to navigation (Fig. 12-9). They are floating devices anchored in position by heavy cast concrete blocks called sinkers, averaging 500 pounds to more than 6 tons. Buoys can be lighted, unlighted or equipped with some form of audible signaling device. Buoys are shown on all charts with notations indicating their shape and color, whether or not they are lighted or emit some form of audible signal. Buoys come in a variety of sizes from little 6th Class types,

Fig. 12-9. Buoys of this type are invaluable to boatmen.

which are just visible a few feet above the water, to enormous Super Buoys that can be 40 feet in diameter and rise to over 30 feet above the water.

Can buoys (Fig. 12-8) look exactly like what they are called, big *cans.* They are cylindrical in shape with a flat top and lifting rings. Newer types have built in radar reflectors which make shipping channels look like lighted airport landing strips at night to boats equipped with radar receiving equipment. Can buoys are always painted black, are odd-numbered and are located on the left side (port) of a channel when entering from seaward.

Nun buoys (Fig. 12-8) are also cylindrical in shape, but the upper half of the cylinder tapers down to almost a point or slightly rounded and with a single lifting ring. Nun buoys are always painted red, are even - numbered and are on the right side (starboard) of a channel entering from seaward. Newer types are also equipped with radar reflectors.

Lighted buoys (Fig. 12-8) are constructed of metal floats with a steel tower-like superstructure atop which a light will be mounted. This light is powered by electric batteries which are kept in the lower float. The batteries will keep the light operating for months. Color of the light can be red, green or white. When used in shipping channels, the red light will always be on the right side (starboard) entering from seaward. The green light, on a black-colored buoy, will always be on the left side of the channel.

A white light can be used on either side of a channel since the color of the light itself has no special significance. The buoy itself, however, will be properly colored for the side of the channel it identifies. It is the intensity and phase characteristic of the light that conveys information to identify the light. White lights have a greater visibility range and are used in situations where the buoy must convey a warning.

Sound buoys are used mainly in areas where fogs are a continuing navigational hazard. In open waters, where there is considerable wave action, bell buoys, gong buoys and whistle buoys are used because wave action itself activates the sound. In whistle buoys, wave action produces compressed air which blows the whistle.

Horn buoys are powered by electricity from batteries rather than wave action, and for this reason are used in quiet waters where there is no wave action. Combination buoys emit a light and produce some form of sound. If you can't see the buoy in heavy fog, you can hear it.

Wreck buoys are placed on either the seaward side or the channel side of submerged wrecks which present a hazard to navigation. Solid colored buoys must be passed only on one side, the *seaward* side. Horizontal banded buoys can be passed on either side.

Wrecks do not always stay where they originally sank. Often after a buoy has been set up, the wreck will shift, and move a considerable distance. For this reason wreck buoys should always be approached and passed with caution.

Special purpose buoys are aids to navigation every boat-man should be familiar with because you will inevitably encounter them when cruising in strange waters. In the Chesapeake Bay area, for example, you will see many black-white horizontally banded buoys which are used to stake off specially designated areas for fish-netting and trapping. These

448

buoys, carrying identification numbers and letters, will be shown on charts (Fig. 12-9).

No matter where you go, the Army Corps of Engineers is dredging. In some areas, like the Detroit River and Chesapeake Bay, they never seem to finish. When you approach a dredging or survey area, you will see many white buoys with green tops. You always pass on the channel side. On the other side will usually be barges and piledrivers (and hardhats shaking a fist at you if you create too much wake as you pass.)

Buoys that are all white indicate anchorages. Buoys that are all yellow indicate quarantine anchorage areas.

If you ever see odd looking yellow-black vertically striped buoys out in the middle of a large expanse of open water, watch out for aircraft, the kind that can land on water. This buoy has no special meaning for boats, other than to warn that the waters are also used by seaplanes.

Dual Purpose Buoys

There are occasions on a passage down the Big Ditch (as it is called by oldtimers) when the Intracoastal Waterway route will coincide with some river which eventually heads off in a different direction. Here you will see buoys with dual markings, serving both ICW traffic and local river boating. On these dual purpose buoys (Fig. 12-10), which are both red and black, you will see either a yellow square or yellow triangle.

To avoid confusion, concentrate your attention only on the yellow squares and triangles, remembering always that the general direction of the ICW is south until you reach Florida. Ignore river markers which go off in other directions. Just keep those yellow squares on your *left*, the yellow triangles on your *right*.

State Buoy Systems

On state controlled waters and rivers you will today find some degree of uniformity in how waters are marked, but not necessarily in a manner used in Federally controlled waters under jurisdiction of the Coast Guard. Before an Act of Congress created the Uniform State Waterway Marking System USWMS), every state had its own system, which was the cause of much confusion for traveling skippers who like to haul their boats from state to state.

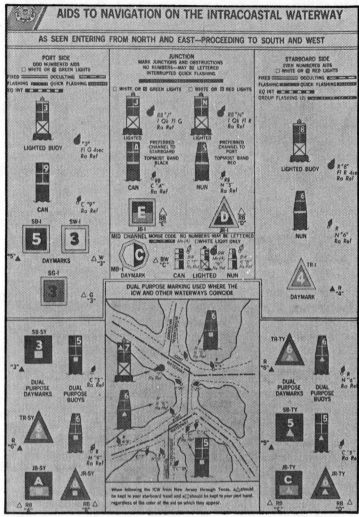

Fig. 12-10. The ICW uses dual purpose buoys because it often coincides with other waterways.

The state marking systems, are in some respects, better since they were designed primarily to help the small recreational boatmen in the state rather than big commercial vessels and the international merchant marine.

If the boatman can read, he can easily understand state regulatory markers without consulting a chart or other publication (Fig. 12-11). All state markers tell you one of four things: beware of danger, keep out, restricted, or official information.

Danger signs will spell out words like: "Dam," "Rocks," "Reefs," or "Snags."

Keep out signs will have words on them like: "Waterfall" or "Swim area."

Restricted signs will read: "No ski," "No anchoring" or "5 MPH."

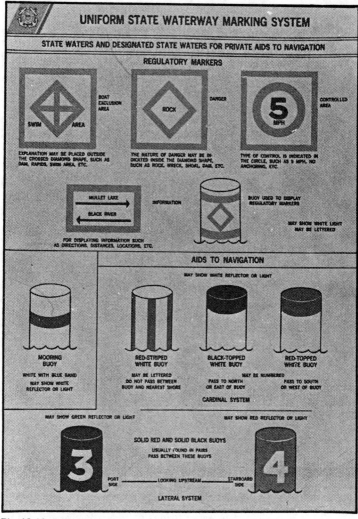

Fig. 12-11. State water markers spell things out for boatmen.

Official information signs will give you distances, arrows pointing to "State park," "Picnic areas" and "Restrooms."

As you can see, this is an easily understood buoyage system for little people in little boats.

State River Buoy Systems

Buoyage in state rivers (Fig. 12-12) follows both the lateral system and, in a few instances, the cardinal system. Going

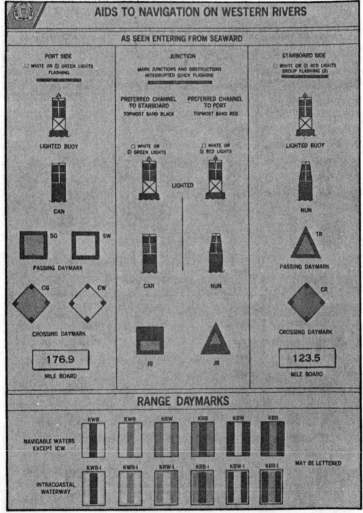

Fig. 12-12. Buoyage in state waters follows both the lateral system and the cardinal system.

upstream, all of the buoys to your left will be black and odd numbered. All buoys to your right will be red and even numbered. It is only in state controlled waters that you will ever encounter the cardinal system of buoyage, and then only with two specific types of buoys—one is white with a red top, the other is white with a black top.

The white buoy with the red top will be to your *left* as you go upstream, where normally you would expect to see black, and this may confuse you. In the cardinal system you pass to the *south* or *west* of that particular buoy. So you just treat it like a black buoy, and keep it on your left.

The white buoy with the black top will be on your right as you go upstream, where normally you only see red. That black top means safe passing is to the *north* and *east*. So you treat it like a red buoy and keep it on your right.

I can understand why the U.S. Coast Guard sticks exclusively to the lateral system of buoyage, which is hard enough for recrational boatmen to understand without adding more confusion. The cardinal system is confusing when it is used by states in their rivers.

An inexperienced boatman knows only that he must keep black on his left and red on his right. Then going up river one day he is surprised to suddenly see *red* on his *left* and *black* on his *right*. He has to be confused. He could even pass the red-topped buoy on the wrong side, which could be a disaster.

THE INTRACOASTAL WATERWAY

There is no need to be fearful of entering the *Intracoastal Waterway* (ICW). You will see the same lateral buoyage system (Fig. 12-10) that is used in all American waters. The only physical difference will be the distinctive ICW identifying color, which is a band of yellow around the top, or a yellow border around a square beacon. When you see that yellow, you are in the Intracoastal Waterway.

When you go south from New Jersey to Florida, you have entered ICW from *seaward*. This means you will see nothing but *red* buoys, fixed aids, beacons and daymarks on your *right* (starboard) all the way to Florida, and to Texas. On your left (port) everything will be black.

Intracoastal Waterway aids to navigation are numbered in the same manner as it is done in all channels. Entering ICS from seaward to go south, buoy numbering starts with a black buoy to port. It will be numbered "1". The first red buoy starboard will be "2". The numbers will never go beyond 99.

INLAND WATERWAYS

The United States has over 30,000 miles of improved interconnecting waterways which give boatmen in all the midwest and eastern states access to the sea. The Great Lakes boatman has two routes to the see by American waters. One from Chicago through the Illinois Waterway to the Mississippi. The other by way of the New York State Canal System to the Hudson River.

There is more than 12,000 miles of wonderful cruising waters in just the Mississippi system alone, which does not include rivers and lakes all over the west which do not have access to the sea, but are just as active in recreational boating. You will see yacht clubs and marinas in areas that have been sage brush-desert backgrounds for old western movies. Today you see 50 foot yachts and big sailboats where buffalo once roamed.

The Inland Waterways are unique. They are *navigable* waters and from Columbus, Ohio, or Zanesville on the Muskingum River, a boat can go anywhere in the world. Navigable waters are under Federal jurisdiction, which means the Coast Guard maintains all aids to navigation.

The one major difference between Inland Waterway cruising and **Big Water** cruising is that you don't need to invest a small fortune in electronics to tell you where you are. You always know. You are rarely far from land. All you really need is a depthfinder, plenty of charts, dividers, pencils and binoculars A VHF radiophone is used mainly to communicate with locktenders. But you don't really have to communicate with them. You already know that they are going to tell you that you must wait until a big string of barges gets through. On the river, everybody waits for them.

Inland River Aids To Navigation

Since the Coast Guard maintains all major river aids, they will be similar in shape and color to aids in coastal waters, with one big difference—they are not numbered. However, some will be numbered, but for a different reason. The numbers indicate *mileage* from a zero reference point that is shown on the chart. This is quite a convenience. It eliminates the need for a speedometer-odometer. The buoys provide you with an accurate daily log of mileage traveled and speed. All you have to do is clock yourself between the buoys. Also, Mississippi buoys have little white tops for improved visibility against shore backgrounds.

"Left" & "Right" River Banks

In river piloting, moving *downstream* establishes "left" bank and "right" bank terminology. In other words, if a city is on the right bank going down river, it is *still* on the "right" bank going up river.

River Charts

Rivers are treacherous waters once you leave the channel. Never cruise any river without charts. They are available in booklet form for all rivers. These booklets, with each page covering only a small section of the river, are very easy to handle and stow. Unlike coastal charts, river charts do not show depth and the location of shoals, rocks or reefs. There is just a broken red line to mark the channel, a shaded blue area to show the river and dark lines to incidate the shoreline.

Eyeball Piloting

You must learn to do a lot of eyeball piloting on rivers, especially when you get squeezed out of the channel by a quarter-mile long string of barges. Rivers are no place to be at night, unless safely anchored off the main channel. During the day you can eyeball the water ahead for the endless trash that you must avoid, like tree trunks and root systems, which often get hung up somewhere and then collect more debris building up a dam behind them.

Some brave skippers, with powerful light systems, risk traveling at night; but that's what it is, a *risk!* There are too many things you just can't see at night, like obstructions just below the surface. Not even with the most powerful light can you see these hazards to small boat travel in the river.

In daylight, these submerged obstacles create a disturbance in the water that you can learn to recognize. The water will boil or ripple in a gentle "V" as it goes around the underwater obstacle. Old experienced river boatmen know how to "read" the river, which is what is meant by "eyeball piloting." Wherever the river changes depth, the surface appearance will change. This is what you look for—sudden ripples and *waves*. Seeing waves on the river ahead should always arouse your suspicion, unless it is a very windy day, in which case the entire river will be covered with waves. The river is a moving mass of water going in one direction. Anything which stands in the way of that moving water causes a change in the surface appearance. That is why you never take your eyes off the water surface ahead of you. In big open water, you eyeball the compass. In the river, you eyeball the river.

Houseboats are ideally suited for river cruising with their shallow draft, low freeboard and close visibility over the bow for the helmsman, which is exactly what you need on rivers (what you do not need on big open water). On the other hand, rivers are a bad environment for the conventional express twin-screw inboard with the helm aft of midship. This is because the bow rides high under moderate power causing the helmsman to look at the sky instead of the water ahead of him. The rudders and propellers on twin-screws are right in the line of fire, where every little piece of debris will get sucked into the wheels.

The outboard drive is far better suited for river boating.

DANGER AREAS

Big bends in rivers should always be approached with caution. They should also be approached *alone*, not alongside commercial traffic. Always try to avoid traveling with commercial vessels. The current does funny things to river bottoms at curves. As a rule, the safest place to be on most river bends is on the outside, which is where the deep water of the channel flows. Most of the shallow water will be on the inside of a big curve.

Warnings

There is no standardization in river charts, which means they're not all alike. Some use different symbols and coloring while some are just black and white. The Ohio River, for example, has its own unique system of symbols and coloring. You better carefully check the Legend of Symbols on any new chart. On the New York State Canal System, for example, buoys on both sides of the canal look alike, except for color.

Range Lights

The compass is rarely needed on rivers, mostly because of

range lights, a valuable aid to commercial traffic, which the Coast Guard has installed on every long stretch of water. Commercial tow pilots use these ranges. Lining up on two lights, fore and aft, is almost like aiming a rifle. Then the autopilot is hooked in and the helmsman has a few free minutes when he can turn his attention to other duties like scanning the waters ahead with binoculars or catching up on paperwork. Binoculars are the river boatman's most used piloting tool.

River Currents

As a general rule, river currents flow in one direction, from headwaters to the mouth, *except* in tidal areas. By judicious timing, a skipper can use the tide and current to save gas—going up river when the tide is flooding, and down river when it is ebbing. Smart skippers do this all the time on the Hudson River. They make that 150 mile run from New York to Albany with the incoming tide and return to New York with the ebbing tide and current.

A great deal of research has been done on river currents, mostly for the benefit of vested interests who use the river for commercial profit. Data from these studies, you can be sure, is available to them and is used by them. For example: going downstream, pilots stay in that portion of the channel where the current is strongest; going upstream they will use a side of the channel closer to shore where the current is slower and weaker. There are always counter-currents flowing behind points of land projecting into the river and the pilots will hug the shoreline headed towards that land to take advantage of the weaker current.

To the recreational boatman this may seem like small potatoes, but to those monsters of the river, it means thousands of dollars in saved fuel costs. Consider the figures: a boat speedometer may show 12 MPH, which is the speed of *water* moving past the boat, but relative to the shoreline the boat is only moving 8 MPH bucking a 4 MPH current.

There are sections of the St. Lawrence River where the current is 12 to 13 MPH. A boat has to burn up gasoline at engine RPMs for 24 MPH just to make 12 MPH headway. This is another reason why houseboats are so ideally suited for river boating. Their shallow drafts and their semi-flat bottoms create less resistance when moving against the current. It was not just by accident that the old stern-wheel riverboats were flat-bottomed.

River Anchoring

Rivers are the worst possible place to take a deep keel sailboat. River channels are kept dredged to a maximum depth of 9 feet, which doesn't leave much clearance for keeled sailboats drawing 6 feet. So long as they stay in the channel, they're safe, but nobody in his right mind anchors overnight in a channel. Small recreational craft have unlimited choices away from channels where they can anchor in water less than 9 feet deep. But this is not true for keeled sailboats. Once the deep-keeler leaves the channel, the mathematical Laws of Probability give him a short life expectancy among the free and the floating before he is stuck in river mud somewhere.

Only a centerboard type sailboat, drawing no more than 3 feet with the board up, is going to be at ease in a river.

Houseboats and outboards, drawing 2 feet and less, have the best of all possible worlds because they can go just about anywhere on the rivers, even close to beaches. In just one weekend on the river, I saw about 50 boats, many of them houseboats, with their bows beached on some small island in the middle of the river. You can't do this with inboards or centerboards, at least, I wouldn't recommend it.

The best place to anchor overnight in the rivers is *behind* something, anything. You will see many dikes projecting out into the river which are constructed to protect river banks from washing away. These are good anchoring spots. There are also endless natural harbors and coves behind land projections which make excellent anchorages and, at the same time, protect you from the never ending commercial traffic and debris that floats in the river current. A thing to remember when anchoring overnight—never beach your boat on the *upstream* side of an island because the current will make it difficult for you to back off.

SPECIAL RIVER PROBLEMS

Rivers are dirty waters, not just during flood times, but at all times. This causes more engine and mechanical problems than the salt in sea water. Engine blocks and water-cooled exhaust manifolds clog up with silt. Water pump impellers wear out, and bronze shaft bearings in struts get chewed up by gritty sand. You don't realize the destructive power of sand until you see sandblasting equipment in action cleaning stone buildings and removing rust and paint from automobile bodies. And remember, sand is what makes sandpaper.

There are special cutlass shaft bearings available with grooves so sand can wash out. They hold up better in muddy water than bronze bearings. Engines can be protected with marine engine strainers which, although they don't remove all the silt, they do filter out most of the sand particles. A filter that removed all the silt would have to be quite large so as not to reduce the flow of cooling water to the engine.

Aids to navigation, like buoys, often become hazards to navigation during high water when currents can pull the buoys under so that only a lifting ring and a V-shaped eddy is visible on the surface as you move downstream. If the current is strong enough, and an uprooted tree gets caught on the buoy, it can be dragged a considerable distance. Frequently when you see a big tree resting motionless in the river, it will be stuck on a buoy. In these situations, you can't be too sure that the buoy is still in its original position but your chart will show you approximately where it should be.

The Mississippi River is an incredible stretch of water and some boatmen just don't give it enough respect. There are stretches on both the upper and lower river where it becomes a sizable body of water, in fact, the river actually becomes a lake. Lake Pepin, for example, is 21 miles long and over 2½ miles wide. The lower river is ½-mile wide during low water and over 2 miles wide during high water. On cloudy, misty days you can't see either shoreline.

These big stretches of water can build up very nasty seas in high winds, especially when the seas run *against* the strong current. This type of sea, current plus waves, can be very damaging to vulnerable craft like houseboats with all that superstructure and those big windows. The twisting, pitching and tossing creates stresses and hull movement which can break windows. This is one of the reasons why houseboats have practically disappeared from Western Lake Erie.

The Army Corps of Engineers is always working on the river, in one place or another, and you will see much equipment, including barges, temporary dikes and pipe lines which must be carefully avoided. Remember, you are responsible for your wake. Slow down, just for reasons of caution and common sense. You are piloting in a hazardous area, which in itself should be enough to slow you down, even if you don't care about all those people working in the river.

If you see hardhats shaking a fist at you as you pass, it means you are going too fast.

River Locks

Locks are the most important aid to navigation on the rivers. Without locks there is no navigation. But as important as they are, lock systems and lock tenders are not one of the endearing aspects of inland waterway boating that some like to remember. You either like it or you hate it. I suppose there are boatmen who like going through locks, but I have yet to meet one.

Order Of Precedence At Locks

There is a VIP pecking order for vessels locking through which is established by the Secretary of the Army, no less, and you can very easily guess who is at the bottom of that totem pole—that's right, the recreational boatman.

Here is the priority list:

1. U.S. Military/Naval craft
2. Mail boats
3. Commercial passenger craft
4. Commercial tow boats
5. Commercial fishermen
6. Non-Commercial

The lock tender can lock you through with commercial craft if he feels there is enough room and if he feels you are competent enough to handle your boat and lines in the surging waters. But he will not run you through with tows or vessels carrying dangerous products.

Locking Through

Locks are dirty places with high concrete walls coated with sludge. You need something to hold you away from that wall going both up and down. Bumpers are no good. They just roll on the wall, picking up the dirt and transferring it to your topsides like the ink roller on a print press (Fig. 12-13).

The lock tender won't allow you to use old tires, or anything else that might foul up his water intakes if it falls into the water. I have seen bales of straw used, but not too well. It's messy, and in some locking systems, if the lock tender sees a

Fig. 12-13. There is nothing wrong with this type of bumper if your boat is painted black. On a white-hulled boat, these bumpers act just like paint rollers, transfering all the crap off the lock wall to your topsides. This stuff is very difficult to wash off.

bale of hay on your decks, and no livestock, he'll wave you off.

Of course, when unprepared, you use whatever you have, which is usually round bumpers. Later, you clean the mess off your topsides.

But after you've been through the locking experience a few times, you eventually learn that there is a better way, a way used by the professionals who ferry boats up and down the Intracoastal Waterway for rich yacht owners who prefer to fly north or south with the seasons. These seasoned old pro boat jockeys know all the lock tenders by their nicknames and they sound like truck drivers talking on CB when they communicate on VHF saying things like: "This is Big Jockey to Herkimer Daddy One. I'm low in the water. Gotta slip for me in that sink basin?"

If you ever lock through with one of these ferried boats, you will see that they use just plain old 2x4 lumber hung *vertically* (up and down) over the side. About two feet will extend above the rub rail and about four feet will extend below it. A ½-inch hole is drilled sideways through the lumber for a loop of line which can be secured to either a cleat or lifeline stanchion post.

The hull side of the lumber on the bottom end will have white fender material to protect the hull. I have also seen rug material used for this purpose.

The lumber, of course, gets dirty in transit but it is easily washed off. At the end of the ferry from Florida to the Great Lakes, the lumber is thrown away. On the next job, they start with new lumber.

One last thing, it is wise to put out fenders on *both* sides of your boat *before* you enter the lock because you never know which side you will be assigned to by the lock tender. I have seen a boat with fenders hanging over the starboard suddenly ordered over to the port wall.

You will need two long lines for locking through. Don't use your regular lines, which may be too heavy and too short. I use 3/8 manila which is cheap, but adequate for the job. This is merely something to hang onto while you go up or down, trying to hold your boat reasonably close to that dirty wall.

With one person up forward and one person aft, the bitter end of the line is lightly secured to a cleat. The bight of the line (the middle part) is run around a bollard or mooring post, and *back* to the boat so that you are holding *two* lines in your hands. As you go down, you play out line; as you go up, you take in line.

There is rarely anybody around to help you with lines, which is why you *do not* drop an eyesplice over a mooring post. If you do, you'll never get it off and you can just wave good bye to your two lines as you leave and hope that you can stop off somewhere to buy new ones. By using a long line doubled back, with both ends under your control, you can pull your line *off* the mooring post when ready to leave.

Lock Signal Lights

Communicating with lock tenders via VHF radio is not a happy or rewarding experience. Forget about the VHF radiotelephone and just watch the lights, which closely resemble traffic signals at major intersections. Red means exactly what red always means: Stop! Do not enter!

When you see that red light, put yourself in a holding pattern or drop a lunch hook if it's a busy day.

The yellow, or amber light means you can approach the lock, but approach *only*, don't enter. The green light means you can enter the lock.

On some rivers there will be a sign warning small craft not to go beyond a certain point. Usually this is quite a distance off, and the lock tender won't hear your horn, unless it's a loud one. This is where a VHF radiotelephone, or a blasting horn, can be helpful. If you have neither, there will usually be a signal cord near the sign for you to pull that signals the lock tender that you want passage.

If you are ever locked through with commercial tows, be careful of the wash directly astern to a jumbo towboat. When they start those big nine-foot propellors in the narrow confines of a lock, the turbulence can bounce you around like a cork. There is always some boiling of the waters in a lock, especially when it is being pumped in, but nothing to compare to the wash from a towboat as it starts to move out.

Dams

It may seem unnecesary to mention that dams are things to stay away from, both at the crest and the lower spillway area below the dam, but this is often an irresistible attraction for fishermen. As obvious as this may seem, about once every season a boat somewhere misses a lock and goes over a dam. If you are wondering how anybody could be so stupid, it's really not that hard to do if you are in strange waters and don't have a chart.

The most dangerous approach is from upstream going *towards* the dam, especially if you are on the opposite side of the river to where the locks are located. Warning signs and rows of big white floating buoys will be on the lock side of the river where you can't help seeing them unless you're blind. The boatmen who miss these signs and go over dams never heard about charts. Surprisingly, there are many boatmen who feel they don't need a chart to just "ride up and down a river."

Speed Limits

There are no speed limits on major rivers and you are free to take all the risks that high speed on debris-filled waters entails. You just never know what may be floating under the surface of that dirty yellow water up ahead, and when you hit a submerged tree trunk at 20 MPH, all the pistons in your engines will change holes.

Not all boating on inland waterways is done on rivers, however. The creation of 42,000 miles of inland waterways necessitated the opening of many artifical waterways to-interconnect and open passageways betwen large navigable bodies of water like lakes and rivers. These artificial waterways are small replicas of the Panama Canal, which consist of big ditches and land cuts that later filled with water, become interconnecting waterways, or canals.

These dredged "ditches" may have a surface width of about 125 feet, but the bottom width may be only 75 feet and the water depth 12 feet.

The shorelines in these land cuts must be protected from the wash of boat traffic or they will erode and wash down again into the area that was just dredged at great expense.

All such waterways have speed limits which, in some areas like the New York State Canal System with a speed limit of 6 MPH, are rigidly enforced.

How do they check on your speed?

Easier than you think. Lock tenders record the arrival time of all boats. There are 58 locks in the entire New York System. From Lock No. 33 to Lock No. 34 is 53.8 miles. It takes 9 hours to travel this distance at a legal speed of 6 MPH. If you make the run in 4 hours, you quite obviously exceeded the speed limit.

The lock tender, in many cases, will have been alerted by property owners along the way who report all speed violations. The lock tender has only to make a phone call to check your departure time at the preceeding lock. If you arrived at his lock in 4 hours instead of 9 hours, you are in trouble. That is how they check up on you.

Chapter 13
Lights/
Rules Of The Road

"Why do I need lights on my boat? I never go out at night."

This is a question often asked by owners of small boats that are used only for water related recreational purposes like skiing, scuba diving, swimming and fishing during daylight hours.

A question is sometimes better answered by another question, like: why do you need lifejackets? Why do you need a fire extinguisher? No boat owner feels a need for these things because he doesn't plan on having a fire or wrecking his craft and being forced to abandon it. Nobody plans these things, they just happen.

WHY LIGHTS ARE NEEDED

You go boating on a Sunday afternoon with the full intention of getting home before dark because you have to go to work Monday. But suppose you don't get home before dark, suppose you don't get home at all. Something screwed up. Maybe that big outboard, all 200 horsepower, just conked out.

The modern outboard engine is no longer a simple piece of machinery with everything exposed and easy to get at with a wrench and screwdriver. Today everything is covered, and when uncovered, anything you touch requires a special tool. Outboard engines, especially in the high horsepower rigs, are complex unserviceable beasts to work "hung on a transom out in the field," (Fig. 13-1) as service people say. If they won't

Fig. 13-1. It is difficult, if not impossible, to service an outboard motor hung out on a transom in this manner, especially in high winds and rough seas.

run, they won't run and if you have only the one engine, you better start waving something on an oar, or better still, start using the oars if you have them, which hardly anybody does.

This is the reason for the increasing popularity of twin-outboard motors. They can sometimes be a life-or-death safety factor in offshore boating.

This is the reason why navigation lights are required on all watercraft, regardless of size.

HAZARDS

When a boat is disabled, dead in the water at night with no lights, it becomes what admiralty lawyers call a *"hazard to navigation."* This is a very serious thing, especially in the corporate boardrooms of big maritime conglomerates whose ships and barges monopolize all navigable waters. If one of their vessels should run down some poor devil at night, it will start all sorts of unpleasant things in motion, like investigations by the Coast Guard, by the insurance underwriters and by boards of inquiry. Before they even get started, the contingency fee lawyers will come in droves like vultures after a lion makes a kill.

When the Coast Guard cutter *Cuyahoga* sank in Chesapeake Bay, after being rammed by the Argentine freighter *Santa Cruz II*, Oct. 20, 1978, before the bodies of the 11 crewmen had

466

been buried, damage suits in the millions were filed on all sides. The litigation on this tragedy will go on for years and many millions will be paid just to the hundreds of lawyers and private investigators involved, not counting the millions that will be paid out when final settlements are reached.

There is no such thing as a small accident in navigable waters, (Fig. 13-2) and even a rented livery rowboat, if run down by another boat, becomes a matter of litigation because *people* are involved. Size of the boats is irrelevant.

CAUSES OF ACCIDENTS

Almost always, when investigations are completed and blame is established, it turns out that the cause of another accident at sea, or on some river, was a trivial little thing like a light that wasn't there, or a light that was there but was not properly identified, which is how the *Cuyahoga* tragedy developed.

According to Coast Guard statistics, the basic cause of over 95% of all boating accidents and mishaps at sea is the same things that caused the *Cuyahoga* accident—*lights* and failure by somebody to observe *Rules of the Road*.

RULES OF THE ROAD

Motor vehicular traffic codes cover both the movement of automobiles and their light systems. Automobile headlights,

Fig. 13-2. Even a minor bump or scrape or another boat on navigable water will bring the contingency fee lawyers after you, especially if the Coast Guard is called by the party you scraped and they cite you for some rule violation.

directional signals, taillights and stoplights all convey information to other auto drivers, both during the day and night. They make automobiles visible at night, they tell you which direction they are facing, when they are moving or stopping and when they are turning left or right.

Maritime Rules of the Road cover both the movement of boats in the water and their navigational light systems, which also convey information to other boats, both day and night. Navigation lights, also called *running lights*, make a boat visible and recognizable as to the type of vessel. They also indicate whether a boat is moving or not and which direction it is going should it be moving. This information is conveyed by position of the lights, points of visibility of the lights and their color. Lights which a boat uses while at anchor or mooring are called *riding lights*.

Day Shapes

During the day, lights are not needed, but there are still special situations where information must be conveyed as to exactly what a vessel is *doing*. The pilot of every approaching vessel wants to know exactly what is going on up ahead. Through binoculars he sees another vessel seemingly dead in the water, perhaps anchored, but he isn't sure until he sees the day shape suspended at the highest mast. At night an anchor light would be displayed. During the day it will be a black round ball or other objects of different sizes and shapes. Vessels display day shapes (Fig. 13-3) to indicate their special

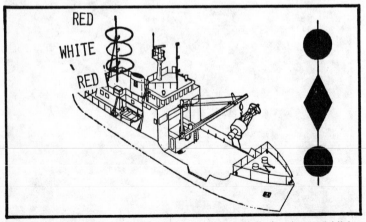

Fig. 13-3. At night the Coast Guard buoy tender will display the special lights shown. But in the daytime it will display instead the black dayshapes shown.

Fig. 13-4. This is the cover of one of the three sets of "Rules of the Road" established by the Coast Guard. There is another set for the Great Lakes and another for the western rivers.

status in the water, such as anchoring or dredging, laying fishnets or a sailboat with sails up but with engines running.

This makes a big difference in a sailboat's status under Rules of the Road. Even with sails up, a sailboat is considered a power-driven vessel when its engines are running and it is treated differently than when under sail alone.

Rules of the Road is a subject of almost wearisome complexity with its own bafflegab language. It is sometimes even more confusing than real estate and contract language. No recreational boatman is going to be interested enough in this boring subject to read any more about it than he has to.

What adds to the complexity is that just in the United States there are three different sets of rules (Fig. 13-4). There are the Great Lakes Rules, the Western Rivers Rules and the Inland Waters Rules. When you leave American waters, the International Rules apply.

Rules Of The Road Boundaries

On all new charts being printed today you will find both boundary lines indicating the limits of U.S. Authority and demarcation lines separating waters under U.S. Inland Waters Rules and International Rules.

The *territorial waters* of the U.S. extend three miles seaward. The next nine miles out to the 12-mile limit are called the *contiguous zone*. This is defined as being an extension of the actual U.S. coastline itself. In other words, any vessel in these waters can be considered as being on United States soil. The U.S. further maintains a *fishing conservation control zone* out to 200 miles which the Coast Guard patrols.

Demarcation lines are printed on new charts in a broken purple line across the entrance to harbors, rivers and bays (Fig. 13-5). You can see such a demarcation line across the entrance to the New York harbor running from Sandy Hook in New Jersey to the western end of Long Beach on Long Island. On the New York Harbor side of that purple line will be printed in capital letters, USE INLAND RULES OF THE ROAD. In San Francisco harbor there is a similar line running across the Golden Gate from Mile Rock Light, just off shore from San Francisco, to Point Bonita Light across the bay. On the bay side of that line Inland Rules prevail. On the seaward side of that line International Rules prevail.

WHEN LIGHTS MUST BE USED

Navigation lights must be used from *sunset to sunrise*

DEPARTMENT OF TRANSPORTATION

U.S.
COAST GUARD

COLREGS
DEMARCATION
LINES

SUPPLEMENT TO
NAVIGATION RULES

INTERNATIONAL—INLAND

CG-169-1   JULY 15, 1977

Fig. 13-5. Demarcation lines are printed on new charts in a broken line across the entrance to harbors, rivers and bays.

regardless of weather. If visibility is reduced during daylight hours, it is a good idea to turn them on just as you do with your car. During hours when running lights are displayed, no other light must be used, or be visible to other boats to cause confusion. This includes bright lights that may be visible through deckhouse or cabin windows. Draw the curtains.

Boat Classifications

There are five general clasifications for boats, with special light requirements for each. They are:

Class A—less than 16 feet (Fig. 13-6).

Class 1—over 16 but less than 26 feet (Fig. 13-7).

Class 2—over 26 but less than 40 feet (Fig. 13-8).

Class 3—over 40 but less than 65 feet (Fig. 13-9).

A fifth class, not listed with the above, is for vessels 20 meters and over which covers everything that travels on the high seas.

Light Options

Most builders of Class 2 stock boats, both power and sail, install navigation lights that comply with requirements of the International Rules of the Road. This is an advantage and a highly desirable feature because such an equipped boat can operate in *all* waters, whereas a boat equipped with Inland Waters navigation lights *cannot* operate legally in International Rules waters without first making some adjustments. This is not always an easy thing to do because navigation lights are permanently installed fixtures.

The builder and the individual boat owner have this option, which it is wise to take advantage of because in coastal areas

Fig. 13-6. Rowing boats, whether under oars or sail, shall have on hand a latern showing a white light which shall be temporarily exhibited in sufficient time to prevent collision.

472

boats are constantly crossing demarcation lines.This is not to suggest that the instant you cross the boundary line to the entrance of the New York Harbor, a Coast Guard cutter will be waiting to pounce on you to issue a citation for a violation under the Federal Boat Safety Act.

On the contrary, thousands of boats violate Federal Boat laws every day because it's so easy to do. In fact, it's often hard to do. For example, many boatmen take guests for a short cruise, forgetting that they don't have a lifejacket for every person. This is a serious violation.

The point is, you can get away with violations so long as your luck holds out. You can operate your boat with Inland Rules lights in any waters just as you can drive a car without a driver's license or without liability insurance. But don't you dare have even a trivial accident or break any traffic law. If you do, that is when your luck will run out and the roof will fall in.

If you scratch somebody's fender, the first thing the cop asks is for your driver's license. If you are taken to court, the first thing the judge asks is do you have liability insurance. If you have a minor mishap on the water, the first thing the Coast Guard boys do when they arrive with their clipboards and boating accident report from OMB No. 04-R3012, is to board your boat for a safety inspection.

If you have nine people on your boat and they only count eight flotation devices (of the approved type), you will be cited for this and any other violation which you may have committed before witnesses, like failing to yield to a priveleged vessel or failing to signal when overtaking a privileged vessel (this term is being replaced by the term *stand-on vessel*).

You can ignore this chapter and you can forget about lights and Rules of the Road if you can be sure that your luck will always hold out and nothing will ever happen to you as you dodge around all those crazy Sunday afternoon cowboys every weekend. If you can't be too sure about your luck, then you better continue reading.

Inland/International Differences

The differences in lights for Inland Waters and International waters is not so great that it cannot be modified on older boats without too much trouble or expense. All it amounts to is the new positioning, or the addition of one more white light.

On boats under 26 feet (Fig. 13-7) you must install a white

light about midship which is 3-feet higher then the red/green bow lights, with a range of 3 miles and 20-point visibility. The stern white light must be changed from 32-point to 12-point and be lowered so it is on the same level as the red/green bow lights.

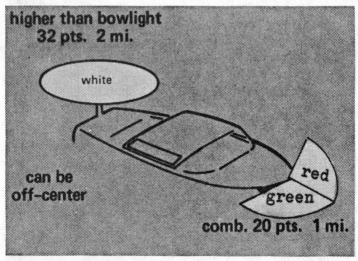

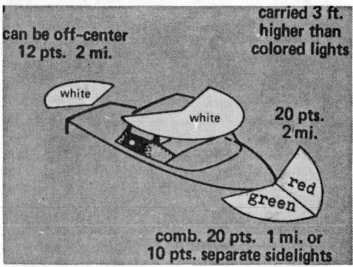

Fig. 13-7. Inland (top) and International (bottom) lights reqired for class 1 boats.

474

On boats over 26 feet (Fig. 13-8) you eliminate the white 20-point bow light by just removing the bulb. Boats over 26 feet usually have masts just forward of the flybridge windshield. On the top of this mast, 3 feet higher then the red/green lights, is where the 20-point 3-mile white light is installed. The

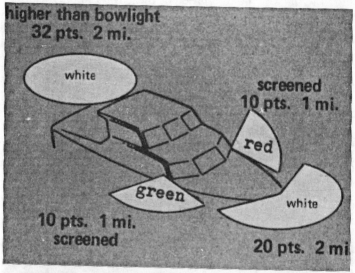

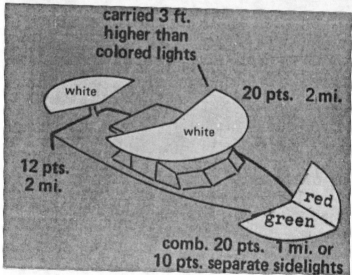

Fig. 13-8. Inland (top) and International (bottom) lights required for class 2 boats.

stern light has to be lowered so it is on the same level as the red/green lights and changed from 32-point to 12-point. The red/green lights can be on the side of the boat or at the bow.

Sailboats under 26 feet, while under sail alone, carry the same lights whether they are on Inland or International waters (Fig. 13-10), which is red/green at the bow, 12-point white at the stern. Under power they add an additional 20-point, 3 mile

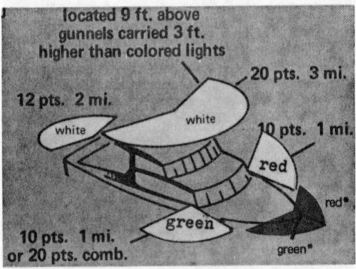

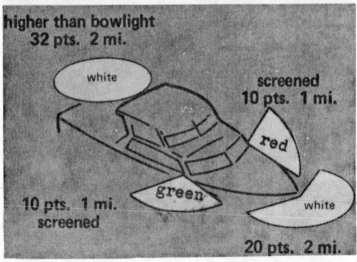

Fig. 13-9. Inland (top) and International (bottom) lights required for class 3 boats.

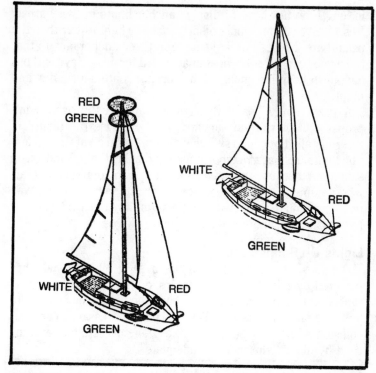

Fig. 13-10. Sailboats under 26 feet, while under sail alone, carry the same lights whether they are on inland or International Waters. The red and green lights on the top of the mast (left illustration) are optional.

white light on the mast, 3 feet higher then the red/green bow lights. Over 26 feet, you eliminate the white bow light.

Anchor Lights

While anchored, boats under 150 feet in length must display a single white 32-point light high in the forward section of the craft (Fig. 13-11) where it can be seen on all points of the compass and be visible for 2 miles. Vessels over 150 feet in length must display two white lights, one forward, and the second aft at a lower height. This is the requirement under Inland rules. However, Great Lakes Rules require *two* lights forward and *two* aft, plus additional lights all around the decks at spaced intervals. You will have no difficulty in recognizing a large vessel anchored at night on the Great Lakes.

On harbor charts you will frequently see an anchor symbol which designates an "anchorage" area. Boats 65 feet and less in length do not have to display anchor lights in these areas. Vessels over 65 feet must display just one light rather then the usual two. There is an advantage in these anchorages in that the owner can leave his boat unattended for a few days without having to keep his anchor light burning continuously day and night.

A great many boats, through no fault of the owner, improperly display their anchor light because the manufacturer installed only one switch which turns on all of the navigation lights. A boat at anchor must not display the red and green side lights because this creates confusion to approaching craft who assume you are either moving or underway with no way on. You should have two switches, one for the white anchor light alone and another for the running lights.

Lights On Small Boats

Dinghies, canoes and rowboats (Fig. 13-12), whether powered by sail or outboard motors, do not require a fixed arrangement of navigation lights, but they must have a white light available that can be displayed when necessary to prevent collision with other boats. The kerosene or gasoline lanterns used by night fishermen are adequate.

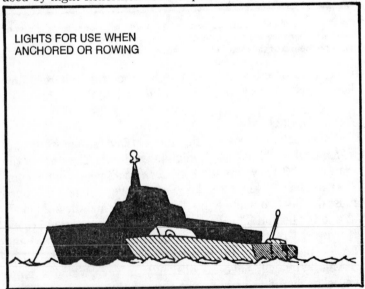

LIGHTS FOR USE WHEN ANCHORED OR ROWING

Fig. 13-11. Power boats under 65 feet and all sailing vessels at anchor must display anchor lights, except those under 65 feet in "special anchorage areas."

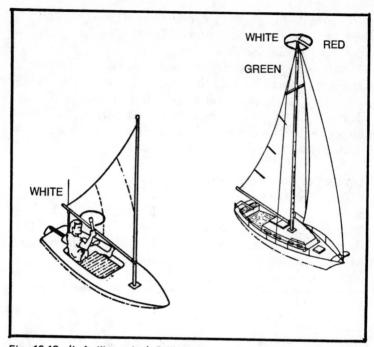

Fig. 13-12. (Left illustration) Sailing vessels less than 7 meters in length require only an available white light. (Right illustration) Optional lighting for sailing vessels less than 12 meters in length.

Light Candlepower

The Rules specify visibility limits on lights as 2-miles or 3-miles, on a dark and clear night. How do you translate that into a bulb that will do the job? You don't, unless you consult a Coast Guard Chart Table which determines more precisely what candlepower bulb is required for the various ranges of visibility. Below is a copy of that Table:

Candlepower	Range in nautical miles
1.0	1 mile
5.5	2 miles
17.6	3 miles
100.0	5 miles

Special Lights

Of particular interest to recreational boatmen are the special survival lights which occasionally both Coast Guard and law enforcement vessels use. For example, waterfront municipalities have their own law enforcement craft which, in addition to carrying the usual running lights for their class, are

479

also permitted to display a special identifying light. This is a blue revolving horizontal beam of light which, at a distance, looks like a pulsating flash of blue.

Coast Guard vessels, while engaged in special duties, like handling or servicing aids to navigation, also display special day shapes during the day and lights during the night. The day shapes will be two orange-white vertically striped balls suspended aloft in a vertical line. At night they will show two red lights suspended in the same manner.

Lights For Other Vessels

The subject of lights for commercial vessels in all types and services is a very lengthy and complicated subject which can fill a book. The recreational boatman has no need for this specialized information, except where it affects him directly, which is realizing that he must *recognize* commercial vessels at night. Since this chapter on lights and Rules of the Road is not

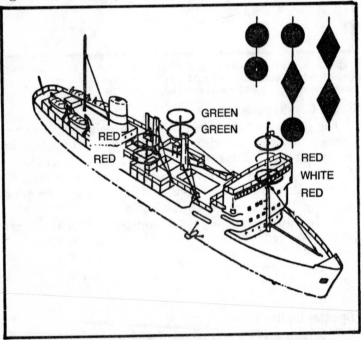

Fig. 13-13. The first time you see these lights on a dark night, it will probably make you very nervous for a few minutes while you try to figure out what the devil it is. Army engineer dredges work around the clock. In the daytime you won't even notice those black day shapes because you will immediately recognize the vessel.

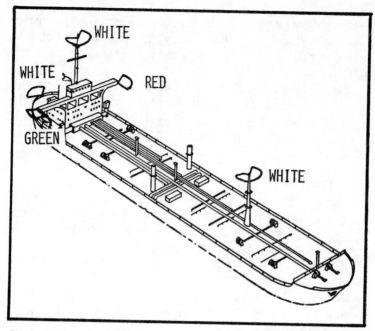

Fig. 3-14. These are the lights that the Coast Guard cutter Cuyahoga saw and mistook for a fishing vessel moving in a different direction.

written for the commercial marine industry, it will provide only the information of use to the private pleasure boat owner.

Of primary interest to the pleasure craft skipper, who chooses to operate his craft at night, is information that will enable him to *recognize* all the lights that he will see on the water (Fig. 13-13). During daylight hours he needs no help in distinguishing between towed barges, freighters, ferries, dredges and tugs. Their identity is self-evident. But recognizing these craft at night, when all you see of them is their navigation lights, is quite a different matter.

Failure to recognize navigation lights is what led to the *Cuyahoga* disaster in Chesapeake Bay when it was rammed amidship by a freighter. A Coast Guard crewman on watch thought he saw the lights of a fishing vessel. The *Cuyahoga* skipper, CWO Robinson, also stated after the accident that he believed the lights he saw was a fishing vessel. They were both wrong. They were looking at the navigation lights of an Argentine coal freighter (Fig. 13-14).

Such a mistake could never be made during the day. But it's a very easy mistake to make at night, which is one of the reasons why I never take my boat out at night. Another reason for this is that I find it hard enough to avoid hitting debris in the water during the day, when I can see the junk, let alone trying to avoid it at night.

Figures 13-15 to 13-26 are intended to show what various types of commercial craft look like at night when all that the pleasure craft skipper sees are navigation lights. He can rarely even see a vague outline of shapes *under* those lights in the dark.

RIGHT-OF-WAY

"Rules are made to be broken," is a silly expression, probably coined by some wag for laughs at a cocktail party. But it's not funny at sea. When Rules are broken on rivers, lakes or oceans, somebody usually gets hurt, and sometimes dies.

A rule was broken when two ocean liners, the *Andrea Doria* and the *Stockholm*, collided off Nantucket in 1956 with a loss of 51 lives. A Rule was broken when the U.S. destroyer *Evans* was cut in half by the Australian aircraft carrier *Melbourne* with a loss of 74 lives.

72 Colregs (Collision Regulations)

The International Regulations for the Prevention of Collisions at Sea, referred to as *colregs*, were adopted in 1972 at international conferences and were established by a Presidential Proclamation and an Act of Congress. These regulations, upon which U.S. Rules are based, did not become effective until 12 noon, July 15th, 1977.

Very few recreational boatmen are totally aware of this. Some boatmen are aware that there were changes in navigation lights, but they assume that everything was taken care of by the manufacturer of their boat, so they give the matter no further thought. But there is more to Rules of the Road then navigation lights and how many honks you give on your horn to raise a drawbridge or pass another boat.

The Rules determine who has right-of-way *to avoid collision*. They also prescribe whistle signals, fog signals and distress signals. But the primary concern, and the main reason for all the international conferences and multi-national treaties, was the enactment of universally acceptable regulations that would prevent collisions like the one that occurred between the *Andrea Doria* and the *Stockholm*.

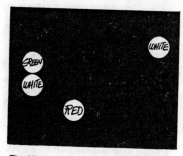

Fig. 13-15. You're looking at a fishing boat from the port side, engaged in trawling. This is a large vessel, about 150 feet in length.

Fig. 13-16. This is a large powerboat underway and seen from port.

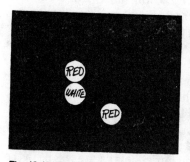

Fig. 13-17. This is a commercial fishing vessel making way and with gear extended.

Fig. 13-18. These are the lights of a power-driven vessel over 150 feet in length as seen from dead ahead and bearing down on you.

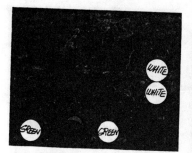

Fig. 13-19. You're looking at the starboard side of the tug engaged in towing or pushing something less than 600 feet long.

Fig. 13-20. You are looking at the anchor lights of a large ship, over 65 feet.

Fig. 13-21. This is a real tough one to identify because it could be five different things. First, it could be a vessel under 65 feet at anchor. But it could also be the stern light of a sailboat, a powerboat or a ship. At least, it's going away from you.

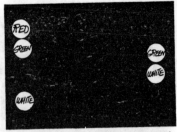

Fig. 13-22. You are looking at the lights of two vessels in the same area. At left is the stern view of a sailboat going away from you. At right is a vessel engaged in trawling, but not making way.

So we have International Rules and the general U.S. Rules, which further break down into the Inland, Great Lakes and Western Rivers Rules. Although there are differences between the three American and the International Rules, they're not really too much different, they're just modified to fit the conditions of each area.

Ship traffic on the Mississippi is not the same as ship traffic in the Boston Harbor or the Chesapeake Bay. A sailing vessel, under sail alone, has the right-of-way over all vessels under power, but God help the poor sailor who takes that too literally and tacks across the path of a jumbo tow coming down river. After his remains are found and buried, his estate will be in the hands of sea lawyers. Before the sea lawyers and courts have finished with this case, and the estate of the deceased can be put in order one recurring question will finally determine the outcome.

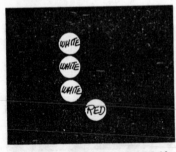

Fig. 13-23. You are looking at the port side of a tow vessel pushing something over 600 feet in length, and you better stay well clear of this baby.

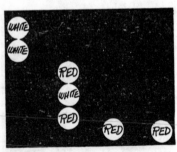

Fig. 13-24. This is another power vessel pushing a tow 600 feet or less, but this one is limited in her ability to maneuver, a warning to you to stay far, far away.

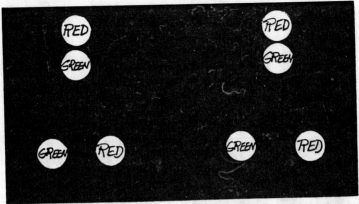

Fig. 13-25. This should be an easy one by now. Obviously, this has to be two different boats, but what kind of boats and what are they doing? With those highly placed red/green lights, it has to be sailboats. And since both lower green are visible at the same time, you are looking at the sailboats head on as they approach.

The General Prudential Rule

Figuring heavily in all litigation, arising from mishaps at sea, is Article 27 of the Inland Rules called the "general prudential rule." This is where heirs of the deceased get the shaft when they go to court to fight for his rights under *law of the sea* as they say around the waterfront bars.

The prudential rule translates down to the simple words: "did the deceased act as a prudent seaman would have acted under similar circumstances?"

Translated down to street language, this says that the safety of a vessel comes first and takes precedence over Rules of the Road. In other words, if your boat is in danger, to hell with the rules, which is what every *prudent* seaman would do under similar circumstances. And that is why courts will rule against you if you try to stand up for your rights as a privileged vessel and continue to sail across the bow of an oncoming freighter in a narrow ship channel.

Regardless of what the Rules say on some specific situation, you, the skipper, are expected to act like a prudent seaman, and everybody knows that jumbo tows on rivers can't be stopped in less then a mile going down river. Therefore, any fool who maneuvers his craft across the bow of an approaching commercial tow just because he has the right-of-way is not observing the prudential rule.

Under the circumstances, the courts will rule that the deceased must share part of the responsibility, if not all of it, and his estate may possibly not get a dime.

Remember that! In all situations of danger, the skipper must act as a prudent seaman. this means no playing "chicken" games on the water (Fig. 13-27). When you find yourself headed on a collision course with another boat crossing your path,

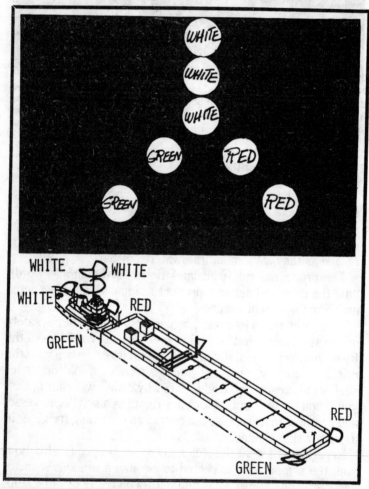

Fig. 13-26. This one I have shown both at night and in the day, purposely leaving it for the last to impress upon all Mississippi River boatmen that if they ever see lights like this at night, they better get their butts outa there in a hurry because they are right in the path of a jumbo tow. If that monster ever runs over them, they will never find two pieces of them to match.

Fig. 13-27. Boating is a never-ending game of confrontation, you meeting another boat head on in a channel, or out in a large body of water where your paths cross and somebody has to give way, but won't. This is the boating game of "Chicken." Boaters who play this game pick up a lot of legal experience because they spend a lot of time dealing with lawyers and dodging process servers.

and you refuse to yield because you are "in the right," then you are not acting like a prudent seaman and you will find the courts not too sympathetic when you bring suit because dangerous confrontations between boats to see who will say "chicken" rarely bring favorable settlements to any of the parties involved. Even the man who was "in the right" winds up a loser because he failed to act as a prudent seaman.

If you hate to be "chicken," and like to stand up for your rights, then you should give up boating because you are going to be confronted with many situations where just saying chicken will keep you alive. Recreational boating, unfortunately, is like that. There are just as many idiots on the water as there are on the highways.

RULES FOR STEERING

Your steering problems in crowded waters will never be with commercial vessels. They are handled by professionals who go by the book. They have to because their license and their jobs are at stake. If you know the "book" yourself, you

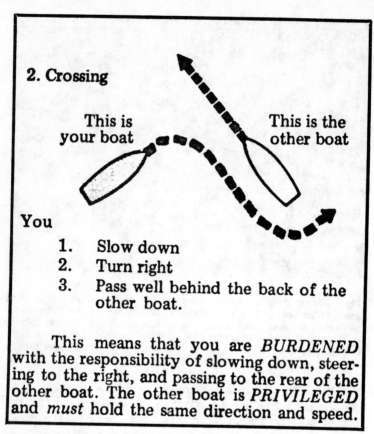

2. Crossing

This is
your boat

This is the
other boat

You

1. Slow down
2. Turn right
3. Pass well behind the back of the other boat.

This means that you are *BURDENED* with the responsibility of slowing down, steering to the right, and passing to the rear of the other boat. The other boat is *PRIVILEGED* and *must* hold the same direction and speed.

Fig. 13-28. This is your classic confrontation, the paths of two boats crossing, a collision is inevitable unless one gives way.

will always know exactly what a professionally handled vessel is going to do at all times. It's only when you approach another pleasure craft that you wonder, you guess and you pray.

A point not too well understood by many boatmen is that the rules for steering and sailing do not apply, in fact they mean nothing, until there is *danger of collision*. For example, you are surrounded out in the bay, or the river, or the lake by dozens of boats—some fishing, some moving. How do steering and sailing rules apply in this situation? They don't. All boats are free to do as they please until one of them approaches your course of travel on a line that indicates a point of collision will soon be reached. And that is when the rules become *rules*, not just rules on paper.

When two vessels are on a collision course, inevitably there comes the moment of truth, as they say, when a decision must be made as to who will say "chicken" and change course. The Rules very clearly define the course of action for two craft approaching each other in a manner that their paths will cross. One of those two boats, because of its position of approach, is *burdened* (this term is being replaced by the term *give-way vessel*). It must slow down or change its course. The other vessel is *privileged*, and has the right-of-way (Fig. 13-28).

In theory, the skipper of the burdened craft is supposed to make a move to indicate that he is yielding. This move must be made early enough that it can be seen by the privileged skipper in time to prevent his zigging when he should have zagged, thereby causing a collision.

Things rarely happen by the book in the world of pleasure boating. I have personally been in the above situation a hundred times and the only time things worked out the way they were supposed to is when my boat was burdened. I always slow down or change course. But when I am privileged, I still am the boat that yields because I am by nature a timid and cautious man. I have said "chicken" so many times I have developed a conditioned reflex and automatically yield to anything that crosses my path, even a covey of ducks. I prefer to play the prudent seaman rather then the resolute seaman who stands up for his rights. History records that prudent seaman live longer then resolute seaman.

DUTY OF PRIVILEGED VESSEL

You have the duty, as a privileged craft, to maintain your speed and course so that the burdened craft *knows* your intentions and can act accordingly. If you waver, and change your course, you create confusion. This may be funny when two people bump on the sidewalk trying to get around each other. But at sea, this is not funny. Your indecision and failure to maintain course, could cause a serious accident. This would weigh heavily against you in court.

On the other hand, if you resolutely maintain course and speed in the face of imminent disaster, it will be argued in court that you did not act in a prudent manner and that *any* action to avoid collision is preferable to *no* action.

Are you confused by all these contradictions? What they say is that no matter *what* action you take to avoid collision, it will be viewed unfavorably in court. In other words, if you are ever involved in a boat collision, you haven't got a prayer in court because there is no solid clear-cut wording in the Rules or Articles on which lawyers can build a sound case. The general prudential rules can destroy almost any argument.

Every boatman has a duty to himself and to his family to stay out of trouble on the navigable waters of the United States because there is no trouble like legal trouble with the federal bureaucracy. I have survived a lifetime of boating only because I have a pathological fear of legal entanglements and sea lawyers. I never hesitate to show my intentions to another craft. I even go a mile out of my way to avoid trouble and a confrontation with the faceless power of the federal bureaucracy.

Beware Of Government Agencies

Agencies of the federal government, somebody once said, are like glaciers, they move one inch a year. The Washington correspondent for a Toledo newspaper wrote to his editor: "There are no people in government, just zombies and gnomes who shuffle papers between coffee breaks."

In the machinery of government, you, as an individual, are nothing but an IBM card with little square punched holes. Your life and your fate is in the control of soulless computers who mail you official-looking, glass-windowed franked envelopes advising you of actions being taken against you in some U.S. District Court a 100 miles from where you live. This goes on for years. Once you get a computer monkey on your back, it never lets go. A computer never forgets.

I write here from personal experience as a newspaper reporter who has covered many United States Courthouses in many districts. I have seen many dazed broken men walking the halls of these stone mausoleums guided by their wives, being so inarticulate that they could only speak through their attorneys.

Boating is most fun but sometimes it can be sheer hell. Make one little mistake some day out there on the water and you'll find all of this out the hard way when the computers start mailing you franked envelopes stamped "Government Use Only."

The Rights Of Fishing Vessels

Encounters with the commercial fishing industry are one of the hazards and annoyances of recreational boating, especially on the Great Lakes and in the Chesapeake Bay area (Fig. 13-29). It's just as bad in coastal waters where lobstermen defend their territorial waters with the savage fury of a jaguar when his hunting grounds are violated.

Fishing boats have special right-of-ways when engaged in the work of setting or tending lobster traps, laying nets, lines or trawls. I know how annoying it can be when you have to go a mile out of your way to get around a half-mile long fishtrap because it screws up your carefully worked out course and estimated time of arrival schedule.

Fishboat skippers will watch you through binoculars and if you approach too close, they write down your registration numbers and boat name if they can see it. If you violate their sacred waters and run through their traps you can be in big trouble!

The ultimate crime is to damage a net.

In all states bordering fishing waters, the equipment and fishing gear of commercial fishermen (Fig. 13-30) are protected by state laws. You are *liable* for any damage you cause with your wake or your propellers. You can get burnt with both damage suits and be cited for violations of federal law.

Fig. 13-29. If you learn nothing else from this book but to stay way from fishboats, you will get your money's worth. Commercial fishermen are not the most sociable people you will ever meet because the very nature of their work puts them in eternal conflict with the nature of your pleasure.

My advice is: whenever you see a fishboat dead in the water, working on its nets, give that vessel wide room.

THE RIGHTS OF SAILING VESSELS

The privileged right-of-way accorded sailing craft is often more theory then fact and if you are the owner of such a craft, don't ever bet your life on it. For example, in a ship channel or river, the burdened vessel may not have the room to maneuver out of the way, and it cannot stop in time. And no burdened vessel is ever going to yield to a sailboat if doing so would place them in a dangerous position, like running aground or on the rocks.

"Rights" Of Sailboats On Private Waters

The "rights" of sailboats can be a touchy issue at yacht clubs where racing and regattas are a major part of the club's activities. I have witnessed violent arguments, with men almost coming to blows, over the question of who exactly had right-of-way in an entrance channel owned by private interests.

Fig. 13-30. When these very expensive trapnets are damaged by the propellers of pleasure craft, as this one was, they must be hauled up, taken ashore, spread over a large field and repaired. This is costly and time consuming. If you ever get fouled up in one of these fishtraps so that you must be rescued by the Coast Guard (which goes into the public records), you will be sued for plenty and your insurance company will settle to the limit of their liability. This will almost certainly end your boating career because any marine insurance you buy after that will be so expensive you will be forced to sell your boat.

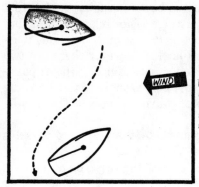

Fig. 13-31. The shaded vessel (port tack) is burdened under International Rules and must yield as shown. But under Inland's Rules it's just the opposite with the shaded vessel being privileged and the starboard tack vessel yielding.

It is argued by some that Rules of the Road apply only to open navigable waters under federal jurisdiction, therefore sailboats without auxiliary power are not specially privileged in channel entrances, bays and mooring basins owned by yacht clubs and private interests.

I have never heard of this issue being settled in the courts. I have never heard of a collision between a sailboat and motorboat under the above circumstances, and the issue is still a puzzlement to me. I have had many close calls coming into narrow entrance channels at the same time 50 or more Lightnings were leaving under sail for the afternoon races. I always stop dead in the water, close my eyes and pray. My wife, however, watches them in awe an admiration as they tack back and forth across the channel, missing us by inches. I have gone through this experience many times, always yielding to them, and, incredibly, have survived without a scratch.

Beyond this, I don't know what else to do or say because I don't care to fight over this with race committees or club membership. It would be a losing battle because sail is the dominant voice on the yacht club scene today. At this writing, they outnumber power boats 2 to 1 at my club. Next year it will be 3 to 1.

Encounters Between Two Sailboats

Encounters between two sailboats can be a journey into madness. What is right on Inland Waters is wrong on International Waters. Sailors must always be aware of the *waters* in which they sail. Under International Rules, starboard tack vessel B is privileged. Under Inland Rules, close-hauled vessel A is privileged (Fig. 13-31).

There are five basic situations between sailing vessels that are specifically mentioned in Article 17 for Inland Waters, but they are not always the same as comparable situations mentioned in the International Rule 12. However there *are* two basic situations, which help to simplify things, if this is possible: One—the main boom of your boat is on the *same* side as the other boat; two—the main boom of your boat is on the *opposite* side of the other boat.

With both booms on the same side, the windward vessel is burdened, and must give way (Fig. 13-32).

With both booms on opposite sides, the vessel on port tack is burdened (Fig. 13-33).

When sail ruled the seas, there was no such thing as Rules of the Road and when vessels collided, as they frequently did, there was much shouting, and often blows were struck in anger. But rarely was anything done of a legal nature because there was nothing on which to base court action.

The old square rigger is an absolute beast to maneuver. Each individual sail has its own two sheets and braces which must be re-trimmed when changes are made in point of sail. It takes a lot of work, climbing, manpower and time to change direction. The square rigger is a beautiful sight on the water under full sail, which is the only nice thing you can say about them.

The first Rules of the Road were based on the concept of *maneuverability*. The vessel that was in the most maneuverable position had to yield to the vessel that was in the least maneuverable position. That concept is still maintained today

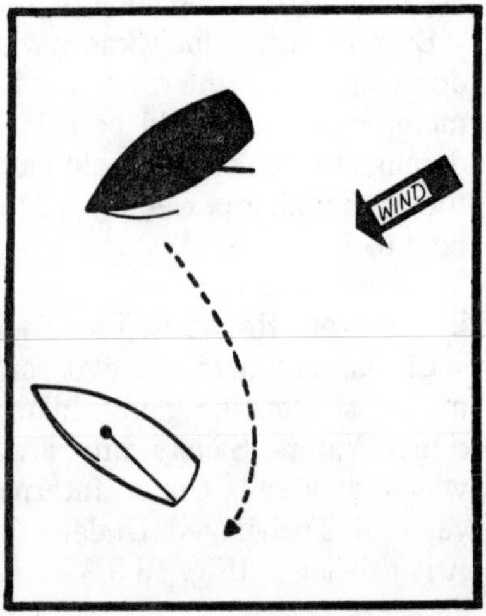

Fig. 13-32. This is an easy one to remember. With both booms on the same side, the windward (shaded) vessel is burdened.

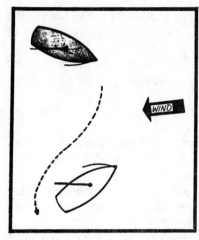

Fig. 13-33. With both booms on opposite sides, vessel on port tack (shaded) is burdened.

where sailing boats are involved and is the reason for all those strange rules which make no sense to non-sailors. The non-sailor never fully understands this. He assumes that two sailboats moving along at the same speed are equally maneuverable. They are not. If you keep that one point in mind, you should have no trouble in understanding the five paragraphs below of Article 17 for Inland Waters:

Paragraph A—*"A vessel which is running free (Fig. 13-34) shall keep out of the way of a vessel which is close-hauled."*

The previous statement is what you must do when sailing on Inland Waters, where the close-hauled vessel is privileged. It is not what you must do on International Waters where the running free vessel is privileged, or just the opposite.

Paragraph B—*"A vessel which is close-hauled on the port tack shall keep out of the way of a vessel which is close-hauled on the starboard tack."*

This is a sticky situation which I would try to avoid whenever possible because there can be differences of opinion as to who *is* and who is *not* "close-hauled." Technically, this means you are pointing as close to the wind as you can get, but the ability to do this varies with different boats and different rigs. If you are slacked off just the least bit, you might be mistakenly considered as running free, thereby making you the burdened vessel.

Rather then take chances in such a situation, with so many new sailors on the water, I would choose to stay out of the way, just as I do driving my car when I see another car with the sign "Student Driver." I always assume that the skipper in the shiny new Cal-30 is a "student driver" who never heard of Rules of the Road.

Paragraph C—*"When both are running free, with the wind on different sides, the vessel which has the wind on the port side shall keep out of the way of the other."*

If your boom is swung over to starboard, you are burdened and must stay out of the way.

Paragraph D—*"When both are running free, with the wind on the same side, the vessel which is to windward shall keep out of the way of the vessel which is to leeward."*

This is that situation mentioned earlier—both booms on the same side, windward is burdened; both booms on opposite sides, port tack vessel is burdened.

Paragraph E—*"A vessel which has the wind aft shall keep out of the way of the other vessel."*

This is the overtaking vessel situation, something even seasoned skippers try to avoid because it takes so long for one sailboat to pass another. When you must pass another sailboat, just remember that the overtaking vessel must always stay clear, regardless of tack. That means stay at least a 100 feet away from the boat you are passing.

Helpful Hints

It is impossible to remember everything you read about Rules of the Road, especially where it concerns sailboats and all that sailor language like windward-leeward, close-hauled and running free. It is just too much for some new skippers to handle. They just want to do a little sailing on weekends

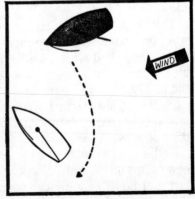

Fig. 13-34. Only sailors can understand certain rules because only a sailor knows when a sailing vessel is most maneuverable, which is the basis for all sailing rules in the first place. A vessel running free is always more maneuverable than one on any other point of sailing, which is why it is burdened, as above.

without getting involved in other things like tying knots, and going to Power Squadron Classes to learn seamanship.

To these casual Sunday afternoon boatmen, I have one little hint that could keep them out of trouble when using the nation's waterways in their mortgaged fiberglass. Rules of the Road were designed for one purpose—to prevent boat collisions. To this end, it is necessary for boats that are maneuverable to stay away from boats that are not maneuverable.

If you own a powerboat, it should be obvious to you that your craft is many times more maneuverable then any sailboat, any barge, any tug, any freighter or any workboat. You can forget about Rules of the Road, if the subject bores you, if you will just remember one thing: a prudent seaman always stays out of the way of craft less maneuverable then his own.

Doing just that one thing will, surprisingly, keep you out of trouble, keep you out of court and keep you out of reach of the computers in the federal bureaucracy.

SOUND SIGNALS

There are two types of boat movement.

On large expanses of water, pleasure craft move around in a helter-skelter fashion, crossing each others paths from all angles. This is the type of boat movement where Rules of the Road are necessary to prevent collisions.

There is a second type of boat movement that is restricted, where boats do *not* move around helter-skelter but stay in designated channels like auto traffic does on Turnpikes and Expressways. All ocean traffic across the Atlantic and Pacific moves in designated east/west *shipping lanes*, which are the 'highways' of the seas. When ocean vessels reach American waters and the harbors of coastal ports, they are even more restricted to narrow little lanes and channels where they must remain.

The largest portion of a boat's lifetime of movement is spent in the confined waters of channels, whether it be a navigable river, lake or sea lane. That means boats are constantly passing each other like automobiles do on highways. And when boats approach each other in these channels, they communicate by sound signals—blasts on their horns.

There is a misconception among many new powerboat shippers that the horn on a boat is used in the same manner as a

Fig. 13-35. There is a vast difference between a boat signal and an automobile signal, a fact which many boaters never learn. Boat signals say something, they convey important information. That's why it is against the law to give improper signals in a harbor area. It causes confusion. (courtesy of the U.S. Coast Guard).

horn on an automobile as a messenger of insult to other drivers and a warning to pedestrians to get out of the way. This is not only wrong, it is a dangerous misconception because when horn signals are improperly given in a harbor, where other vessels can hear, it causes confusion.

Warning! It is against the law to improperly sound a signal "within the harbor limits of any waters of the United States," and any ship's officer guilty of such a violation can have his license suspended or revoked.

Horn signals are a language (Fig. 13-35), not just a big noise. They convey information by the manner and frequency in which they are made. When you go aimlessly blasting away on your horn, signaling greetings to friends on passing boats, you

LENGTH	BELL	WHISTLE OR HORN
☐ < 16′	none required	none required
☐ 16′ to < 26′	none required	mouth, hand or power operated, audible at least ½ mile
☐ 26′ to < 40′	required	hand or power operated, audible at least 1 mile
☐ 40′ to ≤ 65′	required	power operated, audible at least 1 mile

NOTE: *While it is not required that all lengths of boats carry the bell, whistle or horn, Rules of the Road require ALL vessels to give proper signals if a signaling situation develops.*

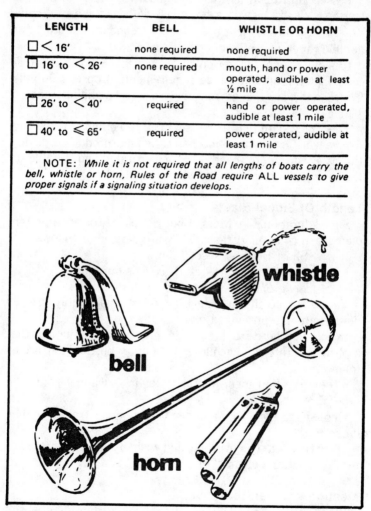

whistle

bell

horn

Fig. 13-36. Horns, bells and whistles are important signaling devices for boats (courtesy of the U.S. Coast Guard).

are sending out false messages which other vessels hear and wonder about.

The Rules refer to ship signaling devices as a *whistle*, but don't be confused by the ancient terminology (Fig. 13-36). Very lengthy and complex specifications are set forth in an annex to the Rules as to what the signaling device must do, what the intensities must be, what bands of audio frequencies must be used and how far the signal can be heard.

Vessels up to 246 feet use the audio frequency of 250-700 Hertz (cycles) which is a low blast with a range of 1 mile. Vessels less then 65 feet use a higher frequency,but still at an audible range of 1 mile.

It is only when you get down to the Class 1 boats, 16 to 26 feet, that the audible range requirements drop to a ½-mile. Class 2 and Class 3 boats must have a signal audibility range of 1 mile.

The Rules state that the vessel must be equipped with an *efficient* whistle, or other mechanical sound producing device, that is either mouth, hand or power operated and suitable for the type and size of boat on which it is used.

Length Of Signal Blasts

Signal duration, like Morse Code dot-dashes, is an important element in communications. They are defined as follows:

Short Blast—1 second duration

Prolonged Blast—4 to 6 seconds duration

Long Blast—8 to 10 seconds duration

You will note that a long blast is of considerably greater duration then a prolonged blast.

In boating, there are three basic confrontation situations that a pleasure craft will encounter with other boats. They are as follows:

Meeting. You meet another boat in a channel going the other direction.

Crossing. You cross another boat's line of travel, or they cross yours.

Overtaking. You overtake and wish to pass another slower moving boat in a channel or river.

Meeting Another Boat

When meeting another boat approaching from the opposite direction in the limited confines of a river or shipping channel,

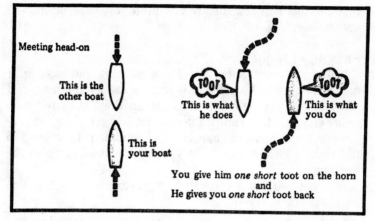

Fig. 13-37. When meeting another boat approaching from the opposite direction, one blast of the horn means you will pass port-to-port (courtesy of the U.S. Coast Guard).

you always pass each other *port-to-port* (Fig. 13-37). This is easy to remember because you do the same thing when driving an automobile. But you don't honk your horn every time you pass an automobile. In a boat you do.

In passing situations, neither boat has right-of-way, and neither boat is obilgated to signal first with his horn. However, precedence established by past court decisions, indicate that when an approaching craft is about 12_ off your port bow, the time has come to give one short blast on the horn. If the other boat does it first, you answer with the same short blast, and *no more*. This is no time to play cute games with your horn, like honking the tune *"shave and a haircut six bits."* This stamps you as a sea clown and a Sunday afternoon cowboy.

When you answer the proper one horn blast for port-to-port passing with *two* horn blasts, you make the other skipper extremely nervous because he immediately wonders if you're kidding or if you really *intend* to pass him on the starboard side.

Two horn blasts is the proper signal to give when boats pass each other starboard-to-starboard (Fig. 13-38). If there is considerable distance between two passing boats, it is not necessary for them to radically go out of their way just so they can pass port-to-port. When you meet another boat directly, almost head-on, and a change of course *must* be made, you always zig to the right for a proper port-to-port passing. If you find this hard to remember, just pretend you're driving an automobile.

Passing At Night

In the above situation, two boats meeting and passing at night, the proper horn signal is imperative, even a matter of life or death. At night you don't see anything but navigation lights coming at you down the channel or river. Give the proper one blast signal and indicate your intentions by veering to the right a little sooner then you would normally do in the daytime.

At night you watch the lights—the colored *side* lights. You pass red-side-to red-side.

Overtaking & Passing

This is a common situation which many new boats in fast hulls never seem to learn how to handle properly. They operate their fast hulls just like they do their fast cars. They come up fast behind a slow moving boat, tailgate for a few moments riding in the wash, and then give one honk and pass to the left.

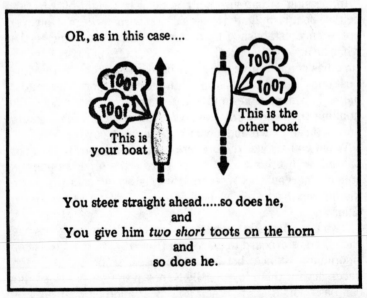

Fig. 13-38. When meeting another boat approaching from the opposite direction, two blasts of the horn means you will pass starboard to starboard (courtesy of the U.S. Coast Guard).

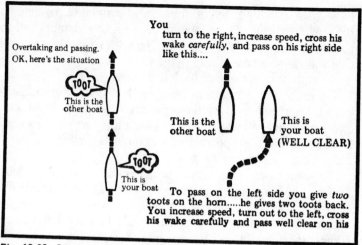

Fig. 13-39. Overtaking a boat from behind requires a different signaling procedure (courtesy of the U.S. Coast Guard).

This is wrong!

The boat being overtaken is *privileged*. The boat that wants to pass is *burdened*. You legally cannot pass a slow moving boat until you get *permission* to do so with an acknowledging horn signal (Fig. 13-39)..You will not get such permission until you ask for it, make known your intentions with the proper signals: two honks to pass the overtaken vessel on her port side; one honk to pass her on the starboard side.

The Danger Signal

If for some reason the overtaken boat does not want to be passed and they respond with the danger signal of five short horn blasts, you must not pass.

It may not be visibly apparent to you, but there is always a reason when danger signals are given by overtaken vessels, especially in rivers when you want to pass a long slow-moving tow.

The skipper in that towboat up ahead is a professional who knows what he's doing. He knows the river and he knows the dangers you face when you try to pass him at the wrong time, and when he signals you off with five horn blasts, you better heed and slack off.

It is customary to pass an overtaken vessel on the port side. However, it is not illegal to pass on the starboard side, after giving the one horn blast and getting a response. I, myself, have many times warned off a boat that wanted to pass me on the starboard side. I was moving up a narrow channel and to the right of me was shoal water filled with rocks. I suspected that the skipper behind me, flying the burgee of some distant yacht club, was not aware of that danger.

If the skipper wanting to pass me had been more experienced, he would have waited a minute, then tried again with two blasts, indicating a wish to pass on my port side. I would have immediately responded with two blasts, indicating that it was safe to pass me to port.

It is sometimes dangerous to pass a jumbo tow, unless there is plenty of sea room. Frequently when you signal your intentions to pass to port, the towboat will warn you off with danger blasts. This may puzzle you. But there is a reason. For instance, there might be another jumbo tow, that you can't see, coming from the opposite direction and will be passing through. If you passed you would have been caught in the turbulent waters between two tows. If you signal to pass on the starboard side, you might be warned off again because in passing jumbo tows, you must stay so far away from them that you can be forced into shallow water. The tow skipper knows of these things and he is doing you a great service and you should be grateful, instead of annoyed.

Crossing

When two boats meet at a point where one must cross the other's line of movement, this is called a *crossing situation* and Rules of the Road clearly define who has the right-of-way. No horn signals are necessary. However, it is permitted for the privileged boat to give one horn blast merely to indicate that it is maintaining its course and speed. The burdeded boat can acknowledge with one blast, but this is not required in the Rules.

River Bend Signal

There is a special warning signal that must be given on rivers when you approach a sharp bend and do not know what is coming from the other direction. If the river is navigable waters, heavy with commercial traffic, you don't have to worry about being surprised because towboat skippers go by the Rules. The Rules call for a special *long* 8 to 10 second horn signal about a ½-mile before a bend in the river is reached. If you hear such a blast when approaching a river bend, respond with a similar 8 to 10 second signal. This guarantees there will be no surprises on either end because towboat horns are unmistakable in their volume and rumbling arrogance. Pleasure boat horns are also easily recognized by towboat skippers.

If you should be approaching a river bend at the same time as a tow, that long blast is also a warning to you to exercise extreme caution. Technically, neither you nor the jumbo tow has right-of-way at a river bend and you are required, under the Western Rivers Rules, to signal and keep to the right of the channel. However, as I have said before, the jumbo tow is "King of the River," an irresistible force that moves relentlessly and all you can do is keep out of the way, especially when it is moving down river in a swift current. On five specified rivers in the rule, a vessel moving down river *with* a fast current has right-of-way over a vessel coming upriver *against* the current.

But I still would not take that too literally if it is you going downriver and a tow coming upriver.

Leaving A Berth Or Dock

The special bend signal, also called *alarm* signal, is used when you back your boat out of a slip, away from a wharf or gas service facility. This is a signal which I hate to give in crowded yacht clubs and marinas, especially when leaving at daybreak for a long trip, because everybody is sleeping late Sunday morning after a hard Saturday night of you-know-what and I always feel like an inconsiderate clown after blasting that horn of mine for 8 seconds and waking up 500 people out of a sound sleep. It just doesn't seem right, or necessary.

This is one Rule I frequently violate—but I do not advise anyone else to do this.

Signals To Open Drawbridges

There is no prescribed signal for the opening of drawbridges defined in Rules of the Road, but signals are given and the manner and number is more a local custom then a requirement and it will vary in some areas. The Coast Pilot, or State publications on boating, will list drawbridges and the proper signals. The usual signal is three short blasts, but in some areas it may be only one blast. Sometimes, the bridge tender, depending on how he feels, may answer your signal. Most of the time he won't.

In some localities the bridge tender will just ignore you and your signal. He will open the bridge only during specified times of the day, usually on the hour and half hour. If you get there a minute late, you just wait for the opening.

How To Go Through Drawbridges

There is a right way and a wrong way of going through an opened drawbridge. You can infuriate a bridge tender when you take your time, moving through his opened bridge at a snail's pace. He is concerned about all that traffic piling up and wants to get the bridge down.

You can relieve the bridge tender's blood presure considerably if you move up slowly as the bridge is being raised, then the instant it is up, open your throttles and shoot through there like a jet plane taking off an aircraft carrier. When you are clear of the bridge, cut your throttles back to normal.

Bridge tenders appreciate this and quite often will give you a "thank you" with two blasts on their horn. As a bridge tender in Port Clinton, Ohio told me: "That's the way the Coast Guard does it, and they're real professionals."

For any given area, the signals for drawbridges will also be the same signal you give at canal locks. Lock tenders and bridge tenders share a common trait, they respect professionalism. If a lock tender treats you with cold indifference, it is because he considers you a lubber and a menace to navigation.

Fog Signals

Before radar, fogs caused more collisions between ships then any other factor.

Today we have radar.

Today fogs cause more collisions between ships then any other factor.

The small boat owner has two legally required devices on his craft that must be used in fog, the horn and the bell. That second device, the bell, puzzles many new boatmen. What is it for? When is it used?

The bell is used mainly when a boat is anchored in fog, or secured to a mooring buoy where she might be run down in fog by another craft that is moving about searching for its own mooring buoy.

The skipper on a boat that is anchored or moored in fog can easily hear the engines of any approaching craft. This is where he rapidly rings his bell for about 5 seconds, separated by intervals of not more then one minute.

When you come into a mooring area in fog conditions, you welcome the sound of that bell. You can home in on it slowly until the boat becomes visible. Once you identify the moored boat, you have a reference point and can calculate where your own buoy will be.

The term "fog" has a very broad meaning because it is applied to situations which do not truly warrant being called fog, like when it is raining or snowing. Visibility may be reduced, but not by true "fog" conditions.

On the water, anytime visibility is restricted to the distance at which side lights are visible (red/green), fog signals must be used. That means, in rain, mist or snow you might still be able to see other vessels at distances of a mile, but this would still be considered "reduced visibility," necessitating the use of proper fog signals. You may feel a little foolish sometimes making all that noise, and listening to even louder noise, when you can see all around you so clearly, and so far.

The small boat owner's personal encounters with "fog" will most frequently be of the "reduced visibility" type where there is mist or heavy rains. Real honest-to-goodness fog, where you can't see much beyond your windshield wipers, is something no boatman should venture into unless there is a pistol pointed at his head.

Pleasure craft are supposed to be used entirely for personal pleasure. They have no time schedules and no work tasks to be performed, no compelling reason that forces them to operate in hazardous conditions as commercial vessels must do. Taking a pleasure boat out into "real" fog conditions is hazardous even with radar. I have known of yacht owners who deliberately took their boats out into heavy fog just to test out new radar equipment. They came back shaken and chastened. They never did that again.

When you run at night with radar, you are able to see buoy lights with your naked eyes and with the radar scope. This gives you a cross check on the radar and you feel more confident, and more secure. In fog, you see nothing but what is on the radar scope. This makes you nervous and less confident because you are not always too sure just what it is you see on

EXAMPLE OF DISPLAY

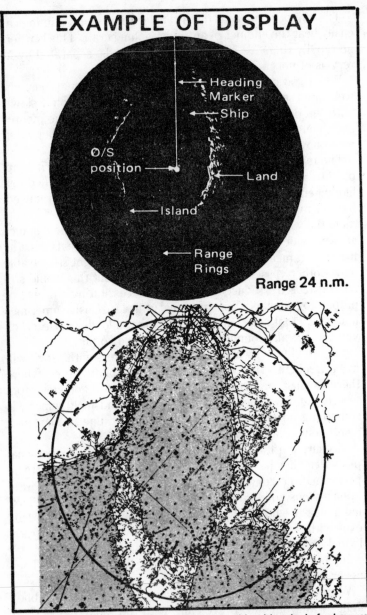

Range 24 n.m.

Fig. 13-40. Inexperienced radar-owners have trouble with radar in fog because they don't have the many cross-checks on visible lights. In mere darkness you can see navigation and shore lights. In fog you are totally blind and so you are totally dependant on radar, which can be terrifying to a novice. Only the experienced radar man can look at the above display and translate it to useful information.

the scope (Fig. 13-40).

Radar is an effective tool only in the hands of an experienced operator. In the Navy, radar men are specialists who perform no other duties.

When any craft is moving on the water in times of reduced visibility (1-mile or less), there are signals that must be given. The Rules specify that the signals must be sounded by the whistle (horn) on power craft, and by an efficient fog horn on sailboats. The reason for the difference in signaling devices is because sailboats are not equipped with horns.

A sailboat underway in reduced visibility must sound its fog horn once on a starboard tack, two times on a port tack and three times when wind is abaft the beam. Timing of the signals is on 1-minute intervals.

For power driven boats, fog signals differ on Inland and Great Lakes Waters. On the Great Lakes you must give *three* blasts on your horn at 1-minute intervals. On Inland Waters you only give *one* prolonged blast (4 to 6 seconds), at one minute intervals.

On International Waters, power driven vessels are only required to give a fog signal at *two minute* intervals, rather then one. If a vessel is making slow headway in dense fog, and water is too deep for anchoring, it must give *two* prolonged blasts, with one second spacing every two minutes. Sailing vessels, under these same conditions and waters, must give *one* prolonged blast, followed by two short ones.

Anchored Aground Or Near A Channel

It frequently happens that a skipper will just give up in thick fog and drop anchor on the edge of a channel to wait for improved visibility. It also frequently happens that a boat will stray out of a channel in fog and run aground.

In the above conditions, Great Lakes Rules have a complicated signal procedure to follow. In fact, they have two *different* signals. Every two minutes you must ring your bell rapidly for about 5 seconds. Then you blast 1 short, 2 long, 1 short horn signals. You repeat this every two minutes. After a few hours of this, you'll never go out in heavy fog again.

Both on Inland and International Waters, you must give the danger signal (5 short blasts), when you hear an approaching vessel to warn them off.

WHEN AN ACCIDENT OCCURS

Rules of the Road were designed to prevent collisions. Radar was supposed to eliminate collisions. But the best laid schemes of mice and men, or as another philosopher said a 100 years before Robert Burns: "There is always something to upset the most careful of human calculations." Collisions still occur at sea and when they do, there are certain things that must be done, both on the State and Federal level.

When your boat is used on navigable waters of the United States, you are subject to regulations of the Federal Boat Safety Act of 1971 (FBSA/71).

On non-Federal waters, you can still be subject to the FBSA because it preempts State Laws in the areas of boat equipment and safety standards. But individual States are not prohibited by the Act from establishing their own regulations in the interest of boat safety, and in the use of boat trailers.

What this all means is that when you have an accident, you can be in violation of both State and Federal regulations and must file an accident report in both areas.

Warning! Ignorance of the laws of any State where you trailer your boat is not acceptable as an excuse. You better *know* them!

If a boating accident results in death, or disappearance of a person, a report must be made *immediately.*

If there are injuries that require medical treatment, hospitalization, or if death occurs within 24 hours, and if there is property damage of more then $50.00 ($100.00 in some states), a report must be made within 48 hours.

If nobody is injured, a report must be made within 5 days.

Your Responsibilities

As a skipper, you have the responsibility in an accident of doing everything humanly possible in rendering assistance to those who may need it on either craft involved in the accident. You must give your name, address and identification of your craft to all persons involved, and to the owner of any property that may have been damaged.

Appendix A
VHF Marine Operator's Guide

VHF MARINE OPERATOR'S GUIDE

CALL SIGN	SERVICE AREA	VHF CHANNEL	MARINE OPERATOR IDENTIFICATION	REGISTRATION INFORMATION
ATLANTIC COAST				
	MAINE			
KOU 620	Camden	26 & 27	(Call sign only)	Dial "0"
KTD 580	Cape Elizabeth	28	" "	(207) 799-4111
KVF 856	Southwest Harbor	28	" "	Dial "0"
	NEW HAMPSHIRE			
KOU 556	New Castle	28	Portsmouth	(603) 668-3000
	MASSACHUSETTS			
KYP 881	Gloucester	25	Gloucester	(716) 894-1763
KJC 737	New Bedford	24, 87 & 26	New Bedford	(617) 994-8523
KOU 634	Hyannis	28	Hyannis	(716) 894-1763
KCD 817	Quincy	26 & 27	Boston	(617) 743-8547
KIZ 309	Nantucket	86	Nantucket	(716) 894-1763
	RHODE ISLAND			
KTR 948	Providence	27 & 28	Providence	(716) 894-1763
KXS 281	Narragansett	84	Narragansett	(716) 894-1763
	CONNECTICUT			
KWB 437	New London	25 & 26	New London	(203) 445-2777
KLU 787	Monroe	24	Bridgeport Channel 24	(203) 372-0373
KLU 785	Stratford	27	Bridgeport Channel 27	(203) 366-4582
	NEW YORK			
KZN 548	Bay Shore	85	Bay Shore	(516) 380-9860
KEA 693	New York	84, 25, 26	New York	(516) 380-9860
KLU 786	Riverhead	28	Riverhead	(516) 380-9860
	NEW JERSEY			
KOU 566	Navesink	24	Sandy Hook	(609) 347-9900
KGW 292	Berkeley Township	27	Tom's River	(609) 347-9900
KGW 378	Sea Isle City	28	Atlantic City	(609) 347-9900
	DELAWARE			
KVF 856	Delaware Bay	27	Lewes	(215) 466-3193
KVR 460	Delaware River	28	Wilmington	(215) 466-3193
	MARYLAND			
KGD 518	Chesapeake Bay	25 & 26	Baltimore	(301) 537-9900
KRS 907	Chesapeake Bay	28	Cambridge	(301) 537-9900
KSK 223	Ocean City	26	Ocean City	(301) 537-9900
KSK 209	Chesapeake Bay	27	Prince Fredrick	(301) 535-1670
KAQ 383	Chesapeake Bay	26	Point Lookout	(301) 537-9900
	VIRGINIA			
KIC 631	Hampton/Norfolk	26 & 27	Norfolk	(804) 461-9911
	NORTH CAROLINA			
KXE 293	Albemarle Sound	24	Elizabeth City	(919) 338-2919
KRS 910	Morehead City/ Beaufort	28	Morehead City	(919) 726-1070
KFT 301	Wilmington	26	(Call sign only)	(919) 762-2444
KMD 258	Nags Head	26	" "	(919) 762-2444
	SOUTH CAROLINA			
KFT 303	Charleston	26	Charleston	(803) 577-4735
KUF 730	Georgetown	24	(Call sign only)	(803) 546-8637
	GEORGIA			
KXC 710	Brunswick	24	Brunswick	(912) 265-0638
KTD 477	Savannah	28	(Call sign only)	(912) 236-6655
ATLANTIC COAST				
	FLORIDA			
KFT 304	Jacksonville	26	Jacksonville	(904) 354-2471
KWS 805	Daytona Beach	28	(Call sign only)	(904) 258-6100
KTR 945	Cocoa	26	" "	(305) 632-3930
KVY 628	Vero Beach	27	" "	(305) 567-3525
KYQ 841	Stuart	26	St Lucie	(305) 283-5660
KGW 294	West Palm Beach	28	Palm Beach	(305) 586-5660
KEW 823	Ft Lauderdale	26	(Call sign only)	(305) 566-2444
KSK 279	Miami	25	Miami	(305) 263-2319
KLU 791	Homestead	27 & 26	Homestead	(305) 248-6456
KQU 411	Key West	26	(Call sign only)	(305) 294-6655
KSK 210	Marathon	25	" "	(305) 743-9081
	PUERTO RICO			
WCT	Loiza	26	(Call sign only)	(809) 723-2520
KRV	Ponce	28	" "	(809) 842-8021 Or 842-4315
	VIRGIN ISLANDS			
WAH	St Thomas	25 & 28	(Call sign only)	(809) 774-5630
GULF OF MEXICO				
	TEXAS			
KLG 376	Brownsville	26	(Call sign only)	(512) 682-3171
KWB 424	Corpus Christi	26 & 28	" "	(512) 884-1915
KGW 304	Port Lavaca	26	Port Lavaca	(512) 552-6751
KGW 304	Freeport/Bay City	25 & 27	(Call sign only)	(713) 245-9151
KKD 742	La Marque	24 & 28	Galveston	(713) 521-8123
KKD 739	La Porte	26	Houston	(713) 521-8123
KKD 741	Port Arthur	26 & 27	(Call sign only)	(713) 521-8123
	LOUISIANA			
KOU 437	Cameron	24	(Call sign only)	(318) 583-2111
KKM 649	Erath	25, 86, 87	Erath	(318) 232-1622
KGN	Delcambre	28 & 85	Delcambre	(318) 685-2344
KKD 732	Morgan City	24 & 26	Morgan City	(504) 872-9001
KSK 317	Cocodrie	27	(Call sign only)	(504) 837-8330
KKO 382	Cenville	25	" "	(504) 693-3111
KSK 316	Leeville	85	" "	(504) 693-3111
KJC 784	Venice	24, 27, 28, 86	Venice	(504) 362-2967
KSK 305	Hopedale	85	Hopedale	(504) 362-2967
KUZ 557	Slidell	84	Slidell	(504) 362-2967
	MISSISSIPPI			
KKM 650	Gulfport	26	Gulfport	(601) 388-9924
KLU 775	Pascagoula	27	Pascagoula	(601) 762-9525
	ALABAMA			
WLO	Mobile	26 & 28	(Call sign only)	(205) 666-5110
WLO	Coden	25 & 28	(Call sign only)	(205) 666-5110
	FLORIDA			
KII 294	Pensacola	26	Pensacola	(904) 432-0034
KW6 455	Ft Walton Beach	26	(Call sign only)	(904) 243-4713
KII 295	Panama City	26	Panama City	(904) 769-1611
KSK 339	Apelachicola	28	(Call sign only)	(904) 229-6000
KUZ 556	Cedar Key	28	Cedar Key	(813) 247-3669
KW6 447	Crystal River	28	(Call sign only)	(904) 795-4811
KUZ 385	Clearwater	24	" "	(813) 229-9111
KWB 426	Tampa	26	" "	(813) 877-6752
KTA 420	St. Petersburg	27	St. Petersburg	(813) 866-5683
KUZ 383	Palmetto	25	(Call sign only)	(813) 247-3669
KTD 563	Venice	26	" "	(813) 960-7702
KYH 550	Ft. Myer	26	Ft. Myer	(813) 542-6001
KQU 410	Naples	25	Naples	(813) 649-8311
KSK 210	Marathon	25	(Call sign only)	(305) 743-9081
KQU 411	Key West	26	" "	(305) 294-6655

CALL SIGN	SERVICE AREA	VHF CHANNEL	MARINE OPERATOR IDENTIFICATION	REGISTRATION INFORMATION
GREAT LAKES				
	MINNESOTA			
KVY 801	Duluth	84 & 86	Duluth	†
	WISCONSIN			
KVY 604	Sturgeon Bay	86 & 87	Sturgeon Bay	†
KVY 605	Port Washington	85 & 86	Port Washington	†
	ILLINOIS			
KTD 564	Waukegan	84	Waukegan	(312) 727-5574
WAY 200	Chicago	26 & 27	Chicago	(312) 727-5574
	INDIANA			
KQU 578	Portage	28	(Call sign only)	(219) 762-1500 or (219) 926-1211
KLU 757	Michigan City	28	(Call sign only)	(219) 762-1500 or (219) 926-1211
	MICHIGAN			
KIL 927	Fair Haven	86 & 87	(Call sign only)	†
KIL 926	Harbor Beach	84 & 86	" "	†
KVY 602	Copper Harbor	84 & 86	Copper Harbor	†
KVY 603	Grand Marais	86 & 87	Grand Marais	†
KSK 263	St Joseph	24	(Call sign only)	(616) 983-0517
KQU 438	Saugatuck	25		(616) 392-2354
KQU 546	Muskegon Hts	26		(616) 733-2007
WLC	Charlevoix	26	Charlevoix	(517) 734-2146
WLC	Sault Ste Marie	26	Soo Marine Opr	(517) 734-2146
WLC	Rogers City	26 & 28	Rogers City	(517) 734-2146
WLC	Tawes City	26	Tawes City	(517) 734-2146
KUF 718	Bay City	28	(Call sign only)	(517) 893-4531
KOB 666	Detroit	26 & 28	Detroit	(313) 569-4880
KAD 806	Monroe	25	(Call sign only)	(313) 241-6202
KAD 836	Marysville	26	Port Huron	(313) 569-4880
KIL 922	Ontonagon	86 & 87	(Call sign only)	†
KIL 923	Hessel	84 & 86	" "	†
KIL 925	Spruce	86 & 87	" "	†
KIL 924	Stevensville	86 & 87	" "	†
	OHIO			
WMI	Loraln	26, 86, 87	Loraln	†
KOU 440	Cleveland	18	(Call sign only)	†
KIL 928	Oregon	84 & 86	" "	†
	PENNSYLVANIA			
KLU 745	Erie	25	(Call sign only)	(814) 455-8014
	NEW YORK			
WBL	Martinsville	26 & 28	Buffalo	(716) 892-5678
KLU 788	Rochester	25	Rochester Channel 25	(914) 831-4290
KIL	Erie	929	84 & 86	†

† Information pertaining to all Loran Electronics Corporation station operations may be obtained by dialing "O" for your local telephone operator and ask to be connected with the Loran Electronics Lakeswide Marine Operator.

CALL SIGN	SERVICE AREA	VHF CHANNEL	MARINE OPERATOR IDENTIFICATION	REGISTRATION INFORMATION
PACIFIC COAST				
	ALASKA			
WXS 77	Boswell Bay	26	(Call sign only)	*
WSX 74	Cold Bay	26	" "	*
WAB 903	Homer	26	" "	*
WRN 40	Juneau	28	" "	*
WRN 41	Ketchikan	26	" "	*
WSX 78	Kodiak	26	" "	*
WSX 78	Nikishka	28	" "	*
WSX 73	Nome	26	" "	*

* For all RCA Alaska locations, telephone (907) 276-6811, extension 224 (Anchorage, Alaska).

CALL SIGN	SERVICE AREA	VHF CHANNEL	MARINE OPERATOR IDENTIFICATION	REGISTRATION INFORMATION
PACIFIC COAST — Continued				
	ALASKA — Continued			
WRN 42	Duncan Canal	28	(Call sign only)	*
WAB 900	Seward	26	" "	*
WRN 43	Sitka	26	" "	*
WAB 902	Unalaska	26	" "	*
WAB 901	Valdez	28	" "	*
WAB 975	Cape Spencer	28	" "	*
WRN 40	Lena Point	26	" "	*
WAB 956	Craig	26	" "	*

* For all RCA Alaska locations, telephone (907) 276-6811, extension 224 (Anchorage, Alaska)

	WASHINGTON			
KOH 840	Bellingham	28	Bellingham	(206) 345-2211
KOH 841	Port Angeles	25	Port Angeles	(206) 345-2211
KOH 630	Seattle	26 & 28	Seattle	(206) 345-2211
KOU 597	Cosmopolis	26	(Call sign only)	(206) 532-6925
KOH 627	Tacoma	28	Tacoma	(206) 345-2211
WXF 646	Tumwater	85	Olympia	(206) 345-2211
	OREGON			
KOF 209	Astoria	26	Astoria	(503) 224-6261
KBA 333	Rainier	26	Rainier	(503) 224-6261
KOE 815	Portland	26	Portland	(503) 244-6261
KTJ	Coos Bay	25	Coos Bay	(503) 269-1141
KZV 784	Newport	26	Newport	(503) 224-6261
KRS 905	Brookings	27	(Call sign only)	(503) 469-2114
	CALIFORNIA			
KTR 967	Klamath City	26	(Call sign only)	(707) 464-3171
KOU 594	Kneeland	25	eureka	(415) 542-4720
KQU 591	Casper	26	Ft. Bragg	(415) 542-4720
KXC 711	Pt Reyes	25	Bodega Bay	(415) 542-4720
KMH 826	Oakland	26 & 84	San Francisco	(415) 542-4720
KUZ 406	Skyland Road	27	Santa Cruz	(408) 354-9000
KTR 860	Salinas	28	Monterey Bay	(408) 424-2903
KLU 727	San Luis Obispo	26	(Call sign only)	(805) 543-3820
KUF 739	Santa Barbara	25	Santa Barbara	(805) 963-0511
KUF 847	San Pedro Hill	27, 85, 87	Redondo	(213) 542-7321
KMB 393	Avalon	24 & 26	San Pedro	(213) 744-1622
KMB 394	San Diego	86 & 86	San Diego	(213) 744-1622
KUF 726	Santiago Peak	84	Dana Point	(714) 547-1250
	HAWAII			
KGW 423	Honolulu	27	(Call sign only)	(808) 521-1424
INLAND WATERS (PARTIAL LIST)				
	LAKE SHASTA			
KUF 732	Redding, CA	28	Redding	(916) 241-5624
	LAKE TAHOE			
KQU 378	Crystal Bay, NV	26 & 28	Lake Tahoe	(916) 546-5057
	LAKE MEAD			
KLU 743	Overton, NV	28	Lake Mead	(702) 293-3353
	MISSOURI RIVER			
KZV 793	Sioux City, IA	28	(Call sign only)	(712) 252-4687
KTD 514	Omaha, NE	26		(402) 341-1529
KFT 310	Kansas City, MO	24 & 26	Kansas City	(816) 221-2720
	MISSISSIPPI RIVER			
KFO 902	St. Paul, MN	26	Minneapolis-St. Paul	(612) 333-2073
KFO 902	Hastings, MN	26	Minneapolis-St. Paul	(612) 333-2073
KWB 426	LaCrosse, WI	26	Lacrosse	(608) 784-3420
KFT 292	Asbury, IA	26	Dubuque	(319) 562-7263

CALL SIGN	SERVICE AREA	VHF CHANNEL	MARINE OPERATOR IDENTIFICATION	REGISTRATION INFORMATION
INLAND WATERS (PARTIAL LIST) — Continued				
KYO 828	Clinton, IA	28	(Call sign only)	(319) 243-4701
KFT 290	Davenport, IA	26		(319) 324-3568
KGW 405	Fowler, IL	26		(312) 727-5574
KLU 732	Grafton, IL	27 & 28	St Louis	(618) 254-1427
WGK	Granite City, IL	24, 25, 26 & 27	St Louis	(314) 436-4781 or (314) 436-5445
WGK	Dupo, IL	24, 25, 26, 27	St Louis	(314) 436-5445
KGW 379	Perryville, MO	26	Perryville	(314) 247-3187
KRS 908	Cape Girardeau, MO	24	(Call sign only)	(314) 334-5816
KGW 320	Cairo, IL	27 & 28	Cairo	(312) 727-5574
KGW 348	Blytheville, AR	26	Blytheville	(501) 371-5347
WJG	Memphis, TN	24 & 26	Memphis	(901) 789-3700
KSK 385	Helena, AR	27 & 28	Helena Radio	(901) 789-3700
KTD 467	Hillhouse, MS	24 & 86	(Call sign only)	(901) 789-3700
KFT 286	Greenville, MS	26	" "	(601) 335-3381
KXS 239	Lake Providence, LA	25	" "	(601) 378-3984
KFT 302	Vicksburg, MS	28	" "	(601) 636-4613
KFT 287	Natchez, MS	26	Natchez	(601) 442-7445
KXE 270	Lebeau, LA	85	Melville	(504) 383-1675
KKM 648	Baton Rouge, LA	27 & 86	Baton Rouge	(504) 383-1675
KZA 917	Convent, LA	25	Convent	(504) 362-2967
KKD 736	New Orleans, LA	24, 26, 27, 87	New Orleans	(504) 362-2967
KJC 784	Venice, LA	24, 25, 27, 28, 86	Venice	(504) 362-2967
KYO 762	Watson, AR	25	Watson	(601) 378-3984
LAKES PONCHARTRAIN/MAUREPAS				
KTR 929	Ponchatoula, LA	85	Ponchatoula	(504) 362-2967
ILLINOIS RIVER				
WAY 200	Chicago	26 & 27	Chicago	(312) 727-5574
KOU 582	Joliet	28	Joliet	(312) 727-5574
KGW 318	Ottawa	26	Ottawa (312) 727-5574	
KFT 288	Peoria	28	(Call sign only)	(309) 674-4749
KGW 322	Beardstown	26	Beardstown	(312) 727-5574

Index

513